THE ILLUSTRATED HANDBOOK OF
WOODWORKING JOINTS

BY PERCY W. BLANDFORD

TAB TAB BOOKS Inc.

BLUE RIDGE SUMMIT, PA 17214

FIRST EDITION

FIRST PRINTING

Copyright © 1984 by TAB BOOKS Inc.
Printed in the United States of America

Library of Congress Cataloging in Publication Data

Blandford, Percy W.
The illustrated handbook of woodworking joints.

Includes index.
1. Joinery—Handbooks, manuals, etc. I. Title.
TH5663.B55   1984   684′.08   83-4953
ISBN 0-8306-0274-7
ISBN 0-8306-0174-0 (pbk.)

Contents

Introduction

YOU CANNOT GET FAR IN WOODWORKING WITH-
out making joints. Some of the simplest assemblies may involve no more than putting one
piece of wood over another and gluing, nailing, or
possibly bolting the two pieces together. Furniture, boats, and houses all require joints.

There have been joints ever since man started
using wood as a construction material. Properly
made joints were used before the birth of Jesus
Christ, and there must have been cruder ways of
joining wood parts long before that time.

A surprising number of today's joints also were
used many thousands of years ago. Some of them
were cruder but basically the same. Precision depends both on the craftsman and the quality of his
tools.

Probably the joint with the longest history is
the mortise and tenon. The idea of a projection on
one part going into a socket in another part must
have occurred to many early craftsmen. The ways
in which the joint has developed are detailed in
Chapter 6.

Wood is not the most durable material, and
some woods have a short life. Some oaks and other
hardwoods may have a long life as can be seen by
church furnishings in many European countries,
where joints can be found that would be made in a
similar way by craftsmen today.

There have been modifications to suit modern
materials and methods. Manufactured boards call
for different joints from those for solid wood, and
the availability of machine tools has brought new
ways of cutting and forming joints. The basic construction material for furniture and many other
things, though, is still solid wood. Much of the final
work on wood is still done by hand. Consequently,
there are very few woodworking joints that may be
regarded as obsolete.

This book covers woodworking joints suitable
for all kinds of construction. The majority of joints is
found in furniture, but there are equivalents in many
other branches of woodworking and a few joints of
special application. Nearly all the joints have practical applications today. A few joints are included
for historical interest only. A woodworking
craftsman should be able to make a variety of good

joints by hand. Some work can be done by using machine tools, but there are occasions when hand tools are essential.

I believe this book contains a larger collection of practical woodworking joints than has ever been published in one volume. Hopefully you will get satisfaction, enjoyment, and practical guidance out of using the book.

Other TAB books by the Author

Chapter 1

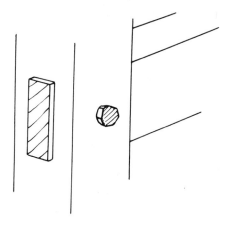

Joints

EVER SINCE MAN STARTED USING WOOD AS A construction material, he has had to develop ways of joining one part to another. At first he may have merely levered parts against each other while they were pushed into the ground. As he began to make simple tools, he managed to cut parts from one piece to take another part.

Joints may provide a mechanical lock between the parts so they will not pull apart—at least in one direction. They may be arranged to provide surfaces for gluing better than if the parts had been laid on each other.

MECHANICAL STRENGTH

Mechanical locking joints came first as glues were not trustworthy until very recent times. A common method of locking is a pin through. This is seen in timber-framed buildings, where mortise and tenon joints form most of the connections. There are holes drilled across the parts so a pin may be driven through (Fig. 1-1A). In a modern joint the pin might be a piece of dowel rod, but in old houses the drill

used was not efficient. The hole might even have been made by burning through with a hot iron rod. Into this went a roughly rounded and tapered peg that held by friction and was usually left with its end projecting, so it could be driven further if the parts loosened.

A more recent development uses the peg to tighten the joint. The hole in the tenon is made slightly nearer the shoulder than in the mortised part, then a tapered peg driven in draws the tenon further into its mortise.

Another way of mechanically locking a joint is with wedges. A wedge may go alongside a part to increase its tightness (Fig. 1-1B), but it is more effective if it spreads the wood to prevent withdrawal. This is usually done by driving one or more wedges into the cut end. If a mortise is cut tapered, the wedges then spread the end of the tenon so it is too wide to pull back (Fig. 1-1C). In old construction these joints can be seen with ends and wedges projecting slightly, so there is surplus length available for driving the wedges further if needed.

SHRINK FITS

Another way of tightening mechanically uses the moisture in the wood. Newly cut wood contains a considerable amount of sap. Seasoning dries most of this out, but there is always a small amount of moisture present in prepared wood. Wood tends to absorb and give out moisture according to the amount in the atmosphere. As wood is seasoned and the amount of moisture is reduced, the wood shrinks. In some woods the amount of shrinkage is considerable. If anything is made from green wood, it will be less in width and thickness in a few months. Shrinkage in the length is not significant. *Green wood* is newly cut and unseasoned wood; it is not green in color.

If a hole is drilled in green wood, it will become smaller as the wood dries out. This property was used in chair making, where the size of a joint might be small and all the strength possible was needed. The legs and back might have been made from green wood, but the rails were seasoned wood. If the rail end was driven into a hole in the leg (Fig. 1-1D), the leg would shrink and tighten the hole on the rail end.

This property could also be used with seasoned wood parts. The small amount of moisture in the rail end was dried out in an oven, then the parts driven together, so subsequent taking up of moisture in the rail would expand it slightly in the hole. Doing this and using an unseasoned leg combined the effect. There was a risk of splitting, and unseasoned wood cannot be relied on to remain true. It may have warped or twisted as it dried out, so sometimes a poorly shaped piece of furniture was produced.

Expansion and contraction due to moisture are also associated with wedges. If a wedge is dried out in an oven just before driving, it can be expected to thicken a little as it takes up moisture again and thus becomes tighter.

As better tools and greater precision developed, man discovered the dovetail principle. In this attractive and very functional joint the slight taper resists pulling apart in one direction very effectively (Fig. 1-1E). Examples, shown later, range from single tails on the ends of strips to multiple joints between wide boards. There are many variations where the joint details are better hidden in one or both directions. The dovetail joint has found a place in mass production. Machines can cut a variation, particularly between drawer fronts and sides.

GLUE

Wood is a porous material. The grain is very open at the end of a piece of wood, and absorption there is very great. A piece of wood with its end in water will soon soak it up for a long way into the grain. If its side only is exposed to water, the amount of absorption is much less. Glue depends on entering the grain on the surface. If glue is used on end grain, though, so much is absorbed that little or none is left to form a film between that and an adjoining piece. Wood glue must enter the grain a little to provide a grip, but there must be some between the surfaces to provide a uniting film. If one or both of the meeting surfaces is end grain, so much glue soaks into the wood that there may be nothing left between the parts. The joint will be weak. It is possible to preglue end grain to seal it, then use more glue in the joint, but it is always better to have side grain for the meeting surfaces.

Many things have been used as wood glue. Early woodworkers tried almost everything that seemed sticky, but none of these adhesives had enough strength to fully resist pulling apart. Joints still had to be primarily mechanically strong, with any glue acting as an aid or a sealer.

In more recent times woodworking glue has been made from hooves and hides of horses and cattle or from fish bones. The manufactured glue was supplied in slabs to be broken up or, more recently, in granules. This glue was and still is prepared for use by soaking in water and heating, so the resulting mixture is thick, sticky, and smelly. The glue should not be overheated and burned. The traditional glue pot is in two parts, with the glue in the inner part and water in the outer one, so the glue never becomes hotter than boiling water (Fig. 1-2).

Modern versions of these glues are available in cans, and it may be possible to obtain the glue in traditional form. Traditional glue should be the

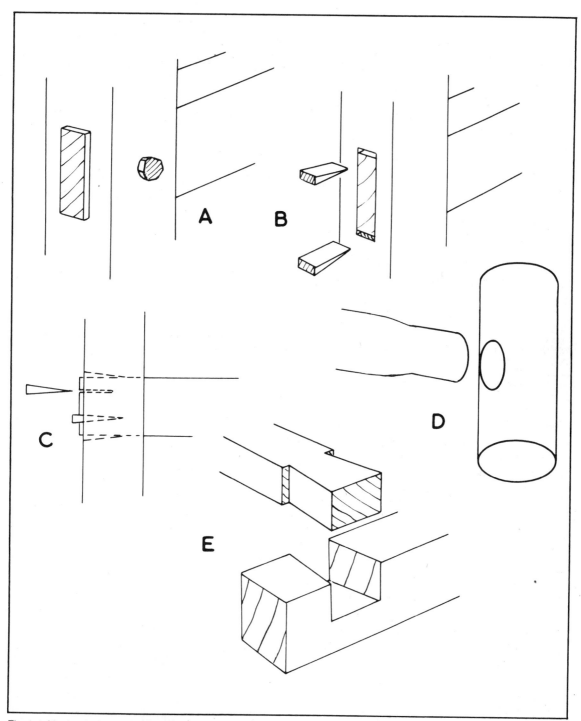

Fig. 1-1. Mechanical strength may be provided by a peg (A), wedges (B, C), or by shaping, as in a dovetail (E). In green wood shrinkage can tighten a hole on to an end (D).

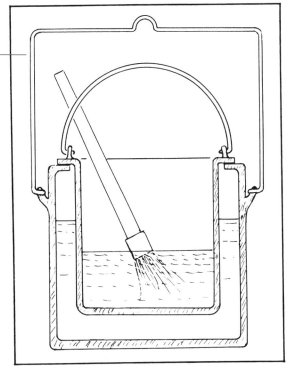

Fig. 1-2. The traditional glue pot or kettle has an inner container for glue and an outer one for water.

choice for repairs to antique furniture, but for general construction it has been superseded.

Traditional glues are not waterproof. They are suitable for furniture, but they can not be used outdoors or anywhere wet or even slightly damp. The furniture surviving for more than 50 years was glued with traditional glue for strength, but if the furniture is examined you will find that there is rarely a joint depending on surfaces meeting with glue alone. There will be a mechanical method of jointing, too.

Synthetic glues which were developed during World War II, are stronger than any traditional glue. Most synthetic glues are fully waterproof. It is possible to put two surfaces together without mechanical jointing and rely only on glue to secure them.

There are many places where joints have to be cut. Even the new glues need side grain to side grain for strong joints. Joints have to be made to suit. A comb or finger joint is an example (Fig.

1-3A). There are good areas of side grain meeting, and the end grain parts in the joint are quite small. A corner dovetail joint has similar good glue areas, with the bonus of mechanical strength one way as well (Fig. 1-3B).

In a mortise and tenon joint the sides of the tenons meeting the sides of the mortises provide the strong glue surfaces. The end grain meetings are fairly narrow (Fig. 1-3C).

There are some compromises to get side grain, or something near it, meeting. Examples will be seen in many joints later, but the point is evident in a plain scarf. End grain to end grain would be weak (Fig. 1-3D) even with modern glue. You could cut half from each piece to make a lap (Fig. 1-3E). That would give a good expanse of side grain meeting, but the narrow pieces of end grain would be the weak points, particularly if subjected to a bending action. It is better to plane both pieces to long slopes and glue them (Fig. 1-3F). The longer the slope, the nearer the surfaces are to side grain. A very short slope would be still too near to end grain to be strong. A slope of 1 in 7 gives a good glue joint (Fig. 1-3G). The scarf could be even longer, but this slope has been accepted in boatbuilding for joining planks end to end when they will be submerged in water.

In modern woodworking the joints to choose are often those that increase glue area. Mechanical strength in a joint may still be desirable, but not so much as it was in the days of inferior glues. If a joint gives good side grain glue area, its actual form may be less important. A simple edge joint may need nothing but glue (Fig. 1-4A). If you feel that more glue area is desirable, there can be a tongue and groove (Fig. 1-4B), or you can work a different shape with a router or spindle (Fig. 1-4C). Besides giving more glue area, these joints are useful in locating parts so one does not ride up on the other as it is clamped. This also applies to dowels. They give a positive location, which may help you avoid misplacing parts when bringing many pieces together in a framework.

MOVING JOINTS

Joints are not always there to hold parts perma-

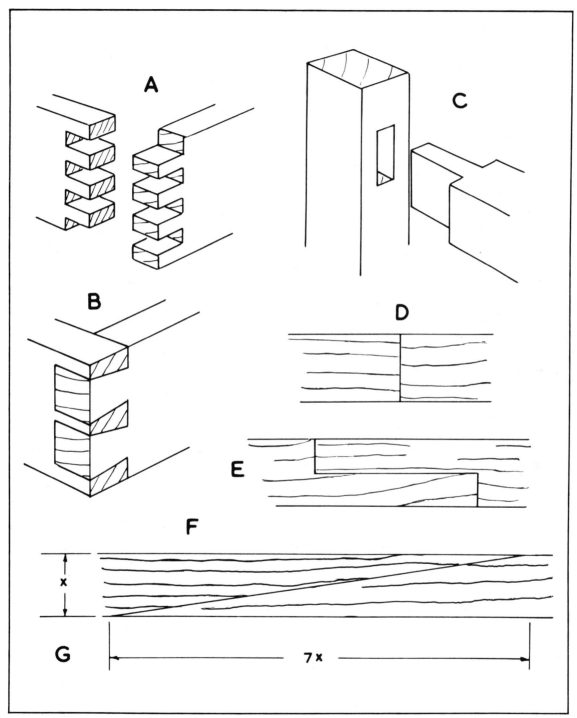

Fig. 1-3. Meeting side grain surfaces (A, B, C) give good glue area. End grain has little hold on glue (D), so end joints may be lapped (E) or scarfed (F).

5

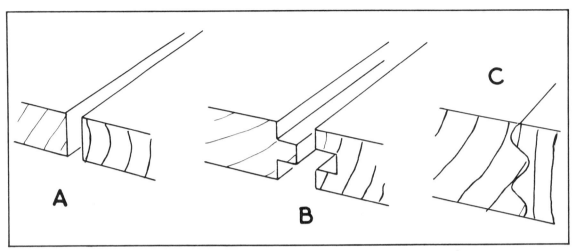

Fig. 1-4. The glue area between edges (A) can be increased by fitting them into each other (B, C).

nently together. Parts may slide or swing on or against each other. Hinges have come a long way from the days when parts turned on wood or metal pegs, then came blacksmith's hinges, but these tended to be massive. There are some beautiful examples of the blacksmith's art in European medieval buildings. Problems came with more delicate hinging needs and with old boxes and small doors requiring leather nailed on, or something equally crude. Smaller metal hinges that could be let into the wood have been available for at least two centuries. Some old furniture pieces are examples of the precision with which doors could swing into

openings or lids could close with the minimum clearance.

You can get hinges that have been produced for mass production. When it comes to making individual pieces of furniture, good quality traditional hinges often are the best choice.

Other joints come where parts meet, as in a pair of swinging doors. In good cabinetry there may be laps and beads that help disguise the meeting edges or give them a pattern that matches surrounding parts. For sliding doors and the fitting of drawers, there are now metal and plastic assemblies.

Chapter 2

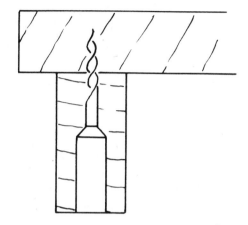

Nailed and Screwed Joints

MOST WOODWORKING JOINTS INVOLVE ONE piece of wood being fitted into another, but there are many situations where the parts are better nailed or screwed. Fitted wood joints may be appropriate to cabinetry or good quality carpentry. They would not be justified for similar construction of lower quality. Nails or screws would be preferred and quite satisfactory. Even in quality work there are places for screws and sometimes nails. In the crudest work, parts are nailed together with little thought for design or the risk of splitting. If nails are chosen and used correctly, they can produce good results.

Screws generally are considered superior to nails. Nails do not have much effect in drawing parts together. The action of hitting a nail at one place may loosen one already driven elsewhere. Screws driven into properly drilled holes will pull and hold parts together, so they can have a clamping effect with a glued joint.

Nails are quicker to use, and less preparation of the work is required. If large numbers of fasteners are required, saving time may be an important consideration. Nails are also cheaper than screws.

The diameters of nails are indicated by a gauge number, with the diameter getting less as the gauge number increases. Common gauge sizes range from number 2 (nearly ¼ inch thick) to number 16 (about 1/16 inch thick) for nails. Screw gauge numbers get higher as the sizes get bigger, from 0 to 24— number 8 is about ⅛ inch.

Common nails and screws are described as iron, but they are actually mild steel. Aluminum, copper, brass, and bronze nails are also used. These nails are resistant to corrosion and can be driven through similar metals. If two different metals are in contact, the atmosphere, particularly if salty, will cause electrolysis. One of the metals will disintegrate. Steel nails may be coated with other metals to protect them from corrosion. Zinc is commonly used, and one method of depositing zinc is known as *galvanizing.*

Screws are made of similar metals used for nails, and they may be protected by coating with other metals. Plating is sometimes applied for the sake of appearance. Brass is considered the cabinetmaking screw metal, and steel screws are not used so often in furniture. Bronze is particularly appropriate for nails and screws on boats. Stainless steel screws, if of a saltwater-resistant alloy, are also used for boats and exposed positions, but they are expensive.

NAIL TYPES

General-purpose nails are usually described as common to distinguish them from other types, although there are box nails that look the same but are slightly thinner for the same length. Both have flat heads and parallel shanks with diamond points (Fig. 2-1A). There is usually only one diameter available for each length. Available lengths go from 1 inch (or shorter) to 6 inches in ¼ inch and then ½-inch steps.

The best way to order nails is by length, quantity, and weight. A system of penny sizes is still in use.

The letter d (abbreviating the old Roman *denarius*) indicates a penny, which is related to the quantity of nails you get in 1 pound. A 2d nail is 1 inch long and about 847 to 1 pound, while a 6d nail is 2 inches long and 167 to 1 pound. At the upper limit a 60d nail is 6 inches long and only 11 to 1 pound.

Smooth shank nails can be grooved in the length with serrations on the parts between the grooves to give better grip. *Barbed ring* or *ring shank* nails (Fig. 2-1B) with raised rings around the nail prevent withdrawal or the pieces of wood from coming apart.

The ordinary flat heads provide a grip to keep the upper piece of wood pulling down against the lower piece, but they are unsightly and unsuitable for many positions. Nails are made with smaller heads (Figs. 2-1C and 2-1D), so there is not so much showing on the surface. They are particularly suitable for setting below the surface and covering with stopping. Others have quite small flat heads in sizes more like pins for such materials as fiberboard and insulation board.

At the other extreme are nails with larger heads (Fig. 2-1E), which are intended for holding down soft materials on roofing and elsewhere. A *roofing nail* for corrugated sheets has a very large

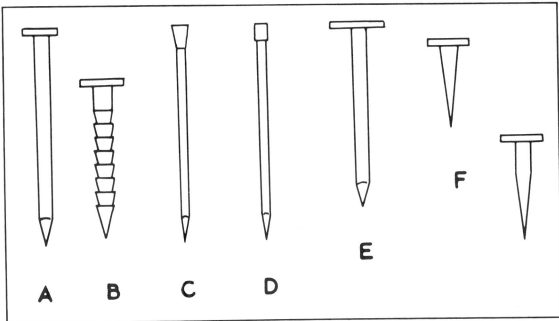

Fig. 2-1. Common nails have flat heads (A). Their grip is increased with ring shanks (B). Heads may be reduced to sink below the surface (C, D). Large heads hold soft material (E). Tacks (F) are used in upholstery.

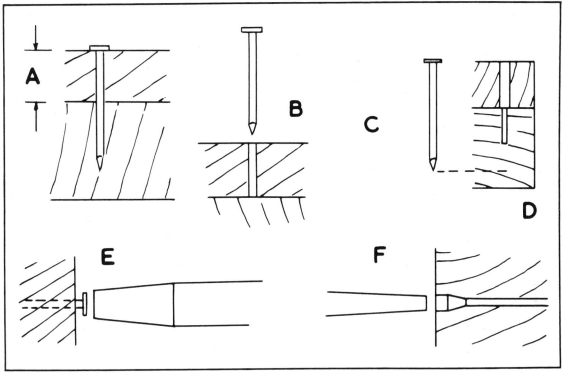

Fig. 2-2. The head and the grip in the lower part hold one piece to another (A). The top piece may be drilled (B), and in hardwood or near an edge the lower piece may be drilled (C). A punch can drive a head tight or sink it (E, F).

domed head. Very small nails may be called *pins* or *brads. Tacks* are small and tapered under large heads (Fig. 2-1F). They are used mainly in up-holstery.

BASIC NAILING

A nail holds by its grip on the lower piece of wood, which is resisted by the head against the top piece (Fig. 2-2A). Any frictional grip in the top piece of wood has no advantage and may even have a nega-tive effect if it prevents the nail from drawing the parts close together. For large nails, it is worth-while drilling the top piece the same size, or slightly smaller than the nail, so strength is not diminished by an unnecessary grip there (Fig. 2-2B).

If the nails are going into a hard, dense wood, an undersize hole may be needed at least partly into the lower piece (Fig. 2-2C). This may be advisable near an edge, even in softer wood where other nails

are driven without drilling, to reduce the risk of splitting (Fig. 2-2D).

A hammer for nailing may have a flat face, but some hammers are made slightly domed. If you drive a nail all the way with a flat-faced hammer, you cannot avoid marking the surface of the wood with the hammer in the final blow. That may not matter in rough construction. With a slightly domed hammer face, a skilled craftsman can drive a nail without marking the wood. If there should be no hammer marks around the nails, you can drive the nail fully home by hammering a punch over its head (Fig. 2-2E).

If a nail with a smaller head is to be punched or set below the surface, the punch used should be about the same diameter as the nailhead (Fig. 2-2F). Some punches are made with hollowed ends, which should reduce the risk of slipping off. Do not set too deeply; about twice the diameter of the head should be enough. When the work is being finished, the holes are filled with a stopping such as plastic wood or a prepared material to suit the finish being used.

There has to be enough of each nail in the bottom piece of wood to provide a grip. The grip is better in dense hardwoods than in open-grained softwoods. A small number of longer nails may be as strong as a larger number of short nails. If there is ample thickness to drive into, nails can be longer than into thinner bottom pieces. As an approximate guide, you could nail down ½-inch wood with 1½-inch nails so there is 1 inch into the lower part.

Nails into side grain (Fig. 2-3A) do not have to be as long as those into end grain (Fig. 2-3B). The corners of a box (end grain) made of ⅝-inch wood might need 2-inch nails, but a bottom of the same thickness might hold with 1½-inch nails.

For grip into end grain, you should space closer than into side grain. It also helps to have a closer spacing near an edge (Fig. 2-3C). There must be enough nails to draw the parts close throughout their length, which probably means between 1½ inches and 2½ inches apart in many assemblies.

If you are nailing in the length of a piece of wood, you may not be able to avoid going into the same grain lines. Splitting may be a risk. If there is enough width, it helps to stagger the nail positions (Fig. 2-3D).

A simple way of getting extra grip with nails is to use *dovetail nailing*. Instead of driving the nails straight, drive them at alternate angles (Fig. 2-3E). The steepness to make the angles depends on the wood. You may tilt the nail more in softwoods than

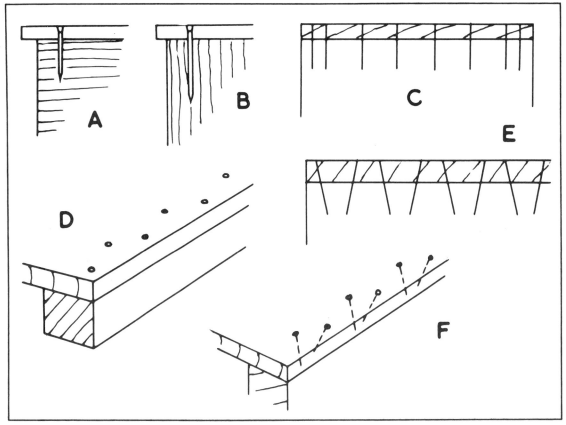

Fig. 2-3. A longer nail is needed in end grain (A, B). Close spacing helps near edges (C). Staggering prevents splitting (D), and driving at alternate angles increases grip (E, F).

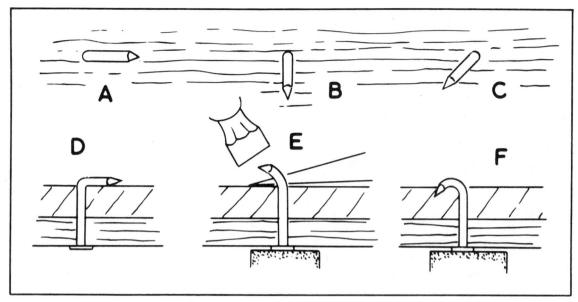

Fig. 2-4. A nail clenched along the grain (A) does not grip as well as when turned across (B) or diagonally (C). The point is exposed when driven flat (D), but it can be buried by bending over a spike (E, F).

hardwoods. It is the spacing where the boards meet that counts, so estimate that the nails go through the meeting surface at about equal spacings. The alternate angles could be across the line if that is more convenient (Fig. 2-3F).

THROUGH NAILING

If you want to nail thin pieces of wood together, there may be little thickness in the bottom piece to let normal nailing provide a grip. You may have to take nails right through and turn over their points. This is *clench nailing*. There is more to it than merely hammering over the projecting points.

Drive the nails with scrap wood underneath, then pull it off. Otherwise, you may get the grain at the far side breaking out. Turn the work over on a flat iron block. If that is impossible, hold a heavy hammer or something similar against each nailhead as you work on the point so the nail cannot move back.

The neatest direction to clench a nail is along the grain, but that is not the strongest. Splitting could result (Fig. 2-4A). It is strongest across the grain (Fig. 2-4B), but you can compromise by clenching diagonally (Fig. 2-4C).

If you merely hammer the nail over, its point will still be exposed (Fig. 2-4D). It is better to curve the end of the nail first, then the point will be buried. While the head of the nail is supported, put the point of a spike alongside the nail and bend the end over it in the direction it is to be clenched (Fig. 2-4E). Remove the spike and hammer the nail end into the wood (Fig. 2-4F).

In traditional lapstrake boatbuilding the overlapping plank edges are held together at intervals with copper nails and roves. The boats are sometimes spoken of as clinker or clench-built. The technique also has uses in other construction where thin parts have to be joined. For boatbuilding the copper nails have square sections and slightly countersunk flat heads. *Roves* are conical copper washers with holes slightly smaller than their matching nails (Fig. 2-5).

Copper is a soft metal, but it is chosen for its ease in riveting and its resistance to saltwater. A hole is drilled slightly undersize for each nail. Otherwise, there is a risk of the nail bending in the wood. A nail length is chosen that will go through and project at least ¼ inch. There is a choice of gauge sizes in each length.

Fig. 2-5. Copper boat nails are square, and the matching conical roves have holes to drive over their points.

After drilling a hole, the man on the outside of the boat drives the nail and holds up with an iron block on the nailhead. Inside the boat his mate puts a rove on the end of the nail and drives it with a hollow punch called a *roving iron* (Fig. 2-6A). As the hole in the rove is slightly undersize, it grips the nail as it goes on and stays tight against the wood with the nail end projecting.

The craftsman cuts off the end of the nail within about ⅛ inch of the rove (Fig. 2-6B). A pair of top cutters (like sharp pincers) is the most suitable tool for this cutting. Then he uses a light ball peen hammer to spread the end of the nail like a rivet over the rove (Fig. 2-6C). Use of a light hammer is important, as heavy blows will cause the copper nail to bend in the wood. It may straighten out later and cause the boat to leak.

A related use is in attaching metal fittings to wood that is too thin to take screws. A hinge can be

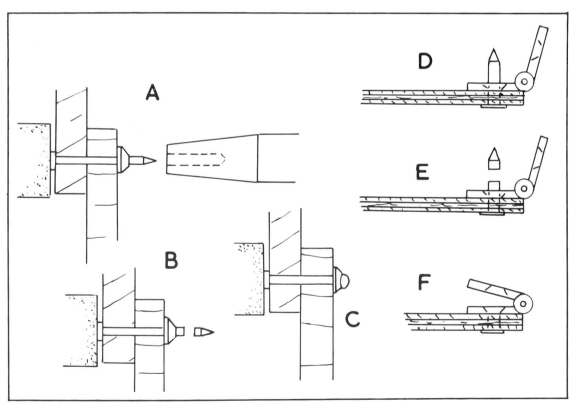

Fig. 2-6. A rove is driven on a boat nail (A), which is cut off and riveted (B, C). A nail can join a hinge to thin wood in the same way (D, E, F).

12

put over thin wood. Copper nails then can be driven through the screw holes, with their heads on the other side (Fig. 2-6D). If the end of the nail is cut off (Fig. 2-6E) with enough metal left to fill the countersunk screw hole, that can be riveted so as to finish flush (Fig. 2-6F).

SCREWS

The principle of the screw has been known for a long time, but there was no satisfactory way of producing screws economically in quantity. Some wood screws of not so long ago were made without points. A hole had to be drilled, and penetration was largely a matter of applying brute force.

Modern wood screws are now produced in uniform types and sizes. With the drill sizes available and suitable tools, screwdriving is one of the best ways of securing many furniture parts together.

Wood screws are made in lengths from ¼ inch by ⅛ inch and ¼-inch steps up to 4 inches or more. Special screws are made smaller and larger. Several gauge diameters are available within each length. The lower numbers are the thinner screws. For instance, 1 inch by 8 gauge is a popular size, but if you need a thinner screw it could be 6 gauge, or for a thicker screw you could have 10 gauge. Except for the smaller screws, you will probably only be able to get screws with even gauge numbers. The smallest practical gauge for most purposes is number 2. That is 0.086 inch in diameter, while number 18 is probably bigger than you will need at 0.294 inches. The gauge size is the diameter of the plain part of the screw under the head.

Common screws have flat heads (sometimes called countersunk heads), which have an included angle of about 82 degrees (Fig. 2-7A). The threaded part is about two-thirds the length of the screw. Next most common are round heads (Fig. 2-7B). The length quoted for any screw is from the surface of the wood, so a round head screw is longer overall than a flat head one. Round heads may be used when the screw will show, and they are often used through handles, ornamental hinges, and similar things. An oval head has the countersink of a flat head screw, but the surface is domed (Fig. 2-7C).

This looks better than a flat head in the countersink of a metal fitment. It is not often used directly into wood.

Wood screws are not the best for use in particleboard. Others are available like self-tapping screws with sharper threads taken to the head (Fig. 2-7D). Some of these have two-start threads. Other screws have single-start threads; one thread winds around the screw. In a two-start thread a second thread starts on the opposite side to the first.

For most of the time that screws have been available, they have been given a slot in the head to take a screwdriver (Fig. 2-7E). These are still the type to be bought for normal individual furniture construction. There are heads with square sockets (Fig. 2-7F) and others to suit Phillips screwdrivers (Fig. 2-7G). These two are meant for power screwdrivers in quantity production, but there are hand screwdrivers for them.

One advantage of screws over nails is the ease of taking apart. It is always easier to withdraw a screw than a nail. If you anticipate having to withdraw screws very often, the screw may be put through a cup washer (Fig. 2-7H) or a screw socket let into a countersink (Fig. 2-7J) to prevent frequent turning, which will mar the surface of the wood.

BASIC SCREWING

Even more than a nail, a screw depends on pulling the bottom piece of wood against the pressure on the top piece provided by the head. If the screw is tight in the top piece, it may screw into that and not draw the lower piece tightly against it. Don't try to drive even the smallest screw into the softest wood without first making a top hole.

If you want to join two pieces of wood, the screw hole in the top piece should allow the screw to slide through (Fig. 2-8A). With a thin screw and softwood, you may be able to put the screw in this hole and give it a gentle tap with a hammer to enter the point in the lower piece, then drive it home. You will have to drill an undersize hole in the bottom piece for most screws. If it is very hard and dense, that hole should go almost as far as the screw will (Fig. 2-8B). With softer wood, the drill need not be quite as large or go quite as far (Fig. 2-8C). Experi-

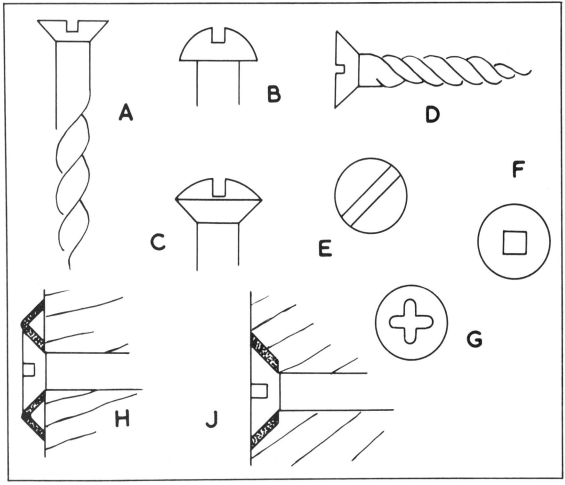

Fig. 2-7. Screw heads may be flat (A), round (B), or raised (C). Screws for particle board have longer threads (D). Screwdriver slots vary (E, F, G). Heads may fit into a cup washer (H) or a socket (J).

ence will tell you what size hole will be needed in the lower piece of wood.

The metalworking type of twist drill will be used for most drilling. A gimlet is not advised because it enters with a splitting action. A *bradawl*, which has a chisel-shaped cutting end (Fig. 2-8D), will make a good hole for the threads of smaller screws as it cuts and pushes aside the fibers of the wood without removing them, so they give a better grip on the screw. Push it in with the cutting edge across the grain, then give it quarter turns in each direction as you push in further.

If you are using flat head screws, you will want them to finish level with the surface of the wood. In many woods a head will go flush with just the pull of the screw and without any preparation of the top of the hole. If you are driving a series of screws, try one before doing any countersinking of the holes. You may find that just a small amount of countersinking will help a head to pull the rest of the way. In a hardwood you may have to countersink fully. Be careful of overdoing it. A screw head pulled below the surface is ugly.

Because screws have a better grip, they can be given a wider spacing than nails. A shelf support 12 inches long could have four screws (Fig. 2-9A),

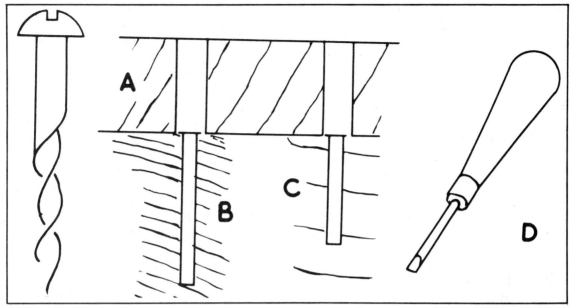

Fig. 2-8. There should be a clearance hole in the top part (A) and a deeper tapping hole (B) in hardwood than in softwood (C). A bradawl (D) will make a tapping hole for small screws.

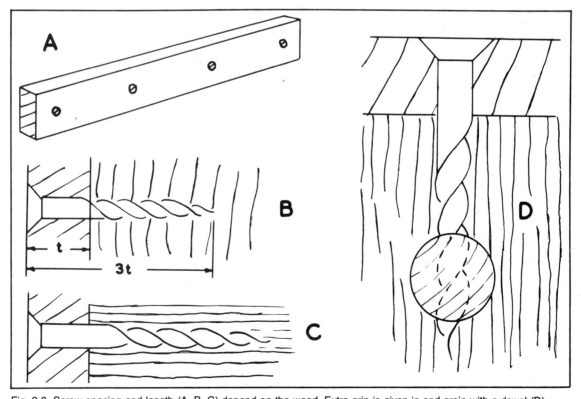

Fig. 2-9. Screw spacing and length (A, B, C) depend on the wood. Extra grip is given in end grain with a dowel (D).

where six or eight nails would be needed. The lengths to use depend on the wood, its thickness, and other factors, but you need sufficient thread into the lower piece to give a good pull. Any thread left in the hole in the top piece is not doing anything useful. As the threads are about two-thirds of the length of a screw, you can choose a screw three times the thickness of the top piece as a guide to estimating your requirements (Fig. 2-9B). If that length cannot be used, you may have a greater number of shorter screws. A screw does not hold as well in end grain, so it may be longer there (Fig. 2-9C).

One way of increasing the grip in end grain is to provide a section of grain going across. You can do this by drilling for a piece of dowel rod (Fig. 2-9D). Position it so the screw will go right through it. If you do not want the dowel to show on one side, you can drill only partly through from the other side.

A screw can be counterbored. Suppose a rail has to be screwed into a tabletop. Because of the rails depth, a very long screw is needed from the surface. Instead you can drill a hole that will clear the screw head, then continue through with a hole to clear the screw shank. Adjust the drilling depth to allow the screw enough thread into the tabletop (Fig. 2-10A). As the underside of the rail will be out of sight, normally the hole can be left open.

A similar idea can be used on the surface if you do not want the screw head to show, or you want it buried so there is nothing for tools to get damaged against on a bench top. The counterbored hole should suit a plug cut with its grain across from a scrap of the same wood. Drill only just enough to allow the plug to be glued in (Fig. 2-10B), then planed off level later. If you match the grain direction, the plug should hardly show.

Another way of driving a screw upward from a

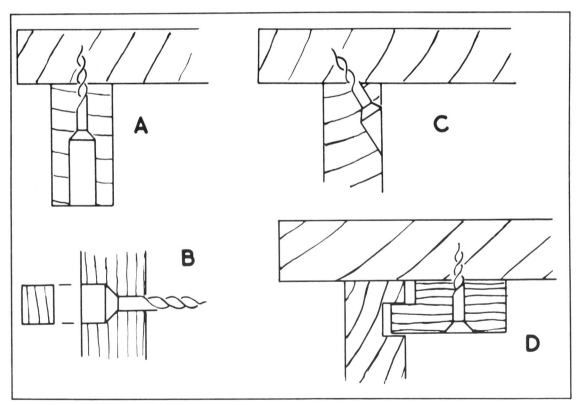

Fig. 2-10. A screw from a rail upward may be counterbored (A) or driven through a pocket (C). There may be a plug over a counterbored screw (B). A button (D) allows for expansion and contraction.

rail into a tabletop is pocket screwing. Drill diagonally from the center of the rail's top to make a hole to take the neck of the screw. With a gouge and a chisel, cut away a pocket that will admit the screw head and allow a screwdriver to be used, then a screw can be driven diagonally upward (Fig. 2-10C).

A problem with a solid wood tabletop is the slight expansion and contraction that takes place in the width. It helps to provide attachments that allow movement. One of these is a button engaging with a groove in the rail. It is usually convenient to plow the grooves full length, but there need be only a short groove each side of each button. Cut the bottom to provide a slight upward pull against the groove when the screw is tightened. Keep the lip of the button back from the bottom of the groove to allow for movement (Fig. 2-10D).

The brass used for screws is sometimes rather brittle. This may cause screws of gauge 4 or under to shear off when being driven, and there is not much you can do to remove a broken piece of screw without damaging the wood. When using these small brass screws, make sure you have drilled adequately to suit the wood. If you have doubts about brass screws of any size, drive a steel screw of the same size first, then withdraw it and put in the brass one. You are never likely to shear a steel screw.

Some woods grip screws more than others. Sometimes it is difficult to turn a screw even with proper holes drilled. If that happens, wiping the threads with soap may help. Wax or wax polish will also help. Do not use lubricating oil, as that may stain the wood around the screw.

Glue is often used in screwed joints. If you are putting together a joint that has a row of screws along it, apply the glue. Bring the parts together and start all the screws, but do not fully tighten them. Commence tightening from near the middle of the row and work outward. Glue oozing from the joint will show you how the work is progressing. Get the whole joint tight, but it is possible to starve the joint of glue with excessive tightening. The screws may provide plenty of strength, but the glue will not be sharing the load properly.

SLOT SCREWING

Wide boards of solid wood are always subject to slight expansion and contraction in their width. If anything is put across with its grain the other way, there has to be some allowance for this movement, or the wood may crack or joints may come apart. Battens or cleats are put across the underside of some wide pieces to stiffen and prevent warping, but they should not be glued or screwed on rigidly. The battens or cleats will not expand and contract in their length as the wide board does in its width.

They should be screwed on without glue, and the screws should be put through slots in the cleats so they can move if necessary. There is no need to make all the holes into slots or to slot them the same amount. If it is a loose board such as a drawing board, with two pieces across (Fig. 2-11A), the center holes can be round so the screw there does not move. The slots should be cut progressively longer further out (Fig. 2-11B). The cleats then will remain central in the width of the wide board whether it gets wider or narrower. The lengths of the slots depend on the width of the board and of what it is made. Most softwoods expand and contract more than hardwoods, but there is not much movement. With a board 24 inches wide, other slots ½ inch long should be more than enough.

If the top piece is a table flap or some other part supported at one edge, it will be better to have a round screw hole at the end of each cleat near the support. Lengthen the slots as you drill outward from there, so any alteration in the top width takes place toward the free edge (Fig. 2-11C).

METAL FASTENERS

Metal fasteners are used for pulling and holding wood parts together. A corrugated fastener or wiggle nail has a corrugated section with one edge sharpened so it will enter wood. The corrugations on the two halves slope slightly in opposite ways, so as the fastener is driven the effect is to pull the parts together (Fig. 2-12A). The fastener can be used on end grain or across the grain and is merely driven in like a nail, preferably in a position where it will not be seen.

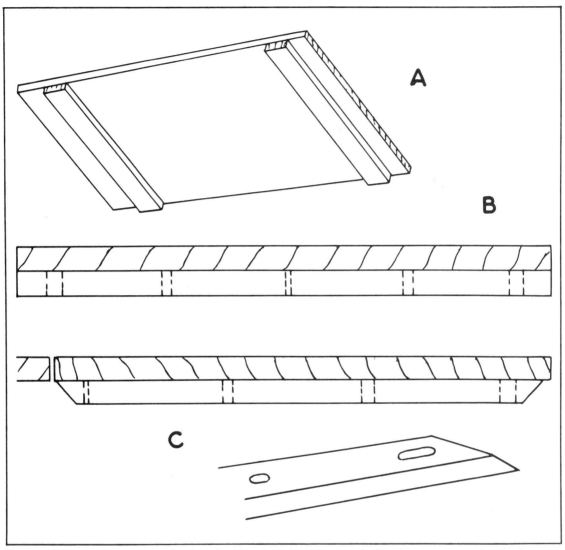

Fig. 2-11. Battens prevent warping, but they should be held with slot screws to allow for expansion and contraction.

It is possible to improvise something for the same purpose from a long, thin nail. Bend over the point with pliers, then cut off the nailhead and bend what is left a similar amount to the point. The two-pronged nail may then be driven into the underside of a miter or other place that needs strengthening (Fig. 2-12B).

A sheet steel shape called a *chevron* (Fig. 2-12C) can be driven into wood to hold joints together. It is particularly suitable across a miter.

There are predrilled metal plates sold as repair plates, but they have uses in construction work when a joint has to be reinforced, or the metal plate can take the place of a cut joint. A *flat plate* (Fig. 2-12D) is intended to go across two pieces of wood that have to be held together. An *angle plate* (Fig. 2-12E) goes between two pieces square to each other. An *L-plate* goes on pieces meeting flat and square to each other (Fig. 2-12F), while a *T-plate* does the same when one part comes to the side of another. Plates can be used with each other and placed on opposite sides of the wood to allow screws through them to provide strength even when there are no fitted joints cut in the wood.

HANGER BOLTS

There are places where something is required with a wood screw end, but the other end is given a metal thread so a nut can be driven on. A hanger bolt (Fig. 2-13A) may be used for attaching a metal part to wood in a position where the opposite side is inaccessible or anywhere that it may be necessary to remove or adjust whatever is held by the bolt.

As there is no screwdriver slot or other way of driving the screw into wood, another way of driving has to be devised. The usual way is with two nuts. Drive the nuts onto the thread, then use two wrenches pulled in opposite directions to force them together. Drill the wood for the screw end, give the bolt a light tap with a hammer to start it,

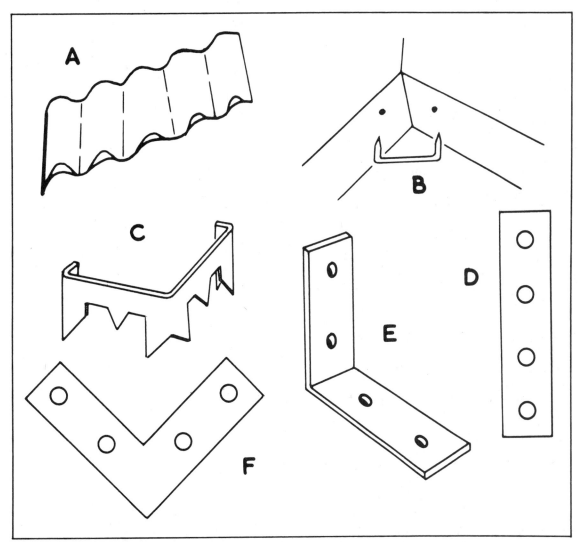

Fig. 2-12. A corrugated fastener (A), a bent nail (B), or a special metal chevron (C) can be driven across two pieces of wood. Repair plates (D, E, F) can be screwed between parts.

19

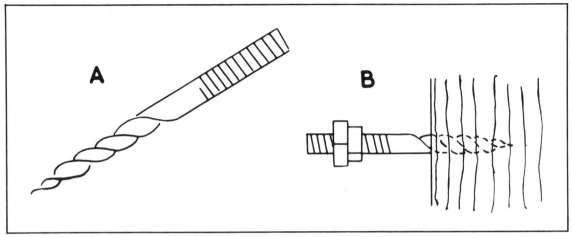

Fig. 2-13. A hanger bolt has a metal thread end. It may be driven with two nuts locked together.

then turn the screw into the wood with a wrench on the top nut (Fig. 2-13B). When it is far enough in, use the two wrenches again to separate the nuts.

LEG BRACE

If a table or similar assembly is to have its legs removable, the rails may be attached to the top and have their ends cut square for the leg to bear against. A brace is then used with a hanger bolt and nut to pull the leg diagonally back against the rail ends (Fig. 2-14). The brace has two bent ends, and the rails are cut across to admit them. That grip may be further supplemented by two small wood screws. When the legs are removed, the hanger bolt goes with the leg, but the brace remains attached to the rails.

For a permanent or nearly permanent assembly, an ordinary nut is used on the hanger bolt. If frequent disassembly is expected, there may be a wing or butterfly nut.

HANDRAIL BOLTS

In some places there may be considerable load on a part, and no wood-to-wood joint may be trusted. One such place is where substantial handrails meet end-on. There is a bolt named after its use in joining these parts, but it may have other uses.

A handrail bolt is double-ended, with points and threads running some way from each end. A square or hexagonal nut goes on one end (Fig. 2-15A). At the other end there is a round nut with notches cut in it (Fig. 2-15B), and that may be used with a locking washer.

To use the bolt, opposite ends of wood are drilled for it. Mortises are cut from the undersurfaces so the pointed ends will be exposed (Fig. 2-15C). The square nut is dropped into one mortise. The bolt is turned in its hole until it has screwed through the nut, leaving enough of the other part of the bolt projecting to go into the other mortise far enough to penetrate the round nut.

The parts are then brought together. The washer and round nut are put into the mortise by

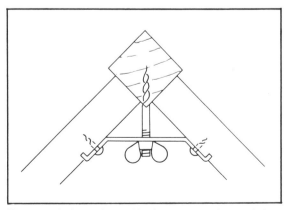

Fig. 2-14. A diagonal metal leg brace uses a hanger bolt to pull a leg against two rail ends.

using a piece of wire with a hooked end to locate them on the bolt end. Tightening is with a long thin screwdriver, which is used in the notches to push the nut round (Fig. 2-15D), followed by a punch with a similar end for final tightening. That could be just the filed end of a large nail.

When the parts are secure and no more adjustment is needed, plugs may be glued into the mortises to hide the bolt ends.

SPLIT RING CONNECTORS

When two parts are bolted together, any sideways loads come on the comparatively small area of the bolt pressing into the wood. The effect of a heavy load is to bend the bolt or cause it to press into the grain of the wood, so the two parts move in relation to each other. More bolts will provide more resistance, but one way of resisting the sideways thrust is to give the joint more bearing area by including a tubular ring let into the wood around the bolt.

The ring may be made from steel tube, and some adjustment is provided by cutting it through (Fig. 2-16A). Use a hole saw to drill for it in the wood, going half its depth into each piece (Fig. 2-16B), with the centers where the bolt will come. Open the center holes for the bolt.

Put the ring into one part, so half projects, then assemble with nut and washers on the bolt in the usual way (Fig. 2-16C). The cut in the ring allows for slight movement if the wood expands or contracts without affecting the strength of the joint.

WOODEN SCREWS

At one time use was made of screw threads cut in wood. The old-time vise or bench screw always had a screwed part 2 inches or more in a diameter. Clamps were also given wooden screws of smaller diameter, but obviously wood cannot take a fine thread in the way that metal can. Screwing tackle for cutting threads in wood is still available, so it is possible to make parts in which joints, particularly adjustable ones, have the two pieces arranged with mating screw threads.

Threads can only be cut satisfactorily in close-grained hardwood. The internal thread must be cut across the grain. The method of cutting

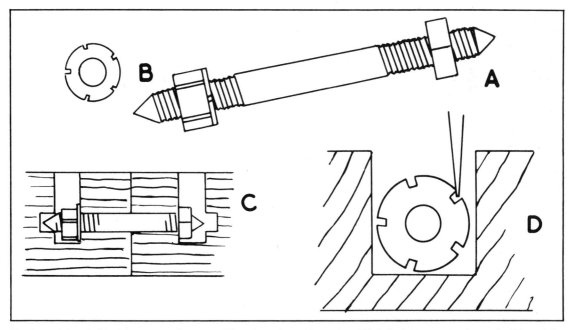

Fig. 2-15. A handrail bolt has one ordinary nut (A) and another with notches (B). It fits between meeting ends (C), and the notched nut is punched round (D).

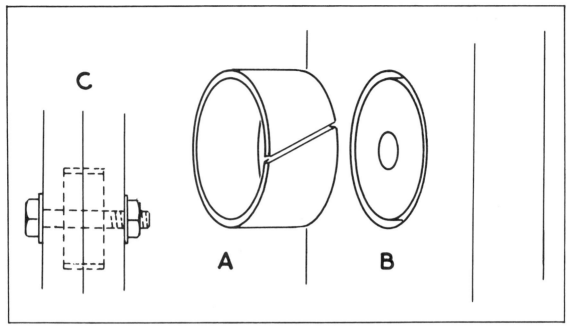

Fig. 2-16. A bolt between overlapping parts can have some of the load taken by a metal ring sunk into grooves.

scrapes, and the wood would break out if an attempt was made to cut into end grain. External threads are made along a cylindrical piece with the grain running lengthwise.

Threads are necessarily coarse so as not to weaken the wood too much by forming parts so fine that they would soon crumble in use. Typically, a 3-inch diameter may have two threads per inch. A 1-inch diameter may have four threads per inch. One-half-inch diameter, which is about as small as advisable, can have six or seven threads per inch.

Threads through holes are made with a tap similar to one cutting threads in metal, but its four lines of cutters taper and work with a scraping action (Fig. 2-17A). The small end starts in a hole, and later teeth scrape more off until a full thread depth is cut at the top of the tap. That means taking the tap right through a hole to get a full thread all the way. The tap cannot be used in a blind hole, unless it is very much deeper than the fully threaded part has to be.

The equivalent of a metalworking screw die is a screw box (Fig. 2-17B), which is made of wood with two handles. Through it is a thread cut with the matching die, but at the entry there is a cutter with its end sharpened in the V-form of the thread section. The end of the wood rod needs a taper, then the box is turned onto it so the cutter makes the thread, which continues through the threaded part of the box. The cutter must be kept very sharp. The depth of its cut is adjustable. It must be carefully aligned to cut the periphery of the thread before the root.

There is no way of altering the thread size cut through a hole with a tap, but the cutter in the screw box can be adjusted to make a thread that will pass through the tapped hole. Threaded wooden parts should not be lubricated with grease or oil. You can use wax or resin, but talc and graphite are also useful.

COUNTER CLAMP

The top of a shop counter or a large bar may have to be made up of two or more wide thick boards meeting end to end. The butt joint must be pulled very tight. One way of doing that is to put strips underneath, which are held with screws and tightened with folding wedges to act as a permanent clamp.

Three strips make a clamp (Fig. 2-18A). Two or more sets of strips are needed for very wide boards.

The sizes of wedges should be determined then three identical strips are made with notches to suit the thickness of the wedges and wider than the wedges will be when both are driven fully home. Drill the strips for screwing underneath the boards. Two screws at each side are shown, but there may have to be more (Fig. 2-18B). To keep the board ends level, a key can be in grooves.

Position the strips on the wide boards with a little clearance between them. Screw the two outer strips to one board and the one between to the other. Leave the other screw holes empty. Position the notches in relation to each other so when the wedges are driven, they will pull the inner strip by pressing against its outer notch edge and thrusting against the other inner edges (Fig. 2-18C). When you have applied sufficient tension to get the board ends tight, leave the wedges in place, but drive the remaining screws to lock the parts together.

BIRD'S-MOUTH

When a piece approaches another square to it at a slope, as many parts do in roof construction, a simple diagonal cut across the end may be nailed (Fig. 2-19A). Location depends on accurate positioning at the time of nailing. Any thrust is taken by the nails, which may bend or move in the wood. It is better to notch the diagonal part in a *bird's-mouth joint*, so the notch pushes against the angle of the other piece. This makes it easier to locate the parts accurately and to make the load wood to wood.

There may be just a small notch (Fig. 2-19B)

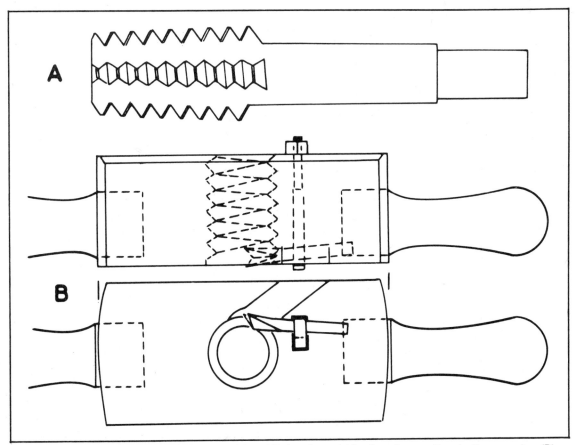

Fig. 2-17. Threads in wood may be cut with a special tap (A), then the matching thread on a rod is cut with a screw box (B).

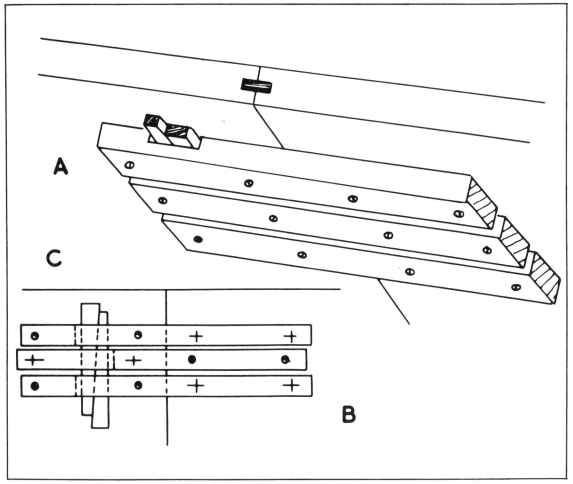

Fig. 2-18. The broad boards of a counter top may be pulled together with wedged pieces screwed below.

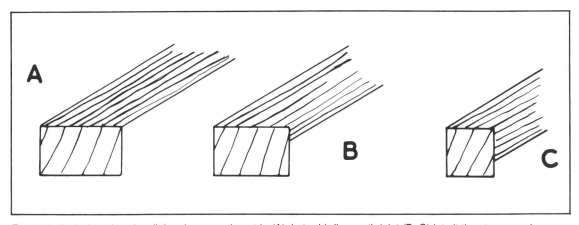

Fig. 2-19. A sloping piece has little grip on another strip (A), but a bird's-mouth joint (B, C) lets it thrust on an edge.

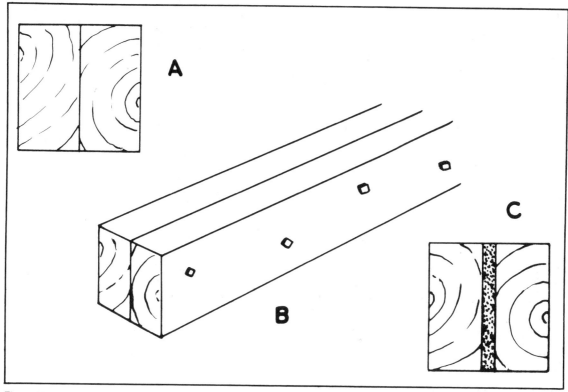

Fig. 2-20. A flitched beam is cut and the parts are reversed (A), with bolts between (B). A steel plate may provide further strength (C).

with all nails driven through the long overlap. If the wood sizes allow for it, a more equal bird's-mouth (Fig. 2-19C) can have nails driven both ways.

FLITCHED BEAM

Flitch may mean a log prepared for conversion into veneers, but it also applies to a side of a built-up beam. When a beam is made from a solid piece of wood, there may be flaws in it to weaken one place, there may be more tendency to bend at one position, or there may just be doubts about its strength characteristics being the same throughout the length. If the piece is cut down the middle and one part is reversed on the other (Fig. 2-20A), the strength of the beam will be equalized throughout the length as far as possible.

Such a beam is assembled with bolts through at intervals, with or without glue between the flitches (Fig. 2-20B). The bolts should be staggered so as to go through different grain lines, but they should be kept fairly near the center of the wood. A further method of strengthening includes a piece of steel plate between the wood sides (Fig. 2-20C).

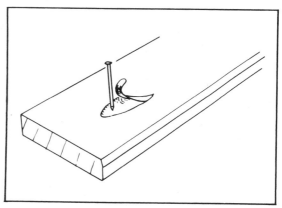

Fig. 2-21. If a sliver of wood is lifted with a gouge, a driven nail may be hidden by gluing it down over it.

SLIVER NAILING

This is of particular use when fitting a baseboard around the bottoms of walls, where exposed nail or screw heads are better avoided. They could be sunk and plugged or covered with stopping, but sliver nailing hides them completely.

At each position a gouge with a fairly deep curve is given one decisive cut along the grain, so it curls up a sliver of wood but does not break it off (Fig. 2-21). Go far enough for the end of the sliver to have lifted far enough for a nail to be inserted. Drive the nail and set it well with a punch, then glue back the sliver over it. If this is done carefully, there will be no obvious mark when the baseboard is stained and varnished or polished.

The technique can be used elsewhere, particularly for repairs, even if the wood has already been polished or painted. If there has to be a nail or screw driven through the surface, this may be the least obvious way of doing it.

Chapter 3

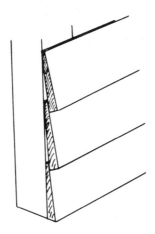

Edge Joints

THE WIDTHS OF BOARDS ARE LIMITED BY THE diameters of the tree trunks from which they are cut. There has to be an allowance for the removal of sapwood and uneven shaping of the log, so a straight board used for carpentry or cabinetmaking may be much narrower than the tree from which it was cut. During milling some boards may be cut down to narrower widths, and what you are offered at the lumberyard could be narrower than the maximum width possible under favorable circumstances.

You will often have to join boards edge to edge for a solid wood top or other part. There are some advantages. A single piece may tend to cast and warp due to the way it was cut across the log. Narrower pieces can be joined so individual pieces don't change shape. A very wide board may not be perfect. You can select good wood for all parts of the assembly with narrower pieces.

Edge joints used for making up widths are usually glued. Satisfactory joints can be made with modern strong glues without complications. There are other edge joints where glue may not be used. These are covered in Chapter 10, while joints designed for machine cutting are described in Chapter 16.

PREPARING FOR JOINING

The boards to be joined should be arranged with their grain the same way if possible. When the finished piece is surfaced, then there is no risk of one part tearing up the grain if it is reversed to the grain of a piece alongside it.

If you look at the end grain of the boards, any with the annual rings across the thickness might get thinner but will not warp. If the rings curve across the board, any warping would be in a direction that tries to straighten the rings (Fig. 3-1A). If you assemble boards so the rings come in alternate ways (Fig. 3-1B), the risk of overall casting of the built-up piece will be slight. The gain direction of adjoining boards should cancel each other out.

Besides getting the planing direction of the surfaces the same and the end grain arranged alter-

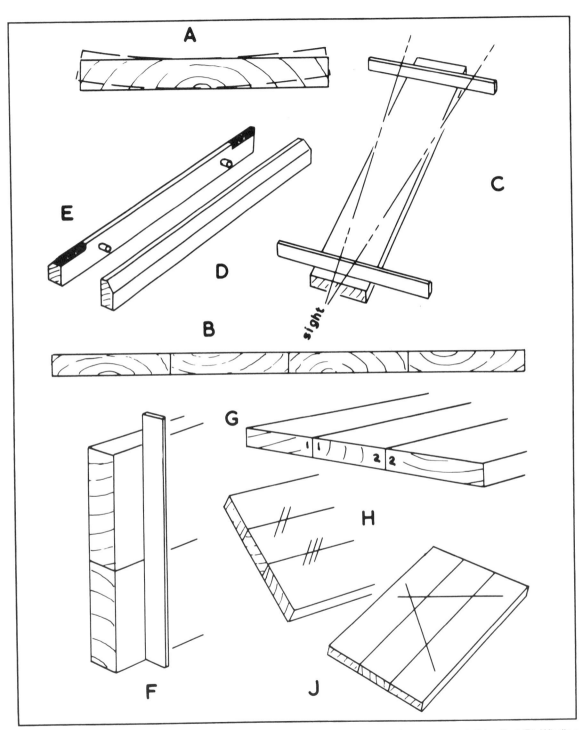

Fig. 3-1. When wood warps, it tries to straighten grain lines (A). Joining boards opposite ways cancels this effect (B). Winding (C, D, E) indicates twist. Joined surfaces may be checked flat (F). Marks indicate mating parts (G, H, J).

nate ways, try to get the surface grains so they will build up an interesting effect. You may not be able to get them matching, but it may be possible to move boards to get a more pleasing pattern. With many hardwoods the surface grain pattern is not very pronounced, so you do not need to worry about the appearance of adjoining boards.

Individual boards should be checked for flatness, and they should also be the same thickness. If a board is glued to others and it has a twist or other poor shape, you will have some awkward surfacing to do on the whole assembly. That could result in the finished piece having to be thinner than you intended.

The flatness of a board or the whole assembly can be checked in both directions with a straightedge. Even if those directions are flat, there could still be a twist. That is best checked by sighting from one end. You can see if the opposite end lines up with the near end. A twisting board may be said to be in winding. The traditional means of testing uses winding strips, which are a pair of straightedges made thick enough to stand on edge. They are fairly long, say, 24 inches. When you put them at opposite ends of a surface, they extend and exaggerate any twist when you sight one over the other (Fig. 3-1C).

A pair of winding strips can be made from close-grained hardwood with dowels in one to engage with holes in the other, so they can be stored together (Fig. 3-1D). A further refinement is to let in pieces of wood of a contrasting color in one piece (Fig. 3-1E) as sighting points.

Edges to be joined must be planed straight and square. With a power jointer or planing machine there should be no difficulty in getting true edges, but check straightness with a straightedge and by sighting along, then use a try square at several places. If the edge has to be made straight by hand, use as long a plane as possible. Its long straight sole bridges over hollows in the edge, so you take off the high spots first. A short plane is more likely to go up and down undulations in the edge.

Even when an edge has been planed straight on a jointer, you should finish it with a hand plane. The rotating cutters of a machine pound the edge and cut it, and this tends to close the pores of the wood so it becomes case-hardened and does not absorb glue readily. Taking off a shaving with a hand plane removes that sealed surface. If you are using a resinous or oily wood, glue immediately after planing while the surfaces are dry.

Although you may get accurate results by hand planing with the wood held in a vise, a *shooting board* can be used as a guide. The wood rests against the stop, and the plane slides on its side to take shavings off the edge (Fig. 3-2). Truth in planing depends on the shooting board being made true. If two boards have to be matched, one may be turned over for shooting, so any error in the shooting board is canceled. The shooting board needs to have a capacity longer than any wood you expect to plane. It can rest on the bench, or the underside may have a strip to grip in the vise.

Match edges to each other and check that the surfaces are flat when one piece rests on the other (Fig. 3-1F). Mark the meeting edges in some way. There could be numbers (Fig. 3-1G), lines across (Fig. 3-1H), or an overall marking on several joints (Fig. 3-1H).

CLAMPING

If a joint fails, it is usually at the ends due to the boards springing apart. One precaution is to plane the edges very slightly hollow (Fig. 3-3A). If they are clamped near the middle, the ends come under slightly more pressure than the center.

Another helpful way of keeping the ends close during clamping is to use *pinch dogs*. These are tapered on the inside (Fig. 3-3B). When the pinch dogs are driven into the end grain of two meeting boards, they press them together (Fig. 3-3C).

Both edges were coated with traditional glues, then rubbed together before clamping. With modern glues, it is better to bring both surfaces directly together after coating them. Follow the glue maker's instructions. Some glues only need enough clamping to hold the edges in contact. Excessive tightening would cause glue starvation and a weak joint.

Except if the width to be made up is excessive and includes many pieces, glue and clamp all the

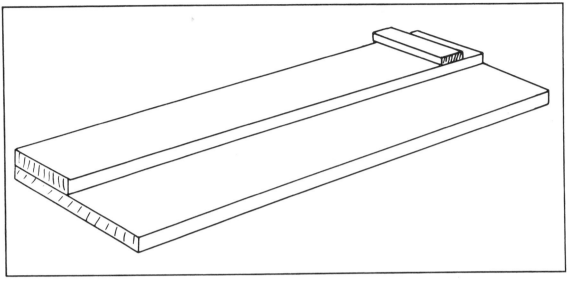

Fig. 3-2. A shooting board with a plane on edge helps in getting edges straight and square.

boards simultaneously. Spread the pressure and minimize damage to edges with strips under the clamp jaws. Besides bar clamps across pieces could be above and below and clamped to keep the assembly flat (Fig. 3-3D). You can improvise wedged clamps with two strips and bolts through to keep the work flat and draw the edges together (Fig. 3-3E).

Most glue instructions suggest a clamping time, then a further period while strength in the joint builds up. You can leave clamps on for this time, but if you want the clamps for another purpose, the assembly can be left without them. Support it so there are no bending strains across the joints (Fig. 3-3F).

DOWELED EDGES

If planed edges meet accurately and gluing is done correctly, the joints should be satisfactory without any other strengthening. Most glues are not gap filling, except for a very small amount, so for a joint to have its full strength the edges should be close for their whole length. If there is any doubt about the closeness of fit, reinforce the joint to compensate for any slight gaps that may fill with glue and not have much strength.

One way of strengthening an edge is to use

dowels at intervals. The size and number of dowels depend on the particular assembly. The dowels should be not more than half the thickness of the wood and could be spaced at about 6-inch intervals, with one fairly near each end of the joint where separating problems are most likely to come (Fig. 3-4A).

Bring the two boards to be joined together with their face sides outward and use a try square to mark across where the dowels are to come. Gauge from the face sides along the centers of the edges (Fig. 3-4B). The depth to take the dowels is not very important, but about three times the diameter into each piece would be about right, so ½-inch dowels in 1-inch boards could go 1½ inches into each half (Fig. 3-4C). Make the holes slightly deeper than the dowels are expected to go. Otherwise, a dowel may touch bottom both ways before the wood surfaces have met when you clamp the joint.

Drill squarely for the dowels. Slightly countersinking the tops of the holes will prevent a buildup of wood splinters that might prevent the joint from pulling closely together. Taper the ends of the dowels and saw grooves along them for excess glue and air to escape. More detailed instructions on dowel joints are given in Chapter 7.

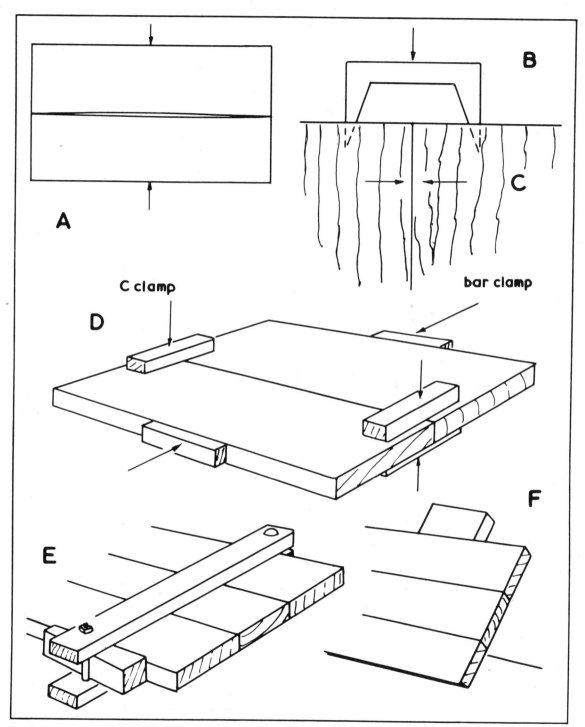

Fig. 3-3. Hollowed edges (A) pull ends tight. A dog pulls edges close (B, C). Clamp glued joints (D, E) and support joined boards flat (F).

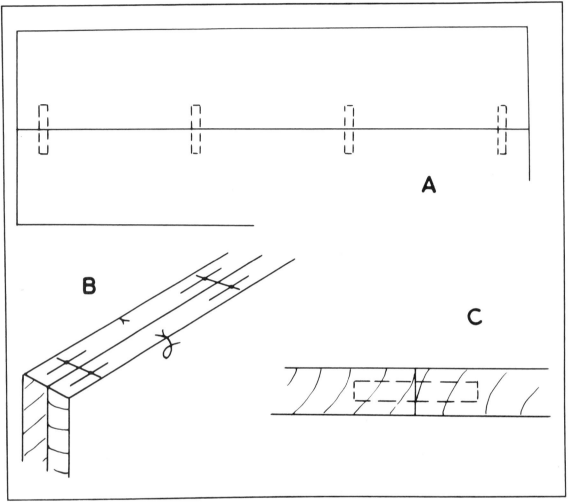

Fig. 3-4. Meeting edges may be strenghtened with dowels.

Glue in the dowels and coat both surfaces at one time, then clamp the parts in the usual way. Watch that the surfaces come together properly in the vicinity of the dowels. The dowels should keep the parts together if you want to remove the clamps almost immediately.

SECRET SLOT SCREWING

Edge joints can be reinforced and pulled together without clamps by *slot screwing*, sometimes called *keyhole screwing*, from the shape of the hole that has to be made. The screws are hidden in the finished joint.

Have the two boards together with their face sides outward in the same way as for marking out dowels. Screw spacing can be about the same as for dowels. The screws should be fairly stout steel ones. You will be driving the threaded part into one board. Much of the plain neck and the flat head will go into the other board at each position. For a tabletop between ¾ inch and 1 inch, you could use 10-gauge screws 1 inch of 1¼ inches long. Slightly thicker screws might be better for softwoods.

Mark the positions and gauge the center lines of each piece (Fig. 3-5A). On the other board, mark another center for each screw about ⅜ inch further along (Fig. 3-5B). At the single positions, drill for and drive the screws until their threads and a short length of the plain neck are buried (Fig. 3-5C). At the offset positions on the other board, drill a hole that will clear the screw head and take it deeper than the projection of the head on the other piece (Fig. 3-5D).

At the position opposite the screw, drill to the same depth with a bit that will make a hole an easy fit on the neck of the screw. Make a few more holes nearer the large hole, so you can chisel out a slot (Fig. 3-5E).

Make a trial assembly. Insert the screw heads in their holes and hammer one board along the other so the screw heads cut their way along to the ends of the slots (Fig. 3-5F). If this is satisfactory, drive the boards back and separate them. Give each screw a further partial turn—not more than half a turn. Put glue on the surfaces and drive the boards together again. It should be unnecessary to use clamps as the tightened screws will pull the joint tight without help.

BUTCHER BLOCK CONSTRUCTION

The popular *butcher block furniture* is made up of panels built to width by gluing comparatively narrow pieces together. Accuracy is needed in planing to width, so the parts are parallel and all the same size. If parts have to be prepared by hand planing, be careful in gauging and planing to the marked lines.

Allow some excess length for trimming to size

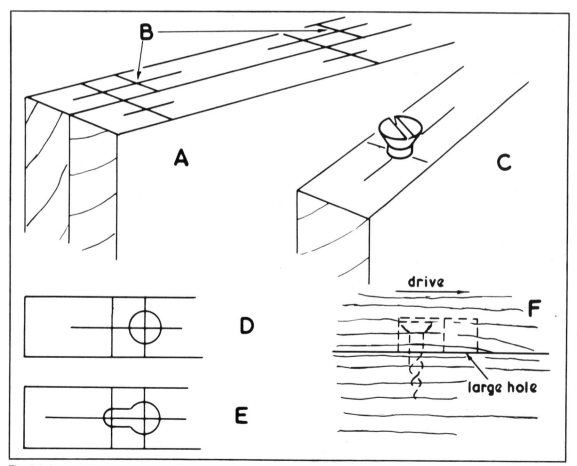

Fig. 3-5. In secret slot screwing an offset screw drives along a prepared groove in the other part.

afterward. Thicknesses should match, but some surface planing or sanding will almost certainly be needed after assembly. Pieces will normally be full length. For the sake of appearance and to carry on the original butcher block idea, though, you can include some short pieces, but don't have many. Stagger their joints (Fig. 3-6A) so they are reinforced by long pieces. It may be sufficient to let the short pieces merely butt together (Fig. 3-6B), but you can get better glue areas by lapping the ends (Fig. 3-6C).

Bench tops and other parts that may have to resist strains and knocks are sometimes made in the butcher block manner. Having many grains and pieces selected for their strength results in a stronger and more rigid top than if it was made of one or two wide boards. The expected loads put a considerable stain on the joints. They could have dowels arranged as already suggested, but there is another way of strengthening this construction.

The parts are assembled one piece at a time. Glue the second piece to the first and lightly clamp it while you drill for dowels (Fig. 3-7A). Go about halfway into the lower piece. Cut the dowels slightly short so you can punch them below the surface (Fig. 3-7B). Remove the clamps and glue on the next piece, which is lightly clamped to position it. Drill for more dowels, again going only partly into the lower piece. Punch dowels below the surface (Fig. 3-7C) and continue adding pieces until you have made up the width. You can include occasional short pieces butted together, but drive dowels each side of the butts (Fig. 3-7D). The last piece will have exposed dowel ends, but that will not usually matter if it is to the back. If appearance there is important, you can mark and drill the meeting surfaces for dowels going a short distance into each part in the way described earlier for joining boards (Fig. 3-7E).

CLAPBOARD

Overlapped boards arranged horizontally provide a weatherproof exterior on a building. They are sometimes called *weatherboard* and may be used vertically to form a fence.

Boards that are parallel in their thickness tend to be too bulky and clumsy, so clapboard is made tapered almost to a featheredge. In its simplest

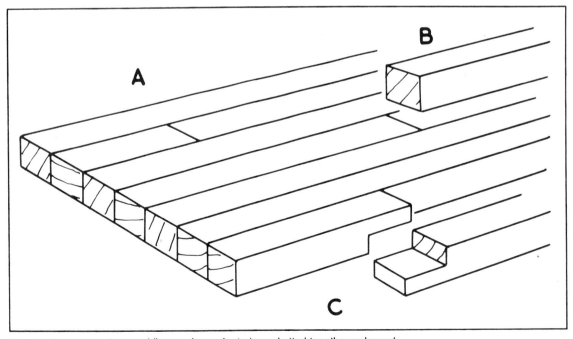

Fig. 3-6. Butcher block assemblies can have short pieces butted together or lapped.

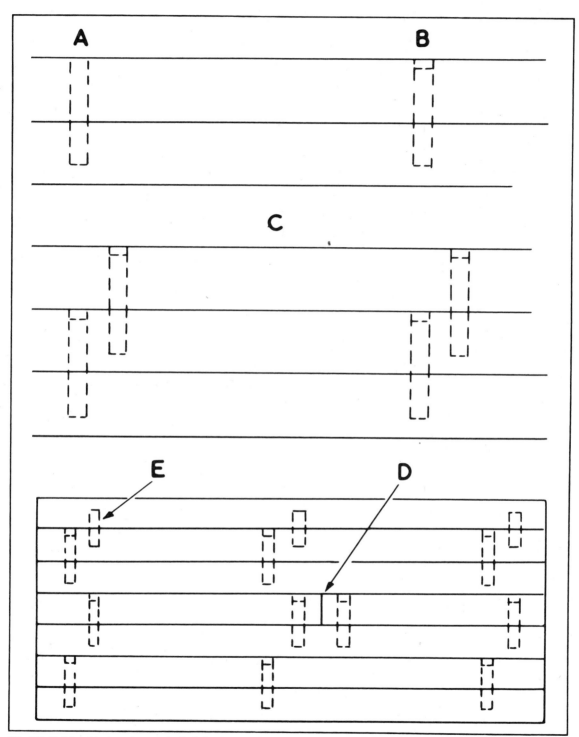

Fig. 3-7. Butcher block parts may be built by doweling strips in place one at a time.

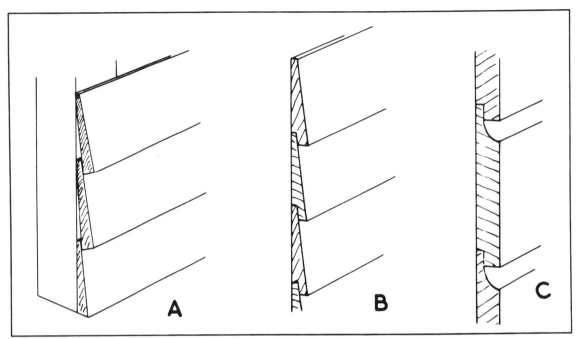

Fig. 3-8. Clapboard may simply overlap (A) or be rabbeted (B). Shaped boards (C) are also rabbeted.

form the edges are overlapped and nailed at intervals (Fig. 3-8A). Such boards may be left with a sawed finish, but if they are to be painted, they should be planed.

For a closer fit, the wide edges are rabbeted (Fig. 3-8B) deep enough for nails to go through the lap. A variation uses boards parallel in their thickness, but cut to fit in the rabbets (Fig. 3-8C). This is *shiplap*. For a neat finish the top board can fit into a rabbeted or grooved capping piece, and then the bottom board can have its rabbet cut off and stiffened with a rail. Ends of clapboard should be covered to prevent water from getting behind or soaking into the end grain. A strip nailed on is simplest. At a corner the boards may be cut back enough for a square piece to fit between them.

Chapter 4

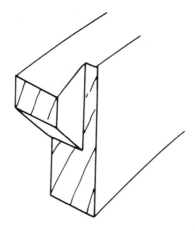

Halved Joints

WHEN TWO PIECES OF WOOD CROSS IN THE same plane, there has to be some joint to allow maintaining the level, on at least one surface, at the crossing. In some cases one piece may be cut completely and doweled or tenoned into the other piece. It is more common to cut a part out of each piece so they go across in continuous pieces. The joint used may be called *halving, half lap, checking* or *checked*, and *half checked*. Variations on the joint may also be used at corners of frames and where an internal member meets an outside one, but for many of these positions there are better joints of other construction.

A typical application of a half lap joint is where two rails cross in the underframing of a table. Another assembly that uses several forms of the joint has framing attached to the back of a plywood or other panel to stiffen it. All of the faces against the panel have to finish level. Corners, T-junctions, and crossings may be halved.

A halved joint is one of the simplest to cut, either by hand or machine. In its simplest form it does not have as good a resistance to pulling apart as some other joints, but with modern glues, and sometimes the reinforcement of screws or dowels, it is strong enough for many purposes. The halved joint must be close fitting. If there are gaps, much of the benefit of mutual support from the pieces is lost. The reduced thickness will be a weak point in the assembly.

A halving joint is the first choice for crossings, but whether to use it or a mortise and tenon or other joint at an outside edge or corner will have to be considered in the particular application.

CROSSED HALVED JOINT

If two pieces of similar section are to cross level, half has to be cut out of each piece (Fig. 4-1A), Except for the altered angles, the joint is the same if the pieces at an angle other than square (Fig. 4-1B).

Care is needed when marking out. Get the widths from the actual pieces of wood and use a knife to cut the lines across the grain. Gauge half the thickness by using the marking gauge from the

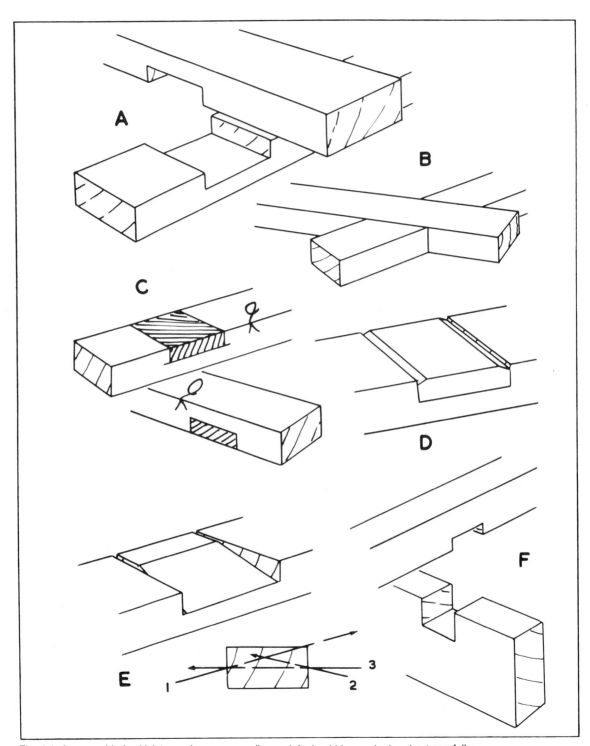

Fig. 4-1. A crossed halved joint may be square or diagonal. It should be marked and cut carefully.

face side of both pieces. If the setting is marginally off-center, it is not compounded if you gauged from opposite surfaces (Fig. 4-1C). The waste can be removed with a router. If you cut the joint with hand tools, use a chisel to pare across inside each cut line to form a guide for the saw (Fig. 4-1D). Chisel out the waste first from opposite sides before leveling the bottom (Fig. 4-1E).

For most applications, it is sufficient to glue a crossed halving joint. Screws or dowels can be arranged centrally or diagonally, depending on the size of the joint.

If the joint is between two pieces of wood of different thickness, but where one surface has to be level, the joint is stronger if not so much is cut from the thinner piece (Fig. 4-1F). That leaves a larger section of it to carry through, so it is not weakened as much as if half was cut out. If there is a considerable difference in depth between the two pieces, you could cut the thicker piece deep enough to take the full depth of the other, but it is usually better to cut quite a small amount of the thinner piece for the sake of accurate location.

HALVED CORNER JOINT

When two pieces of similar section are to meet at a corner, they can each have half cut away (Fig. 4-2A). This is particularly applicable to the corners of stiffening behind a frame. It is not as strong as some other joints for a frame where there is no panel to reinforce it. Dowels or screws through the joint would then be needed for greater strength. In some applications where you want to cut the halved joint at a corner, it may be possible to add a plywood or other gusset (Fig. 4-2B).

In marking out leave a small amount of excess length to be trimmed and planed level after the joint is finished. As with the crossed halving joint, mark out with the gauge against the face side of both pieces, then all cuts can be made with a saw. Keep the saw kerf on the waste side of the lines. Cut across the grain first, then saw diagonally along the grain (Fig. 4-2C). Turn over and cut the other way (Fig. 4-2D) before finally cutting straight through (Fig. 4-2E). You can see the lines each way and avoid letting the saw wander. You can make the

cross cuts with a table saw. Then make those cuts across the end (Fig. 4-2F). Keep the wood upright and tight against the saw fence. This is a useful method if you have a large number of similar corners.

T-HALVED JOINT

Where an internal piece meets an outside one, one piece is cut like a cross halving joint and the other like a corner joint (Fig. 4-3A). This also applies if they meet at an acute angle (Fig. 4-3B), such as when a strut is brought to a horizontal member or a shelf bracket is being constructed. Use knife cuts and a gauge to ensure close fits and leave the end slightly too long for trimming after the joint has been made.

In some assemblies the end grain should not show at the edge, so the T-halved joint can be stopped (Fig. 4-3C). The piece coming to the other can be cut in the same way as the through version, except that it is shorter and the end should be cut to length. The other part can have most of the waste cut away with a router, then the corners squared with a chisel (Fig. 4-3D). Part could be hand sawed (Fig. 4-3E), then the edges squared and waste removed with a chisel.

HOOKED HALVING JOINTS

Although most halving joints have their meeting surfaces flat, there are versions where they are cut on a slope. The joint then has some slight advantage in resisting pulling apart in one direction, but with glued construction this is probably not worthwhile. Halving joints can be hooked at a corner (Fig. 4-4A) or at a T-junction (Fig. 4-4B). There would be no advantage in cutting a crossed halving at a slope. If greater strength is needed at a T-junction, it is better to use one of the dovetail versions of the halving joint.

DOVETAILED HALVED JOINTS

The dovetail form is used in many joints besides pure dovetail ones (Chapter 9) where there is a need to resist a pull in one direction. This is seen in the dovetailed version of T-halved joints. The single leg has a dovetailed end, which resists any

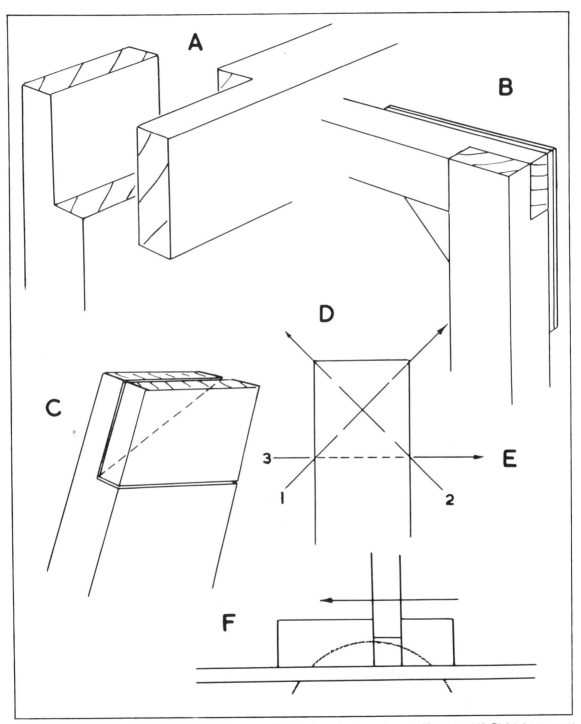

Fig. 4-2. A halved corner joint is similar in form to a crossed joint and may be strengthened with a gusset (A, B). It is best sawed in stages (C, D, E, F).

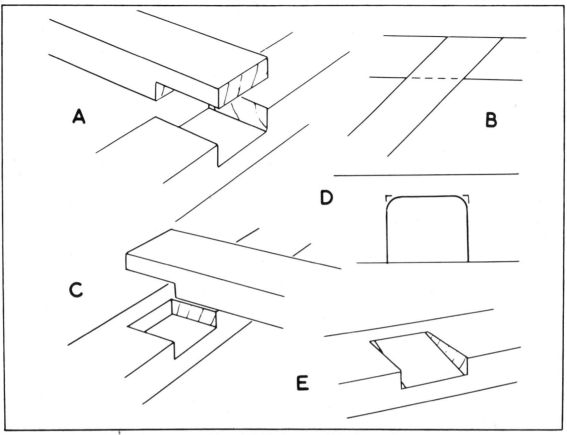

Fig. 4-3. A T-halved joint may be square or diagonal (A, B). A stopped joint (C) can be routed (D) or sawed (E).

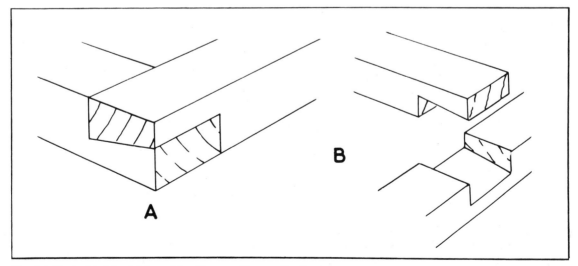

Fig. 4-4. Hooked halving joints resist pulling apart in one direction.

41

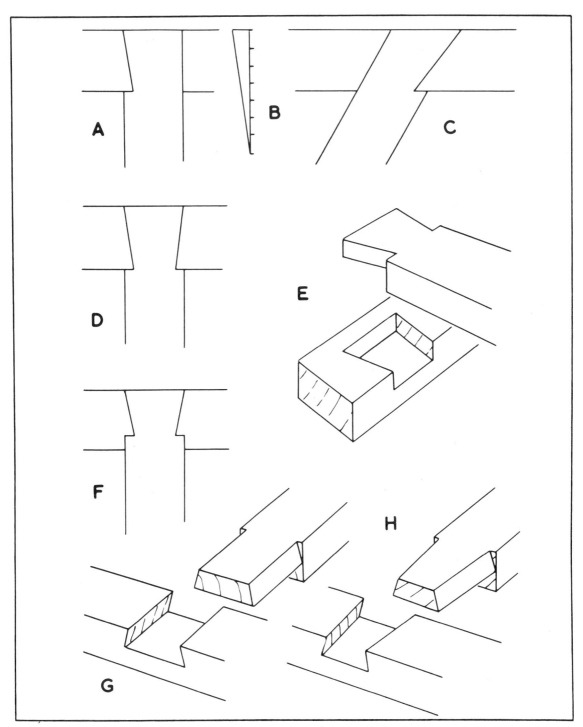

Fig. 4-5. Dovetail halving joints may slope at one or both sides (A, B, C, D) and may be stopped (E) or notched (F). Dovetailing the other way (G, H) resists lifting out.

load that attempts to pull the joint apart in the direction of its length. A less used version resists any load trying to pull the joint apart in a direction square to the meeting parts.

A one-sided dovetail may be needed (Fig. 4-5A). The usual angle of slope is about 1 in 7 (Fig. 4-5B), and the top of the dovetail is started slightly in from the width of the wood to give the saw a starting point. If the parts meet at an acute angle, the joint should be cut with the dovetail edge toward the obtuse side (Fig. 4-5C) to avoid the short grain that would occur at the other side and give greater strength.

The end can be dovetailed both sides (Fig. 4-5D), which should give a greater resistance to pulling part. It removes more of the wood of the single arm, though, and leaves it weaker at the change of section.

Either form a dovetail cutting can be stopped if the construction requires that the end grain does not show on the long edge (Fig. 4-5E).

One way of reducing the weakening effect of cutting dovetail slopes on both sides is to shoulder the dovetailed halved joint, so part of the end goes into the other at the full width and is then dovetailed (Fig. 4-5F). This could be done if only one side is sloped, but that form is not in such great need of reinforcing.

If the need is for a resistance to pulling apart square to the joint, a T-halved joint can be given dovetail slopes the other way (Fig. 4-5G). Sometimes the angle is made greater than 1 in 7, which may be advisable for softwoods, but it is easier to make a close fitting joint if the angle is more upright.

A complication is to give a slight taper across the joint, then as the cut piece is pushed into the slot it tightens (Fig. 4-5H). Both of these versions of the dovetail halved joint are only suitable where the method of assembly allows the T-piece to be pushed into the other. Nearly all other halving joints can be put together by entering the parts flat.

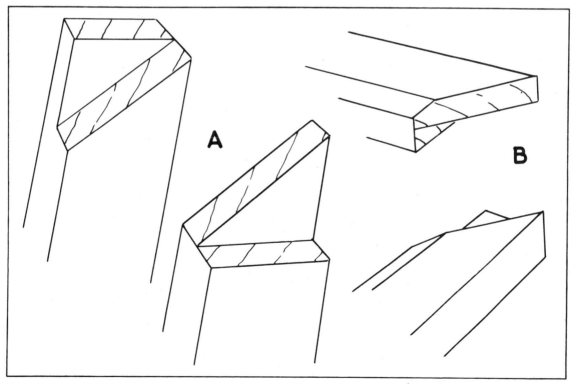

Fig. 4-6. A corner halved joint can be mitered on one face, but that reduces glue area.

MITERED HALVING JOINT

If the framing should have a mitered appearance, one face of the halved joint can be cut back (Fig. 4-6A). As this reduces the areas in contact for gluing, the joint is rather weak. That may not matter if it is backed with a plywood panel. This sort of corner may be needed if the inner edges are molded or simply beveled, then they meet at a miter (Fig. 4-6B). Strength can be given by screws from the back into the mitered tongue.

TIE JOINT

In house construction there is a variation on the cross halving joint where parts cross at an angle other than squarely. One piece fits straight across the other, but that one has the sides of its cut angled inward (Fig. 4-7A). The angles should not be too great, or the cut piece may be weakened too much. Another variation with similar applications is a housed halving joint, where one part has notched shoulders into the other part. As with the first

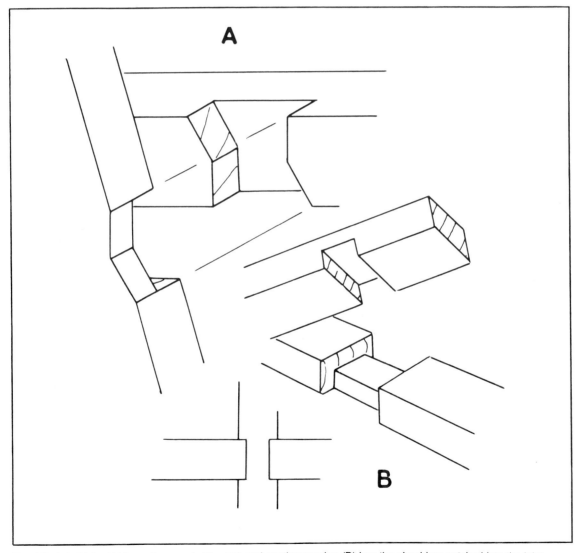

Fig. 4-7. A tied joint (A) has edges angled inward, and another version (B) has the shoulders notched into the joint.

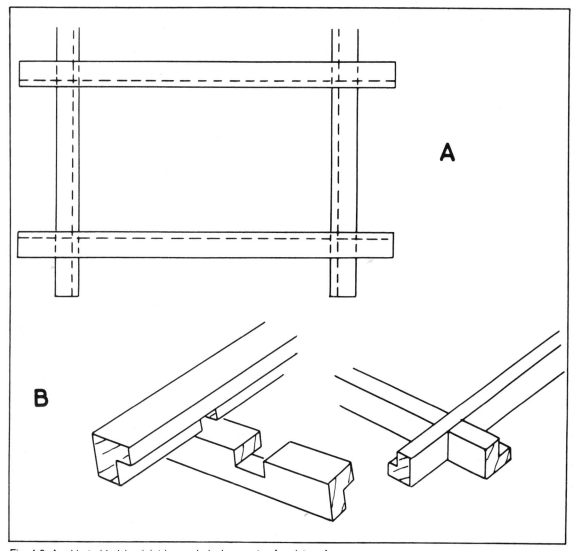

Fig. 4-8. A rabbeted halving joint is needed when parts of a picture frame cross.

example, the notching should only be slight or the cutaway part will be weakened (Fig. 4-7B).

RABBETED HALVING JOINT

In some constructions the crossing pieces have rabbets in them. An example comes in the *Oxford picture frame*, where the arms forming the frame extend past the corners (Fig. 4-8A). This would also apply if a mirror or panel has to be put into a crossed frame assembly, with the need for rabbets in the back. In that case the rabbets would finish at the joints, but in a picture frame it is common to carry them through.

The joint is a basic halving, except you have to cut away at different widths at the two levels. The cutaways should come at the rabbet levels even if these are not halfway through the wood. One part is then cut away on the front to suit the width of the front of the other piece, then that is cut away to suit the wood left beside the rabbet (Fig. 4-8B).

DEEP HALVING

In the making of divisions in a drawer or the assembly of a light display frame, pieces have to cross to form halving joints that are quite deep in relation to their widths (Fig. 4-9A). Providing the wood is stable and there is little risk of casting or warping, this is satisfactory for light loads, but the end grain against side grain will not make a wood glued joint. Where the crossed parts are supported outside by the framing of a drawer or other item, this assembly will probably be strong enough.

If there is enough thickness in the wood to allow grooving and halving, there can be much more mutual support between the parts if they slide into each others' grooves as they are put together (Fig. 4-9B). The grooves need only be quite shallow as their purpose is to prevent the edges in them twisting and to provide slightly more glue area.

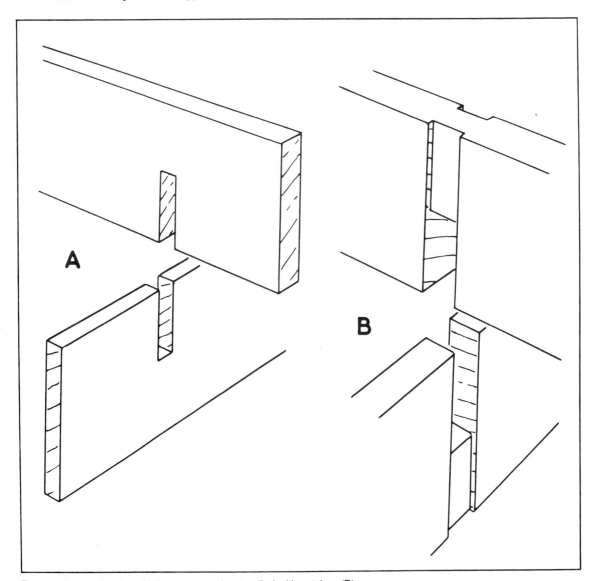

Fig. 4-9. In deep halving (A) the parts may be steadied with notches (B).

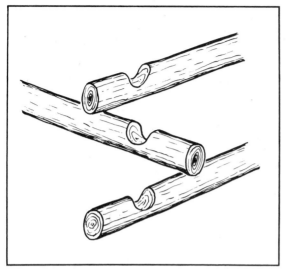

Fig. 4-10. In log cabin construction each log is notched halfway through for the one above.

LOG HALVING

In the corner of a cabin or other log structure, the logs have to be fitted into each other. This is not such precision carpentry as other constructions, although reasonably close fits are desirable. To bring the logs close, each has to be notched about halfway through to take the next log (Fig. 4-10). This is normally done with a saw or ax as the building progresses. The joints can then be adjusted as any leveling of log surfaces is being done.

THREE-WAY CORNER

In framed construction three parts of a frame may have to meet square to each other, like the corner of a cube. If it is nailed assembly, rather than a piece of cabinetry, you can cut the parts into each other in a form of halving joint, which can be drilled for nails all ways to hold it together.

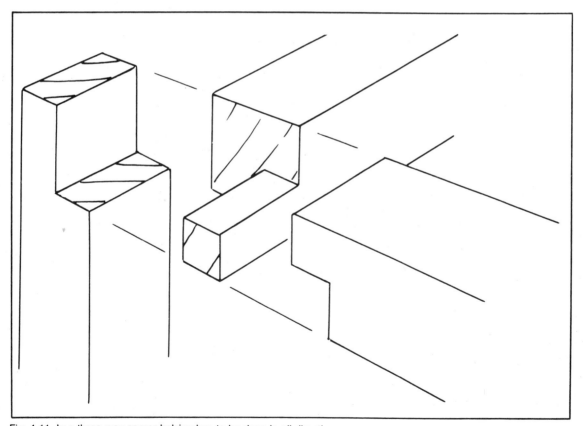

Fig. 4-11. In a three-way corner halving has to be done in all directions.

The upright piece is cut away as if for a normally halved corner (Fig. 4-11). The other two fit into it, using half of each part to fill the space.

THREE-WAY FLAT JOINT

If three pieces have to cross all in the same plane, the joint is a form of halving, but the parts are cut in thirds rather than halves. The pieces may cross evenly divided around a circle, as they would if forming the spokes of a wheel (Fig. 4-12A). They could be part of a wooden wheel, or they might be part of a wooden pattern intended to be used for casting a metal wheel. The spokes outside the joint would be shaped in the way the metal is intended to be cast.

This is a version of the halving joint that is difficult to visualize and make accurately. It is probably best to start with the central part and one side. When they have been cut and fitted, mark out that combination and the third side for the final fitting. Keep the wood overlong to be trimmed and jointed at the ends after the central joint has been cut.

Mark the face sides of all three pieces. Gauge the thicknesses into three, working from the face sides only and carrying the gauge lines far enough to embrace all the later cuts. Make a full-size drawing of the three crossing pieces showing their widths and angles (60 degrees for equally spaced spokes). Set an adjustable bevel to this angle and use it for marking across the wood.

Mark the central piece, with 60-degree cuts on opposite sides, squared down to the gauge lines with knife marks. Cut inside the lines and be careful not to go below the gauge lines, which would weaken this comparatively thin part (Fig. 4-12B).

The pieces that go each side of the central piece have to be cut away to two-thirds of their thickness. One has to fit over the central part and have its edges cut to match the recess of the opposite side (Fig. 4-12C). Fitting this part allows you to see the shape to cut the final piece (Fig. 4-12D). After the parts have been glued and pulled together with a clamp, mark the center of the joint. Use this to measure from to get the lengths of the six spokes or arms.

SLOPED T-HALVING JOINT

When a deep part has to be notched into an even deeper part, as when a beam supporting a boat cabin top has to be joined to a cabin side (Fig. 4-13A), maximum strength in a halving joint can be obtained by cutting away as little wood as possible at the end of the beam. This can be done by sloping the tongue (Fig. 4-13B). How much depends on the sizes of wood, but the angle could be between 30 and 45 degrees.

Besides leaving more wood to take the load in the piece with the tongue, the angle reduces the amount of change in the section of the wood. In any structure whatever the material, and failure nearly always happens at an abrupt change of section. Minimizing the change increases strength.

If there is expected to be a load trying to withdraw the part with the tongue, it may be dovetailed in the usual way on one (Fig. 4-13C) or both sides. Sloping does not interfere with dovetailing.

STRENGTH LAPPED JOINT

When two pieces are notched into each other, the shoulders prevent either piece from moving laterally across the other. There are places where this could be a valuable consideration, yet there is no need to bring the pieces to the same level. An example is the diagonal brace of a gate (Fig. 4-14A) where the parts notched together provide resistance to the gate sagging.

Cutting full half lap joints would weaken the parts by taking out too much, but each piece can be notched slightly to provide strength while leaving most of the thickness of the wood outside (Fig. 4-14B). Notches can be just enough to provide a grip, ¼ inch in a 2-inch thickness should do. A central bolt or dowel can be through each joint in place of or in addition to glue.

NOTCHED JOINT

In some assemblies, particularly in house construction, a full half lap joint or even a strength lap joint may not be needed. There may be value in

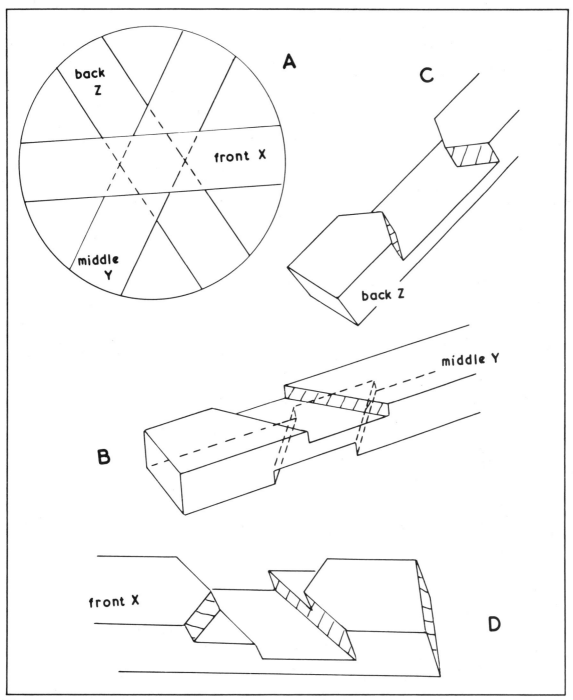

Fig. 4-12. For three parts to cross level (A) the central piece is notched for the others (B), which fit into it and into each other (C, D).

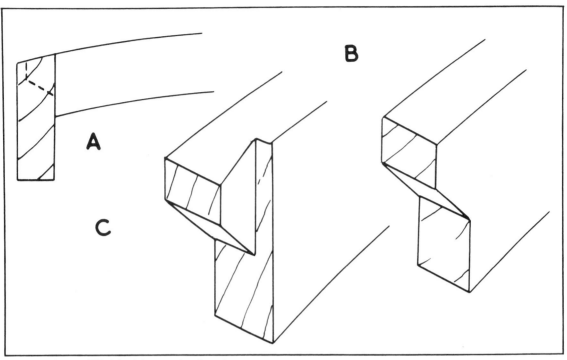

Fig. 4-13. A deep T-halving joint may be sloped.

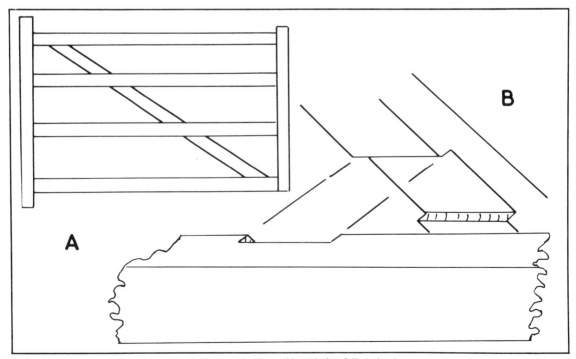

Fig. 4-14. In a gate parts may be notched into each other without being fully halved.

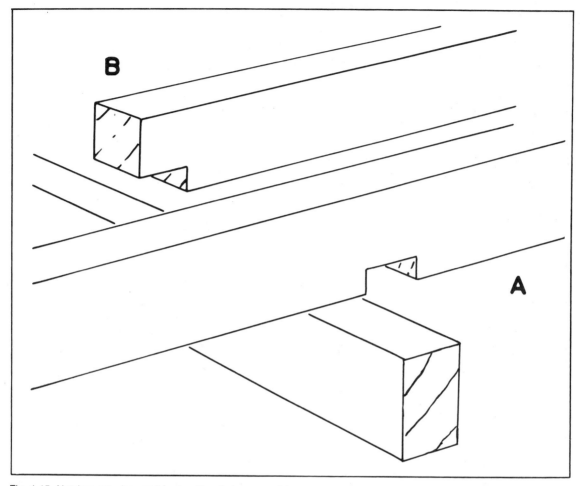

Fig. 4-15. Notches may be used for location during assembly.

locating one piece in one direction against another. In that case it is notched, either in the length (Fig. 4-15A) or at its end (Fig. 4-15B). This may push or pull against the untreated piece, with the notch to resist movement. There may have to be an adjustment the other way during assembly, then locking in position is by nailing or screwing.

NOTCHED AND COGGED JOINT

When a piece of fairly light section has to cross a much more substantial piece, an ordinary lap joint would involve cutting out rather more than is necessary for strength and location. In this case the large piece is notched from both sides to leave a narrow part, over which the lighter piece is notched in the same way as a half lap joint (Fig. 4-16). This is primarily a joint used in building carpentry.

COGGED JOINT

A less common arrangement has the notch worked in the lower piece, then a cog is cut in the top one (Fig. 4-17). A cog is a single projecting piece like one tooth in a cog wheel. This fits the notch and prevents sideways movement in a T-joint, without cutting much out of either piece.

ROOFING DOVETAILED HALVING JOINT

In a roof truss the rafters are stopped from spread-

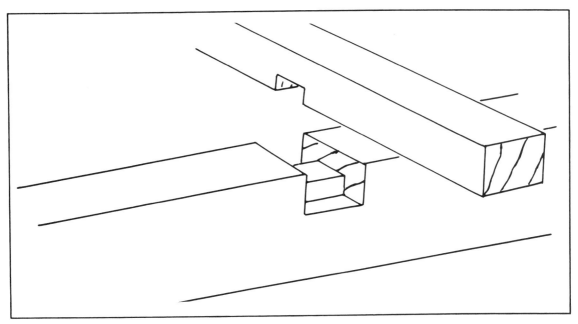

Fig. 4-16. A light piece over a stouter one can go into a notched cog.

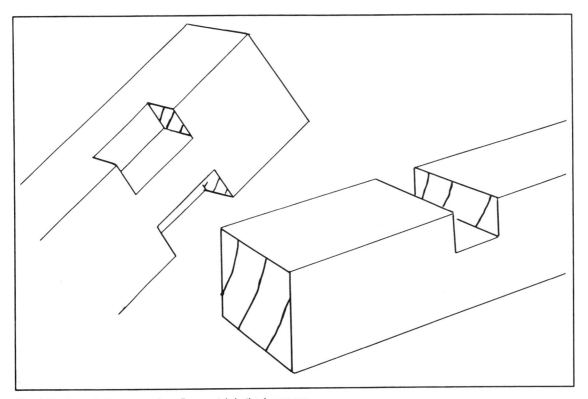

Fig. 4-17. A cog in the upper piece fits a notch in the lower one.

ing under load by a beam called a collar between them. The load at its end tends to pull outward on the joint, and this has to be resisted. One way of doing this is with a dovetailed halving joint (Fig. 4-18A). The parts do not have to finish level, so it is common to cut only a shallow notch in the rafter and make the tongue on the collar fairly thick. Neither piece is weakened much, and the collar stands out of the rafter (Fig. 4-18B). The dovetail slope is on the top edge of the collar only (Fig. 4-18C) and may be about 1 in 7.

WEDGED HALVING JOINT

A T-halving joint with parallel sides depends on glue and screws or dowels to resist withdrawal. It could be made with a dovetail form on one or both sides, but it still has to be an easy enough fit to be dropped in. If the joint is wedged in a similar way to a tenon, a plain halving joint can be spread to match a tapered socket to get the maximum tightness and resistance to withdrawal. The sides of the socket should be cut with a taper for part of the thickness (Fig. 4-19A), and a saw cut is made in the other part to take the wedge (Fig. 4-19B).

Keep the board flat meeting surfaces closely in contact as the wedge is driven, so a clamp over scrap wood could be used while gluing and wedging. Once the wedge is tight, the surfaces should remain in contact.

DOUBLE DOVETAILED HALVING JOINT

If a halving joint can be given a dovetail section both

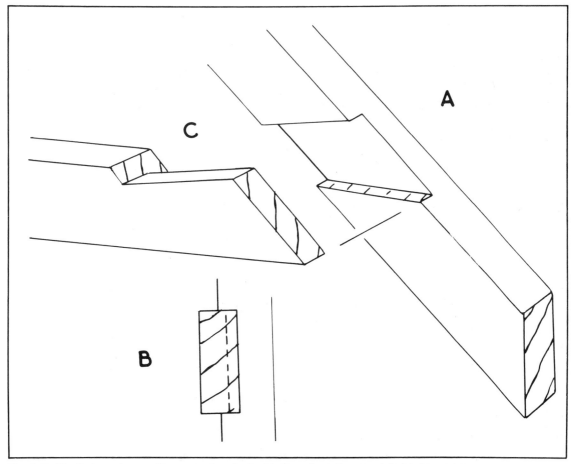

Fig. 4-18. The tie beam in a roof truss may be attached to the rafter with a dovetailed halving joint.

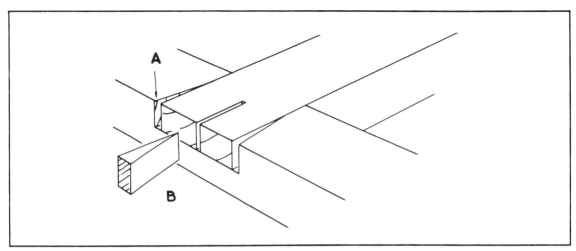

Fig. 4-19. A wedge in a halving joint helps it resist withdrawal.

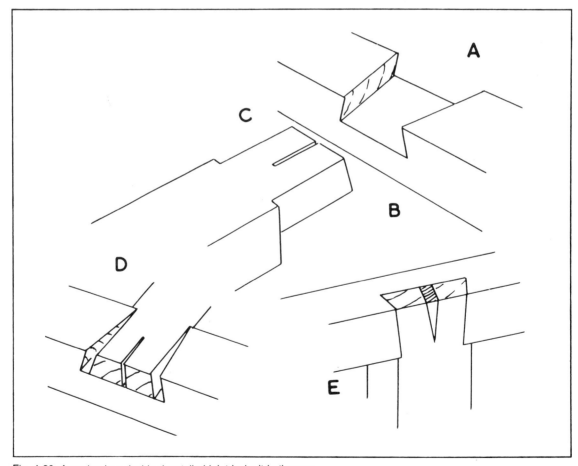

Fig. 4-20. A wedge in a double dovetailed joint locks it both ways.

ways, it cannot pull apart. That can only be arranged by wedging one way. The socketed part is cut to dovetail slopes on both surfaces (Fig. 4-20A). Unlike the normal dovetail halving joint, the narrowest part is not cut back, but the bottom of the cut is the full width of the other piece (Fig. 4-20B), which is cut parallel at the dovetail angle to small shoulders and is given a saw cut for the wedge (Fig. 4-20C). That part should slide in so it fits closely at the bottom of the recess, but there is space each side at the top (Fig. 4-20D). The taper and width of the wedge should be sufficient to spread the tongue to the sides of the recess (Fig. 4-20E).

In this and other wedging, it helps to have the wedge as dry as possible, then it will not shrink and loosen later. The wedge might be dried in an oven.

STOPPED WEDGED HALVING JOINT

A problem with driving a wedge into a saw cut is the possibility of the wood splitting further and the crack showing below the joint. One way of reducing this risk is to drill a hole at the bottom of the saw cut (Fig. 4-21A). Unless the wedge drives into the far side of the hole or the wood is very prone to splitting, there can be a considerable spread with the wedge without risk.

This method could be used for a double dovetailed halving joint (Fig. 4-21B). Use a wedge with a wider taper than would otherwise be advisable.

A wedge cut to a more obtuse angle than usual may be inclined to spring back after driving. If the wedge is roughened or is metal with teeth chopped in it with a chisel, it should hold in place. If you are satisfied that further tightening will not be needed, a plain wedge may be glued in. Another way to hold the wedge in is to line the hole with a piece of metal tube, with a slot sawed in it (Fig. 4-21C). Position

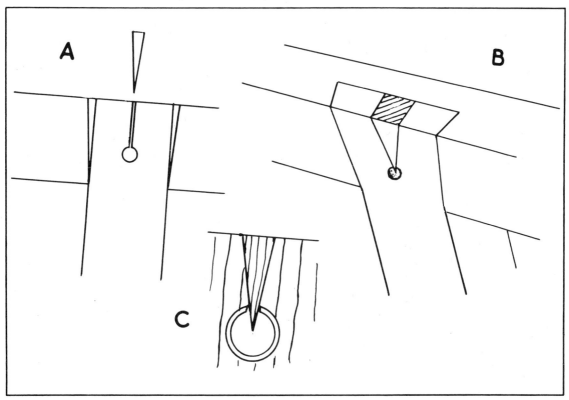

Fig. 4-21. If the wedge slot in a halving joint is stopped with a hole, there is a resistance to splitting. A cut metal tube can provide a lock.

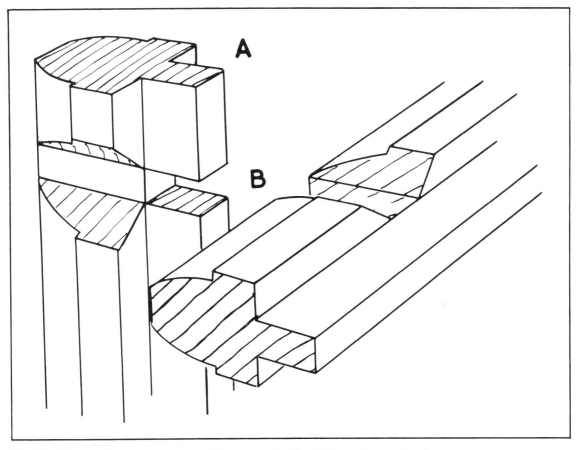

Fig. 4-22. Where sash bars cross, the wood is at two levels. The thicker parts are mitered.

the slot so the wedge will drive into it, and the rough sawed edge should grip the wood.

SASH BAR HALVING

When a window is divided into several panes, the glazing bars have to cross. They must be halved together, but their section has two rabbets for glass and putty with the other thicker side often molded (Fig. 4-22A). Even if the thicker part is not molded, there is the problem of crossing two sections of different thicknesses.

It is best to regard the crossing as being of the thinner parallel sections. The wider parts are mitered, so the crossing pieces can be marked across and cut. The miters are made into them (Fig. 4-22B).

Chapter 5

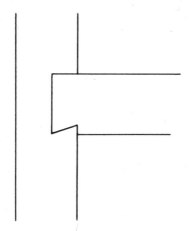

Dado and Housing Joints

WHEN THE END OF ONE PIECE IS NOTCHED IN-
to another piece, as with a shelf into an
upright, the joint may be called a *dado*. The parts
are housed together, and the result is a housing
joint. The notch is a dado groove.

This joint provides positive location for the
shelf and a resistance to slipping down under load in
a way that nailing or screwing through or supporting
on a cleat or batten cannot. There may not be much
strength to resist pulling apart, but in most assemblies there are other parts of the structure that
provide this resistance. If the joint itself has to
resist an endwise load, there are ways of reinforcing it. It may be better to use multiple tenons or
other through arrangements.

SIMPLE DADO

The simplest example has the groove cut right
across (Fig. 5-1A). The end of the shelf should be
cut squarely, but otherwise it needs no special
preparation. The depth to cut the groove depends
on circumstances. Maximum depth gives the

greatest area of contact so the structure of the joint
is strongest, but cutting out to much may weaken
the upright. It helps to have the upright thicker than
the shelf, so a good depth of groove is possible. The
groove must be a good fit on the shelf.

A router is a good tool for making a dado
groove. There can be two passes of a narrower cut
to get the exact width (Fig. 5-1B). If the groove is
cut by hand, gauge the depth and mark the width
with knife cuts taken fairly deep. You can then tilt a
chisel to take out some waste inside the lines (Fig.
5-1C) as a guide for a fine backsaw. When you chisel
out the waste, use a straightedge to check that the
bottom of the groove is flat. The center must not be
higher than the ends if the joint is to close properly.
A slight hollowing would be preferable.

STOPPED DADO JOINT

In many pieces of furniture it is better if the front
edge of the joint does not show, so the groove is
stopped or made blind a short distance back from
the front edge of the upright (Fig. 5-2A). The front

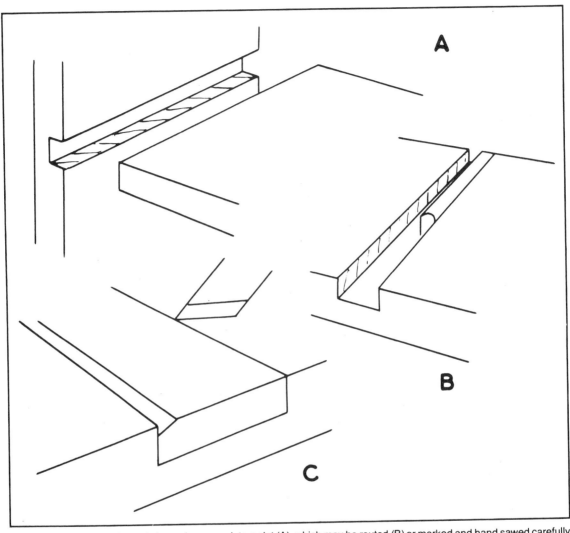

Fig. 5-1. In a dado joint the end of one piece goes into a slot (A), which may be routed (B) or marked and hand sawed carefully (C).

part of the joint does not then provide strength or rigidity, so the cut should be kept narrow—usually not more than ½ inch.

The blind dado is marked out for hand cutting (Fig. 5-2B), then a part of the closed end is cut out with chisels to allow a saw to be used on the two sides. A small amount is left at the end for the saw to hit against (Fig. 5-2C). That is not cut to its final size until all the other cutting of the groove has been done. Saw the sides of the groove with short strokes. Let the end of the saw go into the chiseled

hollow, then remove the waste with a chisel (Fig. 5-2D). A hand router, sometimes called an old woman's tooth plane, is useful for getting the bottom of the groove level. Check the flatness of the groove with a straightedge.

If a router is used, the end of the groove could be squared with a chisel or left rounded. The shelf is cut to match (Fig. 5-2E).

If the cutback on the shelf is machined, it may be rounded and then squared with a chisel, or it could be left and enough groove cut away to suit

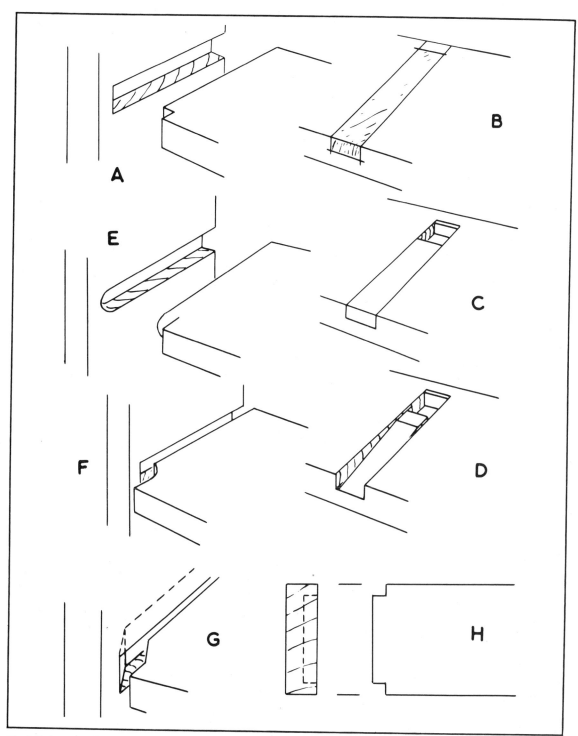

Fig. 5-2. A stopped dado joint may be marked and cut in several ways.

(Fig. 5-2F). The two parts could be cut at an angle where they meet (Fig. 5-2G). It is always better to have a close fit than to leave a gap for convenience in machining. If both edges have to be hidden, the groove may be stopped both ways (Fig. 5-2H), but that presents difficulty in cutting the groove.

STRENGTHENED DADO JOINT

Glue in a dado joint mostly comes between end and side grain. It does not give very great strength, and the dadoed parts have to rely on joints elsewhere keeping them together. If more strength directly in the joint is needed, screws or nails could be endwise into the shelf (Fig. 5-3A) if the outside appearance is not important. Dowels could be put through the same way (Fig. 5-3B) and wedged outside (Fig. 5-3C) for greater strength.

Usually the outside is better left unmarked. The undersides of the shelves are not usually very prominent, so strengthening can be by screws or nails driven diagonally from below (Fig. 5-3D). Heads do not show much if the entry is close into the angle. In many assemblies where there is a back to hold the rear of the joint, one screw at the front of a joint may be all that is needed.

If a resistance is wracking or distortion is needed, there might be a block under the joint (Fig. 5-3E). It could be beveled and kept back from the front to make it less conspicuous.

DOVETAILED DADO JOINT

One way of giving a dado joint a resistance to pulling out is to make the groove a dovetail section and shape the shelf end to match. In section only one

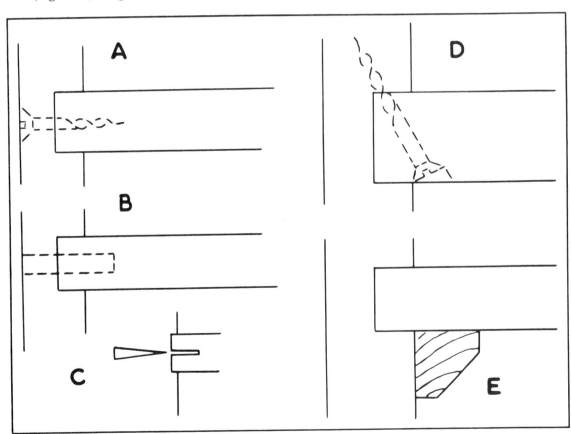

Fig. 5-3. A screw (A) or dowel (B) may go into the end of a dado joint, and the dowel can be wedged (C). A screw may be driven from underneath (D) or a block glued in (E).

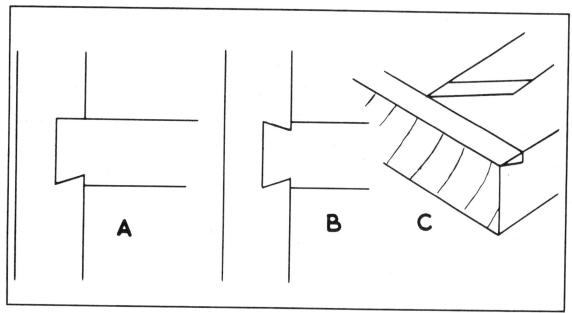

Fig. 5-4. Dovetailing a dado joint helps resist withdrawal.

side may be sloped (Fig. 5-4A), or they both may (Fig. 5-4B). Sloping both sides removes more of the shelf's thickness, so it should only be done if there is enough wood to allow this without weakening. If only one side is sloped, that could be on the underside or the side least obvious, as the straight side is easier to finish neatly.

The sloping edge of the groove may be cut with a suitable router cutter, which would have to be changed to a square cut one if the other side of the groove is to be upright. The shelf end should have a deep knife cut across to guide the saw (Fig. 5-4C). The small amount of end grain to be tapered can be pared with a chisel. Whether it is a through dado or a blind one, the shelf has to slide in from the back. When paring the shelf end, it helps to pare only a short distance from the front edge. Try this before paring a little more and trying entry progressively. This helps to avoid taking off too much and producing a loose joint.

TAPERED DOVETAILED DADO JOINT

A problem with the joint just described comes when you have to slide the shelf across a dado in a wide board. It may be difficult to achieve final tightness

after having to ease the joint so it slides at only partial assembly.

Providing there is enough thickness of wood in the shelf to allow more wood to be cut away, the dovetail part of the shelf end can taper, so it is thinner near the front. This may be done with the dovetail angle on one side (Fig. 5-5A). If you dovetail both edges, both could be tapered. The benefits are the same with the taper at one side only (Fig. 5-5B). This applies whether the joint goes through or is blind. As you assemble the joint by sliding the shelf in from the back, it does not become tight until it is fully home. Intermediate binding is avoided.

For a one-sided taper, mark and cut the end to the amount of the taper first (Fig. 5-5C), then work the dovetail slope on the tapered edge which is usually preferable to the parallel edge. Do the same on the second edge for a two-sided dovetail section.

Mark the thickness of the shelf across the side. Measure the actual thickness at the root of the cut shelf end and repeat these sizes on the part to be grooved (Fig. 5-5D). Cut in these lines and work the groove in the usual way. For maximum tightness, make the joint so it comes within a short

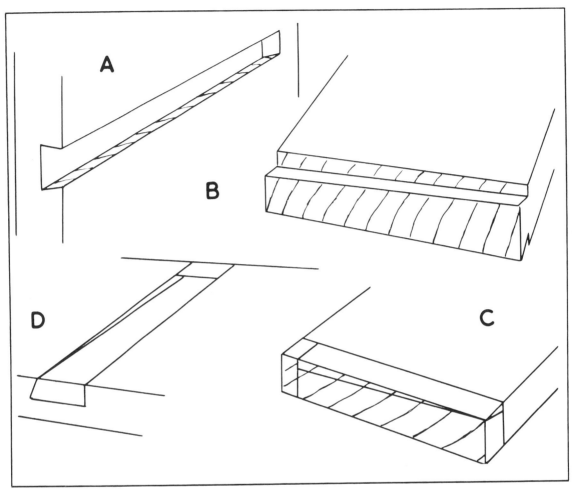

Fig. 5-5. A tapered stopped dovetail dado joint is easy to assemble.

distance of completeness during trial assembly. Make the final assembly with pressure from a clamp.

TAPERED DADO JOINT

A dado joint can have a taper across even if it is not dovetailed (Fig. 5-6). This gives the benefit of tightening by driving the shelf forward from the back, although it can be pushed straight in from the side, which a dovetailed end cannot. Only the last part of assembly is done with back pressure.

PARTIALLY TAPERED DADO JOINT

If it would be preferable to retain most of the full depth of a shelf's end for strength, yet the tightening advantage of a taper would be welcomed, you can keep most of the shelf end full thickness, but have a short taper toward the front (Fig. 5-7A). Just a short piece tapers up from the underside. This could be combined with a dovetail, which is more easily worked on the top (Fig. 5-7B). The tapered part cannot be hand sawed. It will have to be trimmed with chisels. For a blind dado on most shelves, the taper may be about one-fourth of the width and taper to three-fourths thickness.

DADO AND TENON JOINTS

The strength of a dado joint may be increased by

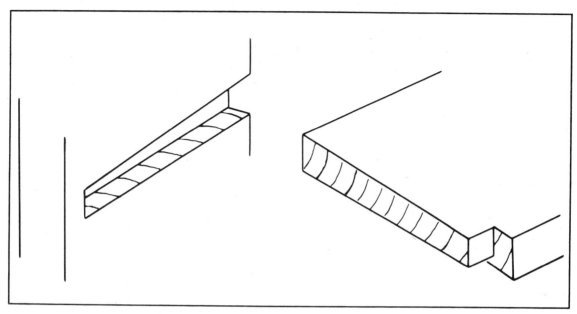

Fig. 5-6. A dado joint may be tapered without dovetailing.

including one or more tenons. If it is a narrow joint, there can be one tenon through (Fig. 5-8A). If that is wedged outside, the joint will be very strong.

Use two or more tenons for a wider joint. They can be widely spaced, and each is not more than twice the thickness of the shelf. It may be sufficient

to have tenons only near the edges (Fig. 5-8B) or only near the front edge if there is a back or other rear part to hold the joint there. A secondary advantage of tenons is that they unite the two parts to give mutual support in resistance to warping.

In many assemblies the ends of tenons show-

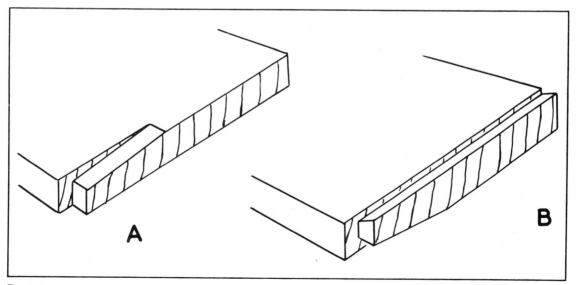

Fig. 5-7. In a wide shelf tapering may only be partial.

ing on the surface would be unacceptable. If there is enough thickness in the end to allow it, the mortises can be blind or stopped. The short tenons secured with foxtail wedging (Fig. 5-8C).

RABBET AND DADO JOINT

If the shelf is fairly thick, taking it into the end a satisfactory amount would involve removing so much from the end that it would be weakened. In a compromise joint the full shelf goes in a short distance, then it is reduced and a narrower tongue goes deeper (Fig. 5-9) to provide more glue area without having to cut away so much wood.

STUDDING DADO JOINT

Most applications of the dado or housing joint are for wide boards like shelves. Most of the variations can be used with thicker and more nearly square material.

Horizontal members between studs that will have panels on one or both sides can have simple dado joints. If the full depth of the horizontal part is to be let in, the dado should not be very deep (Fig. 5-10A). The piece could be reduced in thickness and let in further (Fig. 5-10B). For general carpentry in both cases, a nail driven diagonally will provide sufficient security.

TAPERED STUDDING DADO JOINT

In the previous example the sides of the dado have to be sawed and the waste removed with a chisel. When you are cutting the joint in position, possibly in a situation that is awkwardly placed, it may be difficult to fit the parts accurately. It is possible to use a V-cut so the joint can be cut with a saw only (Fig. 5-11A). If you cut the end of the horizontal piece first, it may be put against the other part and marked round to get the shape of the V-cut.

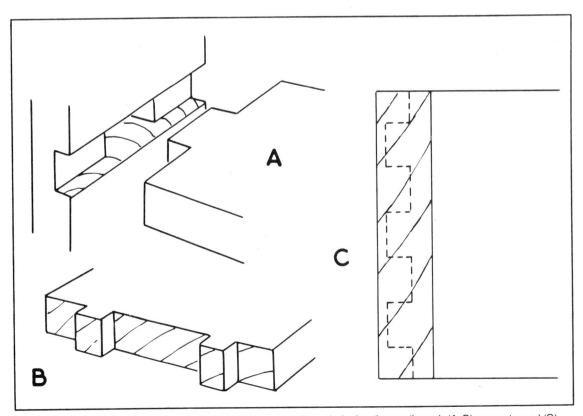

Fig. 5-8. If tenons are taken through a dado joint, it will be strengthened whether they go through (A, B) or are stopped (C).

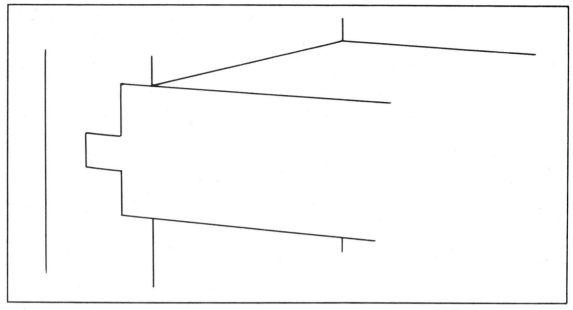

Fig. 5-9. In thick material a dado joint in two steps does not remove as much wood.

This joint also allows you to drop a part into position. If the angle is cut suitably, a horizontal strip can swing down into the other part (Fig. 5-11B).

HOUSED BATTEN

If several boards are glued together to make a large flat surface, such as a drawing board, the assembly needs *battens* across to keep it flat. The battens

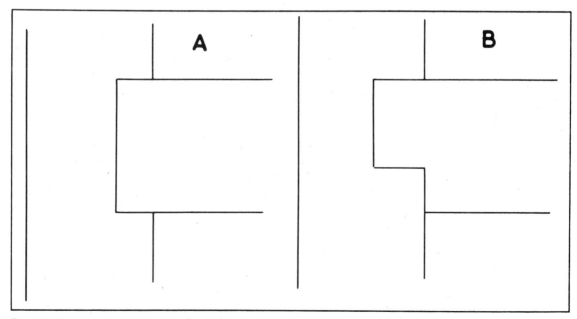

Fig. 5-10. A stud dado joint may take the full depth of a horizontal piece, or that can be notched.

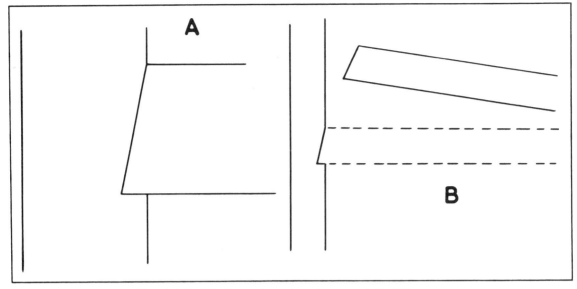

Fig. 5-11. In a tapered studding dado joint the horizontal part can be swung into place.

could be screwed on, with the screws in slots to allow for expansion and contraction. Another method of stiffening uses housed battens.

In the simplest form there is a dado groove across the board that is given a slight taper, then the batten has a similar taper (Fig. 5-12A). Usually the batten is thicker, so it projects and raises the board above the table. Thicker battens also have a better resistance to any tendency of the board to warp.

The batten has to be knocked backward and forward as necessary to allow for changes in the board.

Such a straight-sectioned batten has nothing to keep it in the dado if it loosens. It is better to dovetail it. That can be in its full depth (Fig. 5-12B), or the outer part may be parallel and only the joining part dovetailed (Fig. 5-12C).

A slight taper is needed across the board only. In a width of 18 inches, little more than ¼ inch of

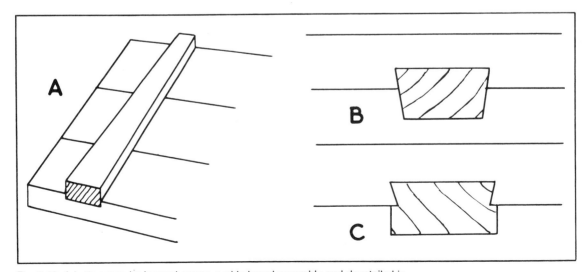

Fig. 5-12. A batten may be housed across a wide board assembly and dovetailed in.

taper would do. The edges toward the ends could be square to the edges of the boards, and only the inner parts are tapered. Make the battens too long at first so they can be driven, then cut to an expected average length.

CORNER DADO JOINT

If a shelf has to be fitted into the corner legs of a table, dado grooves for it are quite small. Some reinforcing is necessary. If too much is cut from the leg to form a groove for the shelf, it will be weakened.

If the shelf does not extend more than half the width of the leg, a simple notch can be diagonally across the inner corner (Fig. 5-13A).

If the shelf goes to the outsides of the legs, don't cut across the leg corner to corner as that would weaken the leg. Cut two tapered dado grooves across the leg (Fig. 5-13B). A small angle could be cut across the inner corner (Fig. 5-13C).

Whatever the form, the amount of glue surface and the fact that it is end to side grain means that the joint is weak. A screw can be driven diagonally upward from near the inner corner of the leg. Cutting away under the shelf will not show, and it will allow the screw hole to be drilled at a more upright angle (Fig. 5-13D).

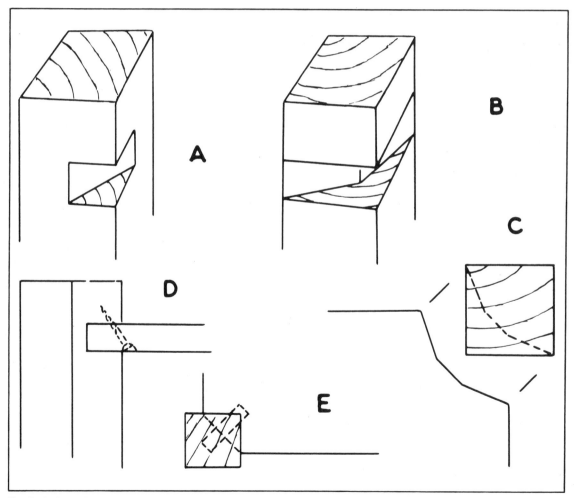

Fig. 5-13. A shelf may be notched fully or partially into a square leg and held with a screw or dowel.

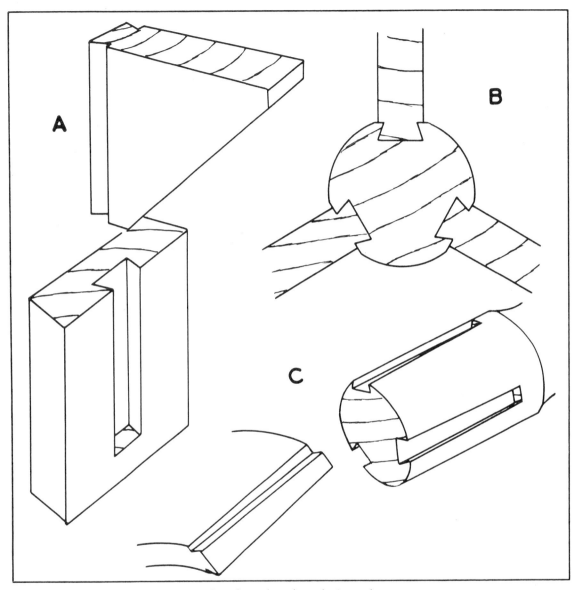

Fig. 5-14. Dovetail dado joints can be cut along the grain and may be tapered.

Another way of strengthening is to use a dowel diagonally (Fig. 5-13E). Keep the diameter of the dowel small, so drilling for it does not remove too much wood from the leg. With 1½-inch square legs and a ¾-inch shelf, the dowel could be ¼-inch.

LENGTHWISE DOVETAIL HOUSING

Most examples of dado or housing joints come across the grain. Similar joints can be used where one or both parts have the grain the same way as the joint.

One example is a bracket that has a dovetailed housing into the back piece (Fig. 5-14A). The bracket may have its grain upright or diagonal to the joint.

Another example is found in the three legs

Fig. 5-15. The three legs of this table are joined to the pedestal with dovetailed dado joints.

They are given tapered dovetail sections, which are very similar to shelf ends. The spindle has tapered dadoes cut to suit, so the legs are slid in from below to pull tight as they reach the top. There is no need for clamps (Fig. 5-14C).

V-HOUSING

When very thin pieces of wood are used to make divisions, there is not enough wood to allow for ordinary dado joints where the divisions meet. It may be possible to use dadoes where the thin divisions meet the outside of the box, drawer, or other container (Fig. 5-16A), but where they meet each other a joint with more economy of wood must be used. If the two pieces cross, a deep half lap joint might be used. If that is very deep, there is a risk of one part moving in relation to the other. It may be stronger to stagger the meetings (Fig. 5-16B) and use the joints described in the next paragraph.

Instead of the weakening dado, use V-cuts (Fig. 5-16C). Taper from the thickness of the wood cut on its end to no more than half through the other piece (Fig. 5-16D). Joints on opposite sides perform a clamping action against each other. Although these joints do not individually have much strength, the usual assembly gives plenty of mutual support.

STAIR TREAD JOINT

Stair treads and the risers below them may be notched into their sides with dado joints, but to avoid creaking stairs they must be very tight. This is achieved by wedging (Fig. 5-17A).

The tread goes into a normal dado groove, except it is cut below to take a wedge to be driven from the back. The thin end is not taken to a featheredge, but it may be up to ½ inch thick. The taper is moderate, as not very much will have to be taken up in tightening. Sizes have to be judged so the wedge is not very far from the end of the groove when fully driven. This gives support over most of the tread width (Fig. 5-17B). It is common to make the wedge too long at first, then to cut it off after driving, leaving a little for further tightening.

If there is a similar wedge for the riser, it does not have to take as much load. It can be kept short to avoid interfering with the wedge under the tread

attached to a single turned upright for a round table (Fig. 5-15). They need strong joints, and there may be difficulty in clamping if dowels are used.

There are three equally spaced flats worked on the parallel round spindle (Fig. 5-14B). The legs have the joints worked before they are shaped.

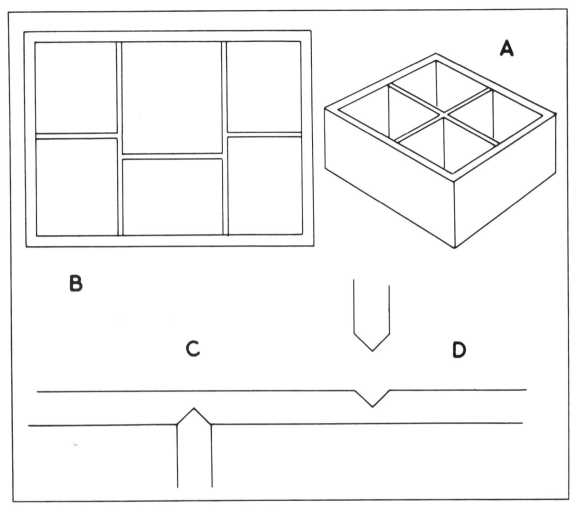

Fig. 5-16. In thin partitions the dadoes may have a V-section.

below. It is common to have the wedge and its slot square across, but you can slope the lower edge of the wedge and its mating surface slightly to reduce any risk of the wedge being driven askew or of it coming away if it gets very loose (Fig. 5-17C).

Although this joint is associated with stair treads, it could be used anywhere that tightening of a dado joint is important, and the presence of a wide wedge would not spoil appearance.

BUILDING HOUSED JOINT

The dado or housing joint is normally associated with assemblies like bookcases, but it can be used

when the parts meet on edge. A stopped joint then uses the notched part to take some of the load. This may happen between floor joists where the notching is aided by nails through.

In a simple form there is a T meeting between two joists, and one is notched into a dado in the other (Fig. 5-18A). The deeper the notch, the greater the bearing and the better the load can be transferred, but notching the long piece takes away some of its stiffness. If the junction is near a support, the notch may go further than if it comes in an unsupported span. The notching can be half the depth of the wood and taken between one-quarter

70

and half the thickness of the long part.

In a variation the notched end is cut at an angle, so not so much has to be cut away from the long part (Fig. 5-18B). More can be cut into the long piece to get a greater bearing without reducing its stiffness as much as the first joint does. As before, much depends on the distance from a support, but up to three-fourths of the way through may be possible.

RUSTIC DADO

When natural poles are joined to make outdoor furniture or garden decorations, such as arches to support climbing plants, the parts are often merely nailed together. It is easier to get an assembly true and make it stronger when in position if joints are used between parts. A simple one for attaching a rail to an upright or similar arrangement is a dado joint adapted to making with outdoor tools (Fig. 5-19). The end of the rail may be chopped to shape with a hatchet or tapered with a drawknife. Do that first, then the dado notch can be made to suite, which is easier than making the parts the other way around. Saw the sides of the notch with a woodman's saw and remove the waste with a chisel. The

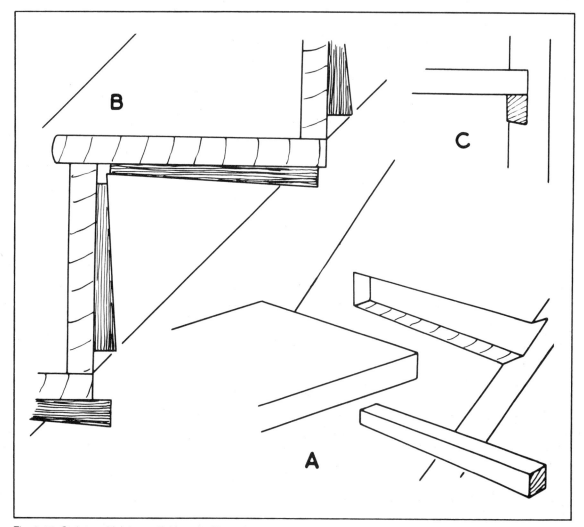

Fig. 5-17. Stair tread joints are tightened with wedges.

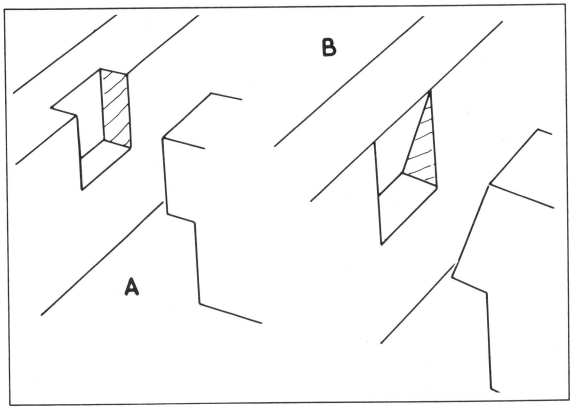

Fig. 5-18. Notched housed joints are used between floor joists.

Fig. 5-19. In rustic work the end of a pole may be notched into another.

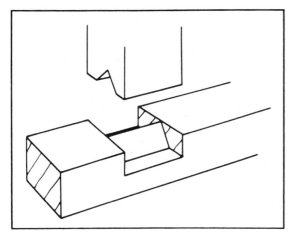

Fig. 5-20. A saddle joint is a dado with a notch to prevent a post from moving sideways.

will stop it moving along the wood. A simple dado does nothing to prevent it from moving sideways out of the groove.

Movement the other way can be stopped by raising a ridge in the groove to match a notch in the end of the post (Fig. 5-20). This is a saddle joint. The end of the post ideally has an exactly matching outline to give an equal downward thrust over the whole area. If the ridge and notch do not make a perfect joint, the load will be taken on the outside flat areas, so they should not be cut too narrow.

STEP JOINT

If two pieces meet at an acute angle, as when a post is to rest on a sloping piece, cutting out to let the end of the post remain square would weaken the sloping piece. If the end of the post is cut to the slope, it will tend to slide even when apparently securely nailed.

The post could be shaped to fit a shallow notch (Fig. 5-21A) in a similar way to that sometimes used for a rafter to a tie, but most endwise thrust is only taken by a narrow bearing surface. A better way uses a form of double dado as two steps (Fig. 5-21B). This puts all the thrust on the full width of

depth to go depends on the wood and the purpose of the structure, but with poles about the same diameter, the neatest joint has a groove nearly halfway through the post. One or two nails are driven from the far side.

SADDLE JOINT

If a post has to stand on a horizontal member, a dado

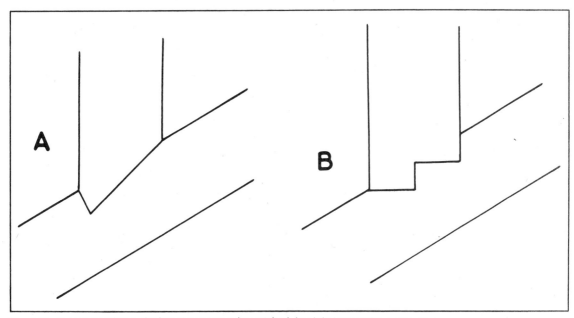

Fig. 5-21. A post meeting a sloping support may be notched, but it is better with a step joint.

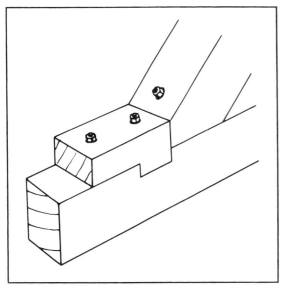

Fig. 5-22. Thrust can be taken with a head block notched in and bolted.

the post without cutting very deeply into the sloping piece.

HEAD BLOCK

If a block has to be attached to one member to resist the thrust coming from another member diagonal to it, it might be bolted on, but the load is more positively taken if the block is keyed into place (Fig. 5-22). Bolts can be used as well, but the keyed block will prevent movement that might have occurred if the bolts alone had been pushed sideways into the wood.

FEATHER JOINT

In the surround of a door the *architrave molding* that forms the framing may finish at a thicker plinth block against the floor with the room baseboard butting against its side. It is important that the plinth block does not move in relation to the archit-

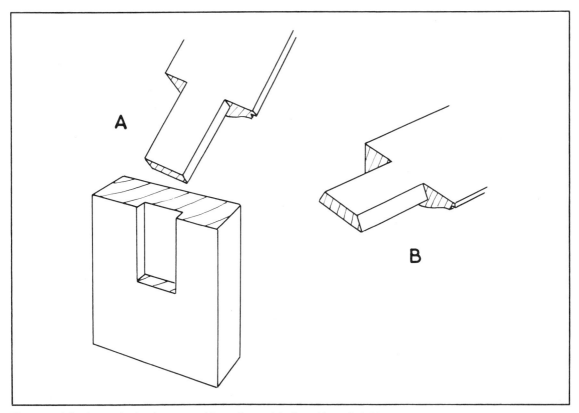

Fig. 5-23. A feather projecting from an architrave keeps it in line with a plinth block.

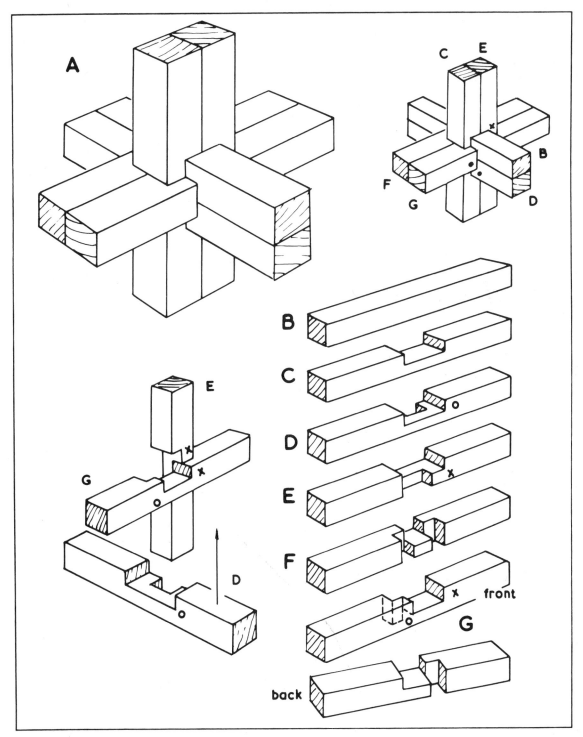

Fig. 5-24. A Chinese cross puzzle uses a variety of notches across the parts.

rave, yet screws through to the wall might spoil appearance.

One way of locating the parts in relation to each other is to let a projecting feather go into a dado groove in the other part (Fig. 5-23A). This need not be large as it does not have to provide much strength. Even better than a feather with a parallel section is one dovetailed to lock the parts together (Fig. 5-23B).

SIX-PIECE CHINESE CROSS PUZZLE

Some cross puzzles are complicated to make and solve because they have many pieces. One with six square pieces is probably as difficult as you will want to deal with. A large one is slightly easier to make, but a small one is easier to handle. For a reasonable size the pieces may be ½ inch square and 4 inches long. Use a close-grained hardwood (Fig. 5-24A). Some of the parts do not have much grain running through the center, so the wood needs to be strong.

The six pieces are lettered for identification in construction and obviously must all be exactly the same section. Cuts across go halfway through the wood and are nearly all as wide as the wood—twice as wide or half as wide. Mark all the cuts with a knife and cut them carefully. Use a file or abrasive paper wrapped around a strip of wood to get the end grain smooth. Two scrap pieces of the same section as the puzzle parts are useful for testing sizes.

All of the parts are different. One piece (Fig. 5-24B) has no cuts in it. The next simplest is a piece with a double-width groove across (Fig. 5-24C). Another piece is cut like that, than a single-width notch cut across it (Fig. 5-24D). Cut another piece with a double-width notch and a 1½-width cut to one side of it (Fig. 5-24E).

Another piece has a single-width notch across, then two half-width ones across beside it (Fig. 5-24F). The last piece has a full-width notch and a half-width one beside it (Fig. 5-24G). Both sides are shown. This and two other drawings have corners of the joint marked for identification in assembly the first time, but do not put any marks permanently on the wood.

Start assembly by holding piece E upright, then hook in piece G with the X corner marks adjoining. Slide piece D upward so it links with the other two and 0 marks are adjoining. Put piece C behind G, then piece F will slide in position and push downward, leaving a square hole to push piece B through.

Chapter 6

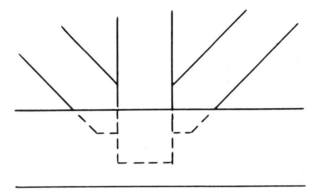

Mortise and Tenon Joints

MORTISE AND TENON JOINTS ARE THE MOST commonly used means of joining parts of wooden structures—from heavy house frames to small pieces of furniture. Doweled joints are an extension of the method used today mainly because of convenience in manufacturing processes. Doweling adapts better to quantity production as the joints can be made easier by machines. For individual craftsmanship, mortise and tenon joints are preferred in many situations. Both methods of joining should have adequate strength for their purpose. As with any type of joint, a good fit is an important contribution to strength, and in quantity production accuracy is more easily achieved in doweling than in tenoning.

In the many variations of the mortise and tenon joint, the *tenon* is a tongue cut on the end of one piece to fit into the *mortise*, which is a hole cut to match in the other part. In nearly all assemblies the grain is lengthwise in the tenon and across the mortise. The side grain in the mortise comes against the side grain in the tenon, which is best for

glue to get a good grip. Only a small area in a joint includes end grain in one part, so the lesser glue strength there is not important.

The idea behind the mortise and tenon joint goes back into history. Early man tapered the end of one piece of wood to go into a hole in another piece. Similar ideas can still be seen in field fences, where the tapered ends of rails go into holes in the posts. More carefully shaped joints followed, and a form of mortise and tenon joint recognizable as similar to ours can be seen in drawings of early Egyptian furniture.

Today there are reliable glues, but earlier users of mortise and tenon joints had to rely on just the tight fit or various methods of using wedges and pegs to keep the joints tight, either alone or to reinforce the inadequate glue that had to be used. These auxiliary methods of tightening still have their uses, as seen in later examples.

Tenons are basically rectangular in section and usually have squared corners, although there may be some rounding. The mortise cavity is cut to

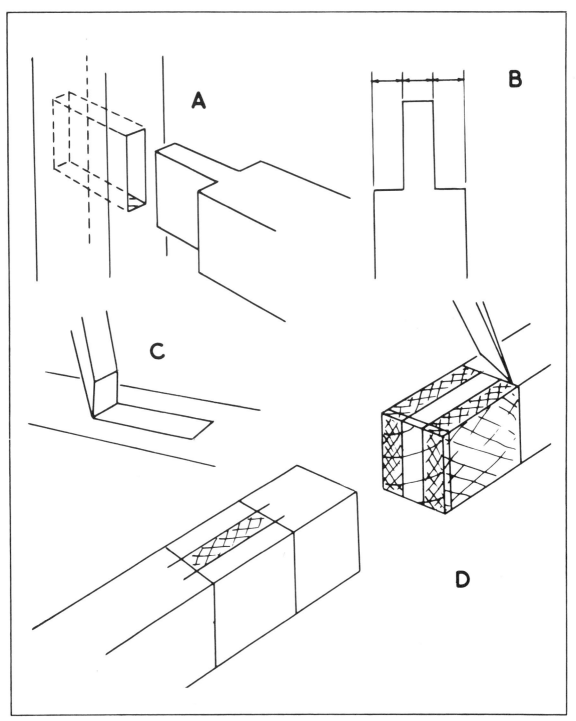

Fig. 6-1. In a through mortise and tenon joint the parts are one-third the thickness (A, B) or the width of a chisel (C) and should be marked to match (D).

match. If the projecting piece is round, even if it is cut in the solid wood, as it often is in turned work, it is better described as a dowel, although most dowels are loose.

THROUGH MORTISE AND TENON

If two parts of similar thickness are to be joined in the simplest manner, the tenon goes right through the mortised piece (Fig. 6-1A). In this case it is common for the tenon to be one-third the thickness of the wood (Fig. 6-1B). It is convenient if the mortise is made the same as the width of the chisel used for cutting it (Fig. 6-1C). Slight variations are permissible to suit this, although too thin a tenon would be weak. At one time mortises were chopped out completely by chisel. Even with the more common method of drilling away most of the waste, though, there has to be some squaring of the shape with a chisel.

The width of both the tenon and the mortise should be gauged at the same setting of a marking gauge, with the limit lines squared around the mortised piece so marking is on both sides. The length of the tenon is marked with knife-cut lines (Fig. 6-1D). Leave a little excess length on the tenon to be trimmed level later. Gauging can be with two settings of an ordinary marking gauge, but special mortise gauges mark both lines at the same time. Usually a brass inset in the stem carries the second pin, so it can be adjusted in relation to the fixed pin to suit the width to be gauged. The stock is set and locked to give the distance from the edge (Fig. 6-2). The two-pin mortise gauge has the advantage that the distance between the pins can be maintained even if you have to move the stock to suit wood of different thicknesses. Some mortise gauges are attractive in rosewood and brass with screw adjustments. A simple gauge is just as effective, and you can make one with wedges instead of screws (Fig. 6-3).

A craftsman does not make trial assemblies of mortise and tenon joints. Pushing together and pulling apart tends to wear the surfaces and loosen the joint. It is better to rely on the accuracy of marking out and cutting, so the first assembly is the last and the joint is as good a fit as it can be. If a trail is

Fig. 6-2. A mortise gauge has two points that can be adjusted in relation to each other and the stock for marking both sides of mortises and tenons simultaneously.

deemed necessary, do not enter the tenon fully into the mortise.

If the mortised part is wider than the tenoned piece, as it usually is when a rail goes into a table or chair leg, the tenon can be made wider to give a stronger joint (Fig. 6-4). If less is cut away from the rail end, that part is not weakened as much. It is not common to make the tennon more than half the width of the rail, unless the other part is considerably wider and only a token shouldering of the rail end is needed to locate it.

STUB MORTISE AND TENONS

In many places it is better for appearance if the end of the tenon does not show on the outside of the mortised piece. If the joint does not go right through, it is a stub mortise and tenon (Fig. 6-5). The distance the joint goes through depends on the wood sizes and the degree of strength required. If the mortised piece is a fairly light section, the cavity may have to be cut as far as you can go without breaking out at the far side to allow for a long enough tenon to give strength. In thicker wood you will have to judge how much to go, and this comes from experience. In most furniture construction a tenon should usually be 1 inch to 1½ inches long.

The tenon is cut in the same way as for a through joint. The mortise should be deep enough for the tenon not to touch its bottom. When the joint is drawn tight, the shoulders of the tenoned piece

Fig. 6-3. A mortise gauge can be made with two sliding parts held in the stock by wedges.

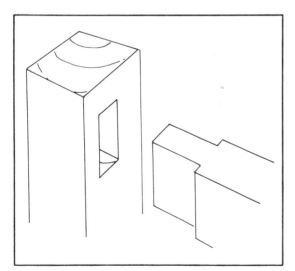

Fig. 6-4. If the mortised part is thicker, the tenon may be more than one-third the thickness of the other piece.

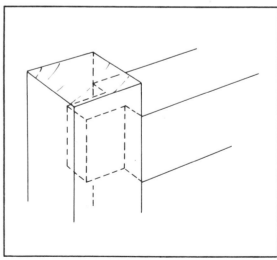

Fig. 6-5. If a tenon does not go right through, it is a stopped or stub tenon.

must close against the surface of the other piece before the tenon touches bottom. The area left void there will not affect strength, as that comes from the meeting side grain surfaces.

A mortise traditionally, was chopped out with a thick mortise chisel. The thickness was needed for strength in levering out the waste. For this method, several cuts are made across the grain, but not right to the ends (Fig. 6-6A). The waste is levered out prior to another line of cuts at the next level until a sufficient depth is cut and the ends, which have been levered against, are trimmed to length (Fig. 6-6B). With a chisel width matching the final width of the mortise, there should be no need for further cuts on the wider surfaces of the mor-

tise. For very deep mortises there are hooked chisels, called lock mortise chisels, that remove the waste from the bottoms of the mortise, which has first been chopped with a straight chisel.

It is more common today to remove most of the waste from a mortise by drilling. With a depth gauge on the drill or the drill press, you can make a series of holes that overlap (Fig. 6-6C) and automatically make the mortise the right depth. With a suitable router cutter it is possible to enter like a drill, the move along for the length of the mortise. In both cases the mortise finishes with rounded ends (Fig. 6-6D). They can be squared easily with a chisel to match the usual tenon, and that is normally preferred in individual work. On production work

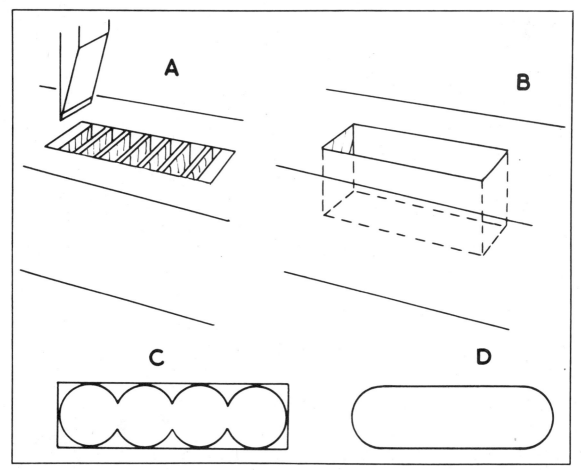

Fig. 6-6. A mortise may be chopped out (A), then the ends squared (B). Waste can be removed with a series of holes drilled (C) or with a router (D).

the mortise is left rounded. The tenon is rounded to suit or even made narrower to avoid the curves.

For large mortises to be cut in large numbers, a machine with a chain that lowers into the wood is used. It is equipped with cutters and looks something like a chain saw. One thrust into the wood makes a mortise of the right length and width, but with a rounded bottom, if it is not a joint that goes through. That is not a tool for the individual craftsman, but another tool is driven in the same manner as a drill, using a fairly substantial press. The outside is square to match the width of the intended mortise. It is hollow and made like four chisels with their bevels inward. Down the center is an auger bit. As the tool is lowered into the wood, the outsides cut out a square and the auger bit removes the waste. The result is a nicely squared hole, and a mortise is made by moving along to make the required number of touching square holes. In both cases standard sizes are produced, so more tools are needed for different sizes. The craftsman doing individual work will prefer a drill, router, or chisel.

BAREFACED TENONS

A tenon may be cut only with one shoulder. The wood carrying the mortise has to be thicker (Fig. 6-7A). This method can be used for rails of light section. With only one shoulder the joint will pull close easier than with the usual two shoulders, which may not be cut exactly in line.

Barefaced tenons should be used if the narrower rail has to come level with one surface of the other piece (Fig. 6-7B). It is the choice if a panel or strips have to go against it to come level with the other side (Fig. 6-7C).

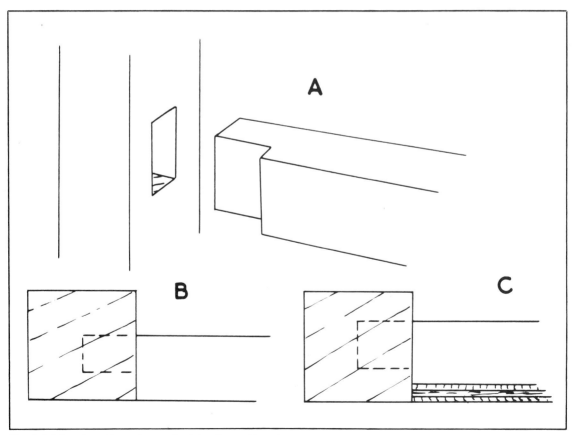

Fig. 6-7. A barefaced tenon has a shoulder at one side only.

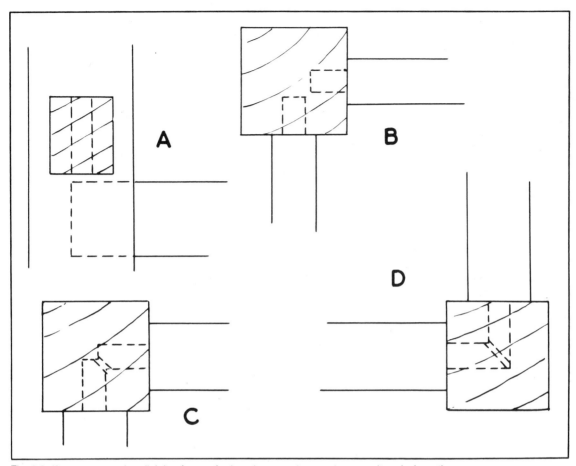

Fig. 6-8. If tenons come in adjoining faces of a leg, they may be cut short or mitered where they meet.

The thickness to make the tenon depends on the relative sizes of the two pieces of wood, but it is often half the thickness of the rail. The tenon may go through, but with the size difference it is better to make it stub.

MEETING TENONS

When rails have to meet at a corner, as they do with rails between the four legs of a table, it is helpful if they are arranged at different levels (Fig. 6-8A), possibly only by the amount of their depth. You can then take the joints as deep as you feel necessary to give sufficient strength. There are many places where the rails and their joints have to be at the same level, as with the rails under a tabletop.

Perhaps you can get sufficient depth without the mortises meeting if there is a large difference in sizes between the pieces of wood (Fig. 6-8B), but more often the mortises have to run into each other if there is to be enough penetration. In that case the mortises are cut to come squarely where they meet. The ends of the tenons are mitered partially (Fig. 6-8C) or completely (Fig. 6-8D), but allow for a little clearance so the ends do not touch. There would be little gain in strength in the extreme corner with miters cut to a featheredge. A partial miter is more common.

WEDGED TENONS

In older construction, much use was made of

wedges to tighten mortise and tenon joints. They provided mechanical strength and would hold without glue. You still can use wedges in many joints. The taper of a wedge is most effective if it is slight, but then it needs to go fairly deeply. A wider angle will achieve a spread with a lesser penetration. If it is too broad an angle, though, it may spring out. Wedges are usually cut by eye as size is not critical, but a slope of about ¼ inch in a 2-inch length (1 in 8) will suit most applications. The width of a wedge is more important for a neat finish, and it should match the tenon with which it is to be used with. Wedges are often cut from the waste after shaping tenons. Cut wedges so there is a little thickness at their points (Fig. 6-9A). Otherwise, a featheredge will crumble as it is driven. There is an advantage in making wedges longer than needed as you have something to grip, which may be cut off afterward.

A through tenon can have its mortise made too wide at the far side to allow wedges to be driven (Fig. 6-9B). The effect is to compress the end of the tenon, but with glued construction that may not matter. It is probably better to spread the tenon to resist pulling back. Make saw cuts in the end of the

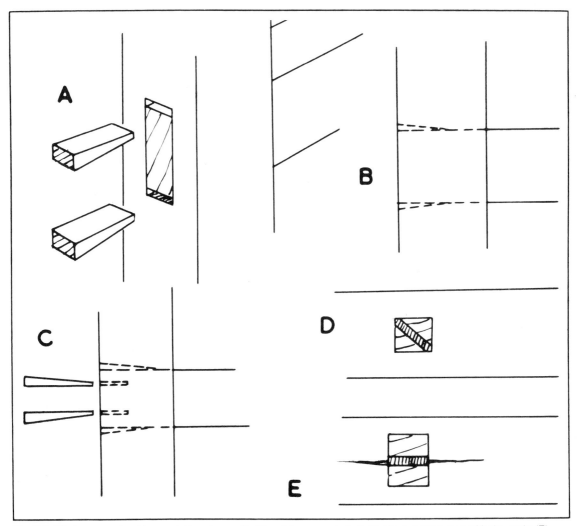

Fig. 6-9. Wedges may be driven outside a tenon (A, B) or into saw cuts in it (C, D), but not in line with the grain (E).

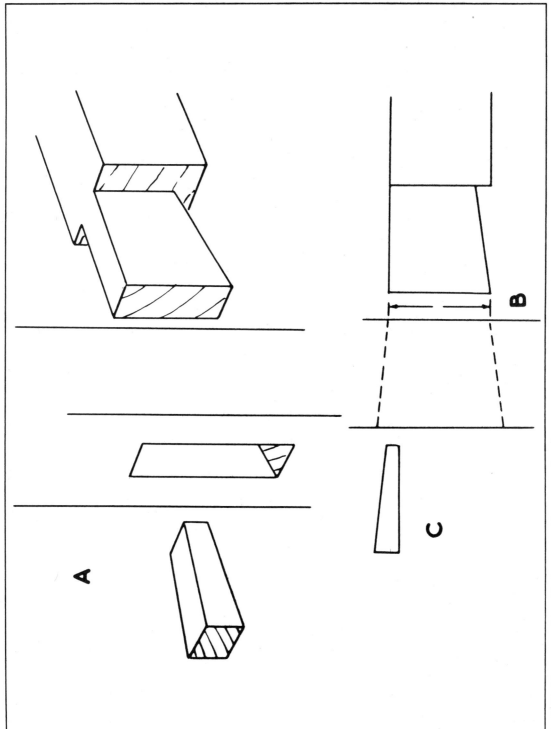

Fig. 6-10. A tenon may be cut to form one of its own wedges.

tenon before it is driven. You may get sufficient grip without widening the mortise, but it helps to have a slightly open angle. When the wedges are driven, the end of the tenon spreads to fill the space (Fig. 6-9C). A small tenon may have a single wedge, but it is more common to use two. For furniture the wedges can be dipped in glue before driving. The wedges and the tenon then are cut off and finished flush. For some exterior work it may be better to drive a wedge dry and leave its end standing above the surface, so it can be driven further if the joint dries and loosens after weathering.

Normally the wedges are driven across the width of the tenon. If the end is near square, a wedge could be driven squarely, but it may be better visually if diagonal (Fig. 6-9D). Even if a tenon is wider than it is deep in relation to the grain of the mortised part, never drive a wedge the long way of the surrounding grain (Fig. 6-9E). That would put a bursting action on the wood and possibly cause cracks, which may not appear until the joint has been in use some time.

You can let the tenon form, in effect, one of the wedges by cutting it to a dovetail edge. It needs a wider mortise so it can be entered, then a wedge is used to fill the gap (Fig. 6-10A).

The dovetail slope should be slight (1 in 8 will do). The entry to the mortise should be just wide enough to admit the tenon (Fig. 6-10B), then the other side and its matching wedge may have a similar slope (Fig. 6-10C). Providing the wedge remains in place, the rail cannot be pulled out.

An interesting method of tightening stub tenons uses fox or foxtail wedging. You have to estimate the necessary size and arrangement of wedges, but this is not critical. The method effectively tightens the joint without any visible clue to how it was done. Cut the joint in the usual way, but slightly widen the ends of the mortise (Fig. 6-11A). Put saw cuts across the end of the tenon and make small wedges to go in them (Fig. 6-11B). The wedges have to be short, so as they press against the bottom of the mortise as the joint is pulled tight with a clamp, they spread the end of the tenon before it reaches its full penetration. Because of this, they may be given a wider angle than wedges driven outside. Much depends on the joint, but after the tenon has spread and the glue has set, nothing can move. A wedge angle of 1 in 5 or 6 in a short tenon may be used.

DEEP RAIL JOINTS

If the part that is to carry the tenon is fairly deep, the amount to cut out of the other piece to make a

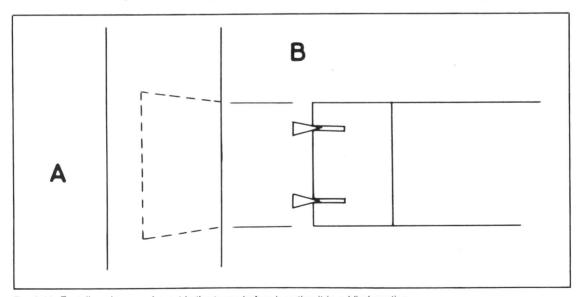

Fig. 6-11. Foxtail wedges can be put in the tenon before inserting it in a blind mortise.

full-depth mortise would probably weaken it excessively. In that case you can cut the mortise in two or more parts (Fig. 6-12A). The part between them remains as solid wood in the mortised piece, tying together the grain across the joint for greater strength. It is common to not cut the spaces right back. Instead, leave a short amount to penetrate the top of the mortise (Fig. 6-12B). This contributes strength and avoids an unsightly gap that might occur if the joint is not cut accurately or pulled absolutely tight.

There may have to be a large number of divisions between tenons for a very wide board. This can happen if a batten or clamp is put across the end of a wide piece to keep it flat. The batten may go straight across (Fig. 6-12C), or its ends could be mitered to give a neat finish (Fig. 6-12D), without stopping the use of a plowed groove to start the joint (Fig. 6-12E).

HAUNCHED TENONS

If a mortise and tenon joint is to come at a corner or the end of the mortised piece, a full-width tenon would make the mortise open. That is sometimes used, but the joint is then more correctly called a *bridle joint* (Fig. 6-13A). In some constructions it is possible to let a piece called a *horn* extend (Fig. 6-13B). For a gate, the hinge stile may have a horn extending downward below the bottom rail, then the horn at the top can be long enough to be decorated (Fig. 6-13C).

There is maximum strength due to the full-width tenon if a horn can be used, but in many corners, such as in doors and window frames, the two parts must have a square outer corner. One way of allowing for this is to cut back the width of the tenon (Fig. 6-13D). That leaves a small amount of wood without a proper joint.

It is more common to provide a haunch, which is the same thickness as the tenon, but is taken only a short way into the mortised part (Fig. 6-13E). This locks the two parts together for the full width of the joint and prevents any unevenness of the surfaces later if either piece has a tendency to warp.

The small haunching shows at the end. For many purposes that does not matter, but if the joint

would look better with it hidden, it can be cut at an angle (Fig. 6-13F). This is nearly as effective as the first example. Joints are often needed at the corners of frames that have been grooved to take panels. Grooves are carried right through when the wood is prepared. The mortised piece will have a groove at its end. The mortise and tenon may be the same width as the groove, but will more likely be wider. The groove at the end is still there, and that is best disguised by the squarely cut haunching (Fig. 6-13G).

When a joint has to be cut at a corner, leave an inch or more of horn on the mortised piece—at least until after the mortise has been cut (Fig. 6-13H). Even with machine cutting of the mortise, there is some bursting load on the end grain. With chisel work, the end grain tends to break out if the wood was cut to length first. If it is a substantial structure and you will wedge the joints, the horns should be left on until the glue has set. If you are making doors or other frames that will not be fitted immediately, leave short horns at each corner to take knocks. They can be cut off just before fitting the door to ensure a true square corner.

For a deep joint with the tenons in parts, the haunchings can be made level with the pieces between (also often called haunches). If it is a full width batten, you can start the mortised part by plowing a groove before deepening to take the extending tenons (Fig. 6-13J).

Haunching is applicable to barefaced tenons (Fig. 6-13K) and may have to be used when rails go two ways into a leg or post top (Fig. 6-13L).

TUSK TENONS

A tenon can be made to extend through the mortise so it forms a tusk. The extension could be rounded or otherwise decorated (Fig. 6-14A), but the tusk is used more often with a wedge. This probably dates from the days when much of the furniture in baronial halls was made to be taken down, either for storage or for the important person to take with him on his travels.

Some modern furniture is made to take down using the same method of construction. The wedged tuck tenon is often used for decoration.

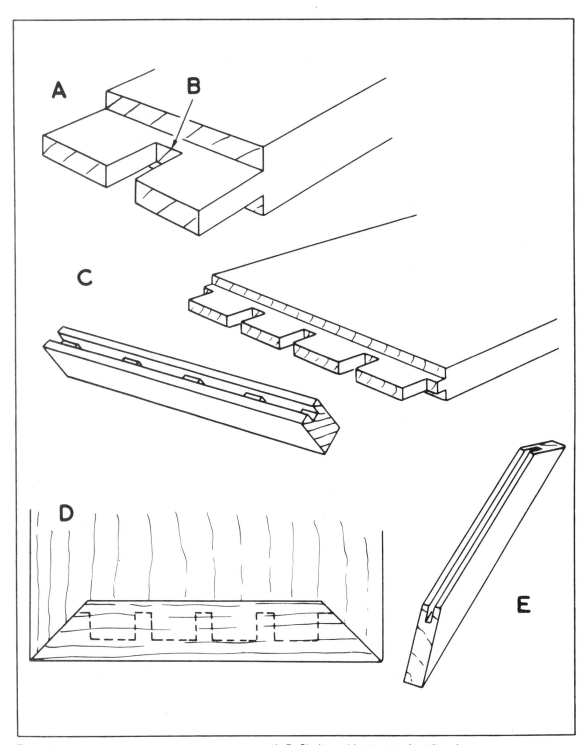

Fig. 6-12. A wide piece may have two or more tenons (A, B, C). An end batten may be mitered.

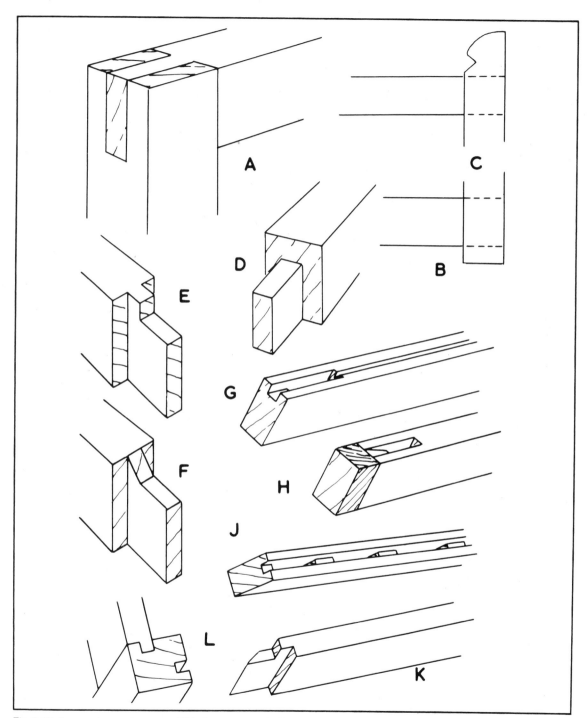

Fig. 6-13. An open tenon at a corner (A) is the same as a bridle joint. There can be a horn to avoid making it open (B, C), or the tenon may be cut back (D) or haunched (E, F), with the mortise cut to match (G, H, J). At a corner the two tenons are haunched (L) and mitered (K).

The edgewise under rail of a table might meet a solid end. In that case the simplest wedged tusk tenon has wide shoulders and the tenon taken through so it is wider than it is deep. The extension is cut to take the wedge (Fig. 6-14B). The wedge only has a moderate slope in this and other versions of the joint. The hole for it is cut to the same angle outside, but kept back a little from the thickness of the mortise (Fig. 6-14C). As the wedge is driven, it pulls against the tenon, presses against the end surface, and yet does not bottom on the hole. Tightening the wedge can put considerable strain on the short grain of the extending tenon end, which should be kept long enough to resist this.

The broadly cut shoulders in that joint do not play any real part in the joint just described. It is stronger if the shoulders also can go into the mortised piece. One way is to taper them in toward the tenon (Fig. 6-14D) above and below it. It is more common to step the lower part, so it can take any downward thrust squarely. That may not be important in a table. If it is a load-bearing structure that is being made, this form is valuable (Fig. 6-14E).

If both parts are deep in relation to their widths, as with pieces of 2-inch by 4-inch wood meeting on edge, cutting away one-third of the depth for a standard mortise and tenon might weaken the mortised part too much. Instead, a thinner tenon goes right through. The stepped part of the lower shoulder shares some of the load, without removing much wood from the other part. In that case the tusk tenon could go right through and be wedged (Fig. 6-15A), or it could be cut off and a dowel or pin put through it (Fig. 6-15B).

Another version, where the purpose is structural rather than decorative, has the shoulder cut at an angle to fit into the mortised part and share some of the load (Fig. 6-15C).

Make the wedges too long at first. Have a trial assembly and drive in a wedge reasonably tight. Mark about an equal amount above and below the tenon, so you can cut it off and decorate it symmetrically (Fig. 6-15D).

A similar idea can be used for shelves. A bookcase or display rack might be made with all the shelves having tusk tenons, so it can be taken down

and packed flat. The shelves go into shallow dado grooves across the ends, then a pair of tusk tenons go through and are wedged (Fig. 6-15E).

DRAW PINNING

One attraction of using tusk tenons is their ability to pull a joint together. This is important where the assembly is too big, or its arrangement does not allow using clamps or wedges for tightening. Another way to tighten mortise and tenon joints is by *draw pinning* (sometimes called drawbore pinning). The method cannot be used when the mortised piece extends some way from the mortise, but it is possible in the majority of mortise and tenon joints.

In a simple example an ordinary mortise and tenon joint is cut, but there is no way that the long piece with the tenon on it can be squeezed into the mortise tightly with a clamp. Mark a hole position on the mortised piece over the mortise—usually at its center. It might be better to be nearer where the tenon shoulder will be, with less risk of breaking out the tenon grain (Fig. 6-16A). Drill right through at that position without the tenon in place. Push the tenon in as tightly as you can and mark through the hole with a pencil. Mark another hole center in the tenon closer to the shoulder (Fig. 6-16B). Drill the same size hole there. Assemble the joint. The inside hole will be offset in relation to the outside hole. Make a peg or pin of the same size as the hole and taper one end so it can enter the holes (Fig. 6-16C). Drive it in. It will pull the tenon further into the mortise.

With softwood, the inner hole needs to be further from the outer hole than it need be in hardwood. The hole size must suit the peg, which may be dowel rod, but the diameter should usually be about one-third the width of the mortise. Offsetting the holes too much may keep the peg from doing its job properly or, in an extreme case, driving the peg could break out end grain in the tenon. As an example, in a joint between two pieces of softwood 1-inch by 2-inch section, the peg could be ½-inch or ⅝-inch diameter. The hole in the tenon could be ⅛ inch nearer the shoulder than the outer hole. Cut off the peg ends when the joint is tight.

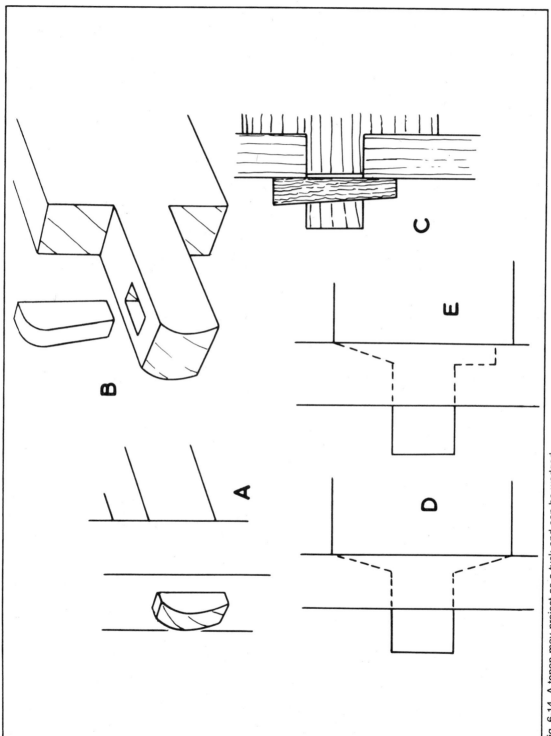

Fig. 6-14. A tenon may project as a tusk and can be wedged.

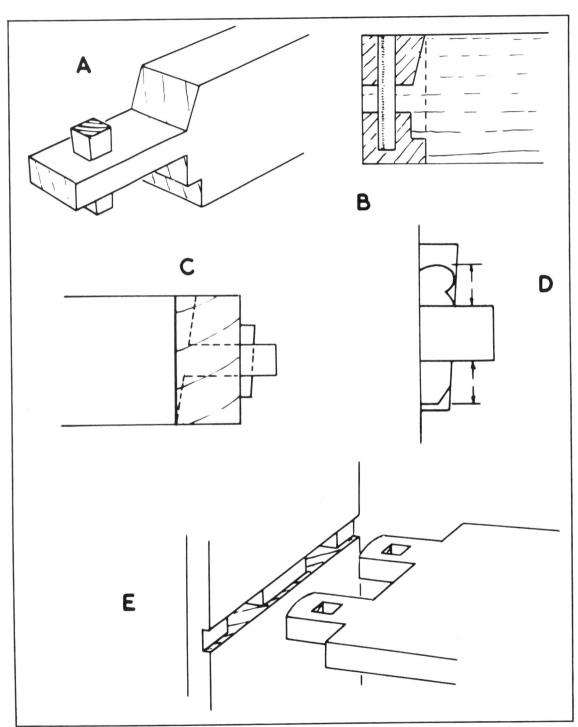

Fig. 6-15. A tusk tenoned piece may be stepped or beveled (A, B, C). The wedge can be shaped (D). A wide piece may have more than one tusk.

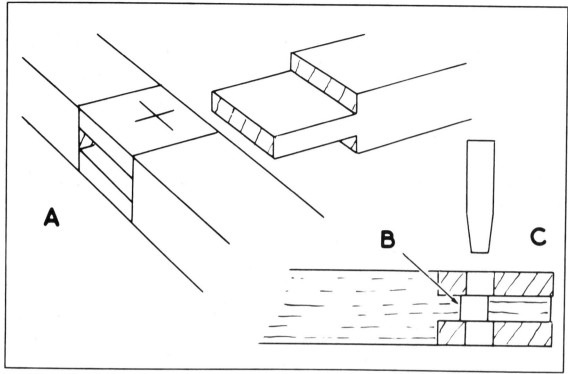

Fig. 6-16. With holes drilled slightly out of line, a mortise and tenon joint can be tightened by draw pinning.

SKEW TENONS

If two parts meet at an acute angle, many versions of the mortise and tenon joint can be used—whether single or multiple tenons. The tenon must continue the line of the piece it is on (Fig. 6-17A). If you make the tenons squarely to the other piece, the shape cuts across grain lines and weakens the joint (Fig. 6-17B). The only concession to the angle may be the cutting of the outer one and of the tenon square to the mortised piece (Fig. 6-17D). This avoids the awkward undercutting of the end of the mortise and probably has little effect on strength.

Instead of cutting the tenon ends squarely or parallel to the mortised piece, they could fit sloped mortises at a compromise angle (Fig. 6-17E) to give an effective glue area.

INSERTED TENONS

When two parts meet as an angle, you can get the grain of tenons square to the mortise piece by in-serting tenons into both parts. Both pieces are cut with mortises, then tenon pieces to fit are made and glued in (Fig. 6-18A). If a hole does not go right through, there could be foxtail wedges to tighten the tenon, while the usual wedges might be used where a tenon end is exposed. This method is comparable in some ways to doweling, and in modern assemblies dowels may be preferred.

Some machine-made mortises finish with rounded ends, which have to be squared by hand or the tenons made rounded. Another method to aid quantity production is to insert the tenons into both parts. The tenon piece is cut to the shoulder length, then it has a mortise cut in the same way as the other piece (Fig. 6-18B). Tenon material is machined in a long piece with rounded edges, then a suitable piece is cut off and glued into both parts (Fig. 6-18C). This is arrangement to suit mass production and is not recommended for one-off furniture.

A loose or inserted tenon may have to be used

93

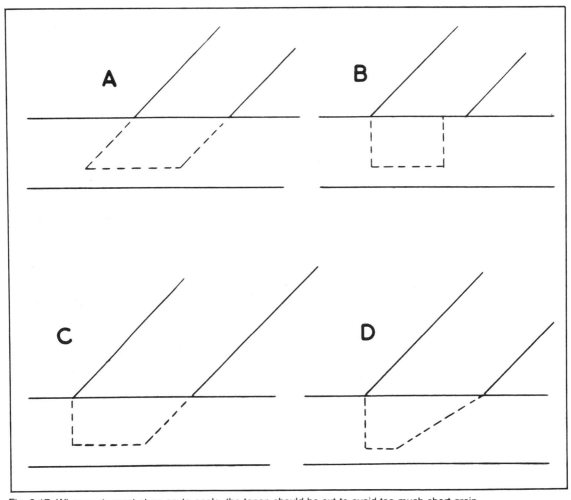

Fig. 6-17. When parts meet at an acute angle, the tenon should be cut to avoid too much short grain.

when the wood has a twisted grain. A piece of straight-grained wood is made into the tenon. A mortise is cut to take it in the part that would have been cut with its own tenon, as well as into the piece intended to be mortised.

Another use for an inserted tenon is in repair work. If a tenon breaks off in a piece of furniture, a false tenon can be made to go into a slot for it (Fig. 6-18D). The finished assembly should then be as strong as before. A lower rail of a table or chair may snap off at an end. As the underside will not normally be visible, a loose tenon can be inserted with a sloping cut on the underside of the rail (Fig. 6-18E). It can be fitted without the need to strain

other parts of the framework to get it in, as the tenon part can go into the mortised leg. The rail is dropped on to the extending sloping part (Fig. 6-18F).

FENCE JOINTS

Rails may go through some fence posts, but where they have to be joined, the tenons have to be cut at an angle to meet inside the mortise (Fig. 6-19A). This can apply to barefaced and ordinary tenons. As the area of contact of each tenon has been reduced, screws or dowels should be across the joint.

A similar method could be used in furniture where tenoned parts come from both sides of the

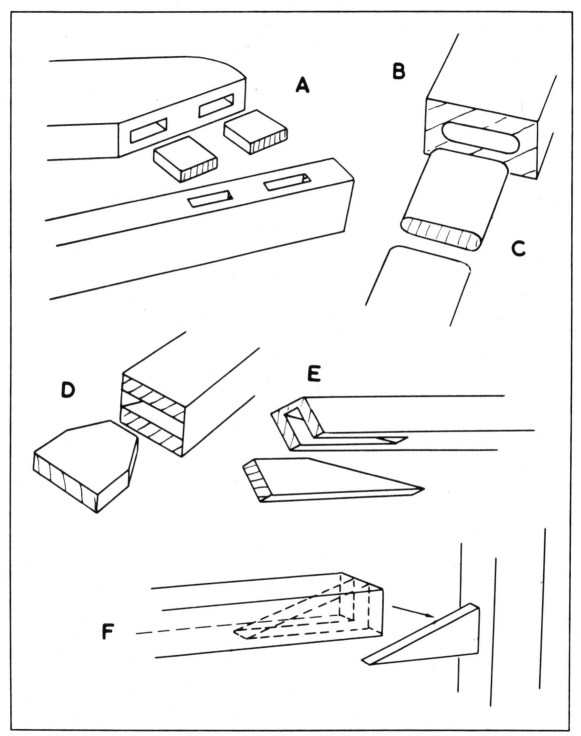

Fig. 6-18. Tenons may be inserted so grain is square to the joint (A, B, C, D). A tenon can be fitted from below for a repair (E, F).

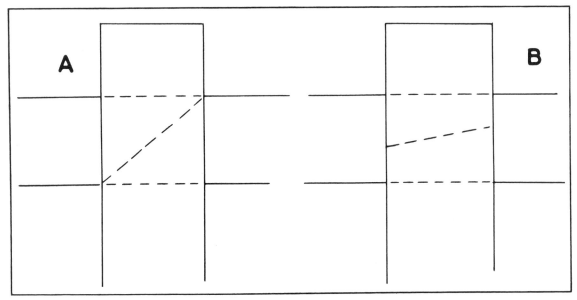

Fig. 6-19. If tenons meet in a mortise, they may be cut to fit together.

mortised part, which is not wide enough for shorter normal tenons. A different way of lapping has the division nearer square, but a slight taper allows for a wedge action in tightening as the parts are driven in (Fig. 6-19B).

WHEELWRIGHT'S TENON

In the construction of a wheel and parts of a wagon or cart the wheelwright favored tenons with a slight taper both ways (Fig. 6-20). The taper was cut so the fit was very close, and the final tightening

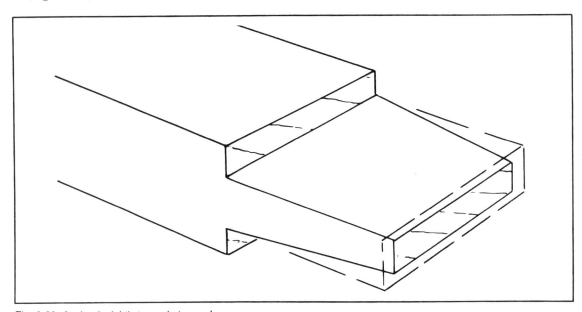

Fig. 6-20. A wheelwright's tenon is tapered.

needed considerable pressure to pull the tenon to its shoulder. In construction of a wheel the spokes went into the *felly* (the wooden rim).

MULTIPLE TENONS

In many constructions only one tenon is needed in the width of a piece of wood. A point is reached in designing a joint where one tenon and its mortise would be rather big, so a considerable amount of wood has to be cut away. In that case there could be two or even more tenons (Fig. 6-21A). Their exact properties depend on circumstances, but for two tenons the width might be divided into five equal parts (Fig. 6-21B). Besides wood of near square section, the twin tenons can be used for wood that is much thinner than it is wide, as in a shelf (Fig. 6-21C). Dividing into five parts equally may still apply, although for a wider piece you may increase the widths of the spaces.

If the boards to be joined are wider, there can be any number of tenons. With comparatively thin material the tenons should be about square, and the spaces between should be about the same width (Fig. 6-21D). If the tenons go through, they can be wedged using saw cuts square across (Fig. 6-21E). If the ends will be visible, putting the wedges diagonally in alternate directions will make an attractive pattern (Fig. 6-21F). If the tenons go into blind holes, they could be fox wedged if extra tightening is desired.

Such a multiple tenon joint can be combined with a dado groove (Fig. 6-21G). This ensures a neater appearance inside the joint and provides extra support and restriction of warping if the piece with the tenons is a shelf or otherwise load-bearing.

Usually the tenons are set in from the edge. If the piece being tenoned would look better with its edge carried through the other piece, outer tenons can be notched in (Fig. 6-21H).

Single or double stub tenons are used on a drawer rail end in carcass construction. There is not much thickness for mortising, and the tenons must be quite short (Fig. 6-21J). The rest of the assembly will hold the joints tight after they are made.

TONGUED-SHOULDERED TENON

In some assemblies there is no space for a wide tenon or multiple tenons. A narrower tenon has to be cut, leaving one or both wide shoulders. The broad end grain will not take glue well, and the joint may show an open gap. For greater strength, splines are inserted in the shoulders (Fig. 6-22A) to serve as small loose tenons. Sometimes plywood is used for the splines, but it is better to cut pieces of hardwood with the grain the same way as that of the tenoned part.

If the exposed ends of the spline would spoil appearance, they can be made shorter and let into slots with closed ends (Fig. 6-22B). You also could use two or more small dowels in each shoulder (Fig. 6-22C).

INTERMEDIATE LEG JOINT

If a leg has to be joined to a rail, as it would at an intermediate position on a long table, instead of the rail being joined to the leg at a corner, a special version of a double tenon is needed. It may be considered a combination of bridle joint with a tenon (Fig. 6-23). The leg does not have to be level with the rail, but the outside part can project. Usually the tenon goes into a blind mortise. To get sizes the rail thickness may be divided into four as a guide to spacings. The particular job may require variations.

The joint can be used either way. If the leg is to go to the top outside and divide the appearance of the rail, the bridle part of the joint goes outside. If the joint is made the other way, the rail outside surface continues across and the leg front stops at its lower edge. The piece on the other side may then go right through the width of the rail or be stopped, allowing a narrow part of the rail to cross above it.

EXTRA TENONED PARTS

If the design requires two or three parts to meet against one another, you can take more than one tenon into a mortise. In a framework there could be diagonal braces meeting at one rail. In that case they can share a mortise equally (Fig. 6-24A). Note that the outer edges of the tenoned pieces continue

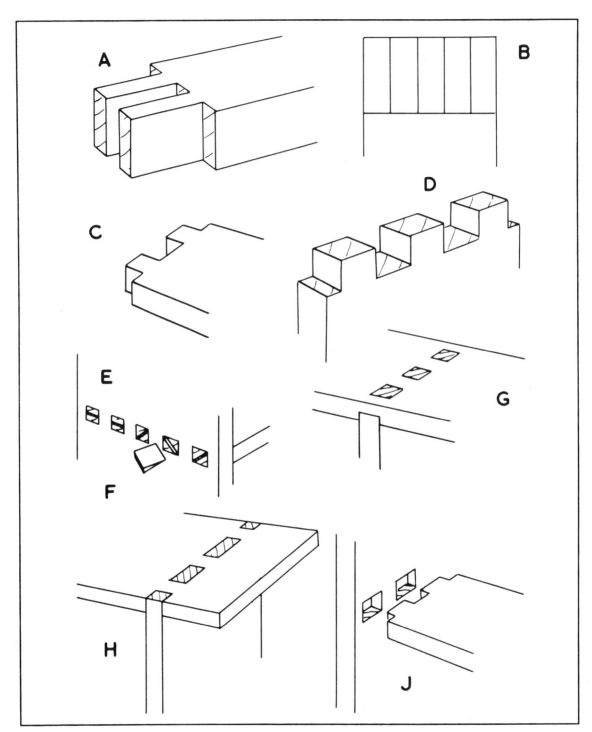

Fig. 6-21. Multiple tenons may be used on a wide piece (A, B, C, D). Tenons can be wedged (F) and partly housed (G). Tenons can be arranged on the outside (H) and may be stub (J).

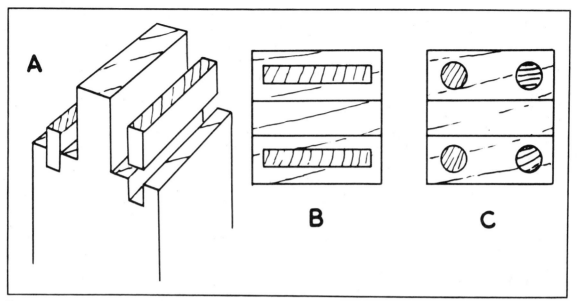

Fig. 6-22. Where there are wide shoulders, splines or dowels can be inserted.

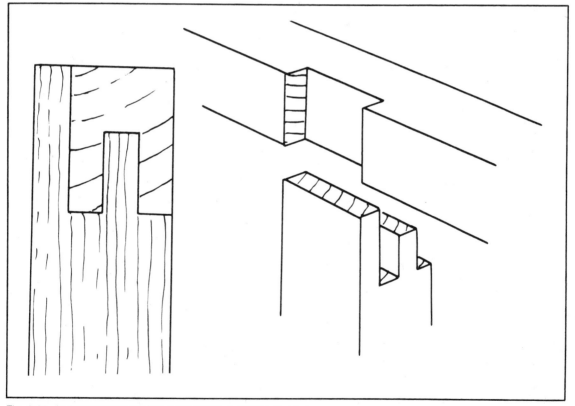

Fig. 6-23. An intermediate leg into a rail needs a special double tenon.

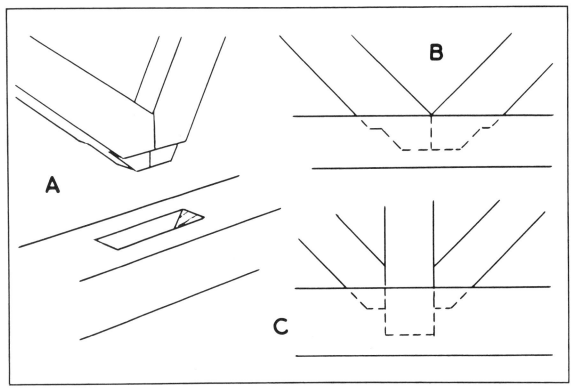

Fig. 6-24. Two or more tenons can be taken into the same mortise.

their lines. Only the meeting edges are cut square to the rail. If the diagonals are very wide, a very wide mortise should be avoided as that could cause weakness in the rails. Short haunched pieces on the outsides of the tenons might be made (Fig. 6-24B).

There could be three pieces meeting, one squarely and the others diagonal to it. This happens in some gate construction, where the upright post is the main load bearer. The diagonal braces keep the assembly in shape and provide decoration. To avoid weakening by cutting out a large mortise, the socket for the squared rail is taken deeply and the others are not taken as far (Fig. 6-24C). In a gate or other assembly where some loads may be expected to put a loosening load on the parts, the joint should be drilled for pegs or dowels across each tenon.

ROOF TRUSS JOINTS

In some wooden roof trusses there is a central upright called a *king post*. At the top the rafters are

joined into it, and near its bottom there are struts angled outward to the rafter. If the roof truss is to be visible from below in the finished roof, as it might in a church or hall, the shaping of the parts is important for the sake of appearance. The joints then have to be made so they are decorative and functional.

In any mortise and tenon joint the shoulders are best able to take thrust if they are square to the length of the tenoned part, as they are in most joints. If the tenoned part meets the other acutely, the ability to take thrust becomes less as the angle gets less. In much furniture there is still more than enough strength, but in a wooden assembly subject to considerable load, it is better if the shoulder can be brought nearer square if it cannot be made fully square to the tenoned part.

In this king post truss, the post is kept full width above and below the joints. It is narrowed between the rafter and strut joints (Fig. 6-25A). It cannot be narrowed enough for the tenon shoulders to be cut square, but they can be at a compromise angle that takes the thrust better than the acute angle they would need to be if the king post was not cut down. The acute angled side of the tenon follows through straight, but the other side is cut square (Fig. 6-25B).

MOLDED T-JOINT

If a plain piece of wood has to meet with a molded edge, something has to be done where the shoulder of the tenoned piece meets the molded edge. Two treatments are possible.

The molding may be cut back each side of the tenoned piece, which is then joined with a normal mortise and tenon joint (Fig. 6-26A). The molding

has to be cut cleanly and close to the other part, or there will be an unsightly gap.

The other method has the shoulder of the tenoned piece scribed or coped over the molding. If it is a complicated section or has undercuts, successful scribing may be difficult or impossible. The other shoulder rests flat on the mortised part, but the scribed shoulder has to be carefully cut across with suitable gouges and chisels (Fig. 6-26B).

THREE-WAY JOINT

If two horizontal rails meet at a corner and have to join an upright post below them, when the rails are upright in section they can be tenoned into the upright, as is usual with the top rails into the leg of a

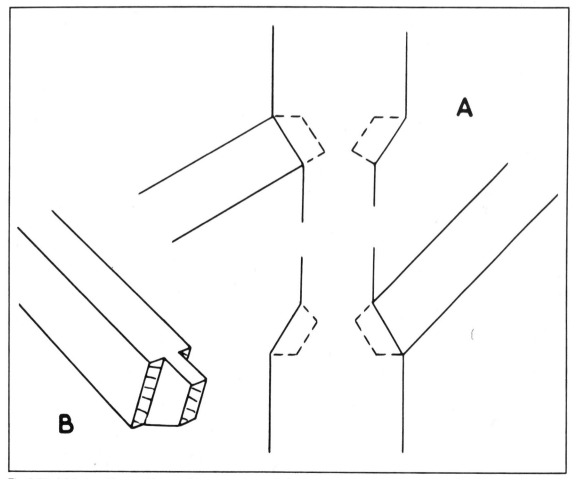

Fig. 6-25. Joints to a king post in a roof truss may be angled.

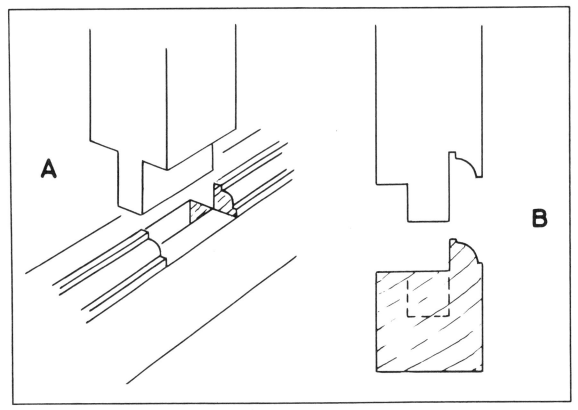

Fig. 6-26. When a joint has to be made into a molded and rabbeted piece, the molding can be cut back or the other piece scribed over it.

table. If the rails have a flat section, they might be joined with two short tenons each on the top of the post (Fig. 6-27A) if the post is of sufficient section.

If the post is the same as or narrower than the rail widths, halve the rails together, then put a tenon from the post through that joint (Fig. 6-27B). The tenon normally would have to be one-third the width of the rails. If it can be wider than this without weakening the other parts, that would increase its strength.

SELF-WEDGED CORNER JOINT

The wheelwright's tenon (Fig. 6-20) shows a method of using a tapered tenon that will tighten the joint as it is forced in, but that method cannot be used at a corner without some adaption. One way this is done uses a haunch wider than usual above a tapered tenon (Fig. 6-28A). There has to be a fairly

wide haunch with enough end grain there to resist the outward thrust of the tapered tenon as it is forced in. A horn should be left on the mortised part until after assembly to further hold the end grain.

That type of joint can be adapted to have mitered surfaces on one or both sides, and it is credited to the Japanese (Fig. 6-28B). The amount of glue area is reduced, but compared with a normal mortise and tenon joint, that is compensated for by the greater area at the haunch.

RABBETED CORNER MORTISE AND TENON JOINT

Frames are often made with the wood rabbeted to hold a mirror or a picture. The front edge may be cut squarely and could be decorated inside the corners with wagon beveling or molding done with a router or spindle, but stopped before the corner. In that case the upright member usually carries through

102

and has the mortise, while the rail is notched into it as it is tenoned (Fig. 6-29A).

The rail end must have the shoulders at two different levels, and it helps in construction work if the rebate is about two-thirds the thickness of the wood, then the side of the tenon matches the inside of the rabbet (Fig. 6-29B). If the rabbet is a different width, the joint can still be out in a similar way, but the mortise will overlap the front width or be cut back from it.

Be careful when marking the shoulders at each side of the tenon that they are cut across at exactly the right distance apart to bed down on the other piece (Fig. 6-29C). The width of the tenon can be gauged all around. You can use the gauge on the flat side of the mortised piece, but you will have to mark inside the rabbet by measuring (Fig. 6-29D). The shoulder of the tenoned part must be cut back to the bottom of its rabbet, but that will cut automatically if the edge of the tenon is also the inside of the rabbet (Fig. 6-29E). This is the important front edge of the joint, so make sure the wood fibers are severed by cutting all around with a knife before sawing.

The usual haunch can be at a corner and either cut squarely or tapered (Fig. 6-29F).

INTERMEDIATE RABBETED
MORTISE AND TENON JOINT

Most assemblies with rabbets only have an outer frame, but in some paneled work other rails may be crossing. If there are similar rabbets on both sides, the joint is comparable to the corner joint, except there are no haunches and there is a cutback for the rabbet on each side of the tenon (Fig. 6-30A). If the rail is wide, there may be two tenons (Fig. 6-30B) to avoid weakening the other part with a long mortise.

In some doors and other constructions there may be a rabbet for glass at one side of the rail,

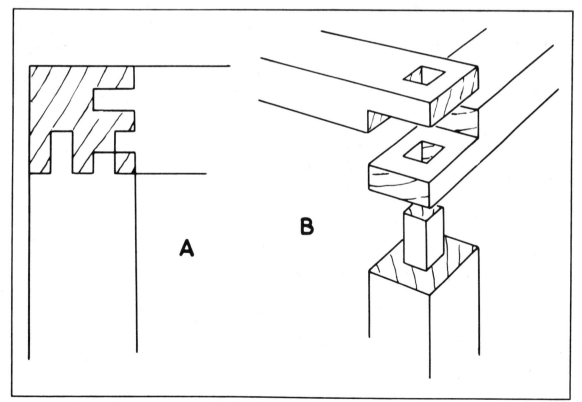

Fig. 6-27. There can be double tenons into a corner post (A) or two parts halved over a central tenon (B).

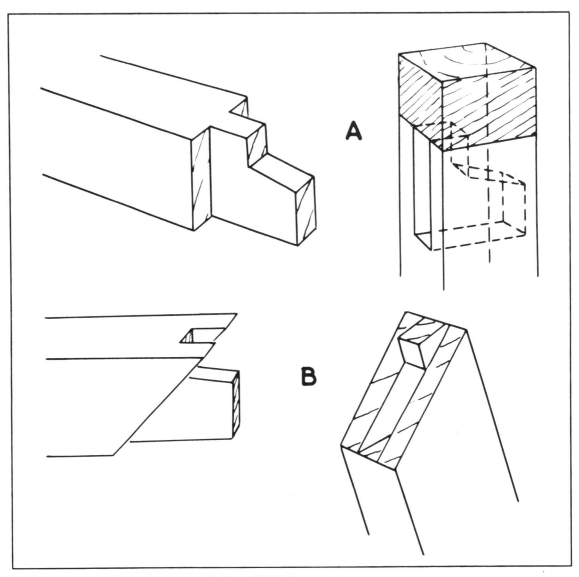

Fig. 6-28. Tapered tenons can be arranged to be self-tightening.

while the parts are grooved to take a panel at the other side. It is convenient to have the side of the plowed groove level with the side of the rabbet (Fig. 6-30C), although it would not matter if it came further back in relation to the rabbet. The other piece has a rabbet on one edge and a groove on the other. The rabbet goes through for the width of the rail (Fig. 6-30D), then the rail can be cut with stepped shoulders and will match at both sides.

MITERED MOLDING CORNER JOINT

If rabbeted wood is prepared with a molded front edge (Fig. 6-31A), there are complications in the design of mortise and tenon joints at the corners. It is common to cut back the moldings and miter them. The molding may be the same depth as the rabbet. If it is not as deep, some of the plain wood will have to be cut back with it to the same depth.

Except for lengths, the actual joints are not

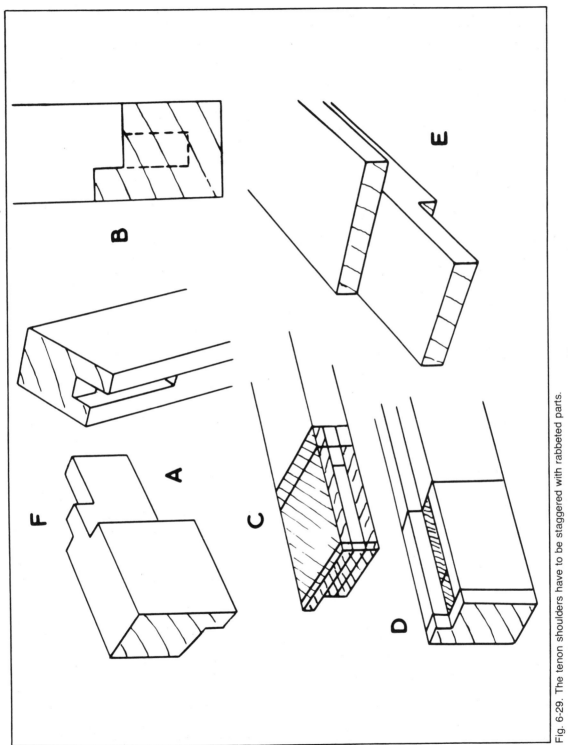

Fig. 6-29. The tenon shoulders have to be staggered with rabbeted parts.

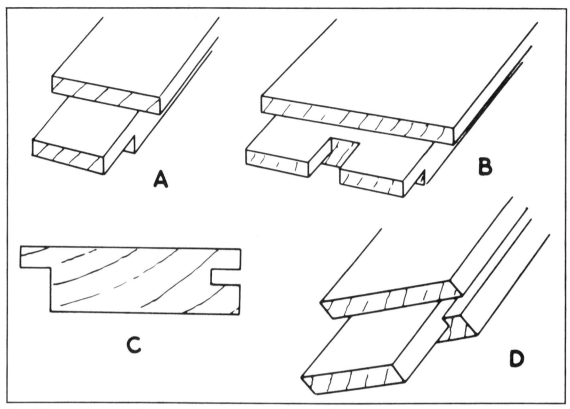

Fig. 6-30. An intermediate rail may have to be tenoned to allow for rabbets and grooves.

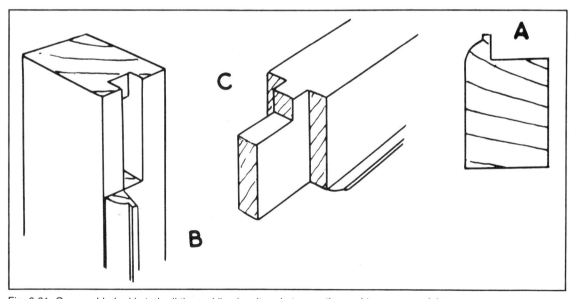

Fig. 6-31. On a molded rabbeted rail the molding is mitered at a mortise and tenon corner joint.

marked out until the miters are cut (Fig. 6-31B). Care is needed in the marking and cutting of the miters, which have to make a close fit when the joint is drawn together. Paring the miters correctly with a chisel is the critical part of the work.

From this point the joint is made in the usual way with a haunched tenon (Fig. 6-31C), stub or through and with or without wedges. It helps in getting the assembly true to have a piece of plywood with an accurately cut 90-degree corner to hold in the rabbet as the tenon is drawn in.

INTERMEDIATE MOLDED EDGE JOINT

If there has to be an intermediate rabbeted rail with matching molded edges, the parts can be cut so the molding is mitered in the same way as at a corner (Fig. 6-32A). When the miters have been cut, the joint becomes a simple mortise and tenon.

Making the joint that way brings the same problem as at the corners in getting the miters cut so they close properly when the joint is drawn together. Here there are two sides to deal with.

Another way of making this joint is to let the molding go through on the mortise piece, then scribe the tenon shoulder over it. If the molding is a simple rounding or just a bevel (Fig. 6-32B), scrib-ing is easy. If the shape is more complicated, there has to be some careful work across the end grain of the shoulder to get a good fit (Fig. 6-32C). A good scribed joint should look better than a mitered one, but if the type of molding makes accurate scribing difficult, a mitered joint will probably finish with a better appearance.

SASH BAR JOINT

In most joints involving rabbets the rabbet is wide enough for the tenon to go into it, and the front shoulder is cut back to step over the other piece. If the rabbet is comparatively narrow, the tenon has to go into the thicker front part. This may happen with window sash bars, which are quite small in section compared with the parts they have to join. The joint is shown with the sash bar going into a piece with square sections (Fig. 6-33A). The tenon is level with the edge of the rabbet. There may not be much thickness in the sash bar for the tenon if it has a molded section. This means the shoulders are rather wide and unsupported, so they are liable to twist. A stronger joint is produced if the shoulders are let in completely or with small haunches (Fig. 6-33B). The tenon holds the joint, but the haunches are there to resist any tendency to twist. If the

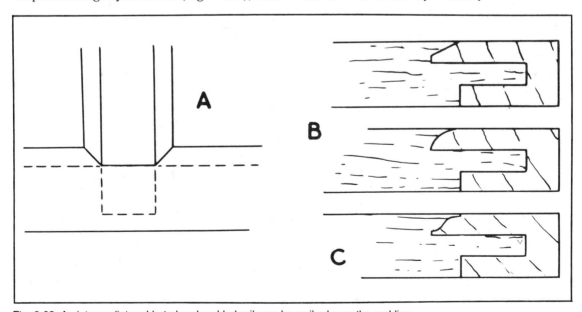

Fig. 6-32. An intermediate rabbeted and molded rail may be scribed over the molding.

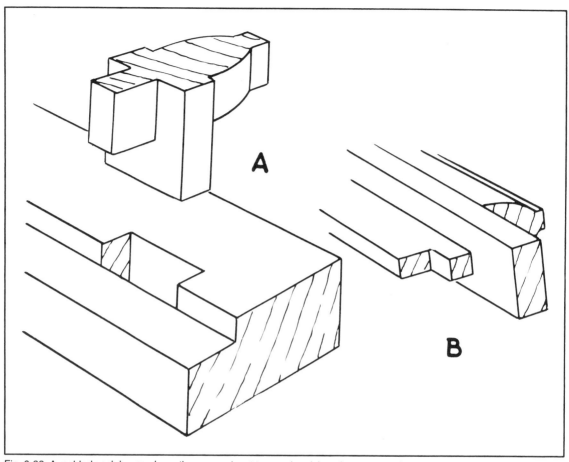

Fig. 6-33. A molded sash bar can have the squared part tenoned and the other parts cut back when it meets a rabbeted strip.

mortised piece is also molded, the end of the sash bar will have to be mitered or scribed to it.

CORNER SCRIBED MOLDED EDGE JOINT

One piece can be scribed over the other at a corner as an alternative to mitering the molded edge. Either part can have the scribing, but it is easier to get a close fit if scribing is done on the wood with the tenon. The mortised piece has the mitered edge taken up to the edge of the mortise and cut squarely. No other work has to be done on that part (Fig. 6-34A).

On the tenoned part the end of the molding is cut off at the position it would be for mitering, then this is scribed to fit over the other piece (Fig. 6-34B). It helps in scribing to first cut the end of the molded part to a miter. The shape shown on the miter is the outline you have to pare away with suitable chisels and gouges (Fig. 6-34C). Pare while viewing directly from above and stop as soon as you reach the limits shown by the edge of the miter. Be careful when the shape comes to a feather-edge as it closes on the curve.

One advantage of scribing over mitering is that changes in the sizes of the wood due to moisture absorption or loss will be less evident.

MITERED SHOULDERED TENON

Some furniture rails have their undersides shaped. If the shaping is stopped before the leg, the rail end can be tenoned in the usual way (Fig. 6-35A). If there is a curve that has to blend into the leg, a normal mortise and tenon joint there would mean having a shoulder with a thin weak edge where the grain could crumble and spoil appearance (Fig. 6-35B).

A better way to deal with the joint has a miter at the lower corner of the shoulder, and this runs off to the top (Fig. 6-35C). The amount of miter depends on the sizes of wood and the amount of curved edge on the rail, but it is not necessarily 45 degrees. It should divide the angle as it comes to give a neat appearance. The haunch could be cut squarely or parallel with the shoulder, or it could be tapered to be hidden if the top is visible when the furniture is finished.

MEETING TENONS

If two pieces of similar section have to meet in another piece so they appear to go through, as in a post passing through a shelf (Fig. 6-36A), they have to be fitted into each other. This is done by letting a narrow tenon on one piece fit into a wider tenon on the other piece.

The thickness could be divided into five equal parts, but that leaves the single tenon rather thin. It

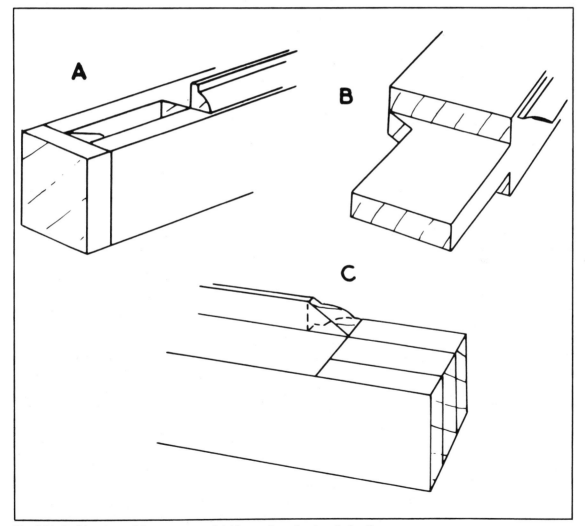

Fig. 6-34. Scribing the molding at a corner joint is an alternative to mitering there.

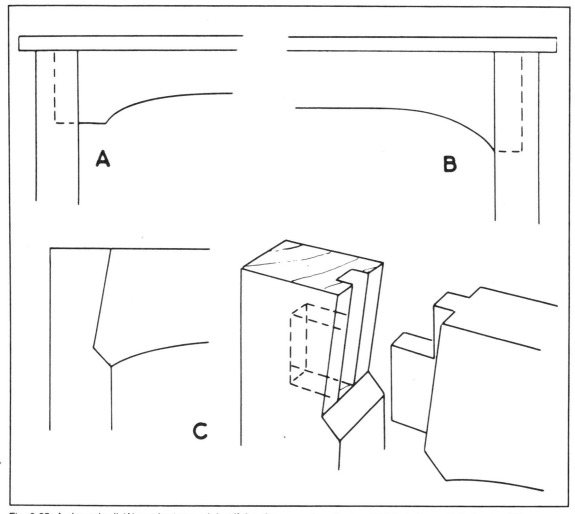

Fig. 6-35. A shaped rail (A) can be tenoned, but if the shape reaches the leg (B) it is better cut into the leg (C).

is better to allow for that tenon to be equal to the total thickness of the two sides of the other piece (Fig. 6-36B), so that is found by dividing the thickness into six equal parts and allowing two of them for the center. The center tenon may go the full thickness of the shelf, or it could be cut back a little so its mortise does not show on the top (Fig. 6-36C).

A similar arrangement of tenons may be used for a handrail into a post or other position where the wood is comparatively thick. It is then possible to interleave two tenons from each piece, so the loads are evenly taken (Fig. 6-36D). The tenons may then

each be one-third of the thickness. If the piece being fitted through is thin, the first version of the joint is preferable.

CHASE MORTISES

If a rail or other part has to be fitted between two pieces that are already in position, it is possible to use a normal short stub tenon at one end. At the other end the tenon must slide into a chase mortise, pivoting on the stub tenon end.

If the tenon can drop in from the top, the chase mortise may slope down to a shoulder for the tenon to rest on (Fig. 6-37A). If it is more convenient or the extended mortise would be hidden better, the chase mortise may be cut to the side (Fig. 6-37B). That could be a barefaced tenon, like the other, or a further part could extend over the surface of the mortised piece (Fig. 6-37C) to give a greater glue area.

The depth and slope of a chase mortise depend on the swing of the rail on its other end and the amount of penetration required on the tenon. The further it is to go in, the longer the slope will have to be. By keeping the rail as long as can be forced in along the slope, the joint balances the shortness of the tenon with the strength that comes from a tight fit.

INTERLOCKING TENONS

Where tenons meet, as in the rails into a chair or table leg, they may be cut short to avoid each other or be mitered, but it is possible to interlock them. In a chair this allows the side rails to be more resistant to being pulled out when the user rocks the chair on two legs—back to front. The rail to be locked extends past the end of the other mortise, so the tenon in that also goes into the side of the extended tenon (Fig. 6-38A).

Both mortises are cut, then the long tenon is inserted tightly so the position of the slot on it can be marked through the other mortise (Fig. 6-38B). If the assembly will be tightly clamped during gluing, the slot can be cut to the lines marked. It is possible to use the second tenon to draw the first tighter in a similar way to drawbore pinning with a tapered dowel in a through mortise and tenon joint. Cut the slot slightly nearer the shoulder of the

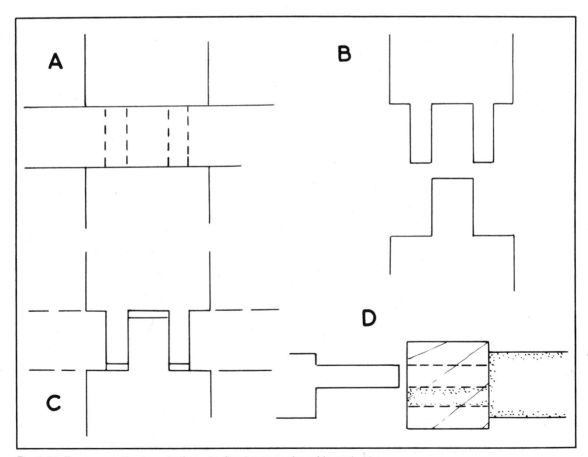

Fig. 6-36. Tenons meeting in a shelf can be fitted over or alongside each other.

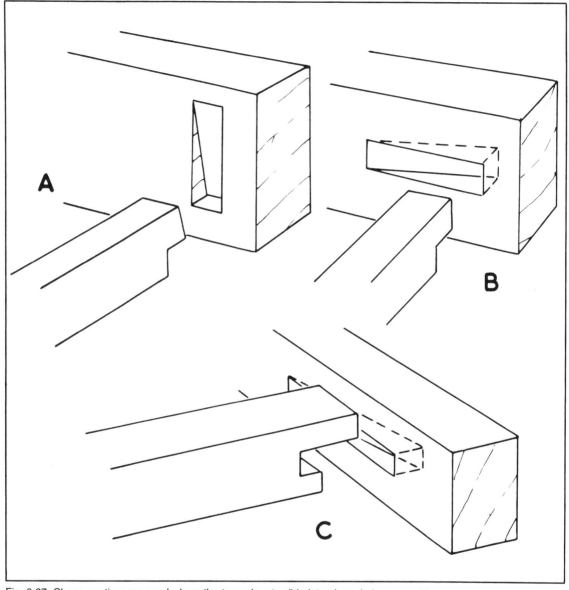

Fig. 6-37. Chase mortises are used where the tenon has to slide into place during assembly.

tenon. Taper the end of the second tenon so it will put against the slot as it is driven in (Fig. 6-38C).

Another version interlocks the tenons edgewise. Two tenons are arranged to cross in a post, with one of the mortises open so that tenon can be dropped in, but the mortises intersect partially. The upper edge of the lower tenon has a notch to mate with a similar one in the top tenon (Fig.

6-39A). The joints may have the tenons through the post or leg, or they can be stopped.

The two parts can be made to tighten on each other by sloping the notches (Fig. 6-39B). As this is only an edgewise pull, there will not be as good a tightening effect as in the first example.

The method can be used with dry joints for a takedown table or bench. The upper rails are attached to the top, and lowering the top assembly into position locks the crossing rails (Fig. 6-39C).

THIN TO THICK JOINTS

A thin piece may have to be tenoned into another much thicker piece. This happens with some chair-back slats or rails into the framing. You may take a very thin sectioned piece into a mortise without cutting it (Fig. 6-40A). If there is slightly more wood, just a slight shoulder could be at the front (Fig. 6-40B). The main advantage of this is in covering any roughness of the edge of the mortise, which may spoil appearance if exposed. If the thin piece is fairly wide, it could have shoulders cut on its edges (Fig. 6-40C). Without shoulders only the

bottom of the mortise limits penetration, which may not matter if surrounding framing sets the sizes. Shoulders on any tenon allow for more precise fitting to size.

ADJUSTABLE SLOT MORTISE AND TENON JOINT

A joint is needed that can be forced outward at the corners of a frame used to stretch an artist's canvas. This is a rectangular frame to which the canvas has to be tacked, but it is then forced outward at each corner so the canvas is fully tensioned for painting on. Tightening is by wedges on the inside surfaces of the joints.

In a simple version the two parts meet squarely at a corner as an open mortise and tenon or

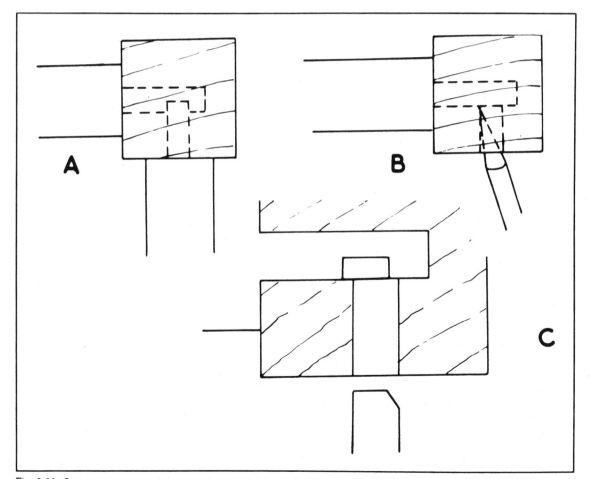

Fig. 6-38. One tenon may notch into another to provide a lock.

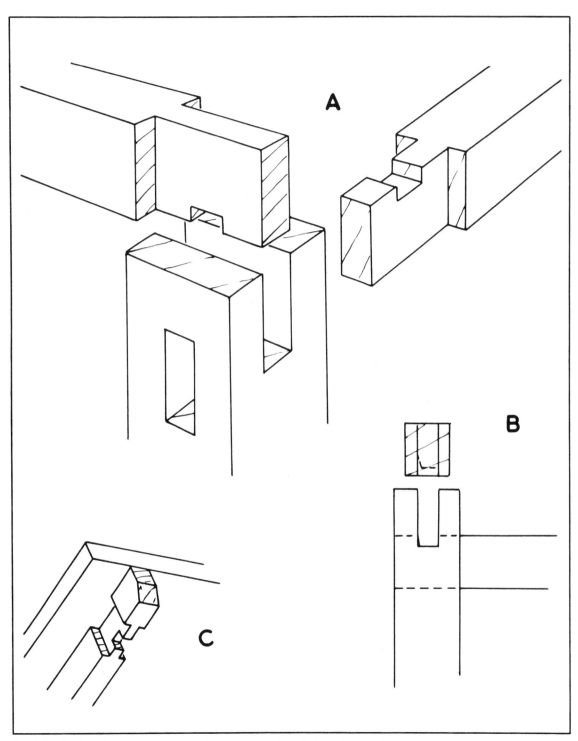

Fig. 6-39. Notched tenons can be used where parts may have to be taken apart.

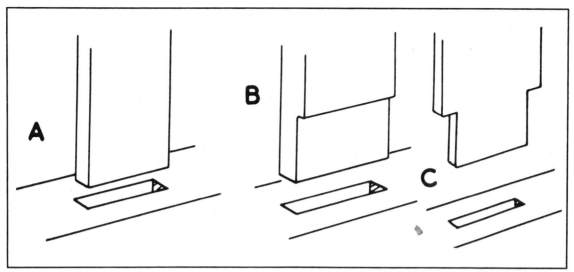

Fig. 6-40. A thin strip can go into a mortise complete (A), be given a shallow shoulder (B), or be notched at the sides (C).

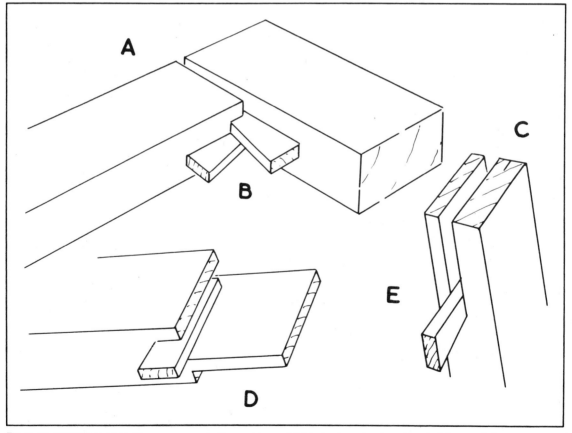

Fig. 6-41. Wedges in slots allow an open mortise and tenon joint to be forced outward to stretch an artist's canvas.

bridle joint (Fig. 6-41A). The tenoned part has a wedge slot below it, and there is another slot to allow a wedge to be driven against the side of the other piece (Fig. 6-41B). The joint could be made with the tenon one-third of the thickness of the wood, but that makes the wedge into its shoulder rather thin. It would be better to divide the thickness into four equal parts (Fig. 6-41C), then the wedge into the shoulder of the tenon part is the same thickness as the tenon (Fig. 6-41D). The mortise in the other piece is offset (Fig. 6-41E).

It is more common to miter the frame corners with a tenon on each part (Fig. 6-42A). The tenons slide on each other, and wedges alongside them push the other tenon outward (Fig. 6-42B). Both parts of a joint are similar. It is common to provide grooves for the wedges to slide, although some frames are made without them.

To mark out the joint, divide the thickness into four for as far as the other piece will come, then mark miters on both surfaces (Fig. 6-42C). Mark further for the wedge slots or leave them until you have made the interlocking joint and can see where the wedges have to come.

Cut the miters and mortise slots to leave the tenons standing (Fig. 6-42D). The wedges and their slots should match and be cut so a full tension can be given without the wedges pushing through the canvas (Fig. 6-42E).

In both forms of the joint the grooves for the wedges can be plowed through the full length, although they are only needed at the ends. You could

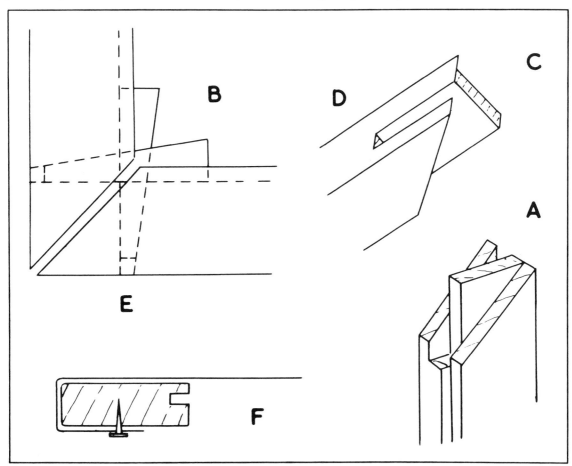

Fig. 6-42. A mitered mortise and tenon joint is another way of using wedges to stretch an artist's canvas.

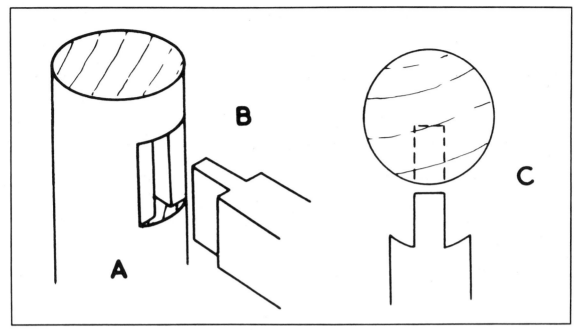

Fig. 6-43. A joint into a round piece can have a flat cut, or the shoulders may be shaped to match the curve.

make the joints with the wedges pushing against the surfaces, but having them in grooves helps to keep the frame from distorting.

In use the canvas is wrapped over to be tacked on the back of the frame (Fig. 6-42F) with a hand tension. Wedges are tapped in tighter progressively with a hammer to get the required even tension for painting. If much stretching is left to the wedges, the corners will open excessively. The first hand tightening should be as much as can be given.

TENON TO ROUND LEG

When a rail meets a round leg and has to be tenoned into it, there are two ways this can be done. A flat can be cut on the leg to match the end of the rail (Fig. 6-43A), then a normal mortise and tenon joint cut (Fig. 6-43B). That is satisfactory if the rail is a much smaller section than the leg. If it is more nearly the same width as the leg diameter, too much would have to be cut away. The leg would be weakened.

For the other method, the leg is not cut back to make a seating for the end of the rail. Instead, the rail has its shoulders rounded to match the leg (Fig. 6-34C). Besides making the joint without cutting much from the leg, this also suits rails of shaped section, such as round or octagonal, to be fitted without any special preparation.

If the rail is very deep, the tenon could be cut back at the top and bottom or divided into two parts to avoid removing too much wood when mortising the leg.

EXPANDED TENON

It is usually possible to get all the strength needed in a mortise and tenon joint by wedging as described earlier, but for large sections of wood it is possible to spread the end of a tenon much more than normal wedging could do. Spreading is by wedge, but the penetration of the wedge is limited by a hole drilled across the saw cut (Fig. 6-44A). This is kept far enough within the mortised part for a short section of the tenon to remain normal width. The mortise is tapered to that level enough to allow for a wedge of a wider taper than in the other joints to be driven (Fig. 6-44B).

The effect is to bend the wood fibers from the

117

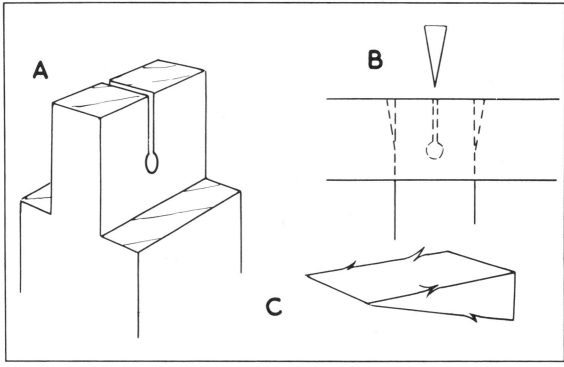

Fig. 6-44. A hole to stop the wedge slot prevents splitting and allows a wider wedge to be used in a tenon. A metal wedge with teeth can be used.

hole level, so the mortise is filled tightly. The wedge may be glued as it is driven. Another way of tightening is to use a steel wedge with teeth chopped into its edges with a cold chisel (Fig. 6-44C), so they resist any tendency for the wedge to come out. Even with a wood wedge, it helps to first drive in a chisel or other wedge-shaped metal tool to open the cut for the wood wedge.

A similar method of wedging is used to secure a handle in a hammerhead. The hole through the head may have a tapered section or be waisted (Fig. 6-45A). The wood handle is sawed lengthwise in relation to the elliptical hole before it is driven in. This is normally done by holding the hammer by its handle with the head downward and a mallet used on the end (Fig. 6-45B). Handles are tapered toward a shoulder so they do not enter too far.

A hardwood wedge of fairly slim section goes into the saw cut to expand the handle end and is cut off level. A chisel makes a cut across its center, then a steel wedge with teeth cut on it goes into that

(Fig. 6-45C). Ax and hatchet heads are fitted in the same way, but because of the very long section of hole, the wood wedge driven the long way may have two steel wedges driven across it.

BOXED TENONS

If two tenons are arranged square to each other, they are boxed (Fig. 6-46). This arrangement might be needed when two rails meet at a corner and the post has to tenon into them, but there are better joints for this purpose.

When the boxed tenons are cut, it usually will not matter if the saw cutting the inside of one is allowed to go through the other. A square at the corner has cuts each side. In some structures that square may be removed. Otherwise, the matching mortises must meet as a hollow L shape.

PLUG TENON

If a tenon is needed for locating rather than

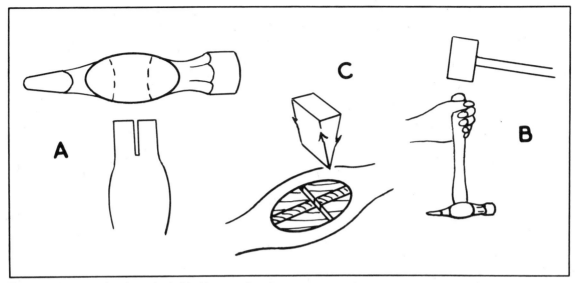

Fig. 6-45. A hammerhead may be held with a metal wedge across a wooden one.

strength, it can be quite small and is then a plug tenon (Fig. 6-47). It might be needed at the foot of a post to position it on the floor, where it will be held down by its own weight or that which it supports. It might come anywhere that another piece has to be manipulated into place, and its mortise dropping on to the plug tenon will give a positive position. The plug tenon need not be square, and it could be anywhere convenient on the wood end.

STUMP TENONS

If a part that is to be tenoned into another part comes under much load across the joint, it might reach a point in an extreme case where the wood sheared at the place where the tenon entered its mortise. That would be the position weakest under a shear load. In this case it is better if all or a greater part of the full section follows the tenon into the other part.

If the load comes the long way of a tenon, the full size of the wood can be taken in a short way before the mortise and tenon are made (Fig. 6-48A). If the mortised part seems too small to be cut out that much, the other part could be tapered to the tenon (Fig. 6-48B) so as not to take away as much wood.

If the load comes across the shorter way of the

tenon, the strain can be spread by making the tenon in two thicknesses. The thicker part must not penetrate the other piece very far, or it would need too much wood cut away. It goes in and resists the shearing load at the surface, while the full tenon completes the joint in the usual way (Fig. 6-48C). If the two pieces of wood are the same thickness, the long tenon may be the usual one-third of the thickness. The thicker part can come to the middle of each shoulder. If the piece with the mortise is thicker, the tenon thicknesses may be increased a little.

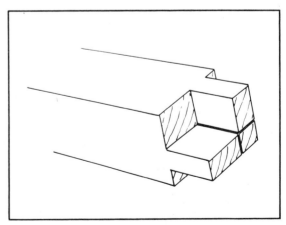

Fig. 6-46. Boxed tenons are two square to each other.

119

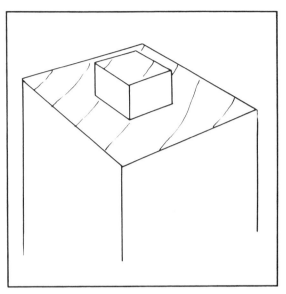

Fig. 6-47. A plug tenon is a small one intended to locate another part.

LAPPED TENONS

When two rail ends are to meet in a post, they can be arranged as shown in Fig. 6-19. If the post is thick enough and the joint has to resist greater loads, particularly those that might break a tenon at the shoulder in a similar way to the need for stump tenons, the tenons can go through alongside each other (Fig. 6-49).

If the post is the same thickness as the rails, the tenons would be rather thin. Otherwise, the rail ends are marked for tenons about half the wood thickness. They step down to one-fourth thickness a short distance inside the post with a length that lets each take up the space left by the other. The mortise is parallel right through. A dowel could be centrally through post and tenons.

TRIPLE TENONS

When there is a T-joint between two parts, the

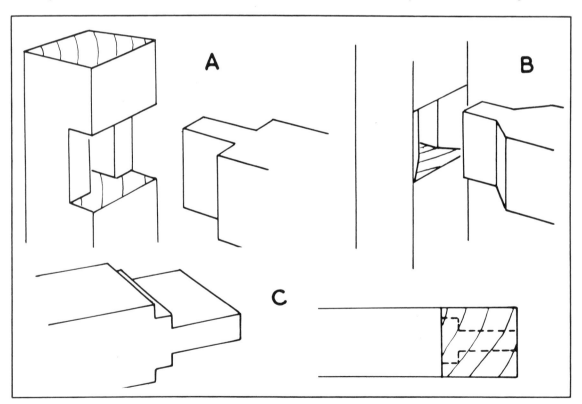

Fig. 6-48. To take a heavy downward load, a stump tenon takes the full-size wood in a short way (A, B). For a heavy load the other way, the tenon may be stepped (C).

120

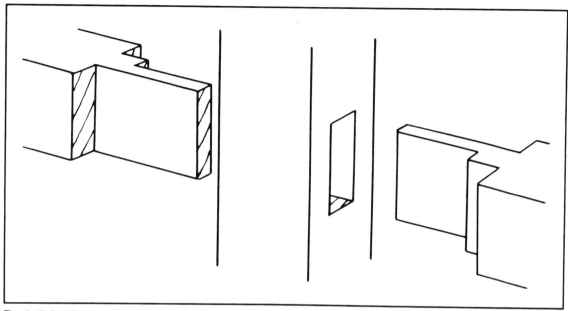

Fig. 6-49. In thick wood two meeting tenons can partially lap each other.

usual strong joint is a plain mortise and tenon. If for visual effect it would be better if the end piece crossed the other on the surface, the joint could be a bridle or halving. Neither may be as strong as a mortise and tenon.

If the wood is thick enough to allow it, there can be three tenons, with two crossing the other piece on the surface and one central (Fig. 6-50A). This necessitates dividing the thickness into five. If the crossing effect is only needed on one surface, the thickness may be divided into four (Fig. 6-50B).

Triple tenons can be used with molded and rabbeted wood. The parts are stepped or shaped to suit, and the end piece is cut back in width. Moldings meet their matching parts and may be mitered or scribed.

FRANKED MORTISE AND TENON

When a mortise and tenon joint comes at a corner, it can be haunched by cutting into the end of the mortised part for a small piece alongside the tenon. Franking the joint uses a projection on the mortised part to go into a gap in the tenoned piece (Fig. 6-51A). This is considered stronger than cutting away the other piece, but it is not always feasible or

advisable. If the mortised piece already has a raised part, that can be used (Fig. 6-51B). Some molded stock with a rabbet may have a flat top alongside the rabbet that can be used. Otherwise, the corner joint with a haunch is simpler and satisfactory.

DIMINISHED STILE

A room door may be made with a wood panel below the lock rail and a wider glass panel above. The upright stiles have to be reduced in width above the rail. This is a *diminished stile*, or a *gunstock stile*, named because of its similarity in form to a gunstock (Fig. 6-52A).

The reduction in width is arranged by sloping shoulders on the rail. Allowance has to be made for a rabbet on the top of the rail meeting a similar rabbet on the stile, with a miter between the parts. On the lower edge there will be a groove for the wood panel matching the groove in the side. That groove is plowed through the stile and runs out in the sloping edge. The depth it cuts into the slope can be used as a guide for a haunch between the tenons. In normal construction twin tenons should be enough (Fig. 6-52B). They go right through and are wedged if the exposed ends are acceptable.

121

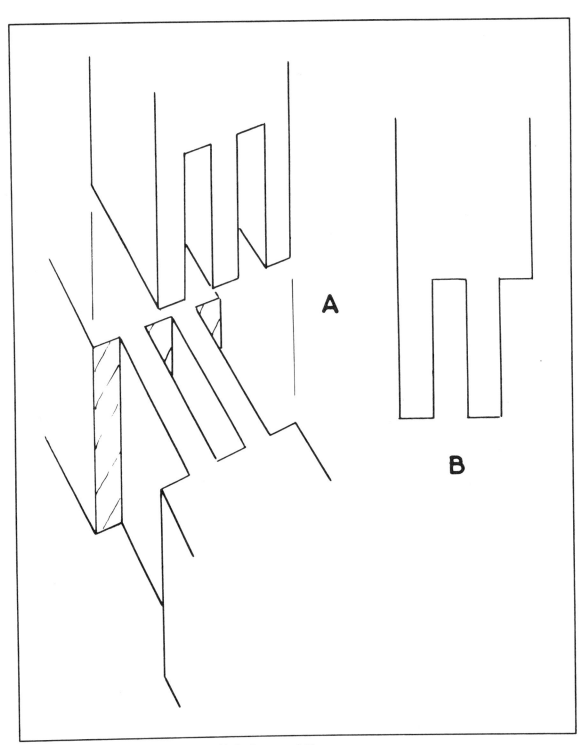

Fig. 6-50. Triple tenons may be arranged with the tenons outside.

122

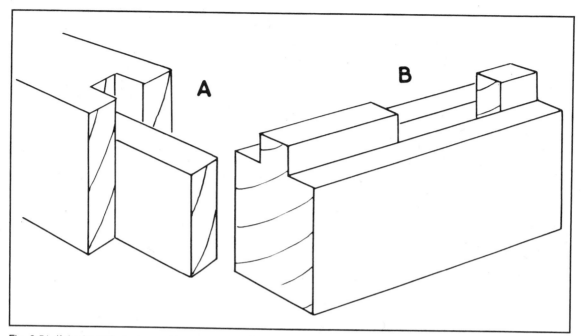

Fig. 6-51. If the haunch is reversed in a corner mortise and tenon joint, the joint is described as franked.

Otherwise, they can be stopped in the thickness.

The lock rail is an important strength member in the door. If the wood is thick—upward of 2 inches—it is better to use double tenons (Fig. 6-52C). In that case the haunching may be a complete cut out between and around the mortises. If any door is to be fitted with a mortise lock, the double tenons should be arranged to clear the opening that will have to be cut for the lock.

COTTERED JOINT

In large construction work where the wood joints may not be strong enough without reinforcement, an iron strap or stirrup may be put around the joint and tightened with folding wedges or *cotters*. An example is the king post above a tie beam in a roof truss.

There is a short stub tenon, but its main purpose is location, as the load is taken by the ironwork (Fig. 6-53). This goes some way up the post, which is slotted and lined with iron pads or *gibs* to spread the load on the wood. Two wedged cotters are driven against each other to thrust down on the post and up on the stirrup to tighten and hold the joint.

PUZZLE CROSS

This is a fairly simple three-part version of the Chinese cross, which may have a large number of parts. There are three mortises that fit into each other (Fig. 6-54A), so the method of assembly is not obvious. Careful work is necessary to get the parts closely fitting, then details of the joint cannot be seen after assembly.

Make the parts of wood three times as wide as it is thick. A width of 1½ inch and a thickness of ½ inch will do, then the length of each part can be 5 inches or 6 inches. Prepare the wood in a long strip to get the sections the same. Make one piece with a mortise that will allow the other parts to slide through (Fig. 6-54B). Make two other parts with the same size mortises, but with cuts into the sides wide enough to take the thickness of the wood (Fig. 6-54C). Check that any part will slide through any mortise and fit into the side cuts. A file or abrasive paper wrapped around a square strip of wood can be used inside the openings. Overall, the strips should be the same size. They can be sanded and given slightly rounded corners.

To assemble the puzzle, slip one of the

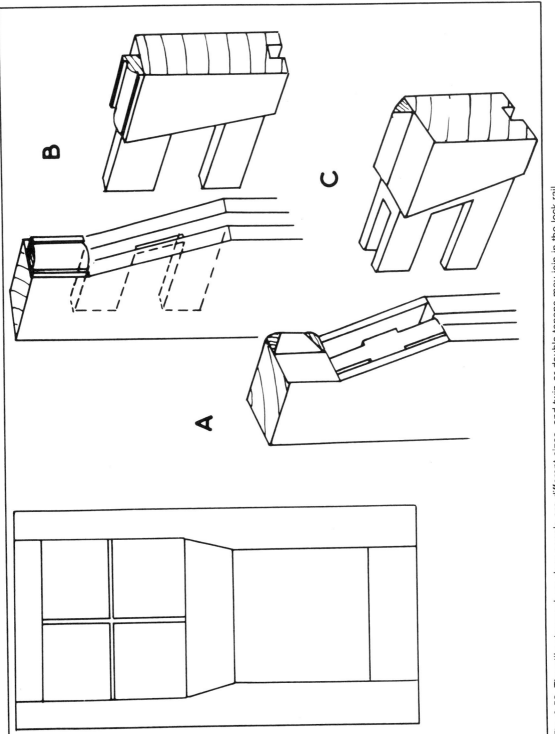

Fig. 6-52. The stiles taper where door panels are different sizes, and twin or double tenons may join in the lock rail.

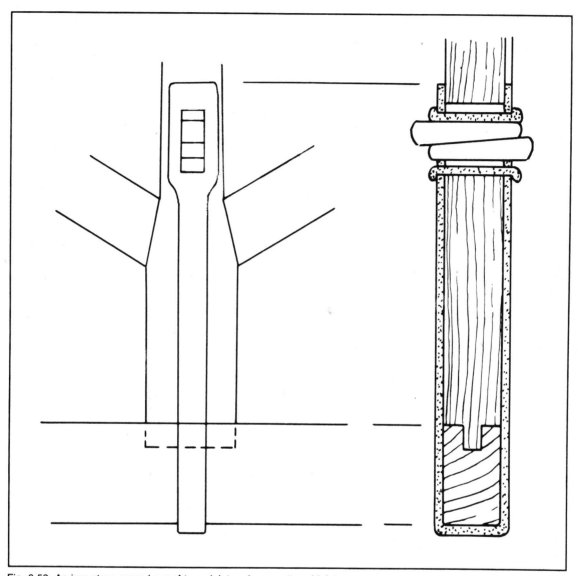

Fig. 6-53. An iron strap around a roof truss joint makes a cottered joint.

notched pieces into the plain mortise (Fig. 6-54D) to the point where the notch comes level with the surface (Fig. 6-54E). Slide the other notched piece on with its notch downward (Fig. 6-54F) until it is inside the cross, then push down the second piece (Fig. 6-54G) to lock it in. To separate, pull one of the notched pieces far enough out to allow the other to slide through its gap and off the plain mortised piece, so the remaining two will slide apart.

THREE-WAY MORTISE AND TENON

If three rails have to meet at 120-degree spacing or at other angles to each other, the joint is difficult to make as strong as might be possible with only two meeting. The following methods give reasonable strength.

If the rails are square or wider than they are deep, a tenon can be on one part, with its mortise cut half into each of the other pieces (Fig. 6-55A).

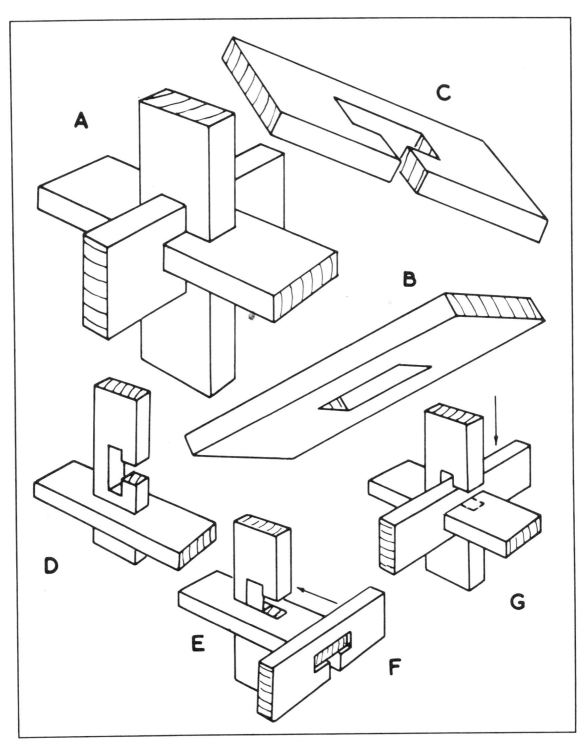

Fig. 6-54. This three-part cross puzzle has all the parts mortised.

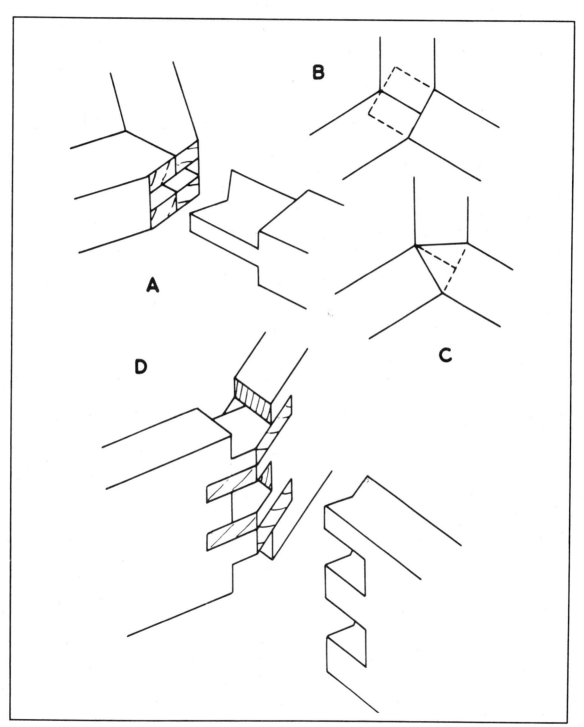

Fig. 6-55. For a three-way mortise and tenon joint two parts may be mortised to take a tenon on the other part (A, B), or the two may go into a mortise in one (C). For deeper parts, two pieces interlock and leave mortises for tenons on the third piece (D).

Greatest strength comes from taking the tenon through. If the exposed end grain is to be avoided, it can be stopped at the junction of the other two pieces (Fig. 6-55B). If appearance is more important and the surfaces would look better mitered, one piece can have the mortise between cheeks cut to match the other two parts. They have short shaped tenons meeting between cheeks (Fig. 6-55C).

When the rails are deep in relation to their width, there can be a system of interlocking tenons (Fig. 6-55D). Two pieces are cut so their tenons overlap, leaving open mortises for the other part to enter. To equalize the loads on the three parts, the tenons on the third part should be a little thicker than those on the other parts, and there should be outside mortises for it. Joint the first two parts and trim their tenon level before adding the third part, which may have its ends trimmed after assembly.

Chapter 7

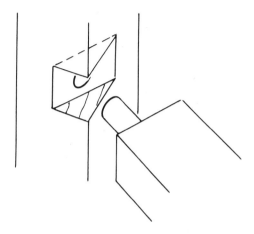

Doweled Joints

DOWELS HAVE BEEN USED UNDER OTHER names for a very long time. In most doweled joints used now, the dowels are alternatives to tenons or tongues. In earlier days, when nearly all woodworking was done with hand tools, dowels were more often used as reinforcements across the grain. Early dowels had to be made individually and usually did not have the precision of modern dowel rods. They did not fit as well, and joints were not always as strong.

Very early dowels were pared with a chisel or drawknife on the end of a piece of scrap wood. The hole a dowel was to enter might have been burned through or drilled with a crude bit that left a rough, uneven surface. In this case the dowel, with its many flats rather than a round surface, forced the hole sides to conform as it was driven in. If the dowel had a slight taper and was sized properly, it could make a strong joint. Examples can be seen in many old European timber-framed houses where the mortise and tenon joints have dowels driven across them, usually with the dowel end left above the surface.

Dowels often were used in boatbuilding. In many countries boats were made with their planks overlapping in lapstrake or clinker construction. Today there are metal fastenings, but boats, at least into medieval days, had dowels at fairly close intervals through the overlapping plank edges. The dowels were called *treenails* and pronounced *trunnels*. The Vikings crossed the Atlantic in boats with their planks held together in this way.

Where dowels of more exact shape were needed for cabinetmaking, the craftsman used a dowel plate or pop, which is a steel plate with holes of several sizes through it. Such a plate is thick enough to be stiff (about ⅜ inch). The holes are tapered slightly to present cutting edges (Fig. 7-1A). Usually there are screw holes so the plate can be mounted over a wood block (Fig. 7-1B). Pieces of wood are roughly shaped slightly oversize. Their ends are pointed and driven through the plate with a hammer. The resulting dowel may not have the smooth exact surface of a machine-made dowel. If the wood is allowed to go out of perpendicular, it may not finish straight. It could usually be

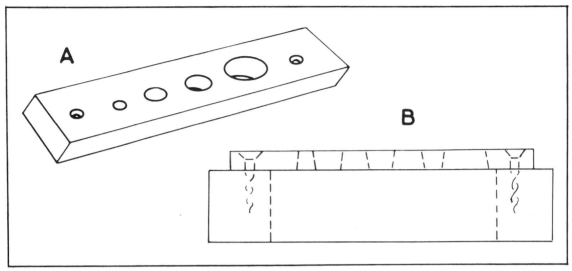

Fig. 7-1. A dowel plate makes dowels from pieces of wood driven through holes.

expected to make a strong glued joint. An advantage of making dowels in this way is that pieces of the same wood being joined can be used. If the dowel end will show, it will look the same.

Dowels are turned on a lathe. You can use the same wood as for the parts being joined. The dowels can be turned to the exact length required and given tapered ends for easy driving into holes.

Most doweling is now done with prepared round rods obtained in long lengths and cut as required. They are of close-grained hardwood and should be truly round and of the exact diameter to fit a standard size hole.

When a dowel is driven into a blind hole (Fig. 7-2A), it is like a piston going into a cylinder. If the dowel is a close fit and smeared with glue, the air below it is compressed. This could cause splitting. Cut a groove along the dowel (Fig. 7-2B) for air and surplus glue to escape. The dowel can be held in a vise. A backsaw can be held with its teeth upward and the dowel pulled along it. The ends should also be given a small bevel for easy entry into the hole (Fig. 7-2C). That could be done with a chisel, but a reversed countersink bit (Fig. 7-2D) can be used in a brace and is particularly useful for large dowels. Ready-made dowels can be bought with their ends beveled and grooves pressed into them, usually around the wood (Fig. 7-2E). Dowel plates have

been made with a spur at one side of each hole, so a groove is scratched in the wood as it is driven through.

MARKING OUT

Holes in doweled joints should match exactly if the parts are to go together properly, particularly when there are many dowels involved. This can be done by careful marking so far as possible with the parts together. If the parts can be held with the meeting surfaces level and their face sides outward, lines can be squared across and a gauge used from the outside surfaces (Fig. 7-3A). It helps in exactly locating the point of the drill to make a dent with a spike or machinist's center punch on the line crossings.

That is easy where the parts are the same thickness and suitable for bringing together. Otherwise, it is useful to make the edge of a piece of scrap wood into a rod for checking that spacings are the same (Fig. 7-3B).

Doweling jigs have bushes through which the drill can be entered. They can be moved to various positions in relation to adjustable guides to press or clamp against the wood edges. Once set, a jig can be moved to different pieces of wood. Hole spacings will be the same.

Some simple dowel markers are metal plugs

130

with small central points projecting (Fig. 7-4). Holes are drilled in one part, and the plugs are pressed into them. If the piece is then brought into position on the other wood and pressed, the points make dents to indicate the centers of holes to be drilled (Fig. 7-3C). If dowels go right through one piece, holes can be drilled in that first. It may be positioned, then the holes are used as guides for the drill into the other piece (Fig. 7-3D).

DRILLING

Besides being accurately spaced, holes in opposite parts should be in line, which normally means square to the surface. If you can use a drill press or a stand for a portable electric drill, there should be no difficulty in drilling squarely. If a doweling jig is used for freehand drilling, the bushes are usually deep enough to guide the drill squarely. If the work is in a position where you have to drill without guides, either with a brace or an electric drill, get an assistant to sight the drill. You can see if it is square to the surface one way, but have your assistant viewing squarely to your view, so he can tell you how to hold the drill truly.

If the dowel end will be visible, the hole around it should be clean. It should be drilled with a bit that has spurs to sever the fibers as it enters. A similar bit could be used for dowels elsewhere in positions where they will not be seen. You could use a metal-working twist drill, particularly if it is to go through the bushes of a jig, as its outside has more bearing surface and is easier to keep straight. Another advantage is that these drills are made with more precision and in sizes that differ by only a few thousandths of an inch. You can find such a drill that is a better match to the dowel than a woodworking bit may be.

If a doweled joint is strained to the breaking

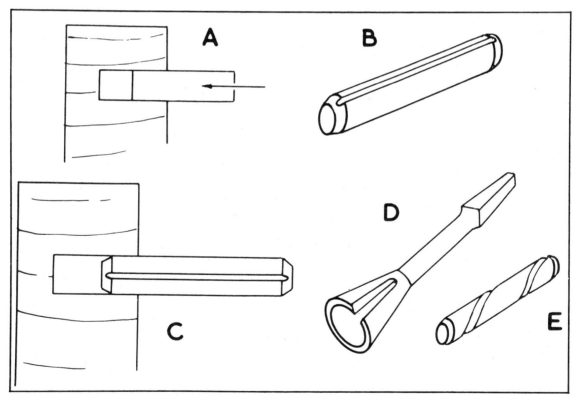

Fig. 7-2. A dowel acts like a piston in a hole (A). Air may be released if it is grooved (B). Beveling the ends helps assembly (C, E). A special tool can be used to make the bevel (D).

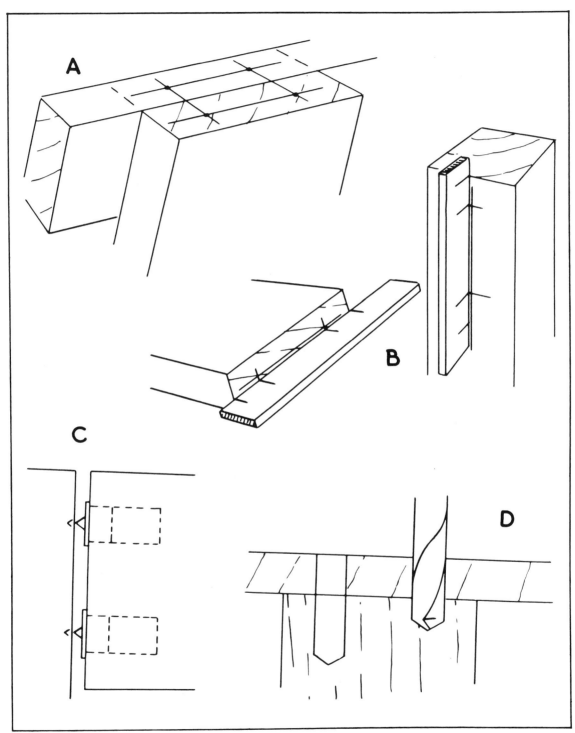

Fig. 7-3. Dowel parts should be marked together (A, B). Markers can be used (C) or holes drilled through (D).

Fig. 7-4. These dowel markers have points to push into dowel locations in one piece, which is brought to the other piece and pressed to mark hole centers.

times the diameter into end grain preferable (Fig. 7-5A). If there is plenty of thickness of wood, the holes may go deeper. In any case it is common to have the holes deeper than the length of the dowels (Fig. 7-5B). This avoids the dowels bottoming before the surfaces have met and provides a place for excess glue that may not have escaped via the dowel grooves.

Dowel diameters have to provide about the same glue area as would tenons in similar situations. There could be many thin dowels or fewer thick dowels. It is easier to make a joint with the minimum number of thick dowels. Unless there is a particular need for thin dowels, it is common to have diameters as thick as can reasonably be accommodated. Normally slightly more than half the thickness of the thinnest piece of wood involved will do. In ¾-inch or ⅞-inch wood the dowels could be ½-inch diameter. In thinner wood they would have to come down to ⅜-inch or ¼-inch diameter.

point, it may collapse between the meeting surfaces, so what is actually in the holes is normally more than enough. Going twice as deep as the diameter of the dowel is a minimum, with three

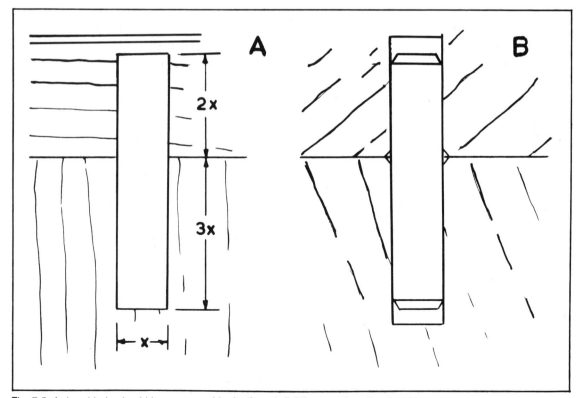

Fig. 7-5. A dowel hole should be a reasonable depth and slightly more than the dowel is expected to reach.

Prepared dowel rods usually are made in ⅛-inch steps.

Hole spacing is a matter for experience rather than calculation. There should never be less than two dowels in a joint. The space between the edge of a hole and the edge of the wood should not be less than the diameter of the hole, although that may have to be reduced in small joints. The space between the edges of holes should not be less than the diameter of the holes. For convenience in marking out or the use of a jig, dowels may be in a straight line. If one piece is square, it might be better to arrange the holes diagonally. If the narrowest piece is wide enough to permit it, the dowels can be arranged zigzag. This avoids getting many holes in one line of grain, with a consequent risk of splitting.

Most of the strength of a doweled joint is usually in the dowels and the bond they make with glue. If the meeting surfaces have the grain lengthwise, there should be a good glue bond between them. If one is end grain, glue on it will not be very effective. The end should be cut square so clamping pulls it close to the other piece. If the angle is other than square, take care to get a close fit for the sake of appearance, even if the end grain will not hold glue strongly.

When two surfaces have been drilled and will be brought together with dowels, it helps to slightly countersink the holes to stop fibers rising around the dowel and prevent the surfaces from pulling tightly together.

THROUGH DOWELS

If two pieces meet, either at a corner or at a T-junction, a row of dowels can be in the end grain of one piece going into holes in the other piece (Fig. 7-6A). If the exposed ends of the dowels are acceptable, they can go right through. The position of the end grain piece is marked on the other, then holes

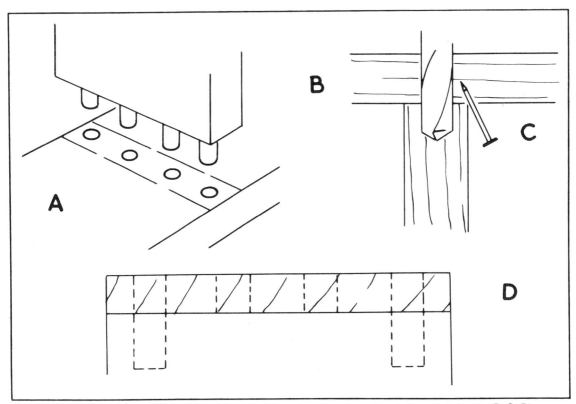

Fig. 7-6. A row of dowels at a T-joint (A) may be drilled through, with nails or dowels through to locate (B, C, D).

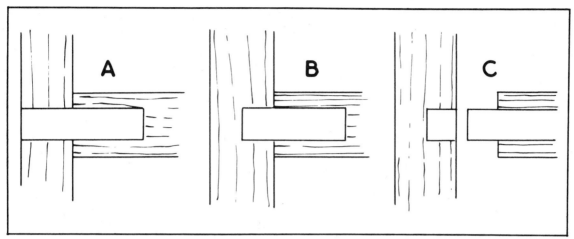

Fig. 7-7. Dowels may go through (A) or be stopped (B, C).

drilled in it first. If you put it in place on the end of the other, you can drill through (Fig. 7-6B). Two or more nails will help to locate the parts (Fig. 7-6C). If there are many dowels in the joint, you can drill through the end holes only first, then put dowels in them to stop the parts moving while you drill the end grain for the other dowels (Fig. 7-6D). Have the dowels slightly too long, then you can plane the ends flush with the surface after making the joint.

STOPPED DOWELS

If it would be unacceptable for dowel ends to show through one part (Fig. 7-7A), they have to go into blind holes. If there is sufficient thickness, the holes may be of adequate depth. If it is a thin piece and holes have to be shallow (Fig. 7-7B), glue area will have to be made up with a larger number of dowels.

In this sort of joint glue the dowels into the end grain piece (Fig. 7-7C) and quickly check that the amounts projecting are less than the depths of the blind holes before putting on more glue and pulling the joint together. If the meeting surfaces come close and excess glue oozes out, you know that the joint is properly made.

FRAMING DOWELS

Dowels are often used instead of mortise and tenon joints in the framing of tables and chairs, where rails

have to be joined to legs. If only one rail and leg are involved, the joint is similar to the previous one (Fig. 7-8A), with sufficient dowels arranged to suit the depth of the rail.

If it is a corner with rails both ways, the arrangement of the dowels depends on relative thicknesses. It may be possible to get holes deep enough on the same level without them meeting (Fig. 7-8B). Otherwise, the holes can meet, and the ends of the dowels can be mitered so they go in as far as possible (Fig. 7-8C). In this sort of assembly it is common to put opposite pairs of sides together first, square them, and let the glue dry before adding the rails the other way. The dowel holes the second way can be left until this stage, then the drill may be allowed to go into the first dowels.

If the rails are deep enough and the dowels are to go so deep that they would meet on the same level, it may be possible to stagger them, so the dowels one way miss those the other way (Fig. 7-8D). If you cannot allow for them missing each other completely, it may be possible to let them overlap only slightly. Drill and assemble one way, then drill in the other direction so as to remove only part of each first dowel (Fig. 7-8E).

DIAGONAL STRUT DOWELING

If a piece comes to another at an angle, tenons would have to be cut so as to keep the grain

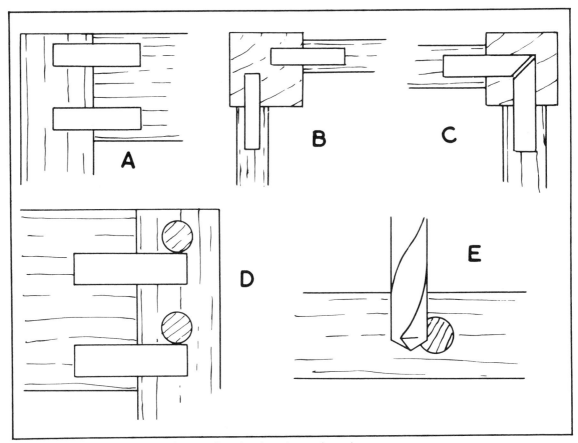

Fig. 7-8. Framing dowels may be short or mitered and can be overlapped.

lengthwise through them. If dowels are used, they are better arranged square to the meeting surfaces (Fig. 7-9A).

If the angle is not far from square, there is no difficulty in arranging a good spread of dowels. If it is more acute, there is a long thin end that will not take much length of dowel (Fig. 7-9B). If there is much width, you can use two or more thinner dowels side by side or staggered near the end. If an exposed dowel end does not matter, you can make the joint with concealed dowels in the thicker part and drill for a dowel square to the edge of the strut near the thin end (Fig. 7-9C).

DIAGONAL BRACE DOWELING

In the underframing of a table or chair, braces may be taken diagonally between legs. Because of pos-

sible loads to be resisted when the furniture is tilted, the joints need to be as strong as possible. The alternative to a mortise and tenon joint is a dowel joint. It does not matter if the meeting is at 45 degrees or any other angle.

Cut a notch across the corner of the leg, so its bottom is the same width as the brace (Fig. 7-10A). Drill this and the end of the brace for one fairly thick dowel. You can get plenty of depth as you drill the leg diagonally (Fig. 7-10B). Usually the brace is of fairly light section, and it will only take one dowel. If it is deeper, two dowels, even of smaller section, should give a better joint.

WEDGED DOWELS

If a dowel fits closely into a hole and is adequately glued, it should have ample strength. It can be

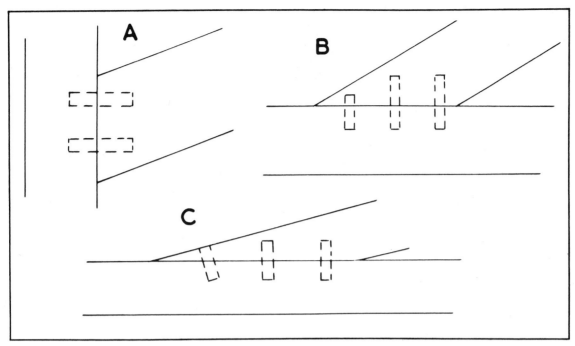

Fig. 7-9. At diagonal joints the dowels may be of different lengths.

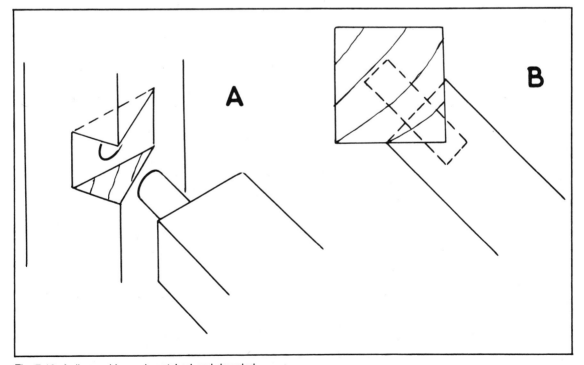

Fig. 7-10. A diagonal brace is notched and doweled.

strengthened by wedging in a similar way to tenons. This may be advisable in some circumstances with glued interior joints, but it would be particularly useful when dowels are used dry in housebuilding or other external woodwork.

If the dowel passes through wood, it could have a saw cut made across its end before insertion. This should be arranged as you assemble so it comes across the grain (Fig. 7-11A). It may have to be levered open with a chisel, then a wedge driven in (Fig. 7-11B). For a glued assembly, the wedge may be dipped in glue before driving. Finally, plane the dowel end and wedge level with the surface.

Two wedges could be arranged as a cross (Fig. 7-10C). Make two saw cuts before driving the dowel, then arrange them so they come diagonal to the lines of grain in the piece with the hole. Drive one wedge, then split it with a chisel in line with the second saw cut before driving the second wedge (Fig. 7-11D). This may be regarded as decorative when planed level, particularly if the wedges are in hardwood of a contrasting color.

If the dowels are into blind holes, they can have foxtailed wedges. As with tenons, make a saw cut in the dowel and arrange it so it comes across the grain of the other part. Use a small wedge to spread it as it is driven in (Fig. 7-11E). The bottom of the hole cannot easily be widened as suggested for a mortise, so use only a slim wedge inside. If dowels are to have foxtail wedges at one end, deal with that first, then level the other projecting ends before making the joint the other way. If there are internal wedges at both ends, you will have to estimate the sizes of wedges needed. Allow for the holes being slightly deeper than the lengths of the dowels.

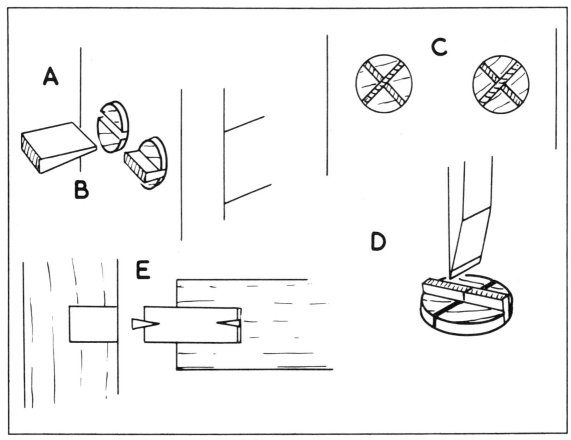

Fig. 7-11. Through dowels may be wedged (A, B, C, D), and foxtail wedges can be used in blind holes.

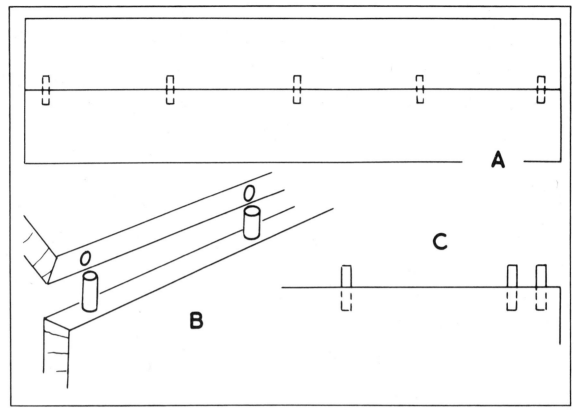

Fig. 7-12. Dowels in edge joints can be widely spaced, but with extra strength at the ends.

BUTT JOINT DOWELING

If two boards are to be glued edge to edge, fairly widely spaced dowels in the joint will strengthen it. Dowels near the end of the joint provide a resistance to the joint opening if the boards shrink or warp (Fig. 7-12A). Mark out the two board edges together and drill squarely in the marked positions. The holes need not be very deep. The dowels may go in about the same distance as the thickness of the wood. Put the dowels in one part (Fig. 7-12B), check the amount of their projection, then add more glue and draw the parts together with clamps. In heavy construction there may be closer spacing of holes near the ends (Fig. 7-12C).

MITER DOWELING

Strength can be given to a plain miter joint with dowels. The dowel holes have to be square to the surface of the miter, so cut the miter first and mark out the two surfaces together (Fig. 7-13A). At the outer corner there has to be a compromise between having the dowel near enough to the end of the joint and getting a sufficient length. That dowel will have to be shorter than any others (Fig. 7-13B).

In another version of a doweled miter, the dowels go right through. Where the parts are deeper than they are thick, they can be brought together and drilled through (Fig. 7-13C). Position the holes so they go fairly close to the inner corner, but do not break through there. When the ends of the dowels are planed level, they will be elliptical (Fig. 7-13D). This could be used as a decorative feature if the dowels are in a color to contrast with the main parts.

CLAMPED ENDS

Where a wide board or several boards glued to-

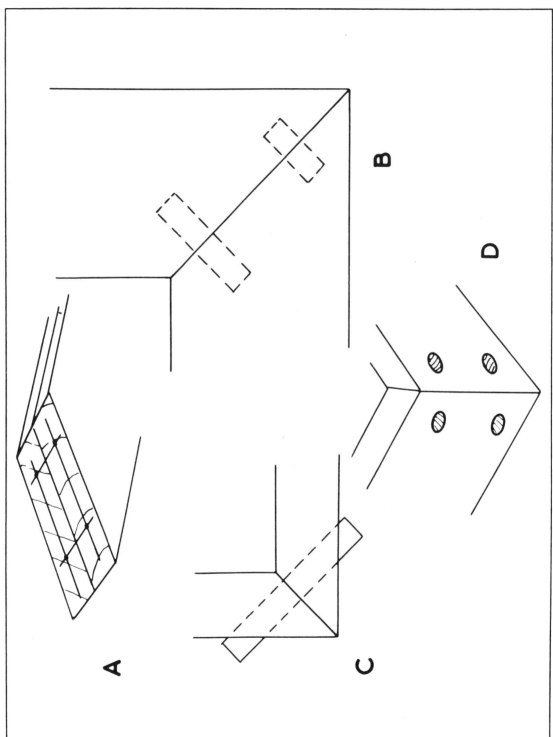

Fig. 7-13. A miter may have dowels stopped or through.

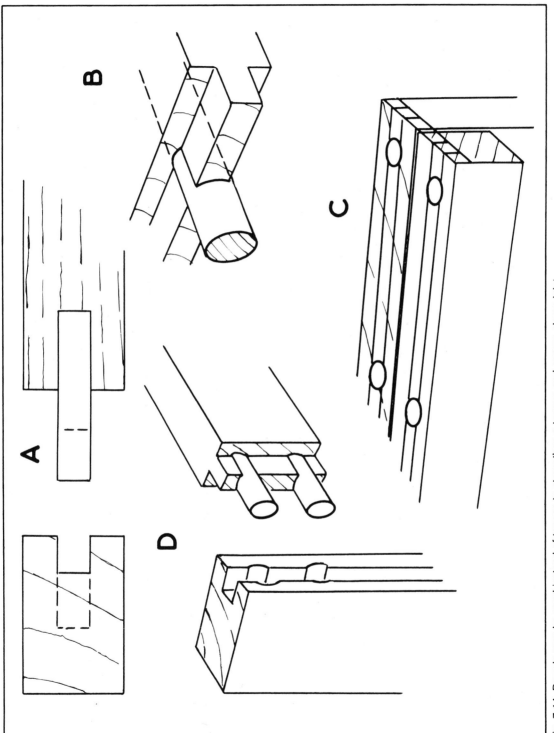

Fig. 7-14. Dowels may be used instead of tenons to strengthen a tongue and groove clamp joint.

gether have to be prevented from warping by clamping pieces across the ends, one way is to have a tongue and groove with tenons projecting at intervals. Dowels may be used instead of tenons.

If the wood is thick enough, the dowels may be the same thickness as the tongue so they go wholly into the groove (Fig. 7-14A). With thinner wood it is better to have the dowels thicker than the tongue (Fig. 7-14B). In both cases cutting the tongue and groove first would present drilling problems. Instead, it is better to mark out and drill for the dowels first (Fig. 7-14C), then make the tongue and groove to cut through the holes. In that way the holes will be correctly registered, and the joint should pull together securely.

A similar problem comes when a grooved frame has to be assembled with dowels. Drilling should be done before grooving (Fig. 7-14D).

RABBETED DOWELING

In a frame with both parts rabbeted, the possible arrangements of dowels depend on the thickness of the wood and the size of the rabbet. If the rabbet is wide enough, the dowels can go wholly into it (Fig. 7-15A), even if they are not then centrally placed in the thickness of the wood.

The rabbet usually is not wide enough to permit this, and the dowel has to come partly into the shoulder (Fig. 7-15B). Like the previous example, this would be difficult to drill after the parts had been rabbeted, so the hole positions should be marked out and drilled before cutting the rabbets (Fig. 7-15C). Allow for the difference in depth due to the long and short shoulders, so you are left with enough penetration of the dowels in each part. The number of dowels depends on the size of wood, but do not have less than two.

MOLDED FRAME CORNER

If a rabbeted frame is to have the front corners mitered (Fig. 7-16A), or it is a frame without a rabbet that is to show a partial miter (Fig. 7-16B), the two parts are cut to make the miter. This leaves the meeting surfaces full width, and the method of laying out the dowels becomes the same as for two meeting plain pieces (Fig. 7-16C).

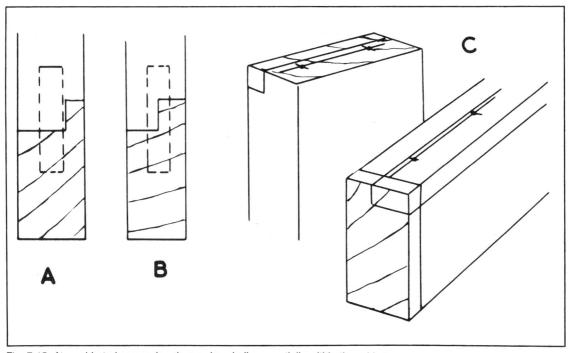

Fig. 7-15. At a rabbeted corner dowels may be wholly or partially within the rabbet.

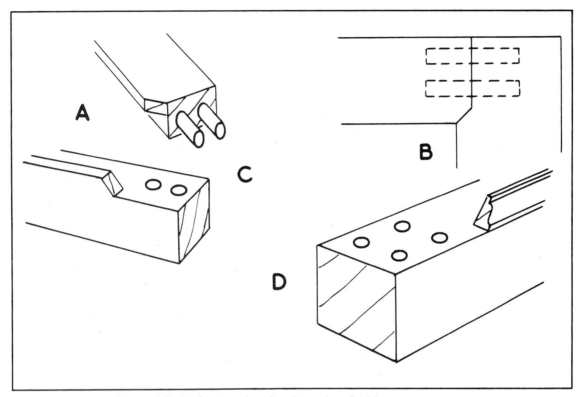

Fig. 7-16. In a rabbeted corner joint the front may be mitered to make a flat joint.

If the wood sections are largely or nearly square, four smaller dowels (Fig. 7-16D) may be better than two larger ones. Leave one piece over-long to be trimmed to size after assembly.

DOWELED INTERIOR TABLE LEG

Where an extra table leg has to come partway along the top rail or it joins a curved rail under a round tabletop, one form of joint uses a bridle at the front to allow the leg to go the full height and a tenon inside. The mortise and tenon may be difficult to cut accurately, and dowels can be substituted (Fig. 7-17A).

Make the bridle part of the joint first, then mark and drill for the dowels (Fig. 7-17B). Use a pair of dowels and take them reasonably deep into the rail.

TABLE LEAF DOWELS

In some extending tables a leaf may be arranged to lift out so the remaining parts of the top can be brought together to make a smaller area. The leaf has to be located so it cannot slide, yet it must be removable. Dowels are arranged in its edge (Fig. 7-18A). They are glued in, but their extending ends are slightly tapered and rounded so they can fit into holes in the other part of the tabletop fairly easily (Fig. 7-18B). At the other side of the leaf are holes similarly spaced so dowels on the other side of the table can engage when the parts are pushed together. Both sides must match so the outer parts of the top can be linked together when the leaf has been removed.

SHAPED PARTS DOWELING

If many pieces have to be joined end to end to make up an irregular shape, dowels are often the most convenient way of making the joints. Suppose straight parts have to be linked with curved pieces making rounded corners (Fig. 7-19A). The pieces that will make the rounded corners are probably

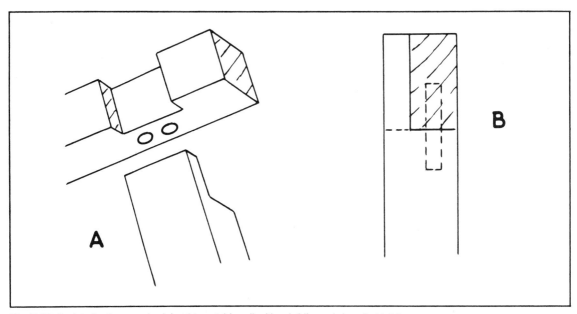

Fig. 7-17. An interior leg may be joined to a table rail with a bridle and doweled joint.

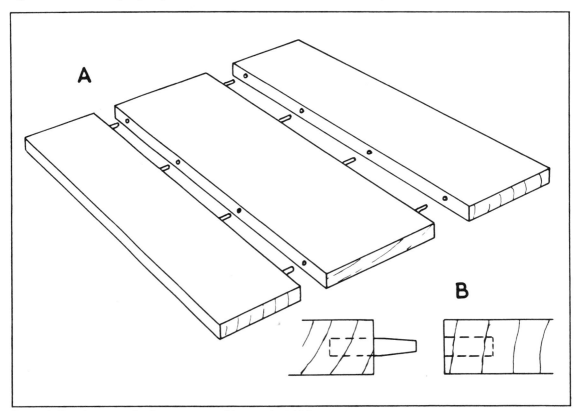

Fig. 7-18. Dowels are used to locate a removable part of a tabletop.

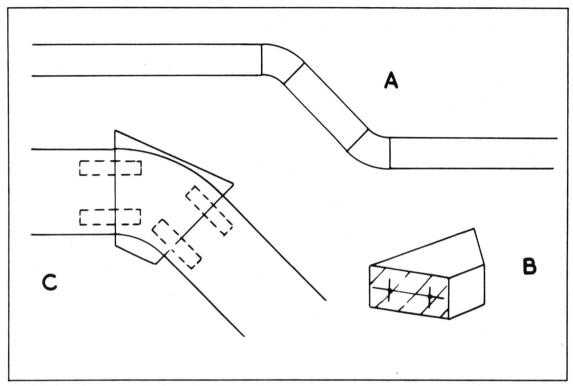

Fig. 7-19. In a shaped assembly dowels are fitted before curves are cut.

best left angular and larger than their final shape until after drilling for dowels (Fig. 7-19B). The number of dowels depends on the sections of wood, but there should be at least two at each position. Cut the surfaces to meet squarely and drill square to them (Fig. 7-19C). After the joints have been prepared, the corner pieces can be brought close to their final shape and ready for finishing to match the other parts after the joints have been glued.

INTEGRAL DOWELS

When parts are made on a lathe, it is usually better to turn dowels on the solid piece to link with other parts than to drill holes for loose parts. Usually a dowel end may be turned (Fig. 7-20A) with its chamfer ready to go into a hole. If possible, use a hole made with the same bit in a thin piece of scrap wood to test the size of the dowel. This may be done at the tailstock end, but if there is a dowel at the headstock end, its size will have to be checked with calipers. If the dowel is to go through the other part,

make it too long for trimming after assembly. This is important if there is a hollow from the tailstock center in its end, and that will have to be removed.

An interesting arrangement of turned dowels is when there is a shelf between turned parts, which appear to extend through it. In this case there is a dowel of large diameter turned to fit a hole in the shelf, the it has a hole made in it to take a smaller dowel turned on the other part (Fig. 7-20B). The smaller dowel can go as far as necessary for strength into the other piece. There could be foxtail wedging to hold the parts together. Do not expand the inner dowel excessively, or it will crack the other turned part.

If parts have to be turned longer than the capacity of the lathe, it is usually possible to arrange joints between patterns and turn a dowel on one piece to enter a hole in the other piece. If the positions are carefully chosen and the meeting surfaces make good contact, the final joints should be invisible.

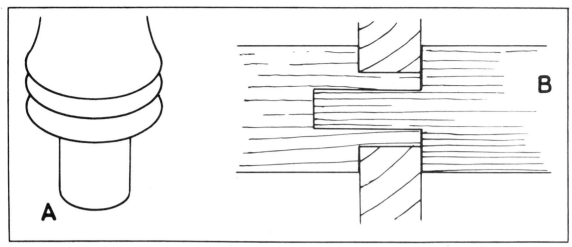

Fig. 7-20. Turned parts are made with their own dowels, which may fit into each other.

RUSTIC DOWELING

Natural poles, possibly with their bark still on, can be joined to make arches and fences for climbing plants and decoration in a garden. Although they can be nailed, there is a better method using joints similar to those used for turned parts on a lathe.

A hole is drilled in one piece, and the end of another piece is tapered to drive in (Fig. 7-21A). The work can be done with an auger and drawknife (Fig. 7-22). An auger is a woodworking twist bit with its own handle. The drawknife has two handles for pulling, and the blade is sharpened with a bevel

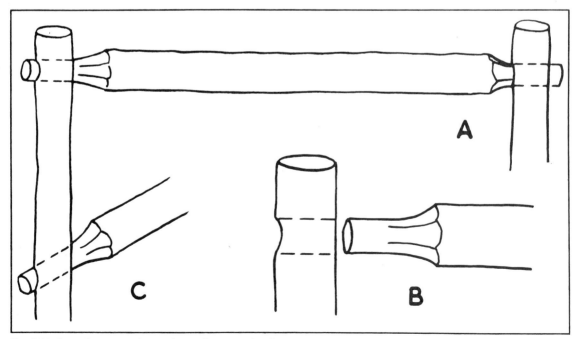

Fig. 7-21. In rustic construction ends may be tapered to form dowels to fit holes.

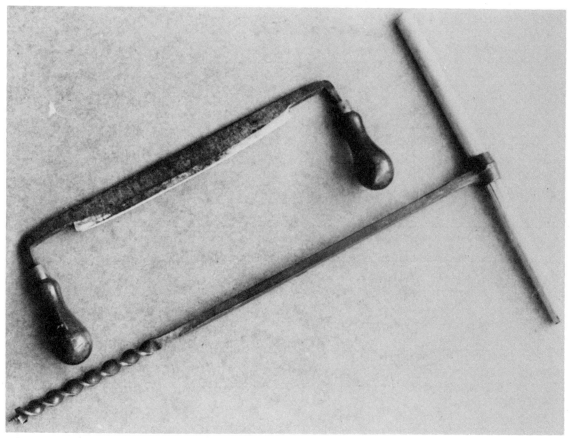

Fig. 7-22. A drawknife has two handles for pulling. An auger is a long drill with its own handle.

on one side. Using the tool with the bevel downward, you can alter the angle of pull to take off thin or thick shavings.

The hole goes right through and is obviously parallel. The other piece need only be made approximately round, but the shaping should be done so the taper terminates in a part that is near parallel for the length to go through the hole (Fig. 7-21B). In most assemblies the parts are driven together so a short end projects from the hole. A nail could be across the joint if it seems necessary, but each joint should drive tight.

Joints need not be square. Parts of arches or braces can be arranged diagonally (Fig. 7-21C). Consider assembly. You cannot drive in a strut diagonally at both ends at the same time as you make square joints in the frame. One end may have to be notched.

THROUGH DOWELS

If two parts have to come opposite each other on another piece and there is sufficient thickness, use two dowel joints (Fig. 7-23A). This may happen with rails going into a leg or post, but if the part between is thinner, dowels will have to go right through to provide enough strength (Fig. 7-23B). This is easy to mark and drill except that the opposite sides must match. Mark the central piece on opposite sides and drill partly from each side, so there is no risk of the drill wandering to finish slightly out of true.

147

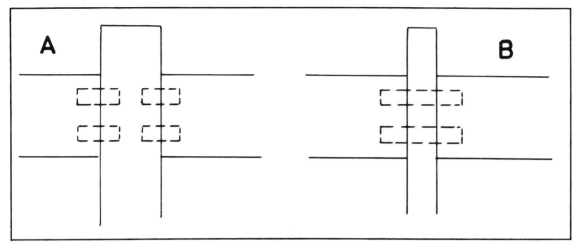

Fig. 7-23. Parts coming to opposite sides of a post may have their own dowels or can share dowels going through.

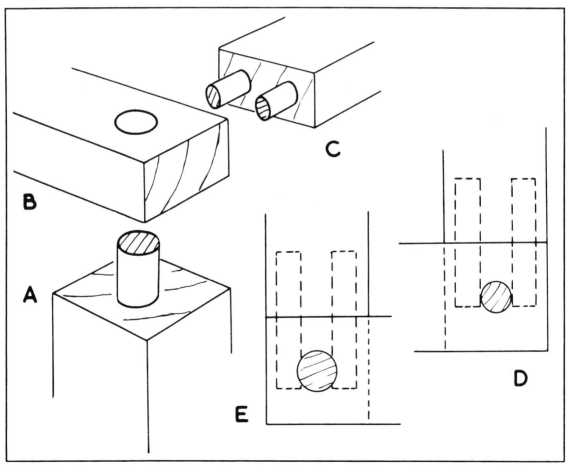

Fig. 7-24. In a three-way doweled joint, two parts are doweled together and fitted over one dowel in the upright.

THREE-WAY DOWELED JOINT

If two horizontal rails meet at a corner, then they have to be attached to an upright post. You can dowel in all directions if there is enough thickness to allow for it.

The upright post carries a single central dowel long enough to go through the other parts (Fig. 7-24A). One other piece can go over it and have a matching hole (Fig. 7-24B). The other piece has dowels into it (Fig. 7-24C). These dowels would probably have to be thinner than the central one. If possible, arrange the horizontal dowels far enough apart to clear the central one (Fig. 7-24D). If space is limited, it would not matter if you joined the horizontal pieces and drilled slightly into those dowels for the central one (Fig. 7-24E). If the top pieces are too small or thin for dowels, they could be halved together. The upright dowel could be put through the joint.

DOWEL HANDLE

A piece of dowel rod may go across the top of a piece of square or round rod to form a handle (Fig. 7-25A). If possible, the ends should be rounded in a lathe. Otherwise, the sharpness of the ends can be re-moved by sanding. It should be possible to use glue to keep the handle in, but you cannot drive in the dowel with enough glue without getting surplus glue outside where it has to be cleaned off.

A nail or screw could be driven from the front (Fig. 7-25B), but if the handle is fairly near the end you can drive a nail down through or even use a thinner dowel there to secure the handle (Fig. 7-25C). In a darker color in a rounded end, it would improve appearance.

SHELF DOWEL PINS

If a shelf in a bookcase or similar assembly is to have alternate positions, it can be supported on short pieces of dowel rod pushed into holes (Fig. 7-26A), with several possible heights in regularly spaced holes. The pins may come entirely below the shelf, or they can go into half holes (Fig. 7-26B).

If shouldered dowels can be turned on a lathe, the enlarged part may be given a flat surface to come against the shelf (Fig. 7-26C). The dowels should be an easy push fit into the holes, but the weight of the shelf and its load should keep them in place. Metal and plastic supports are available, but they work in the same way.

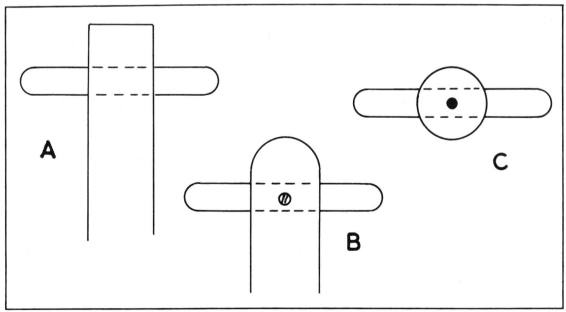

Fig. 7-25. A cross dowel can make a handle.

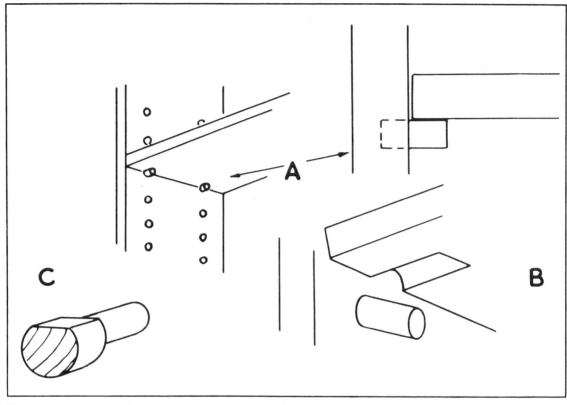

Fig. 7-26. Shelves can rest on dowels so their heights may be adjusted.

DOWELED TENON

When fairly wide boards have to be joined on edge, a deep mortise is needed if a tenon of normal proportion has to be inserted. This brings the problem of waste removal as the cut gets deeper. An alternative that gets comparable strength from a much shallower tenon uses dowels to extend it (Fig. 7-27A). The tenon goes as far as can permit an easily cleared mortise, then the dowels continue to provide a greater glue area.

Mark and drill both parts (Fig. 7-27B) to get the dowel holes true before-cutting the rest of the joint. The dowel diameters should be less than the thickness of the tenon, but not much less, providing the wood does not break through. The dowels could be glued in before cutting the sides of the tenon. In grooved parts the tenon might only go as deep as the groove, but the dowels would have to be somewhat longer.

DOWELED CHAIR ARMS

Some armchairs have their arms tenoned to the back uprights, but that is only satisfactory when the arm is fairly straight. In many chairs the arm is given considerable shaping and may come into the back from the side when any attempt at tenoning would result in cutting across the grain and leaving the joint weak. In that case it is better to use dowels.

If the arm comes to the back fairly straight, it may be possible to use dowels into the end grain instead of tenons (Fig. 7-28A). If the arm is more curved, it may be better cut to fit against the back and dowels driven at an angle. This strengthens across the grain where it may be weak (Fig. 7-28B). In many chairs the back is quite narrow in relation to the other parts, and the arm curves into its side. Dowels make good joints and provide strength across the grain (Fig. 7-28C).

150

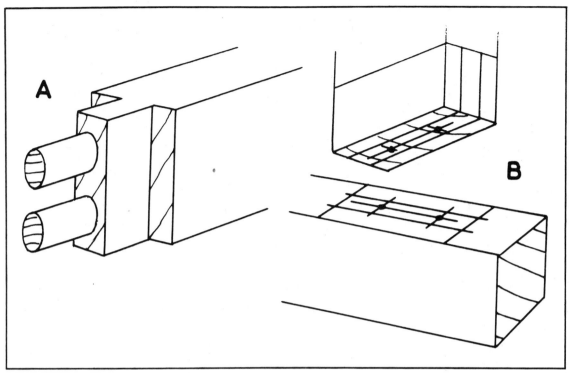

Fig. 7-27. Dowels may be used to extend tenons.

For clarity single dowels are shown, but it is always better to have at least two. They prevent sideways movement of a joint, and the stiffening is better. Two thinner dowels are better than one thicker one.

CLAMPING EARS

Parts of curved or irregular outline may be doweled, but their outline is unsuitable for letting any form of clamp exert a direct pressure in line with the dowels, without a risk of it slipping or damaging

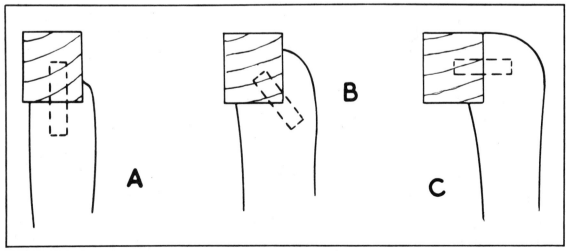

Fig. 7-28. Chair arms are doweled according to the way they meet the back.

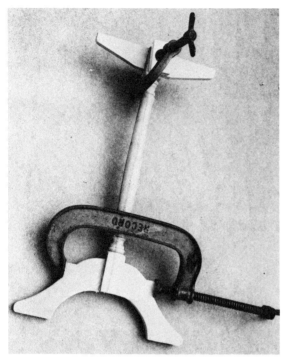

the shaping. Added blocks could be glued on to take the clamp jaws and removed later, but a better way is to leave lugs or ears on the solid wood when cutting the outline, providing they are in positions that will take the thrust and be easy to cut off and trim the outline after gluing (Fig. 7-29). This gives you the benefit of solid wood to allow maximum pressure on the doweled joint, with no risk of damage to prepared surfaces.

DRILLED SHELF SUPPORTS

This method of providing adjustable shelving is not strictly doweling, but it is closely related. Adjustable shelves with actual dowels are shown in Fig. 7-26.

The shelf supports rest across strips fitted to back and front edges of the uprights (Fig. 7-30A), with the shelf end notched to fit between them. The size to make the strips depends on the size of the assembly, but they should be hardwood and need not be very wide or project much. They are made as a pair from one piece of wood drilled through on its center line (Fig. 7-30B). The spacing of the holes determines the intervals by which the shelf can be moved. If you are able to drill with a drill press or an

Fig. 7-29. The ears on the feet are temporary for clamping the doweled joints and will be cut off later. The top clamp is holding a bridle joint, with scrap blocks to avoid marking the wood.

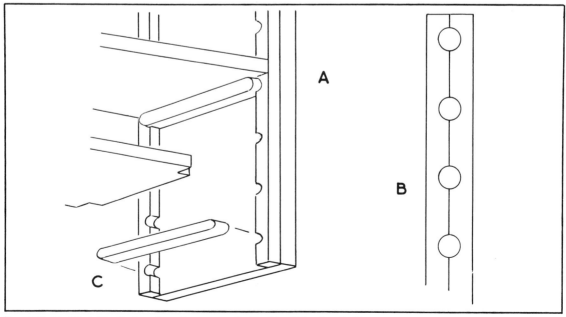

Fig. 7-30. Shelf height adjustment can be arranged with strips fitting into half holes.

electric drill on a stand, the pieces for the opposite ends of the shelves can be drilled through at the same time to ensure uniformity. Have a sharp drill so the holes are made cleanly. Saw exactly centrally and clean up the edges to remove only the minimum amount of wood.

To give the shelf supports a good bearing, make them to project about twice the thickness of the strips. Their depth should be the same as the diameter of the drill used, and the ends are rounded to press in (Fig. 7-30C).

When assembling the strips to the bookcase ends, use supports between at various places to ensure there is no distortion. Check the squareness across. The supports ideally are identical and will fit by hand pressure anywhere.

Chapter 8

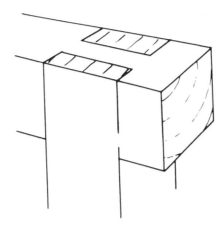

Bridle Joints

BRIDLE JOINTS MAY BE REGARDED AS VAR-
iations on mortise and tenon joints or as reversed mortise and tenons. In most of these joints,
what is left solid in a mortise and tenon joint is cut
away in a bridle joint. There are not as many uses
for bridles as for mortise and tenons, but they may
give a better appearance in particular positions or
suit special constructions. Mortise and tenon joints
generally are stronger and are to be chosen if there
is no special reason for having bridle joints.

In some ways a bridle joint is like a double half
lap joint. A bridle joint has a better locking action
and gives a greater glue area. Where strips are used
to make framing to back and stiffen a plywood panel,
bridle joints would be better than halved joints. At
corners a glued bridle joint may be satisfactory. A
lapped joint would need screws or dowels.

BASIC BRIDLE JOINT

A bridle joint where one piece meets another of the
same thickness squarely (Fig. 8-1A) can have the
thickness divided into three equal parts (Fig. 8-1B).

It is then marked out in the same way as a mortise
and tenon, but different parts are cut away (Fig.
8-1C).

STOPPED BRIDLE JOINT

If the end grain is not to show through the long
piece, the joint can be stopped (Fig. 8-2A). This
leaves more strength in the long piece. If the stopping is only to hide the ends, it need not be very
wide. Sometimes the bridle provides a location, as
when a post has to be positioned over a horizontal
member (Fig. 8-2B). Small notching is required for
the two short ends (Fig. 8-2C).

DIAGONAL BRIDLE JOINT

The parts need not meet squarely. If the angle is
only moderate, the joint can go through (Fig. 8-3A)
or be stopped in the usual way (Fig. 8-3B). If the
angle is more acute, it then weakens the part with
the central web because of the very long notches.
The end could be squared to reduce the amount cut

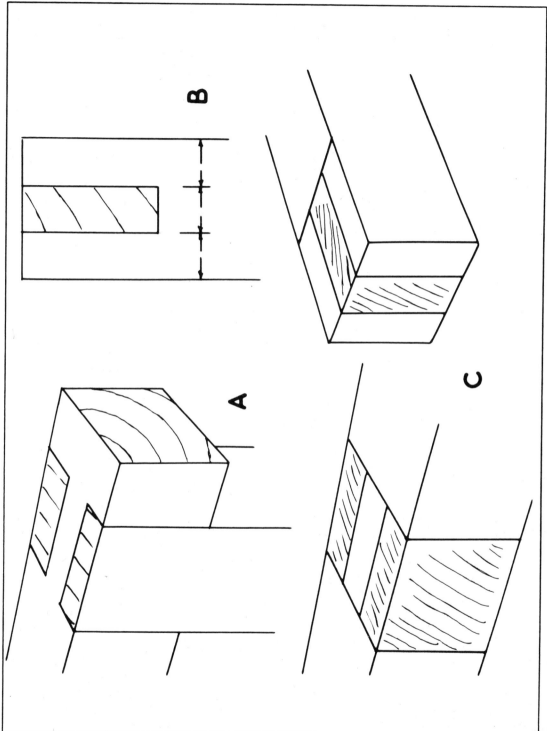

Fig. 8-1. A bridle joint is formed in the opposite way to a mortise and tenon joint.

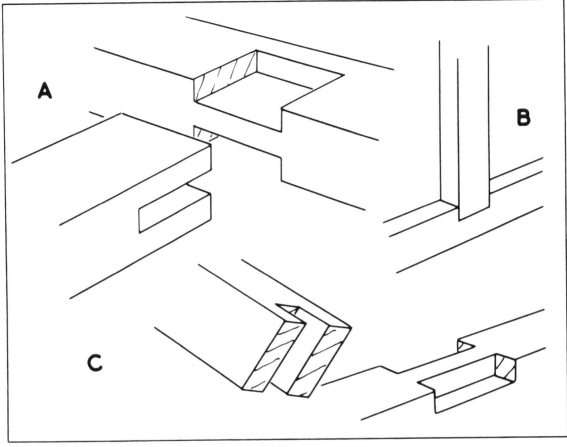

Fig. 8-2. A bridle joint can be stopped if the far side is to be left clear.

out (Fig. 8-3C), or the joint might be stopped, with the end cut squarely or nearly so (Fig. 8-3D).

CORNER BRIDLE JOINT

In a basic corner joint the parts are cut similarly to a T-bridle joint (Fig. 8-4A). The arrangement might be called an open mortise and tenon joint. It is best marked out with a little surplus on the ends (Fig. 8-4B) to be trimmed later. Glue may be all that is needed to secure a joint, particularly if the assembly will be attached to plywood. Otherwise, one or two screws or dowels could be across the joint (Fig. 8-4C), not necessarily right through, but driven from the least important side.

If you want to hide the end grain in one direction, the joint can be stopped in a very similar way

to a T-joint (Fig. 8-4D). Hiding the grain both ways is possible, but it reduces the effective size of the joint and therefore the glue area and its strength.

MITERED BRIDLE JOINT

A mitered appearance can be arranged on one surface (Fig. 8-5A) by cutting the meeting surfaces to a mitered match (Fig. 8-5B). This reduces the useful glue area on that side. If miters are needed on both sides (Fig. 8-5C), the glue area is even less. If the appearance of one side is unimportant, screws or dowels could strengthen the joint.

MULTIPLE CORNER BRIDLE JOINT

One way of strengthening a joint by increasing glue area is to let the joint have more tongues. If taken

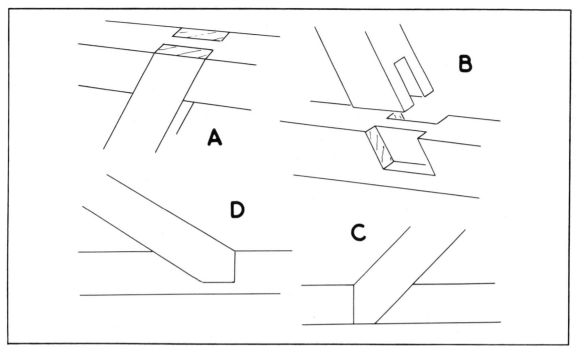

Fig. 8-3. Diagonal bridle joints may be through or stopped.

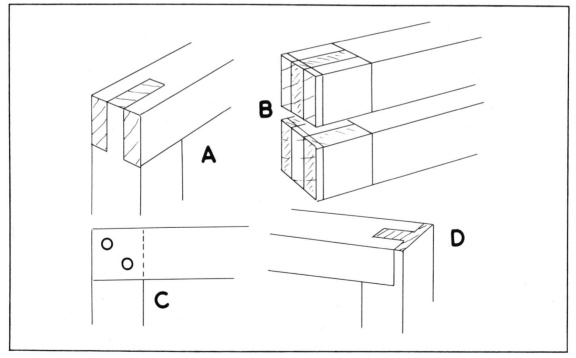

Fig. 8-4. A corner bridle joint may go through and be doweled, or it may be stopped.

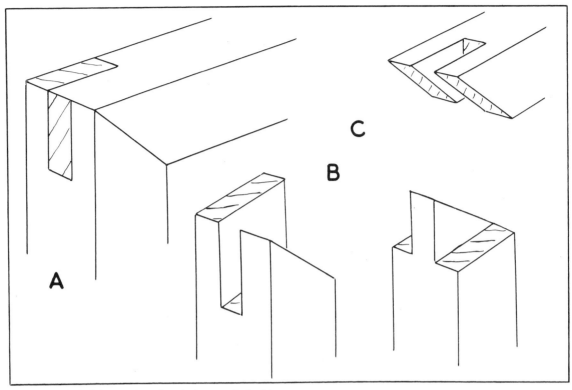

Fig. 8-5. A bridle joint may be mitered at one or both sides.

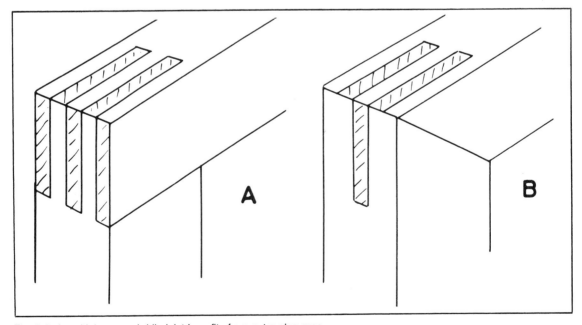

Fig. 8-6. A multiple corner bridle joint benefits from extra glue area.

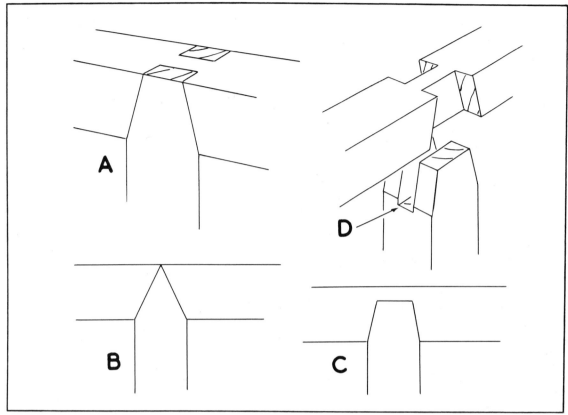

Fig. 8-7. A tapered bridle joint does not cut as much from the notched piece.

too far, the tongues might be so thin that the re-maining wood fibers are weak at the expense of more glue surfaces. A part that could be divided into three might often just as well be divided into five. This could be done at a T-junction, but it is particu-larly valuable at a corner (Fig. 8-6A).

It can be used with miters on both sides (Fig. 8-6B) where the pieces going through keep much of the strength that would be lost in a three-part bridle joint.

TAPERED BRIDLE JOINT

One of the objections to bridle joints is that they weaken one part by reducing it to one-third thick-ness over a large part. There may be much more strength proportionately in the other part. Strength can be balanced by tapering the joint. It may be sufficient to include a slight taper (Fig. 8-7A) right

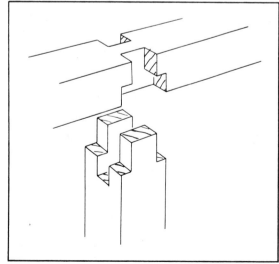

Fig. 8-8. A stepped bridle joint reduces the amount cut from the notched piece.

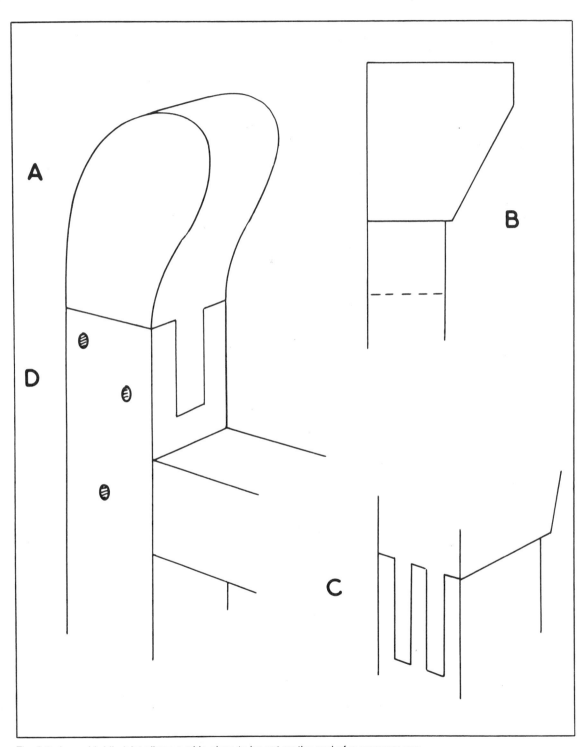

Fig. 8-9. An end bridle joint allows a wide piece to be put on the end of a narrower one.

across, or it could go almost to a point (Fig. 8-7B) or be stopped (Fig. 8-7C).

One advantage of a tapered joint is that it can be self-tightening. If you cut back the space between the outer tongues a little too much (Fig. 8-7D), the joint can be pushed together until the tapers come close.

STEPPED BRIDLE JOINT

Another way to lessen the weakening effect of the narrow part is to take the full width of the other piece in only a short distance. Cut down to about half size (Fig. 8-8).

END BRIDLE JOINT

The bridle form of construction is not the best choice when two pieces of similarly sized wood are to be joined end to end. Other more suitable joints are described in Chapter 12.

One example of an end grain joint better made with a bridle is where a wider or shaped piece is to be added to a long parallel piece to avoid cutting down a wide large piece for the sake of the shaping. This may happen at the decorative top of a gate (Fig. 8-9A).

The projecting piece can have a shaped outline or be carved, but the part for the joint must come down to the size of the other part. The tongues in the joint should be at least as long as the width of the wood (Fig. 8-9B). If the wood is very thick, there could be five divisions instead of three (Fig. 8-9C). Gates of this type usually have dowels through other joints, so they would be appropriate in this one (Fig. 8-9D).

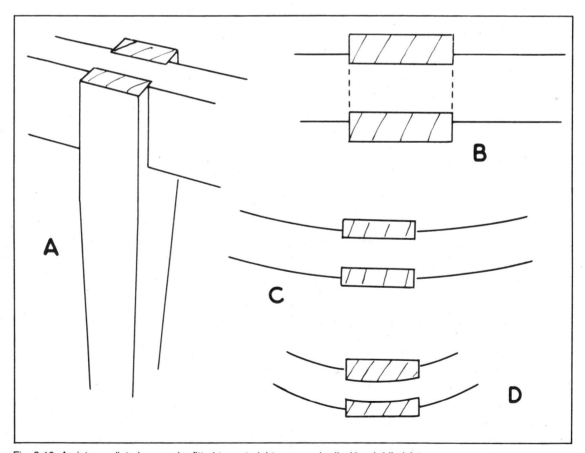

Fig. 8-10. An intermediate leg may be fitted to a straight or curved rail with a bridle joint.

TABLE LEG BRIDLE

At the corner of a tabletop, rails are best joined to the legs with mortise and tenon joints. If there is an intermediate leg under the side of a table, it may be better to let the rail go through and attach the leg to it. One suitable joint is a bridle. Because the leg is thicker than the rail, less needs to be cut from the rail than would be done for parts of the same thickness (Fig. 8-10A). The amount cut out depends on the relative thicknesses, but no more need be cut away than is required to provide shoulders to keep the leg upright (Fig. 8-10B).

A similar joint may be used for legs under a round or elliptical tabletop when the top rail is made in a continous ring. It if is a thick ring or a large-diameter table, the joint might be cut straight across (Fig. 8-10C). Otherwise, the meeting parts must be curved (Fig. 8-10D).

NOTCHED BRIDLE

In a T-bridle joint between parts of the same thickness, the simple form is all that is required in most circumstances. In another form the center web can be cut thicker than one-third of the thickness, but it is reduced in depth slightly by notching. The other piece does not have to be cut away as much (Fig. 8-11A). In its stopped form it can be used to position the base of a post on a horizontal member (Fig. 8-11B).

SHAPED BRIDLE JOINT

Bridle joints are suitable where the meeting parts have shaped outlines and where straight parts join. Corners may be between concave or convex curves or between curves and straight parts. Sometimes it is necessary to carry a curve through for the sake of appearance. You may have to cut curved shoulders (Fig. 8-12A), but in most shapes the shoulders can be straight. Let the interleaved parts be too long. Cut them to shape after the glue has set (Fig. 8-12B).

ROOFING BRIDLE JOINTS

Joints used in roof trusses and other parts of build-

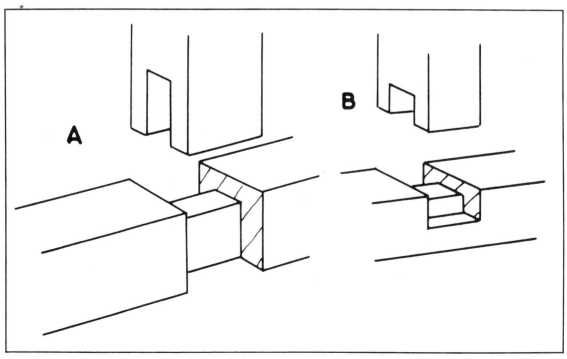

Fig. 8-11. A notched bridle joint has the inner part cut down.

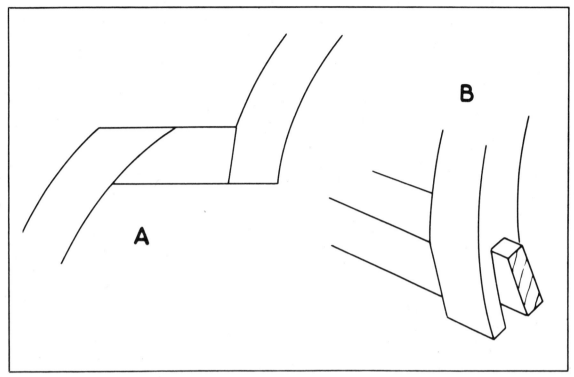

Fig. 8-12. Bridles can join curved parts and may be trimmed after joining.

ings are adaptions or combinations of standard joints to suit special situations and to take loads in particular directions. In many parts one piece has two tongues fitting over a single tongue on the other part, so the joint is a bridle. If the parts are arranged the other way, the result is very similar, but the joint becomes a mortise and tenon.

If a sloping rafter has to join to a tie beam, the parts can be either way. Loads tend to thrust down and outward. In the bridle version the outer tongues are cut square at the end and parallel with the tie beam (Fig. 8-13A).

In a slightly more complicated version the rafter runs over a little, and the cutout is stepped so the sloping bottom is nearer the angle needed to resist thrust (Fig. 8-13B). Not as much wood is removed from the tie beam. In all roof construction care is needed at all stages to avoid cutting away one part too much when another will be thrusting against it. Otherwise, a bend may develop if not a split or fracture.

DOVETAILED BRIDLE JOINT

When the end of one piece fits into another in the form of a T-halving joint, it is possible to strengthen the connection by cutting in a dovetail manner instead of squarely to the surfaces.

If the parts are the same thickness, cuts may go straight across (Fig. 8-14A). The piece with outside tongues has small shoulders. Both parts can be cut mainly by careful sawing and a little paring with a chisel.

With parallel cuts there may be some difficulty in driving the end part in, particularly if the parts are cut to fit tightly. One way to ease assembly and ensure maximum tightness when the parts are fully assembled is to give the joint a slight taper across the long part (Fig. 8-14B). The taper across need only be slight; 1/8 inch in a 2-inch width should be enough.

If the piece with the outer tongues is thicker than the piece it joins, as when a rail under a table or bench top passes through the top of a leg (Fig.

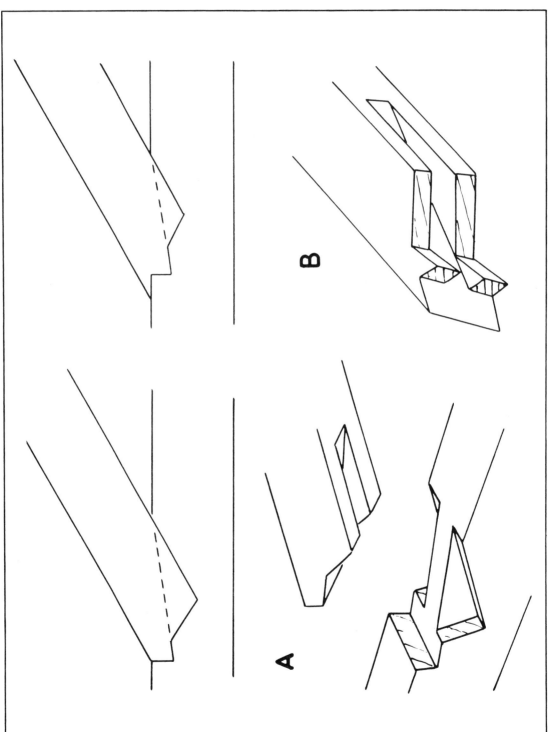

Fig. 8-13. A roofing bridle joint takes a thrust diagonally.

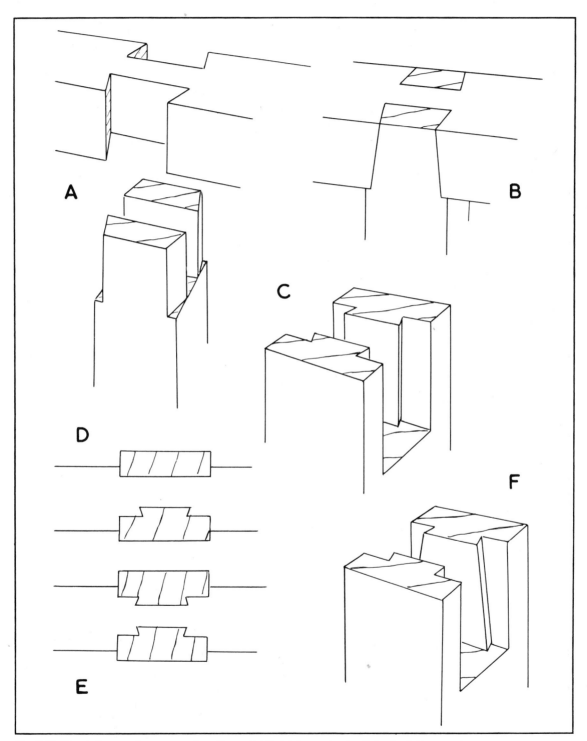

Fig. 8-14. Dovetailing can be used to strengthen a bridle joint or make it suitable for taking apart.

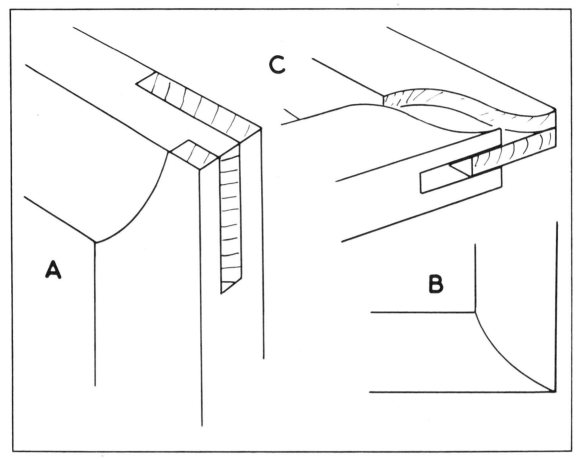

Fig. 8-15. Instead of a straight miter, the face of a bridle joint can be shaped.

8-14C), the dovetail linkage can be made internally. The rail cutout is similar to the previous joint, but the dovetailing comes inside the leg. Dovetails may be on one (Fig. 8-14D) or both sides (Fig. 8-14E) when viewed from above. Inside the joint both sides may be parallel, both may have a taper, or one could be parallel and the other tapered. Tapering both sides is preferable in most cases (Fig. 8-14F).

The rail joint is easily cut with a saw and chisel. The center part of the other piece can be cut in the usual way. The dovetails must then be marked on the inside surfaces. Very little can be cut with a saw. There is no way to machine the dovetails, so they have to be shaped by careful work with chisels. It may be advisable to complete this

part first. It is easier to make the other piece match if the dovetails do not finish exactly as you first intended.

Tapered dovetailed bridle joints have a use in takedown parts. The shape allows the joint to push together tightly when dry in a way that most other joints would not. It should be possible to retain rigidity after many assemblies and disassemblies. Hardwoods are better able to stand up to this treatment than most softwoods.

CURVED CHEEK CORNER BRIDLE

When two pieces meet at a corner with a normal or a multiple bridle joint, it is common for one piece to go through and the other to butt against it on the front surface. Appearance may be improved by mitering the front cheeks. This has been the usual limitation of frame decoration, but with the increasing use of power routers it is possible to alter the meeting surfaces to curves by using the router, with a plain cutter, in a suitable shop-made guide. For doors and frames with attractive, prominently marked hardwood, this technique adds to the decoration.

The outer cheek may partially curve (Fig. 8-15A). This leaves more of the overlap to provide useful glue area than in a straight miter. A corner to corner miter could be cut on a curve (Fig. 8-15B) or be allowed to follow a wavy line (Fig. 8-15C).

Chapter 9

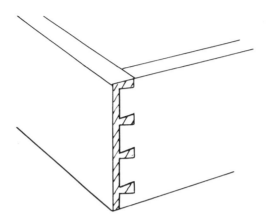

Dovetail Joints

DOVETAIL JOINTS HAVE BEEN USED FOR A very long time. The principle of resisting pulling apart in one direction by a reversed wedge action has been used since early days. Wood does not last long, but examples of stones interlocked in this way are in existence showing that dovetails were known thousands of years ago and would have been used for wood and stone.

In wooden construction dovetail joints are nearly always used where two pieces of wood meet with their end grains. Dovetails are strong when the wood grain runs along the tails on one piece and the pins on the other. If the grain runs across, there is a great risk of cracking or breaking.

The name comes from the shape of a dove's tail. One or more tails cut to this shape are fashioned on one part, then they fit between pins in the other part. A simple example has a single tail to make a corner between two fairly narrow parts (Fig. 9-1A). Any pulling load on the piece with the tail will be resisted by it. In the other direction there is no mechanical strength provided, other

than closeness of fit, and resistance to separation that way has to be provided by glue.

If the angle at the side of a tail is too acute, a pull might squeeze fibers. If the angle there is too obtuse, the short grain may break at the corners of the tail. The slopes for hardwoods are generally more upright than those for softwoods.

The angle is not usually quoted in degrees. It is more common to quote a slope of one in a number. For hardwoods, 1 in 8 is often chosen (Fig. 9-1B). For softwoods, it may be broadened to 1 in 6 (Fig. 9-1C). This can be set out by drawing the angle on a piece of wood, then setting an adjustable bevel to it (Fig. 9-1D). It is useful to have templates cut to the angle you use. If you make templates to mark 1 in 6, 1 in 7, and 1 in 8, you will have all you need for various woods.

A simple template is a bent piece of sheet metal (Fig. 9-2A), or you could make it of wood (Fig. 9-2B). Sometimes it is made with the angle the other way (Fig. 9-2C), but that does not give a very wide piece to bear against the wood and it may

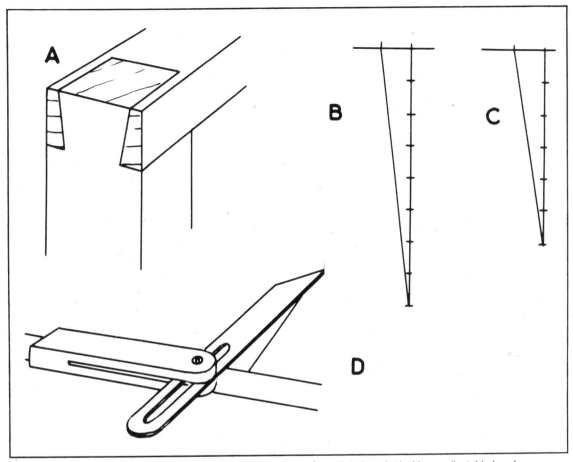

Fig. 9-1. Dovetail angles may be adjusted to suit hardwood or softwood and marked with an adjustable bevel.

wobble. Another way of making a broad-based template is to cut the angles internally (Fig. 9-2D). A more sophisticated template can be made with a blade adjustable across its stock (Fig. 9-3). The template is not intended to mark both sides at once, so the width between the two sloping sides does not matter. Each slope is marked individually. After the sloping tails have been marked, the cut lines have to be squared across the wood. That is usually done with a try square. The open gauge could be made to mark that way as well (Fig. 9-2E), but as squaring across is often done over several boards at once, use of the open gauge is restricted.

THROUGH DOVETAILS

When the tails and pins go right through the other piece, the joint is often called a through dovetail. The number of tails to use in a particular width is largely a matter of experience. You may find it worthwhile to examine joints in furniture and elsewhere. Check on the numbers in relation to wood sizes and the function of the joint. Note the type of wood.

As a rough guide to planning the layout of a dovetail joint, the widest part of each tail could be between 1½ and 2 times the thickness of the wood. The pins might be half that width (Fig. 9-4A). Consider actual widths of wood and how they can be conveniently divided. Some craftsmen favor narrower tails than others for the same purpose. Theoretically the maximum strength would come with the pins and tails the same width (Fig. 9-4B),

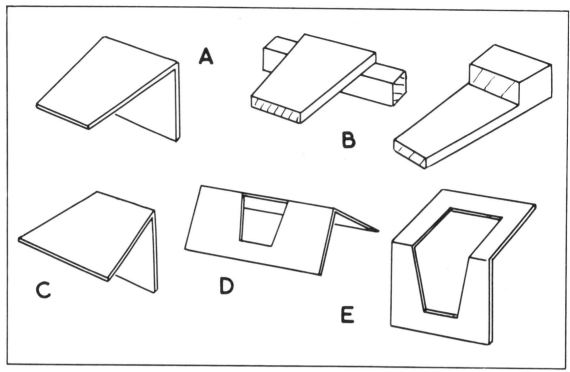

Fig. 9-2. Templates can be made for marking dovetail angles.

but that is not considered very pleasing visually. Some Victorian cabinetmakers made the pins so narrow that their outer ends were almost points (Fig. 9-4C). That may have exhibited their skill, but there is little otherwise to commend the arrangement. There is no record of these joints failing due to pins fracturing, so almost any arrangement of pins and tails should have adequate strength in furniture.

Unless there is a need for another arrangement, pins could be on the outsides of the tails (Fig. 9-4D), but there could be part of a tail at one or both edges (Fig. 9-4E). That may be done if there is a groove to be hidden, as when a plywood bottom is let into the sides. The part tail hides the groove better than a pin and avoids the awkward arrangement that would occur if the groove came partly in a pin and a tail.

Dividing the width of a board's end may be by direct measuring, but usually it will not divide evenly. When you have decided how many tails to

Fig. 9-3. This adjustable dovetail template has angles for hard and soft wood joints on opposite sides.

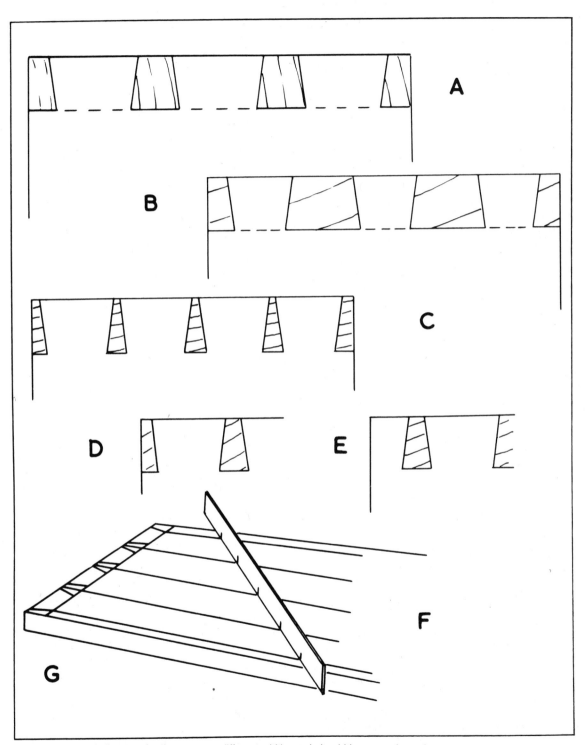

Fig. 9-4. Tails and pins may be the same or different widths and should be spaced evenly.

have, one way of getting even divisions is to mark the widths of the outer pins. Allow half the width of pins and project these lines along the wood, then tilt a rule between them until you get a size that will divide easily (Fig. 9-4F). Project those divisions to the end of the wood. Those points are the centers of the pins. Mark the widths of the pins about these points and draw the sides of the tails (Fig. 9-4G).

A dovetail joint may be just as strong with tails that vary in width, but lack of uniformity would offend the eye. It is common to mark out a joint carefully and symmetrically. If you examine dovetail joints in parts taht are not normally within view, you may find some uneven tails, but properly fitted, in the backs of drawers and similar places in furniture maybe 100 years old. In the days before mass production, a skilled craftsman might spend much of his time sawing and chopping out dovetails by hand. He reached the stage where he could go straight into cutting with little or no marking out, yet what he produced had the required strength.

To mark out dovetail joints, have the ends of the wood squared to length. There might be less than the width of a saw kerf left on the end for trimming level after assembly. If you leave much excess on the length, it will interfere with cutting the joint. On each piece mark all around at a distance from the end the thickness of the other piece (Fig. 9-5A). This is better cut with a knife, so the fibers are severed and will not break out where you have to cut out. If the outer surface will be exposed when finished, cut lines may spoil appearance. In some cases they can be planed off, but otherwise it may be better to mark in pencil. It will still be possible to cut where the spaces come.

There will normally be at least two pieces with similar dovetails. The tail shapes need only be marked on one. Two or more are cut together while held with their ends upward in the vise. Mark out all the tail shapes on one piece as just described, then mark all the parts that are to be cut out (Fig. 9-5B). Without moving the wood, saw across on the waste sides of the lines with a fine backsaw, or keep the pieces together and make the cuts with a band saw. The sides can also be sawed, but the spaces between the tails must be chopped and pared with a

chisel, except for large joints where some of the waste can be removed with a coping saw.

Put the dovetailed piece on the end of the other piece, with the cuts level with its inner surface. Mark the sides of the tails, either with a sharp awl or a finely sharpened pencil (Fig. 9-5C). Square down these lines on the surfaces (Fig. 9-5D). Mark the waste parts.

Saw down on the waste sides of the lines (Fig. 9-5E). Some waste can be removed by diagonal cuts, but final trimming to size will be with the chisel. Remember the slope and be careful to avoid chopping the corners of pins. Work from both sides in both parts to avoid cutting below the bottom lines. Putting together and taking apart may wear surfaces and result in a loose joint. If you want to test your joint, do not enter the parts fully.

Another way of marking the pins can be used before chopping out between the pins. Put the sawed, but not chiseled, tail piece in position and use the saw to scratch through its own kerfs (Fig. 9-6A). This gives you duplicate saw marks across the end grain, which can be squared down the surfaces. Remember that what you have marked is a repeat of the cuts on the other piece. If you continue to saw down in these positions, the joint will be slack at each position by the thickness of each saw cut. Instead, keep the saw cuts for the pins on the waste sides of the first saw marks (Fig. 9-6B).

It does not matter if the tails or pins are cut first. Some craftsmen prefer to mark and cut the pins, then mark the tails from them. In that case mark around the width of each piece on the other. Have the pin piece end upward for spacing and marking, which can be done with a bevel or template (Fig. 9-6C). Cut the sockets between the pins and stand that part over the other to mark the shapes of the tails (Fig. 9-6D). Keep saw cuts just on the waste sides of the lines so the parts will go together tightly, but not so tightly that the wood splits.

STOPPED DOVETAILS

In some places it is better if the tails do not go through the other piece, but stop to leave a narrow part of solid wood outside. This is a stopped or

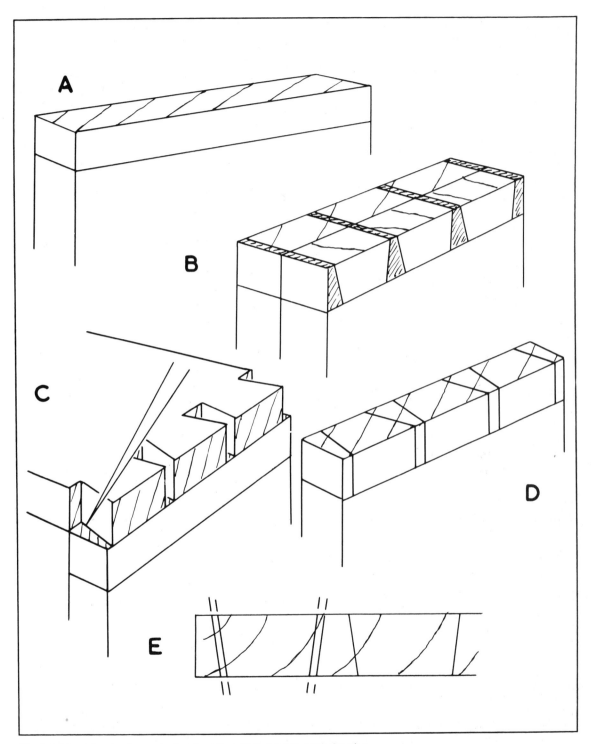

Fig. 9-5. The tails may be marked and cut first, then used to mark the pins.

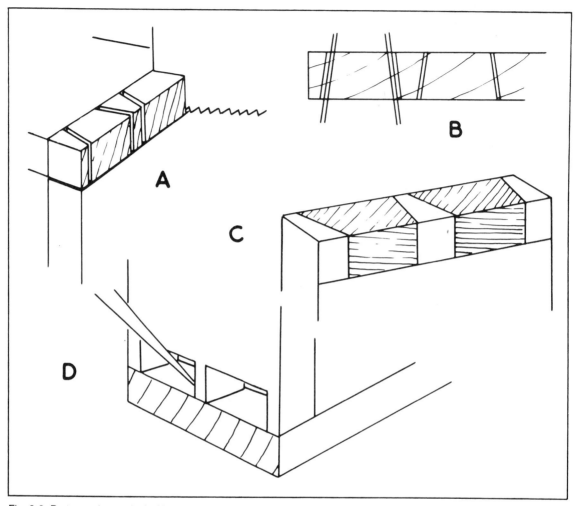

Fig. 9-6. Parts can be marked with a saw or the pins cut first and used to mark the tails.

half-blind dovetail. Other versions have the joint details hidden and are fully blind. The most common example of a stopped or half-blind dovetail comes between a drawer front and its side (Fig. 9-7A). In a drawer, a bottom half pin may hide the groove for the bottom (Fig. 9-7B).

In a hand-cut stopped dovetail joint the layout of the tails is very similar to that for a through dovetail, with the tails at least twice as wide as the pins. These joints can be cut by machine. Inside the cuts are curved, and on the surface there is the usual shape, but the pins and tails are the same width (Fig. 9-7C). Mechanically-cut dovetails can

be recognized by their evenly divided appearance. Tools acting as guides for cutters driven by a hand drill are used to make these joints. A closely fitting mechanically-cut dovetail joint may be stronger than a poorly made hand-cut joint, but anyone making individual pieces of furniture is not normally satisfied with anything but a hand-cut joint.

The distance the tails go through the other piece depends on its thickness and type of wood, but usually the tails need to go as far as possible. This means you have to estimate how thin the solid part can be made without the risk of breaking out as you cut the joint. The front of a drawer is usually

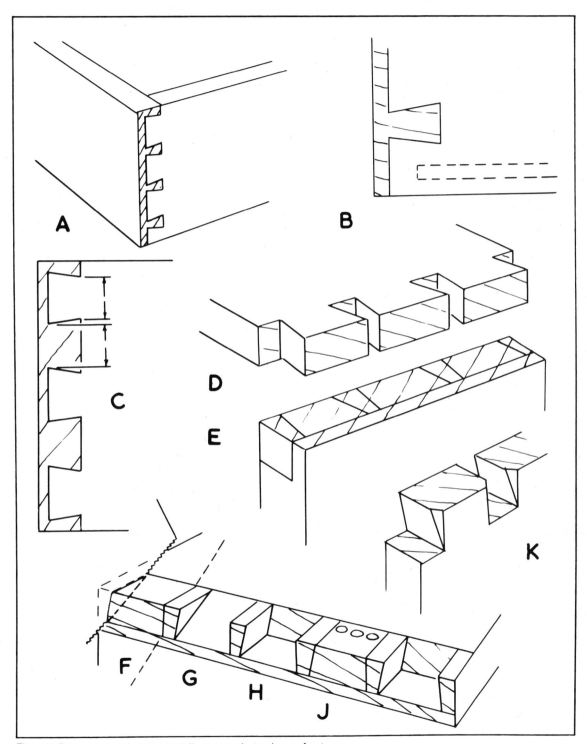

Fig. 9-7. Stopped or half-blind dovetails are used at a drawer front.

thicker than the side, so it is often possible to make the tails as long as the thickness of the side.

Gauge across the end of the piece with the pins. Mark the thickness of the other piece and mark around that in the same way as for a through dovetail joint (Fig. 9-7D). Mark and cut the dovetails. If you prefer to deal with the pins first, that is possible. It is not so easy to mark the tails from them as it is with through dovetails.

Mark the pin part from the tails (Fig. 9-7E). You cannot saw through, but you can make diagonal cuts and remove small wedges (Fig. 9-7F). Some of the waste between may be pared at an angle (Fig. 9-7G), then you can chop across the grain and pare inward (Fig. 9-7H).

Another way of removing waste is with a drill or router. With a depth stop on the drill, you can make a line of holes to chisel into and set the depth to work to (Fig. 9-7J), with less risk of breaking through the thin solid part. Make sure you cut right into the corners of the recesses. A knife may have to follow the chisel. To prevent the tails from binding there and stopping the joint from pulling tight, they can be lightly chamfered on the corners (Fig. 9-7K) without weakening the joint.

BLIND LAP DOVETAIL

If the dovetails must be hidden, both parts can be given outside solid pieces. This may also be called a double lap or a stopped lap dovetail joint. It can be visualized as something like the previous joint, but with the part having the pins provided with an extended cover that takes in the solid back of the part with the tails (Fig. 9-8A). When the joint is closed, there is just a narrow piece of end grain of the front part showing as it overlaps the side. No details of the joint are visible (Fig. 9-8B).

Cut a rabbet across the end of the part that will

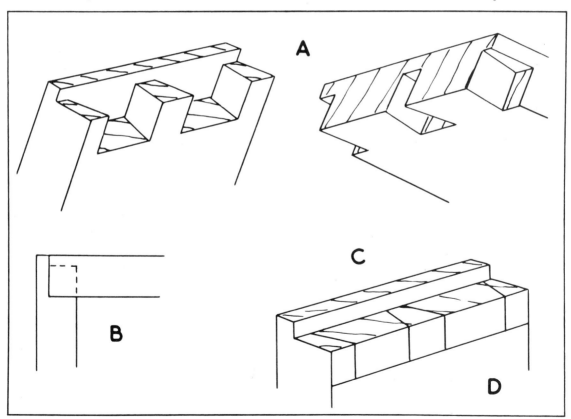

Fig. 9-8. In a blind lapped dovetail the joint details are hidden both ways.

176

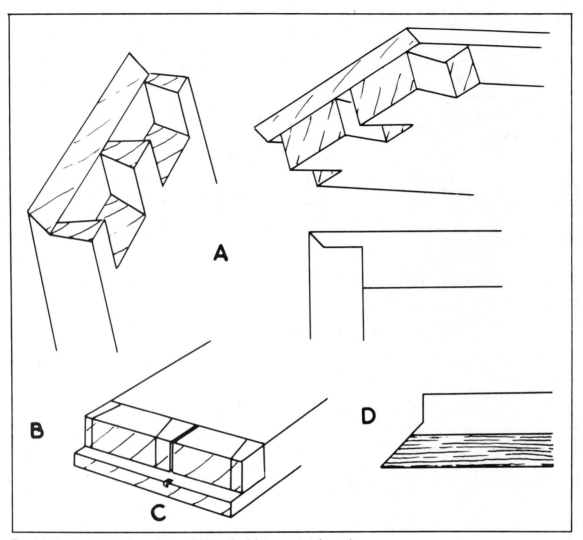

Fig. 9-9. A mitered blind lapped dovetail hides the joint except at the ends.

have the pins. Allow for the depth that will be left solid on the other piece (Fig. 9-8C). Mark the amount each piece will take up the other piece, then mark the tail shape on whichever piece you prefer. Transferring outlines from one piece to the other in this joint is awkward, but probably less so if you mark and cut the pins first (Fig. 9-8D). There cannot be much sawing of the joint, and care is needed to avoid blemishes. You can drill out some waste. The rest can be removed with chisels. Remember to make cross grain cuts first, so cuts along the grain do not cause splits.

This joint is used in places where the open dovetail shapes would not suit the design, but where the narrow piece of end grain would not be noticed. In much modern furniture through dovetails are often left fully exposed as part of the design.

MITERED BLIND LAPPED DOVETAIL

You can convert the previous joint to one in which the outer corner is mitered. The solid pieces outside the dovetail cuts have to be extended and mitered to each other. The layout of the joint may

177

be imagined as a through dovetail with solid mitered wood on the outside (Fig. 9-9A).

When cutting the joint, allow both parts to have squared extensions until the dovetails and pins are shaped (Fig. 9-9B). If your saw or chisel marks this part slightly, it will not matter because any damage will be trimmed off as you cut the miter (Fig. 9-9C).

The miter needs careful cutting as it goes to a featheredge on each piece, and these must meet neatly if the joint is to be effective. For hand paring it helps to have a guide piece clamped under the work, with its edge already at 45 degrees and straight (Fig. 9-9D). This prevents the thin edge from breaking out and tells you when you have pared far enough.

Along the miter there is no clue to the construction inside. At the ends the pins can still be seen fitting into the edge of the other part.

SECRET MITERED DOVETAIL

Any of the previous joints will be all that are required for many assemblies. If the joint is not to have its internal construction visible anywhere, the edges of the boards have to be mitered as well as the end grain corners. This dovetail joint is a secret mitered dovetail and is a test of your skill.

The joint is very similar to the previous one, but you have to mark out and cut it so the outer pins are set in enough for miters outside them (Fig. 9-10A), which have matching sockets in the piece with tails (Fig. 9-10B). As with the previous joint, you can visualize a normal through dovetail joint

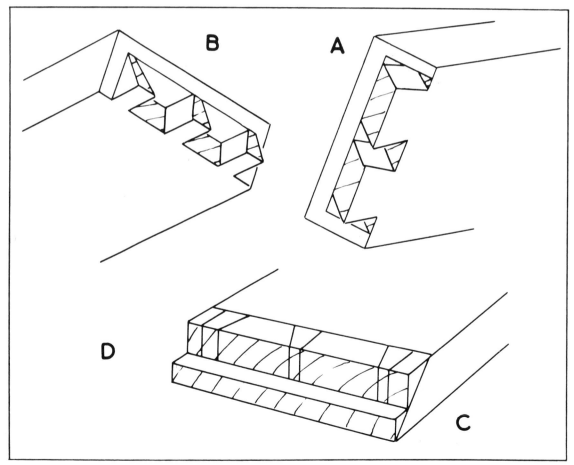

Fig. 9-10. In a secret mitered dovetail all the construction is hidden.

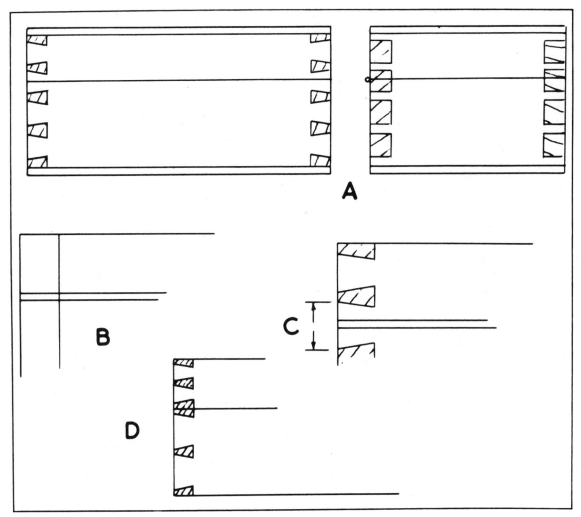

Fig. 9-11. A dovetailed box can have its lid cut off after joining.

with solid pieces outside, but this time you allow for solid mitered pieces outside at the edges.

Cut back both pieces for the amount of the miter and draw the miters on the edges (Fig. 9-10C), but do not cut them yet. Mark the side pins and their sockets, then space dovetails between them (Fig. 9-10D). It may help to cut away part of the mitered edges, but do not go close to the final line at this stage. Drill out and chisel away the dovetails and pins. With these to shape and all inner corners trimmed of odd fibers and anything else that would interfere with pulling the joint tight, pare the miters. Be careful not to take off too much from the

miters. They must meet as the dovetails tighten in their sockets. Leaving a miter slightly too thick is better than taking off too much, then the surfaces should close together tightly.

BOX AND LID DOVETAILS

If a box and its lid are to match, the two parts may be made as one and then separated. If one is not reversed on the other during assembly, they will match exactly. The corners could be made in any of several ways, including the versions of the dovetail joint already described, but as an example a box is shown with through dovetails (Fig. 9-11A).

179

When laying out the four sides, gauge two parallel lines where the cut will come. The gap between the lines must be judged enough to allow for the saw kerf and few shavings to be taken off with a plane (Fig. 9-11B). You could mark out dovetails as if the wood would remain uncut, but then you may get the joint across a line between tail and pin or in some way that leaves a poor edge where top and box meet.

The cut should come across the center of a tail, which may be planned slightly wider than the others to allow for the cut (Fig. 9-11C). If the lid is to be comparatively shallow, it may be better to space its tails differently from those of the box's body (Fig. 9-11D).

Make up the four sides. When the glue has set, trim the joints and smooth the exterior surfaces as if they were to remain one thing. Saw between the lines after making reference marks across the lines at one side, so you know which way the lid has to go on the box. Plane the edges carefully, with the gauge lines as a guide. It is easy to plane in a twist so the parts do not close properly all around.

TRAY CORNER

A small tray or open box may have through dovetails at the corners, but it will usually have a bottom rabbeted in and looks best if the top edges meet with miters. Both requirements involve modifying the plain dovetail joint.

Have the wood rabbeted sufficiently. Make the bottom pin deeper than the rabbet. Above that the parts fit together in the usual way, but you will have to hide the edge of the bottom with an extension on the tail part into the rabbet exposed on the end of the pin (Fig. 9-12A). This is better than taking the other piece through and exposing end grain (Fig. 9-12B).

There are at least two ways of arranging the miter at the top. You can miter directly above the tail. That means the upper edge of the last tail does not show on the outside (Fig. 9-12C), but its end shows below the top mitered pin. Inside, the edge of the pin could follow the usual dovetail slope, and the pin could be made to match. It would be easier

and just as satisfactory to make parallel cuts (Fig. 9-10D).

Another way is to let the pin above the top tail go through. Its upper edge is kept straight and flat, but what remains above it is mitered (Fig. 9-12E). The piece the other way extends over it with a matching miter (Fig. 9-12F).

That type of tray may have its upper edges well rounded. That does not present any complications, except that the part mitered must be deep enough to allow for it.

REDUCED DOVETAIL

In any joint between wide boards meeting on their end grain, the greatest stresses due to internal action come near the edges. As wood absorbs or gives off moisture, it may tend to shrink, expand, or warp. The joint has to resist this. If any part is to fail, it will be near the outside.

One way of providing extra strength near the edges in a dovetail joint is to make the outer dovetails narrower (Fig. 9-13). Glue grips best where side grain surfaces meet, so in a dovetail the finest bond should come between the edges of the tails and pins. If more glue surfaces of this sort are provided, the strength should be greater. Narrower tails will provide more suitable glue surfaces, but very narrow tails would not look right and would be tedious to cut. A more reasonable width can be used across the joint, but at each end there may be a narrow tail possibly half the width of the others.

FLY JOINTS

In furniture construction a fairly narrow rail may be all that is needed between two parts, but at its ends there may not be enough width to cut strong joints. In that case an extra piece of wood may be jointed on to take an extra tail. Taper it off acutely (Fig. 9-14A). Allow enough width at the end for enough grain lines running through to minimize any risk of splitting.

Glue and clamp the parts together. Screws could be inserted from the fly piece into the other, or dowels might go through. Secret slot screwing also could be used (Fig. 9-14B).

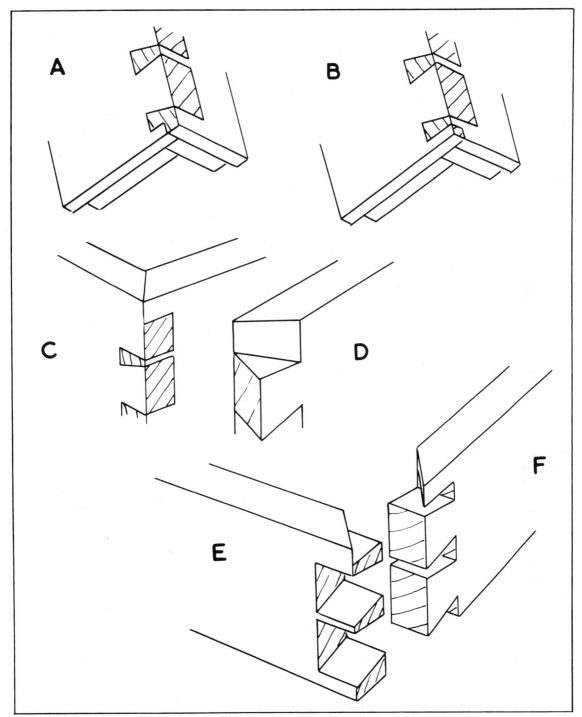

Fig. 9-12. Allowance can be made for a rabbeted bottom and mitered top corners on a through dovetail joint.

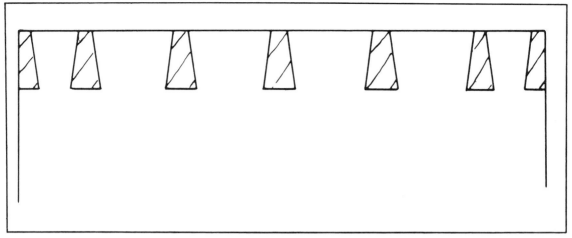

Fig. 9-13. A wide board joint can have narrower dovetails at the end to provide greater glue area there.

LEG AND RAIL DOVETAILS

In much furniture a rail on edge goes into a leg that is wider and usually square. In some constructions there has to be a rail that is flat on top and joined to the edge rail and leg. This should be cut around the leg top so there is enough extending to dovetail into the other rail (Fig. 9-15A). The tail into the leg top should be as large as can be fitted in without cutting into the tenon of the other rail. The tenon into the rail does not usually go through, but it should be taken as far as possible. This is one of the few places where a dovetail joint goes into side grain, but with the support from the joint at the leg, there is no fear of the side grain breaking out under load.

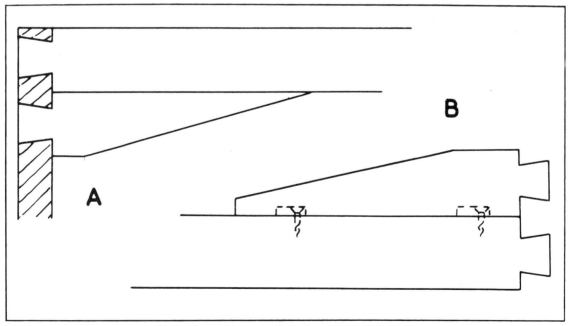

Fig. 9-14. A fly piece may be added inside a rail for extra dovetails.

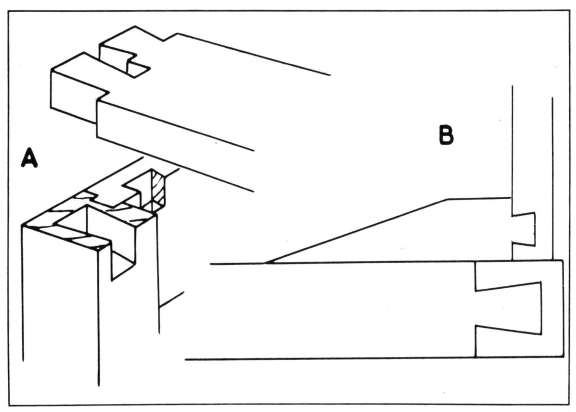

Fig. 9-15. A front rail may go around a leg to dovetail into a side rail.

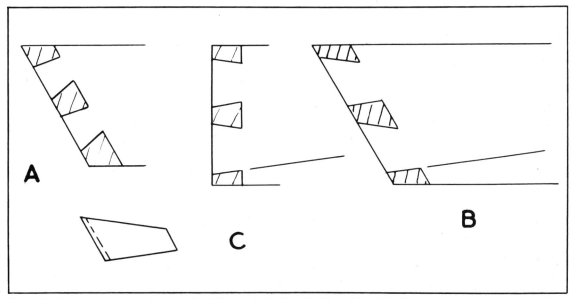

Fig. 9-16. Dovetails into a sloping part should be angled to the direction of the straight piece.

If the rail is not wide enough to go around the leg with enough there for a dovetail, it can be fitted with a fly piece to give enough width (Fig. 9-15B). It would not matter if the glued edge joint came through a tail, as that would act as a clamp.

SLOPING DOVETAILS

If a part like a drawer front slopes instead of being square to the side, but the side is square to the front when viewed the other way, cutting dovetail joints is very similar to dealing with square ones.

It might not matter how the angles of the tails are arranged with only a slight slope but as the angle gets more it would be wrong to angle the sides of the tails in relation to the sloping piece (Fig. 9-16A). Some of the grain lines come across tail edges, so the short grain might break out. The edges of the tails toward the longer corner will come in line with the length of the side of even slope the wrong way, so they do not contribute the usual strength.

Instead, the angles of the tails should be related to the edges of the sides. If checked against the top and bottom edges, the angles should be the same as if the piece they meet is at 90 degrees, so you cannot use one of the usual templates against the end. Slopes can be marked with an adjustable bevel against one of the edges (Fig. 9-16B), or you can make a special template (Fig. 9-16C) if many of these joints are needed.

The method applies to any form of dovetail, but there are complications if you choose to miter outside the linking parts. If there is a slope both ways between the pieces, the joints may be cut in a similar way. There is some geometry involved to get sizes and angles. See the oblique details section later in the chapter.

HOUSE DOVETAIL

A less common use of a dovetail comes where the resistance to pull is needed, but there is no way of using a conventional one. An example is a shelf or rail between stout uprights that could be subject to considerable spreading loads, which the shelf has to resist.

The end of the rail is given one or more dovetails long enough to go well into the upright, but not through it (Fig. 9-17A). Above the level at which the rail finally comes is a recess cut (the housing) large enough for the tail(s) to be passed in (Fig. 9-17B). Below this a socket is cut to take the dovetail. Pins are used if it is a multiple dovetail. The tail can be inserted in the housing, then pressed down into its socket (Fig. 9-17C).

After the rail has been glued into place, fill the housing with a plug (Fig. 9-17D), preferably with the grain the same way as the upright. The joint could be made the other way up to hide the plug underneath without affecting strength. A similar joint could be used where parts may have to be knocked down at some future date.

If a leg is to go into a solid top, there can be a housing, then a dovetail for the leg (Fig. 9-17E). After the leg has been fitted without glue, a plug is held in place with a screw (Fig. 9-17F). Removal of the plug allows the leg to be knocked out. In a table assembly a pair of legs might be permanently braced together. The tops are fitted as described. Lower rails between the leg assemblies are joined in as first described, but without glue and with screw plugs (Fig. 9-17G). By removing the plugs, the parts of the table can be reduced to a flat package.

LONG AND SHORT DOVETAILS

If the wood is comparatively thick, normal through dovetails look rather large and clumsy, although they are quite strong. If through dovetails are visible in a joint between wide and thick boards, there is a way of cutting tails of different lengths that is decorative and breaks down the clumsy appearance of large tails alone (Fig. 9-18).

Mark out the joint for the large tails, with an equal spacing and narrow pins. Inside each large tail mark one or two more smaller tails, depending on the width. Usually a central tail with a pin each side of it will do. Do not make the inner tails too small—not less than half the depth of the large tails.

From this point marking and cutting are similar to any other through dovetails, except in the other part of the bottom of the large socket will have to be

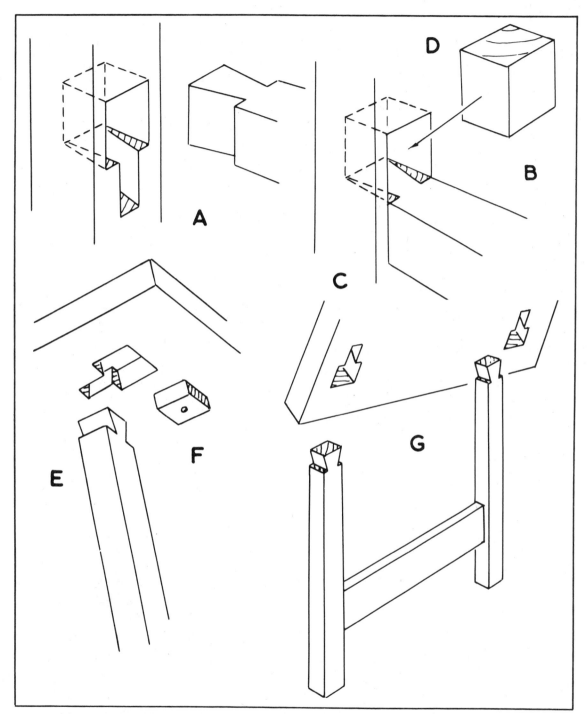

Fig. 9-17. A dovetail may be housed and covered with a plug (A, B, C, D). The joint can be used to make legs removable (E, F, G).

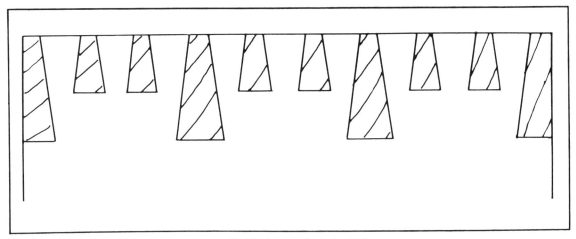

Fig. 9-18. In thick wood decoration may be provided by intermediate short tails.

cut back to suit the narrower pins and tails. A complication is to step up at the small tails, so they do not go as deep into the other piece.

CURVED DOVETAILS

When two flat boards meet, the usual through dovetails are parallel to the corner throughout their depth. An interesting variation still keeps the corner square, but the inner edges of the pins and tails are following a curved track, from full thickness to about half thickness at the center (Fig. 9-19A). This is only done for visual effect and possibly to show the craftsman's skill. It will be strong enough, but so will a plain through dovetail.

Something has to be done about the reduced thickness near the center of each board, where the joint uses only about half the wood. This is taken care of by an inner miter, which is at 45 degrees, but the width of the slope increases toward the center of both pieces (Fig. 9-19B).

The curves the inner lines will take are marked on both sides and ends of both pieces (Fig. 9-19C). What goes on the face of one must match what goes on the end of the other. Hollow the ends to the inner curves, squarely at first (Fig. 9-19D). Draw a straight line across between the ends of the curve. This will serve as a guide to paring the slope on each piece (Fig. 9-19E).

From this point you have to mark and cut tails and pins in a very similar way to making a normal joint. The curves give you the bases of the cuts to work to. Keep these accurate and avoid breaking out fibers on the outside (Fig. 9-19F). The best visual effects comes from accurate and close work, with the end grain leveled accurately with the adjoining side grain parts.

SLOT DOVETAILS

In most dovetail joints the board with the tails is wider than it is deep. Dovetails can also be used when the wood is on edge. The form is then something like a dado or housing joint and is found where parts, such as stretchers, have to be built into furniture in a way that provides some resistance to pulling apart.

In the simplest form the joint is cut right through and is barefaced; dovetailing is on one side only (Fig. 9-20A). In furniture this is a common form and is often reinforced with a glue block on the plain side (Fig. 9-20B). The alternative is to dovetail on both sides (Fig. 9-20C) if there is enough thickness to prevent the wood being weakened by the double cutting. The dovetail could taper slightly in the depth, so it tightens as the tail piece is lowered into its socket (Fig. 9-20D).

The joint may have to be cut blind or stopped, so the form of the joint does not show on one surface (Fig. 9-20E). Dovetailing of this could be on one or both sides, but for hand cutting the groove, stopping means it cannot be sawed through. You need to

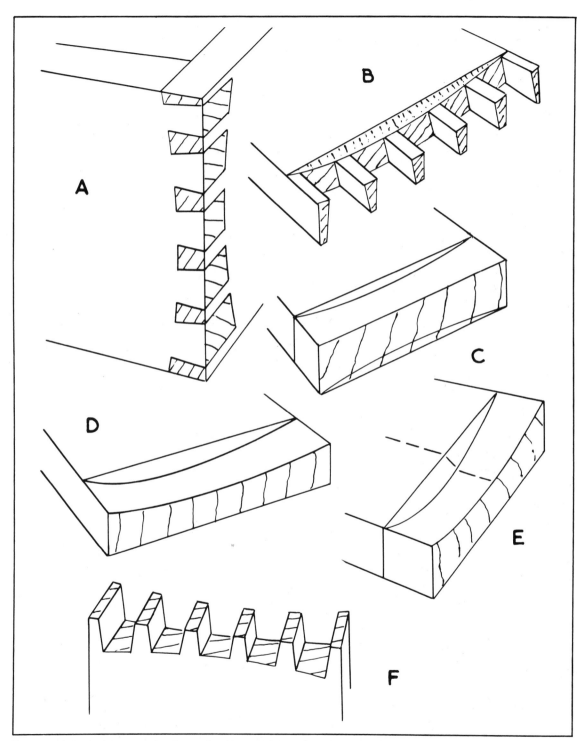

Fig. 9-19. A decorative corner can be made with curved dovetails.

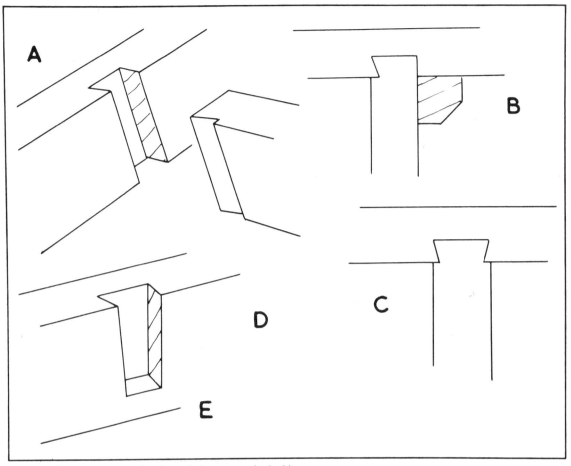

Fig. 9-20. Slotted joints may be dovetailed on one or both sides.

do some careful work with chisels. The work is simplified with a suitable dado cutter, and only the end of the groove has to be trimmed with chisels. The dovetailed piece could be rounded to match the end as it comes.

If the stretcher is narrower than the other piece, its width sets the position of the stopping of the slot on the other piece. If it is the same width as the piece it joins, it must be cut back in a similar way to a shelf into a dado joint.

DEEP SLOT DOVETAIL

While slot dovetails have a place in furniture construction, there comes a stage in house construction where a similar resistance to pulling apart is needed. The sizes of the wood involved mean that more support than just the dovetail is needed to take the weight of the beam and any load on it.

The joint used has a dovetail, either barefaced or double-sided, but the pieces of wood are also notched together (Fig. 9-21A). If the beam with the tail is not as deep as the other, it can go into the cutout fully (Fig. 9-21B). If they are the same depth, it will have to be notched (Fig. 9-21C).

The depth to make the dovetail depends on the available thickness for the socket. It is easier to cut the tail right across the end, so the socket can be full depth, if that does not take too much out of the other piece (Fig. 9-21D). That gives the maximum resistance to pulling apart. If it would be preferable to

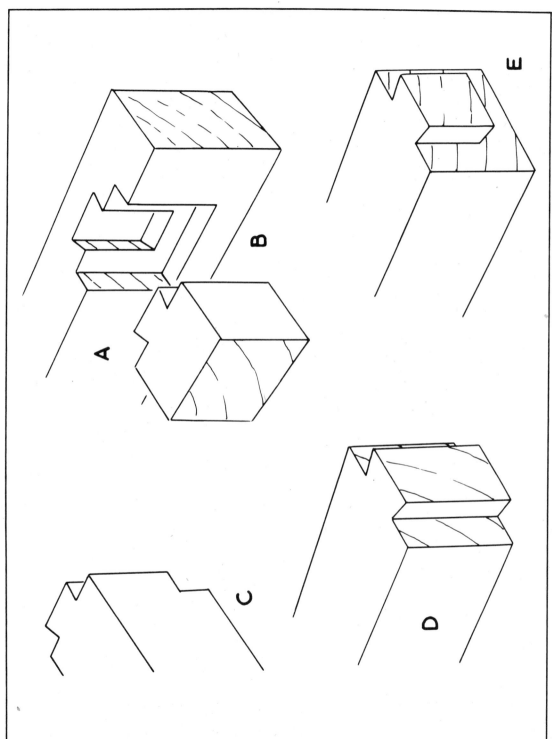

Fig. 9-21. In large construction a dovetail may lock the end of a notched beam.

not remove so much wood, the dovetail can be reduced (Fig. 9-21E).

WEDGED DOVETAIL

The deep slot dovetail or a larger plain dovetail can be made easier to assemble, yet capable of pulling parts tight, by using a wedge. This has an advantage in housebuilding where the wood is of large section and difficult to position to fit a precision dovetail exactly. Attempting to bring a closely cut joint together when one part is swinging from a rope or otherwise temporarily and unsteadily supported may be impossible. It is likely to result in corners of the tails being broken off or the joint damaged in some other way.

The joint can be made very loose for easy fitting by using a wedge. A wedge is driven to tighten the joint (Fig. 9-22). The side of the socket can be tapered slightly, so the wedge goes home neatly.

DOOR FRAME DOVETAIL

If it is expected that the inside of a frame may have to be altered in size slightly, it is helpful to use corner joints that allow for adjustment. This can happen with a house door, which may vary slightly in width with changes in the moisture content of the wood due to weather.

If the frame in which the door is hung is rigid in size, the only way of freeing a tight door is to plane its edges. If it shrinks later, it may become excessively loose. If the frame has adjustable joints, the uprights may be moved in and out slightly, so the gaps around the door can be kept to neat and reasonable limits.

One way of joining the parts of the door frame uses a variation of the through dovetail joint. The door fits into a rabbet (Fig. 9-23A). That has to be allowed for, with the dovetailing only in the other part. Dovetails, as many as the thickness warrants, are made in the upright (Fig. 9-23B), then shouldered back to the depth of the rabbet (Fig. 9-23C). On the other piece the rabbeted part goes over the matching upright part, and the sockets for the dovetails are shaped to match the tails (Fig. 9-23D).

When the joint is drawn together tightly, it is like any other through dovetail. If the opening has to be widened and the sides knocked out, the joint will still look the same inside, at least as far as the depth

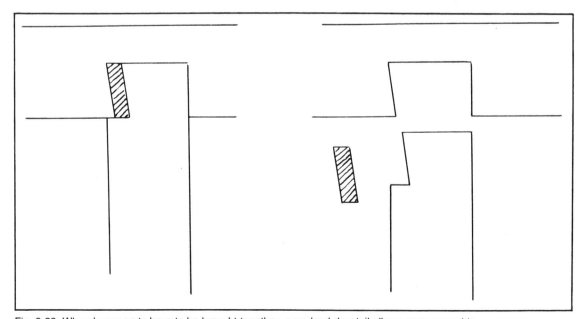

Fig. 9-22. When heavy parts have to be brought together, a wedged dovetail allows easy assembly.

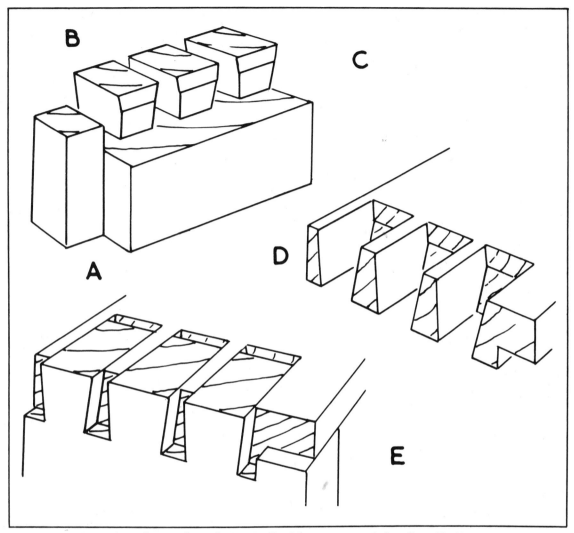

Fig. 9-23. Door frame dovetails may allow adjustment without the appearance being affected inside.

of the rabbet, although outside, where it does not matter, the joint appears open (Fig. 9-23E).

Such a joint obviously has to be assembled without glue, so it should be a close fit. The edges are usually covered with molding, so that has to be easily removable to permit adjustment.

SLIDING DOVETAILS

If one part has to slide on another, yet keep close to it under pressure, the first part can have a dovetail to travel along a matching groove in the other part.

The moving part needs to be fairly wide so its dovetail has a good bearing surface in the groove. A short dovetail would tend to move about in relation to the groove and allow the piece to take up positions that were not intended or to let it slip.

An example is a sliding pair of bookends that are cut from thick solid wood (Fig. 9-24A) and move on a flat base. Have the tails as deep and long as the thickness of the base will take without being weakened or bent. The groove is most easily cut with a router, but it could be sawed and chiseled

(Fig. 9-24B). Under pressure from the books, there should be enough friction between the end and the base for the dovetail to hold in any position. With the pressure relaxed, each end should slide easily to a new position. Wax in the grooves will aid smooth movement without being messy.

To prevent the ends from coming right out, a screw could be standing at each end of the groove (Fig. 9-24C). If the groove is routed, it could stop short of each end, but then be widened near the center so the bookends can be inserted (Fig. 9-24D).

DOVETAIL KEYING

A small piece of wood cut as a double dovetail may also be called a *butterfly* (Fig. 9-25A). It can be used in many ways for joining parts, limiting damage, or pulling pieces together. It can be used across

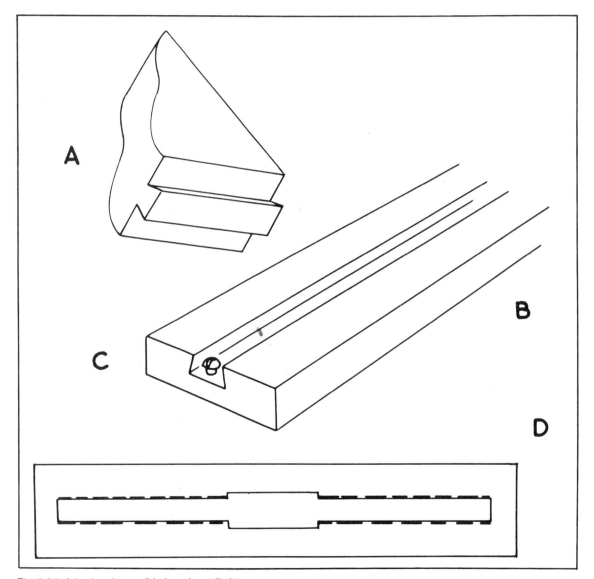

Fig. 9-24. A bookend may slide in a dovetail slot.

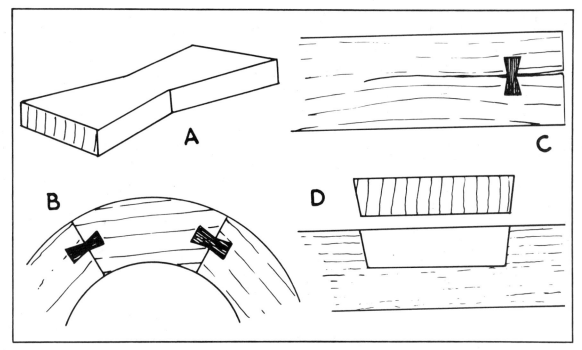

Fig. 9-25. A dovetailed butterfly key will strengthen across a joint or split.

boards to prevent warping or casting. Usually the key is a hardwood, even if the parts it fits into are softwood. In some cases the butterfly shape can be used for decoration as well as a strength member by choosing a wood of contrasting color. The slopes of the two parts should be the same as other dovetails—about 1 in 7.

A dovetail key can be used to join pieces end to end where they make up an angular or curved border (Fig. 9-25B). The key may be up to half the thickness of the parts being joined.

Another application is in securing a shake or crack from developing further along a board (Fig. 9-25C). Where boards are joined edge to edge, butterflies could be inserted on the underside to strengthen the joint.

To be effective, butterflies have to be tight in their sockets, particularly if they are for decoration. One way of securing a close fit is to give the butterfly edges a slight taper, with the socket tapered similarly (Fig. 9-25D). Squeezing in should bring all edges close. If a butterfly is made slightly too thick,

it can be leveled with the surface after the glue has set to get a perfect appearance.

DOVETAIL SPLINED MITER

If a corner between two boards, meeting like a box corner, is mitered, the joint has little strength if it is merely glued on the mitered surfaces. It has to be reinforced in some way. One decorative way is to insert dovetail splines (Fig. 9-26A). The appearance is something like through dovetails, with the different color and grain of the splines coming between dovetail shapes in the boards.

Spline material is made in a long length (Fig. 9-26B), with the usual dovetail angles each side. The mitered parts are brought together in a vise. Cut one end of a spline to 45 degrees and use this as a template for marking the shape to be cut out (Fig. 9-26C). Mark the wood with a knife to prevent grain from tearing out then cut carefully inside the lines. Choose a section of spline that will go well into the miter, but not break through inside the corner. Glue in splines that are overlong, then trim them level after the glue has set.

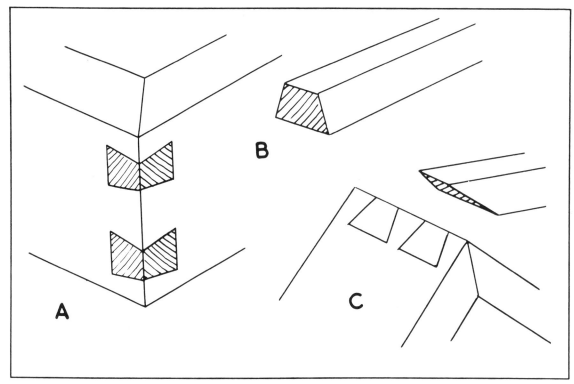

Fig. 9-26. Dovetail splines may strengthen and decorate a miter joint.

OBLIQUE DOVETAILS

If two boards meet so that both are flared or splayed outward, there are complications in arriving at the angles between the sides and the shapes and angles of the dovetails. Such a joint can be made with almost any dovetail joint already described once the angles to work to have been found, but the examples is a through dovetail.

Although the corner is square when viewed directly from above, the actual angle between the sides, taken squarely from the line of the corner, is not. The more the splay, the greater the angle there increases above a right angle. Angles have to be found geometrically. Nearly all marking is done with the aid of an adjustable bevel, where you would normally use a try square.

It is assumed that the amount of splay is the same both ways. It could be different, but once the equal splay geometry is understood, it may be adapted to suit unequal slopes of sides.

Draw a whole or half layout of side and end elevation over a plan (Fig. 9-27A). This gives you the appearance in three directions, but does not take into account that front pieces in the two elevations slope toward you. You have the width of the wood in its side view. For the actual shape of the outside of the end, project the wood width from the wide elevation on to the plan and join the corners at the new distance (Fig. 9-27B). The wood is actually wider than this by the amount needed to make up the angle at the bottom (Fig. 9-27C). Find the actual sizes of the sides in the same way. Prepare enough wood for the four parts, with tops and bottoms planed to the angles shown in one of the elevations (Figs. 9-27D and 9-27E). Mark the shapes of the pieces, but allow a little extra at each end until you have finished marking out.

To obtain the angle between the sides, on a plan view of the corner (Fig. 9-27F, 1-2-3) draw a perpendicular line (1-4). Join 3-4 and project 2-5

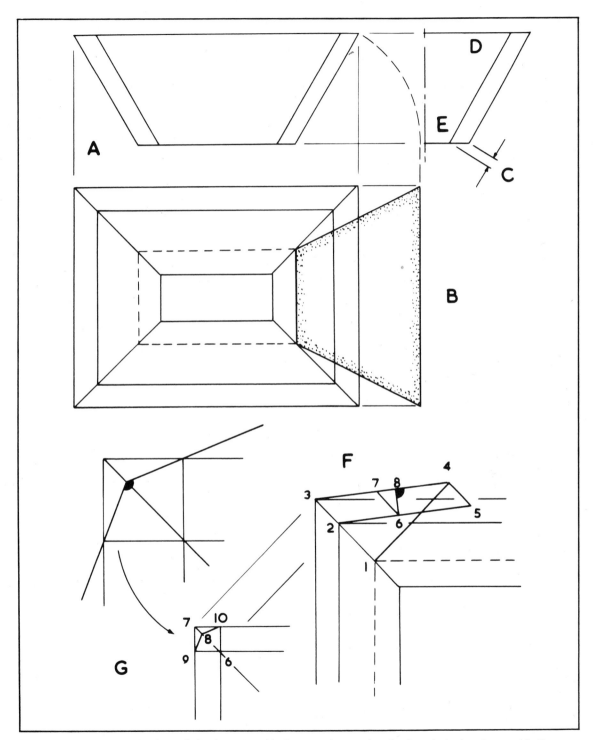

Fig. 9-27. Where parts to be dovetailed splay outward both ways, sizes and angles have to be found geometrically.

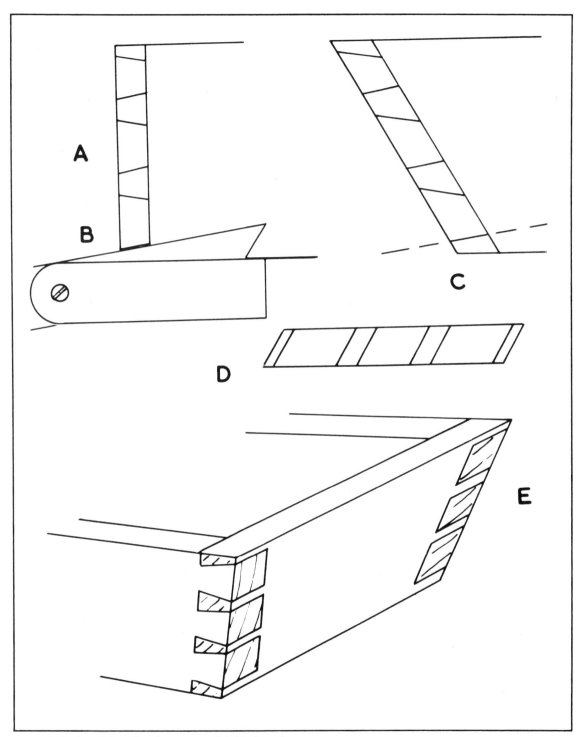

Fig. 9-28. Angles of the splayed parts are related to the edges.

parallel to it. You have a true side view of the thickness of a corner. Draw 6-7 parallel with the base and 6-8 square to the corner line.

Draw a square corner with a miter line in it, either under the corner elevation or elsewhere. Measure the same as 6-7 along the miter line and draw two more square lines. Measure the same as 6-8 out from the inner corner and join this point with the crossings of the lines at 9 and 10. The angle 9-8-10 is the actual angle between the two sides (Fig. 9-27G). Use an adjustable bevel set to this instead of a try square for marking the angles of the

ends of the four pieces. If the splay is only slight, this will not be much different from square. If parts are to fit properly, the bottoms of cuts between pins and tails should be angled. Otherwise, there will be gaps in the assembled parts.

The actual shapes of the dovetails should be related to the sides of the wood and not to the cut ends. Take the developed shape of a side and make the sides of each dovetail the same in relation to its edge. If the end had been square, you would make the angle 1 in 7, or other chosen angle, to the end (Fig. 9-28A). Set an adjustable bevel to this, with

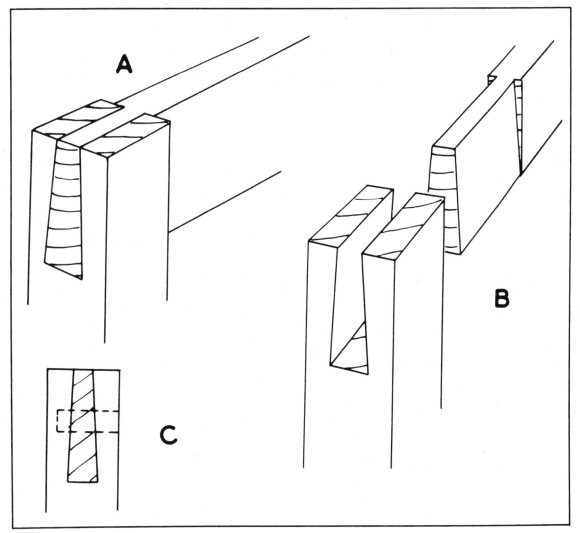

Fig. 9-29. A bridle joint may be strengthened by cutting it with a dovetail section.

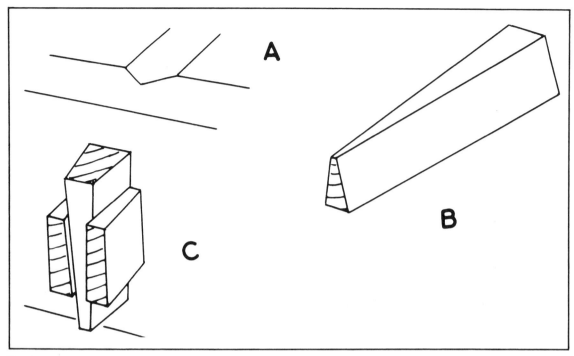

Fig. 9-30. A dovetail wedge may be used as an alternative to the usual tusk tenon.

its stock on the edge of the wood (Fig. 9-28B). Use that to mark the tails (Fig. 9-28C). If you angled to the beveled end, dovetails would cut across grain lines and even be reversed in relation to the direction of pull if there is much splay.

In the other direction, cuts across will come parallel with top and bottom bevels (Fig. 9-28D). The ends will have already been cut to the angle 9-8-10. Mark all around for the depth of the cuts between tail. Be careful to cut to these lines and the correct angle—not straight across. Mark the pins from the tails and use similar angles for marking across the wood. You can leave a small amount of excess wood on the ends, but too much will interfere with cutting the joints. Leave only enough for a few shavings with a plane after assembly (Fig. 9-28E).

DOVETAILED BRIDLE

When two parts are joined with a bridle joint, there is nothing to resist pulling apart except glue and dowels, screws, or other fastenings. If the joint is given a dovetail form, that can assist in resisting separation one way. The amount of taper possible in the dovetail is determined by the relative sizes of the parts. It is best where the wood with the central projection is narrower than the other, as in a top rail meeting a leg (Fig. 9-29A).

The ideal slope of 1 in 7 for a dovetail may not be possible, but the maximum width of the dovetail should be a little more than one-third of the thickness of the leg (Fig. 9-29B) and be given a taper that comes to a fairly narrow piece at the top. Completely remove any stray fibers in the corners of the leg slot with a bevel-edge chisel or knife, so the parts fit closely. Make both pieces slightly too long, so they can be planed level after assembly. One or more dowels might be put across the joint—partially through (Fig. 9-29C) if you do not want them to show on one surface.

DOVETAIL WEDGING

An alternative to the wedged tusk tenon can have a dovetailed piece to provide locking, so it offers decoration or can be removed if the table or other piece of furniture has to be taken apart. The vertically sectioned rail notches into the other part (Fig. 9-30A). It could be square across or notched in steps, as described for the tusk tenon in Chapter 6.

When the wedge is thrust home, it has an expanding effect on the end of the tenon, which should be thick enough to resist this. The wedge should be kept as narrow as possible, so too much wood does not have to be cut from the tenon. The limit is set by its taper, which can be to almost nothing on the bottom (Fig. 9-30B). Design that part of the joint about the wedge, which is given a dovetail taper in its thickness and a moderate slope in its length, depending on the thickness of tenon it is to go through. A slope of 1 in 10 may suit.

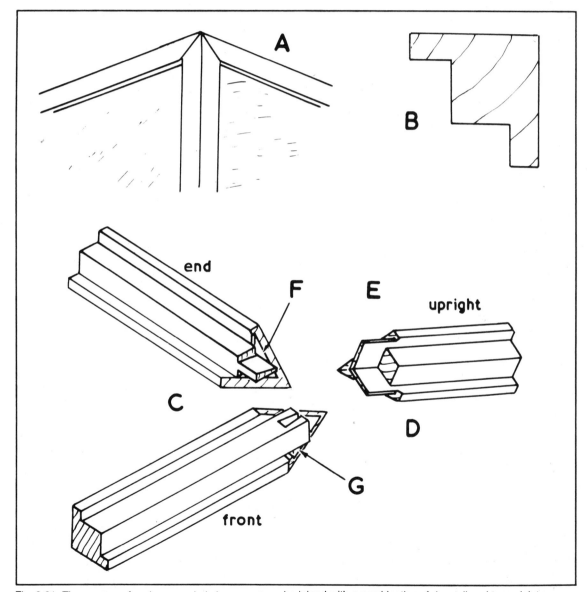

Fig. 9-31. The corners of a glass-paneled showcase may be joined with a combination of dovetail and tenon joint.

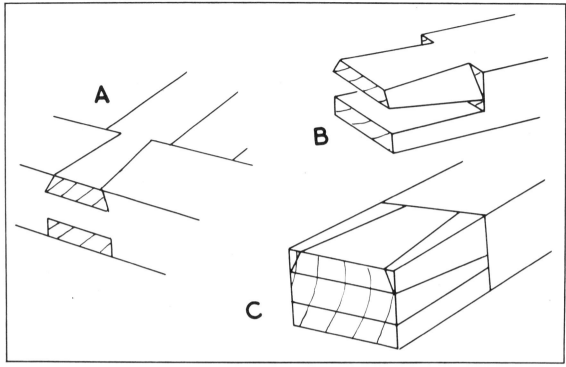

Fig. 9-32. A trick dovetailed bridle joint appears to be impossible to take apart.

If the parts are to be notched, the notch should not go very far into the mortised rail. If it is thick enough, the notch could be at 90 degrees, but it may have to be more obtuse so as not to cut too much away. One-third the wood thickness is about right. The tenon can be about one-third the depth of the rail, but the projection looks best if slightly deeper than it is wide (Fig. 9-30C).

Make the wedge too long, so you can cut it off after fitting and leave equal amounts above and below. The finished joint may be left angular, or the wedge and tenon may be rounded a little.

THREE-WAY SHOWCASE CORNER

A showcase with glass panels all around has to be framed with wood of thin section, so the framing does not detract from the case and its contents or look too massive. This creates a problem of joining at the corners, where three similar rails meet (Fig. 9-31A) and there is not much wood for making the joint. This example shows one way of using a dovetail to lock two parts and a double tenon to bring in the other piece.

The wood is cut from square stock with rabbets to take the glass and its fillets (Fig. 9-31B). All three pieces are mitered on their outer surfaces. Mark and cut these through to the rabbet line on the front and end bars. Inside this mark and cut the dovetail joint in the projecting parts of the core (Fig. 9-31C). They have to meet in line with the neighboring parts of the miters, but the ends should be kept back slightly so they do not prevent the miters from coming close during assembly.

That completes jointing between these two parts, but they have to be prepared for the tenons from the upright. Cut back the core of that piece (Fig. 9-31D), but make two thin joined tenons in the miter thickness, then cut what remains outside to the miters. The thickness of the tenons depends on the section of the wood, but they will probably have to be at least ⅛ inch to allow for getting a chisel of that thickness into the mortises (Fig. 9-31E). Cut the ends of the tenons back a little, so they will not bottom before the miters are tight. Trim the mortises within the thickness of the miters in the meeting surfaces of the other two parts (Figs. 9-31F and 9-31G).

PUZZLE DOVETAIL BRIDLE JOINT

This joint (Fig. 9-32A) appears to be impossible to make or separate due to the double slopes of the dovetail part. The secret is inside the joint, where the bottom of the dovetail is parallel (Fig. 9-32B) and sloping. The amount of slope controls the amount of bevel on the sides of the dovetail.

Draw the side of the joint on the wood (Fig. 9-32C). It does not matter if the lower piece is parallel or sloping. Draw the dovetail shape on top and bevel the sides with a saw and chisel.

The other piece is cut to match. The only awkward parts are inside the acute angles at the bottom of the dovetail, where the corners must be cut cleanly. To make it difficult for a viewer to see how the joint is formed, be careful with the cross grain cuts so they do not break out and show the slope at the side of the dovetail.

This is really only a trick joint, but some users claim it has practical uses. It might form a point of interest if built into an assembly where it is prominent. It would certainly be as strong as a normal bridle joint.

PUZZLE END DOVETAIL

This is purely a puzzle (Fig. 9-33A) without any practical use. Like the previous puzzle, it appears to be impossible to make or separate. It is best made of close-grained hardwood that will not crumble when cut acutely, as broken grain would show

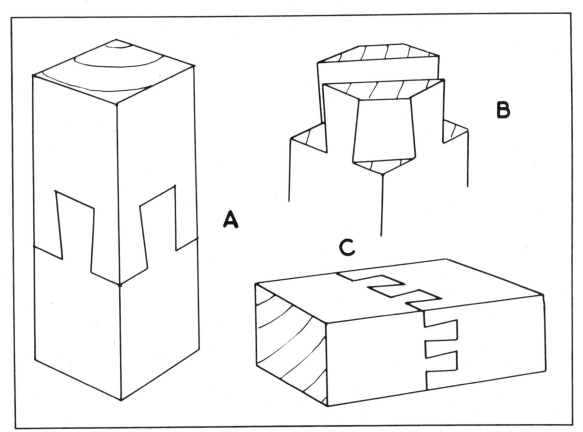

Fig. 9-33. The apparently impossible and dovetail will slide diagonally.

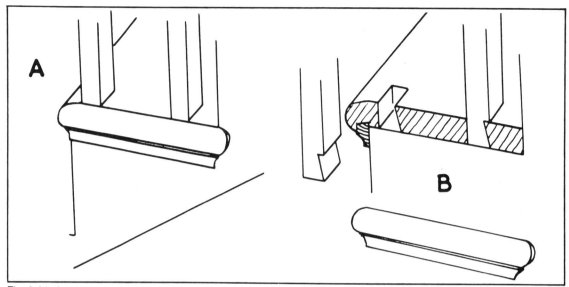

Fig. 9-34. A baluster end is dovetailed and hidden by the molding.

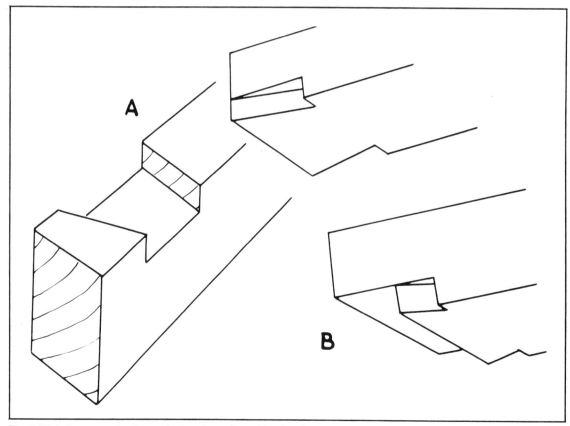

Fig. 9-35. In large construction a shallow dovetail provides location.

how the joint is cut. The secret is in the way the dovetails are cut diagonally (Fig. 9-33B).

There may be a single dovetail on each face. One is easier to make, but there could be two (Fig. 9-33C), so the puzzle looks even more complicated. Do not bring the dovetails too near the corners, or you will make some fragile pieces there that will not stand up to sliding in and out for long. How far the parts extend into each other is up to you. Having tails twice as long as they are wide looks about right. Cutting needs care, particularly where the diagonal cuts meet the surfaces, and a gap might show the slope below and tell a smart observer how the joint is made.

BALUSTER DOVETAIL

In a staircase the upright rails in the banister may have their feet set in the treads. They could be tenoned in, but for strength it is better if the joint resists withdrawal. If the ends of the treads can be open until the joints are made, square-ended balusters may be dovetailed. The joints are then covered with a molded piece that follows around the pattern of the tread nosing (Fig. 9-34A).

Cut the dovetail on one side of each piece (Fig. 9-34B), with open-ended notches in the ends of the tread. The return nosing should be molded to match the front edge of the tread and cover the joints.

BUILDING DOVETAIL

When one large piece of wood has to rest on another during the assembly of a building or other large structure, it helps to have a positive location. This is particularly important if the piece on top also has to prevent the lower one from moving. In that case there can be a shallow dovetail (Fig. 9-35A).

Usually it may go the full width of the lower piece and will then give a good bearing surface. It could be stopped (Fig. 9-35B) so as not to remove as much wood from the lower piece if the joint is some way from supports, and cutting away might cause the beam to sag. The depth the dovetail is cut depends on circumstances. A shallow one will prevent the lower part spreading, but you have to consider how high the top piece needs to project above the other.

Chapter 10

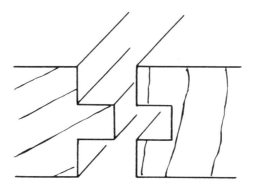

Tongued and Grooved Joints

JOINING BOARDS EDGE TO EDGE WITH A TONGUE on one piece and a groove on the other had two main purposes. When glue was not as trustworthy, the tongue and groove provided some additional mechanical strength and extra glue area. Before plywood and other manufactured boards in considerable widths came along, backs of cabinets and shelves were often made by using available boards joined with tongues and grooves without glue. As the wood expanded and contracted in width, the tongues slid in their grooves. If the exposed edges were beaded or otherwise shaped, variations in width were not very apparent as the joint looked like part of the molding pattern. If this arrangement is used, one problem is the color in the joint. If the finished work is stained or painted, the tongues should be colored in the same way before assembly. Otherwise, shrinkage will show bare wood of a different shape in the gap. For a broad assembly of tongued and grooved boards, the ends should be nailed or screwed near their centers, so they are free to expand or contract. Widely spaced nails at the ends might lead to cracking.

PLAIN TONGUE AND GROOVE

In a simple joint the tongue is usually one-third the thickness of the wood (Fig. 10-1A). The depth to take it varies, but the minimum would be about the same as the width of the tongue. In thin wood it should go deeper, and ⅜ inch is a size to use as a guide.

In very thick wood where the purpose is to provide extra glue area, it may be better to use two tongues (Fig. 10-1B). The total thickness should be divided into five equal parts.

Both of these joints may be used when joining boards to make up a greater width. They could be used dry to allow for expansion and contraction where the surface has to be flat, as in floorboards, where beads on the surface would be unacceptable. Yet the tongue has a value in preventing dust and drafts passing through.

LONG AND SHORT TONGUE AND GROOVE

Sometimes there is an advantage in stepping the joint so the pieces each side of the groove extend

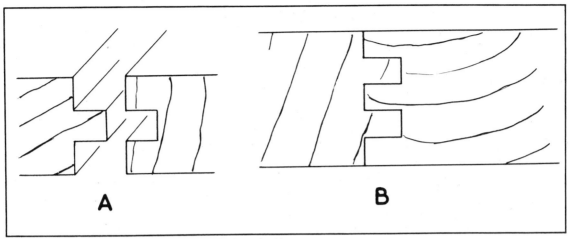

Fig. 10-1. Tongue and groove joints may be single or double.

different amounts (Fig. 10-2A). One way of concealing nails is to drive and punch them diagonally through the tongue. With a normal tongue there is not much space, but with long and short legs a nail through the long one does not have to be driven at such a sharp angle (Fig. 10-2B). Floorboards thus can be laid without nailheads showing anywhere.

FLOORBOARD JOINT

A variation of the long and short tongue and groove tilts the surface the nail goes into and lets the nail go through a more substantial piece of wood. The result is a gain in strength and a reduction in the risk of splitting (Fig. 10-3). The sloping cuts have to fit, but there can be clearance at the others. Too much movement would cause one board to ride above the

other, so this joint is more suitable for stable hardwood than for softwood flooring.

MATCHED BOARDING

Prepared boards with tongues and grooves may be described as match or matched boarding (Fig. 10-4A). Various treatments are used to disguise the joints when the boards are put together dry to make up panels. The simplest is a chamfer on both sides of the joint (Fig. 10-4B). If only one side will be seen, this is only done on that side, but if both sides will be visible the boards may have a double V (Fig. 10-4C).

A common type of joint uses a bead on the tongue piece (Fig. 10-4D). Any movement makes the gap look much the same as the groove worked

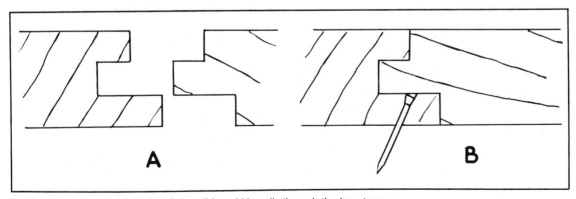

Fig. 10-2. With stepped tongues it is possible to hide nails through the long tongue.

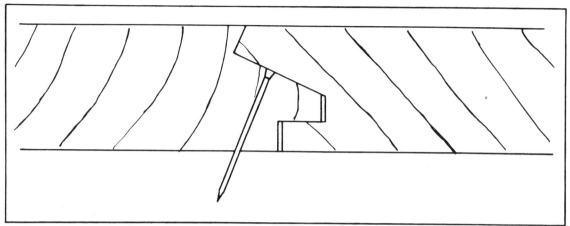

Fig. 10-3. A special joint for floors allows diagonal nailing.

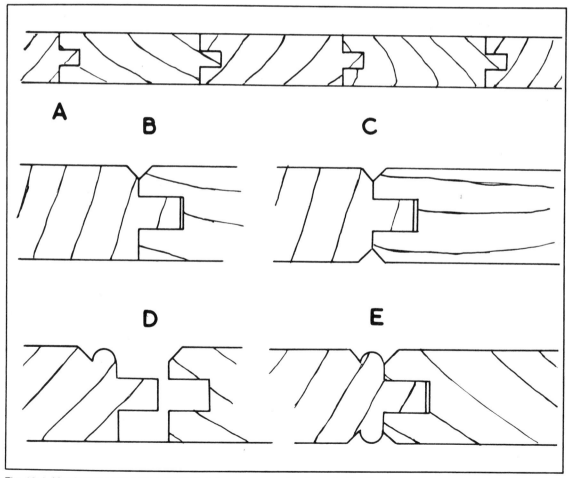

Fig. 10-4. Matched boarding uses tongues and grooves may be decorated to disguise the joint on one or both surfaces.

206

the other side of the bead. The bead could be on both sides (Fig. 10-4E). Beads are best done on thicker boards (⅝ inch and up). They have to come close to the root of the tongue of thin boards and could cause splitting. With very thick wood there could be double tongues, but beaded matched boarding is usually fairly thin as cabinet backs or door panels. A ledged and braced door might be completely of matched boarding.

Pairs of special planes were used to produce matched boards before power tools came along. They looked like molding planes, but had soles and cutters matched to each other and to suit particular thicknesses of wood.

SPLINED JOINT

A variation of the tongue and groove has grooves in both parts and a separate tongue or spline inserted. The spline could have its grain the same way as the grooved wood (Fig. 10-5A). This is comparable to working a tongue in the solid wood. It is also the easiest type of spline to prepare.

There is a gain in strength if the grain of the spline goes across the joint (Figs. 10-5B and 10-5C). That does not affect strength, but preparation of the splines could be tedious.

One way of cutting the splines to get a greater length in each piece is to make them diagonal to the grain (Fig. 10-5D). This still has grain lines crossing the joint so there should be enough strength, with the advantage of fewer pieces in a given length of joint.

Splines are better for glued joints than those made dry to allow for expansion and contraction, where the spaces between sections of spline might become visible. The depth they are taken into each piece of wood may vary according to thickness and purpose, but for average construction about ⅜ inch into each board should be satisfactory. Make the grooves slightly too deep so there is no risk of the

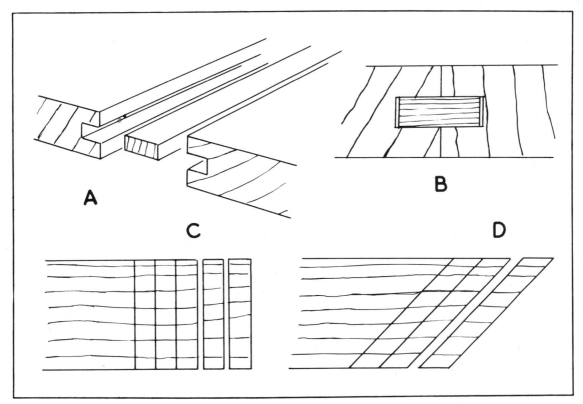

Fig. 10-5. A spline, preferably cut across the grain, can be used in two grooves.

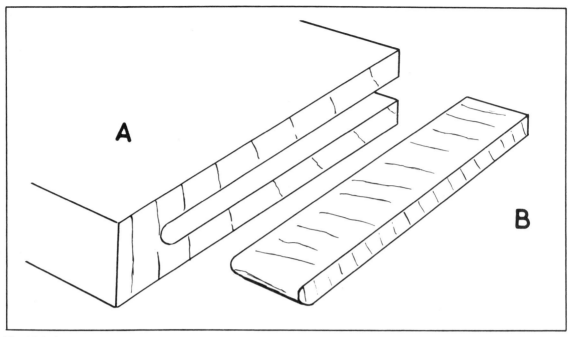

Fig. 10-6. A splined joint may be stopped at one end.

spline bottoming before the wood surfaces have met.

STOPPED SPLINE

In all the foregoing examples the joint runs through to the ends of the boards. There are places where a spline or tongue may make the best joint, but its end should not show at one or both ends. This can apply to quite short joints and those with long runs. The method is applicable to end or side grain.

A router is a convenient tool for making the grooves, and rounded ends need not be squared (Fig. 10-6A). The spline should have its grain across or diagonal. It may be rounded to match the groove end or be cut short (Fig. 10-6B).

DOVETAIL TONGUES

If a tongue and its matching groove can be made wider at the bottom, the joint will be pulled together mechanically. A dovetail section may be

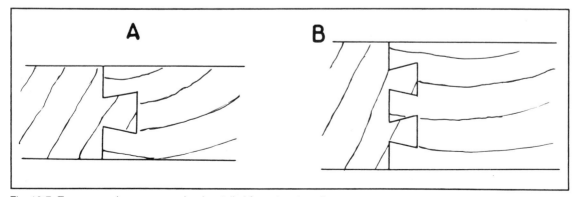

Fig. 10-7. Tongues and grooves may be dovetailed for extra strength.

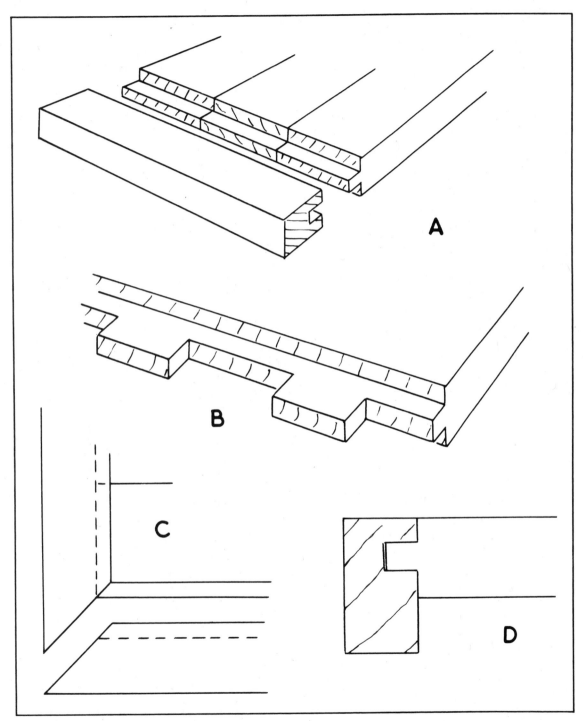

Fig. 10-8. Tongues and grooves may be used at the ends of boards into a clamp, and this can be carried all around or thickened.

used (Fig. 10-7A), but the joint obviously has to slide together. The longer the joint, the more difficult it will be to produce an assembly that will slide the full length without snags. For boards making up a tabletop or something similar, careful work should result in a tight fit.

Double dovetails could be used for thicker boards (Fig. 10-7B). There is increased difficulty in cutting for a good fit, particularly with hand tools.

FRAMED PANELS

A built-up board can be stiffened with strips at the end only or all around using tongue and groove joints or grooves with splines. After boards have been joined to make up width, the ends are given tongues. Cutting a tongue across end grain is easier than grooving it. Mating pieces are made to go across the ends (Fig. 10-8A). For large and heavy construction, the tongues may be continued at intervals as tenons (Fig. 10-8B).

Side pieces could be added in a similar way, with the corners mitered (Fig. 10-8C) or joined by one of the other framing methods. This assembly is effective if the panel and framing are different colored woods. It could also be used with framing thicker than the panel (Fig. 10-8D) to give an effect of solidity while actually being kept light. This could be done with a tabletop; the legs and top rails would be inside the deeper framing.

EDGED SHELF

Any wide board that only has one prominent edge could be lipped with a strip. That allows the greater part to be cheap or plain, while the edge is of better quality. You could create a decorative effect by using contrasting colors of woods. A nearly-white lip on a nearly-black board, or the other way around, would be effective.

If the lip is narrow, the groove must come in the shelf or wide board and the tongue on the lip (Fig. 10-9A). It helps to make the lip slightly too thick, so it can be planed level after gluing. If possible, cut the tongue on a wider piece first, then cut it off (Fig. 10-9B). More examples on manufactured boards are covered in Chapter 17.

TONGUED SHAPED PARTS

If several flat pieces are used to make up a curved or involved shape, tongues or splines may make the most convenient joint. If strips have to follow a curve and grain running off is to be avoided, there have to be joints like miters. Where they meet, there can be tongues and grooves or splines in grooves (Fig. 10-10A) taken right through or stopped if their ends would affect appearance.

There is a similar problem where a rounded corner for a cabinet or similar assembly is made separate from the adjoining sides. Tongues can be worked on the sides, or both parts may be grooved for splines (Fig. 10-10B). Grooving of the curved part is most easily done after it has been marked on a square section and before it is shaped.

CORNER TONGUE AND GROOVE

If two boards meet on edge with grain parallel, as at the rear of a corner cabinet, and something better

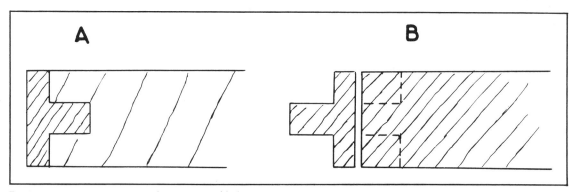

Fig. 10-9. An edging piece may be cut on a wide board and used to form a lip.

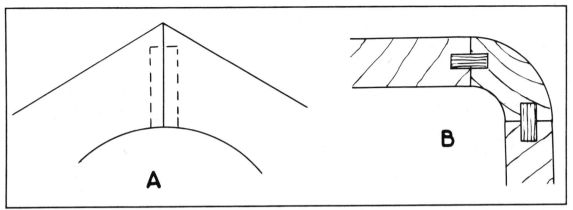

Fig. 10-10. Tongues or splines can be used between shaped parts.

than a nailed or screwed butt joint is needed, there can be a tongue and groove (Fig. 10-11). Unless the wood is very thick, the tongue is level with the inner surface of its board, so this is not a place where a spline could be an alternative. The tongue usually is about half the thickness of the wood. A very similar joint for parts meeting with their end grain, but for machine cutting, is described in Chapter 16.

MOLDED CORNER TONGUE AND GROOVE

If a suitable molding section is chosen, you can disguise the joining surfaces of two boards meeting with their grain parallel. In the example (Fig. 10-12) there is a tongue into a groove, as in the previous joint, then the outer piece is worked to a curve that leaves similar flats each side of it—one on each board.

BEADED CORNER TONGUE AND GROOVE

Another way of disguising the joining surfaces of a tongue and groove corner between boards with their grain parallel uses a bead worked so the gaps each side of it are the same (Fig. 10-13A).

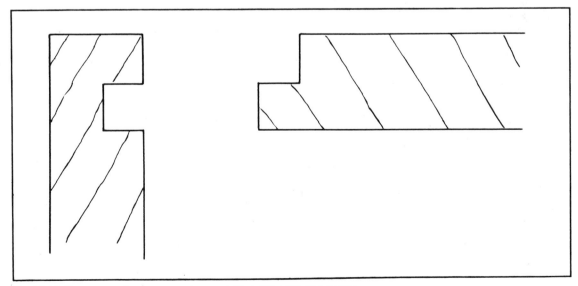

Fig. 10-11. Tongues and grooves can be used along the grain at a corner.

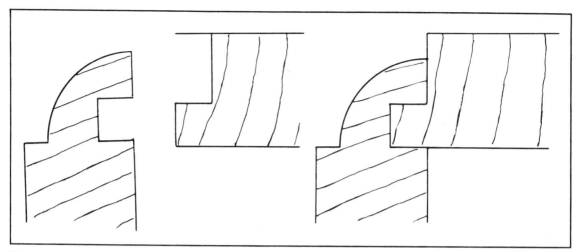

Fig. 10-12. The corner joint can be disguised with a molding.

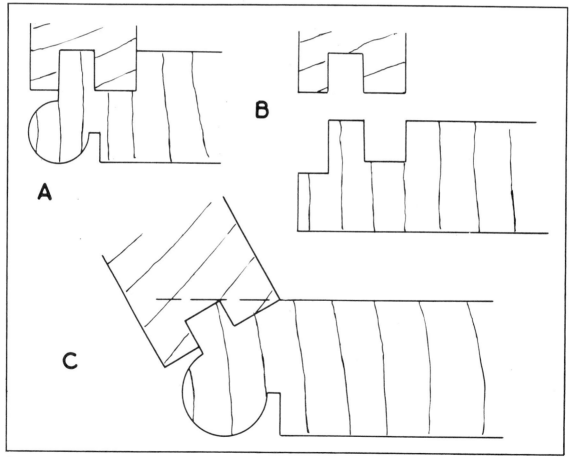

Fig. 10-13. A bead can be worked into a corner.

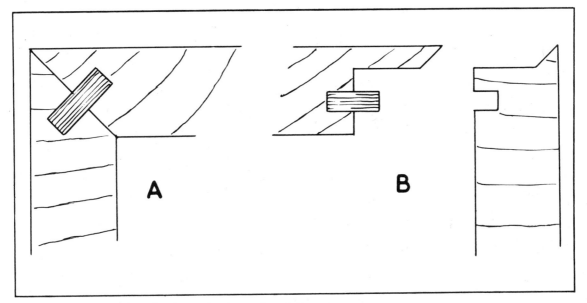

Fig. 10-14. A miter may be splined or made stronger by notching.

For a square corner, one piece has its edge groove to match a tongue formed on the side of the other piece (Fig. 10-13B). The bead then has equal grooves and border each way.

You can make similar joints where the boards do not meet squarely, as in a hexagonal or octagonal assembly, providing there is enough wood to allow the tongue to be cut in the thickness (Fig. 10-13C).

NOTCHED MITER

If two boards are to meet with their grain parallel, but without any thickness showing, the outside corner has to be a miter. It could be a complete miter through the thickness with a spline (Fig. 10-14A). A miter is not a strong structural joint, however, even with its spline, and cutting grooves and matching in the angled surface are difficult to do accurately.

One alternative stronger joint has the splined part cut square and only the outer corner mitered (Fig. 10-14B).

BUILT-UP MOLDING

Elaborate moldings are not usually cut from one solid piece, but they are built up from several pieces. The technique reached its peak in Victorian days, but the method is useful today for more modest moldings and is essential when making reproduction Victorian furniture or refurbishing a home of that period (Fig. 10-15).

An advantage of using many parts is the economy of wood. Cutting some moldings from solid wood might result in more wood going to waste than is left in the finished piece. Another advantage is the ease of working. A shape can be made on a strip of wood of a size easy to handle, yet it will build into a complex section. You can work shapes that would be undercut in a solid molding, but the cutting can be done with normal hand or power tools when worked in a part.

In the assembled section the parts must be kept in the correct relation to each other. That can be ensured by working tongues and grooves between most of them. They need not go very deep as their purpose is location rather than strength. In some parts of the section they may disguise the meeting of two pieces of wood, where there might be a gap visible if they were merely brought together and glued. A tongue that is not pulled as tightly into its groove as it should be will still present a clean appearance to the front, where a

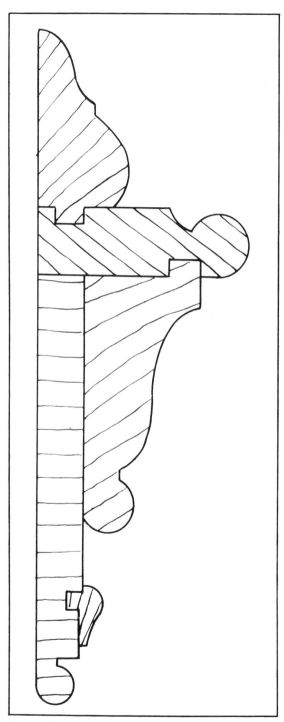

Fig. 10-15. Large moldings may be built up using parts tongued together.

slight discrepancy in meeting flat surfaces would be obvious.

FALSE EDGES

Besides putting on a solid wood edge to cover the edges of the veneers in plywood, it is sometimes necessary to give a more massive appearance to an edge, so the whole thing looks bigger and thicker than it is. This may happen at the base or top of a cabinet or block of shelves. Even when fairly thick plywood is used, the piece of furniture may look better if its edge is increased in size.

There may be a solid molding with a tongue into a groove in the plywood (Fig. 10-16A)—not projecting much and with a section anywhere between a simple curved nosing and complex mixture of beads and quirks. This may have to extend further, possibly to take an adjoining piece that would be better joined to solid wood. The edge may project some way, and the joint to the plywood would be better hidden further back. In that case the molding can have a more elongated section (Fig. 10-16B).

If the plywood and its surround are to form the base for a decorative veneer, the veneer might go to a suitable edge on the surround (Fig. 10-16C) for all-over coverage. If the added solid wood is to form a border to the veneer, that might be added to the plywood first and the whole thing enclosed by the border (Fig. 10-16D). Another way, which reduces the risk of the levels not all matching, takes the veneer over into a shallow rabbet in the solid wood (Fig. 10-16E).

These borders make the plywood look thicker than it would without the edging, but to actually make the edge thicker, the border should extend below the plywood and go further under it than the top reaches (Fig. 10-16F). This gives valuable extra glue area. Besides letting a tongue of the solid wood go into the plywood, this construction also allows the plywood to be rabbeted to go into a groove plowed in the border piece (Fig. 10-16G). Apart from the more solid appearance, the thicker front may be useful in providing stiffness that might otherwise have had to come from a strip put across underneath.

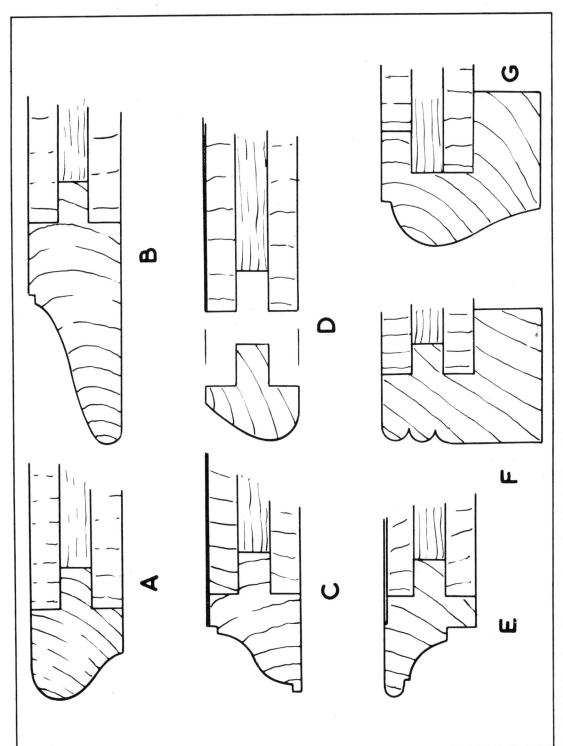

Fig. 10-16. False edges of many sorts may be added to plywood.

215

Chapter 11

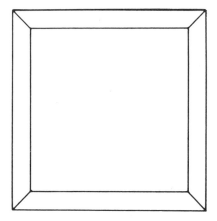

Mitered and Coopered Joints

A MITER IS THE LINE BETWEEN TWO PLANE surfaces meeting. The most common form is seen in the corner of a picture frame where two pieces of molding of equal width meet at 90 degrees. The angle of the miter is then 45 degrees (Fig. 11-1A).

A coopered joint gets its name from barrel-making. The craftsman who makes wooden barrels is a *cooper*. The joints are similar to miters, except their angles depend on the number of parts (staves in a barrel) making up a circle (Fig. 11-1B).

GEOMETRY OF MITERS

If two parts of equal width meet, the miter between them bisects the angle, so with a square corner half of 90 degrees is 45 degrees (Fig. 11-2A). The same rule applies if the joint is other than square. Geometric bisecting gives the angle. From the corner mark arcs of the same radius on the sides, then with these crossings as centers strike two crossing arcs (Fig. 11-2B). A line from the corner through this crossing will be the miter line,

whether it is an acute corner (Fig. 11-2C) or an obtuse one (Fig. 11-2D).

A miter can be between parts of different widths meeting in the same way. The miter line joins their outer and inner face crossings squarely (Fig. 11-2E) or at another angle (Fig. 11-2F). The sides of a frame may taper, but the corner angles are marked by drawing the lines to cross (Fig. 11-2G).

If a plain curved piece meets a straight piece, you can draw a line between outer and inner corners (Fig. 11-3A). If the two parts are molded and you do this, comparable parts on the two pieces will not meet correctly on a straight miter. Instead, the miter that will bring the molding parts together has to be cut with a curve.

To get this curve, set out full-size a section of the molding with the key parts projected to the corner (Fig. 11-3B). Do the same with the curved part; draw the outside first. If it is part of a circle, use compasses or trammels (Fig. 11-4) or a strip of wood with a pencil at the end and an awl for the center (Fig. 11-3C).

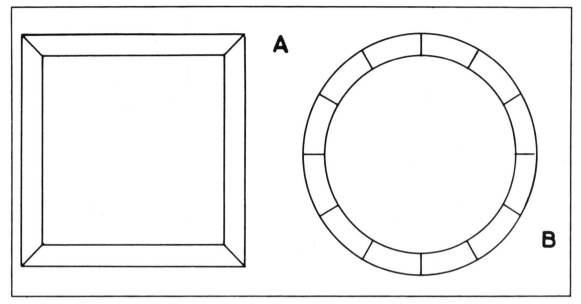

Fig. 11-1. A miter comes at a corner. It is a coopered joint where the parts make up a circle.

If the curve is not part of a circle, draw the outside and make other lines parallel to it by measuring at intervals and drawing curves through the marks.

Draw from a section of the molding on the curve lines to cross similar ones projected on the straight side. If it is a molding with wide curves in it, draw lines across the curve at the same locations each way (Fig. 11-3D). Bend a piece of steel or plastic through the crossings and draw along it to get the curve of the miter (Fig. 11-3E). If the line does not go cleanly through all crossings, check your drawing again. The amount of curve may only be slight. You may decide that a straight line will be a sufficient approximation. If there is much curve in the developed miter, it should be followed in top-notch work.

In some cabinetwork the curved molding may be wider than the straight one, but the shape of the miter is found in the same way (Fig. 11-3F). The same methods apply if two curved moldings meet; their sections are projected to the corners. If the curves are similar, the miter will be a straight line (Fig. 11-3G). Equal curves meeting have similar miters to straight parts meeting.

MITER CUTTING

If the parts are fairly large, a miter may be marked out, sawed and planed. There are miter squares (Fig. 11-5A) for the common 45-degree miter, or the angle may be included in a combination square (Fig. 11-5B). The square corner of a piece of paper folded on itself will give you 45 degrees (Fig. 11-5C). An adjustable bevel can be set with a protractor for this and any other miter angle.

A traditional saw guide for 45-degree miters is a miter block, which is cut from solid wood or built up (Fig. 11-6A). A better guide is a miter box, which controls the saw in two places (Fig. 11-6B). The better miter boxes have metal guides to bear against the sides of a backsaw blade (Fig. 11-6C).

Other miter guides have developed from the block and box. Most have the important metal parts, and there are clamping arrangements to hold the wood. In some the saw blade is part of the device. Others are intended for use with a fine backsaw.

Although the sawed miter may be used as is in some assemblies, it is too rough and ragged for good quality work. A sawed miter could be planed freehand, but it is better to have a guide. One is a

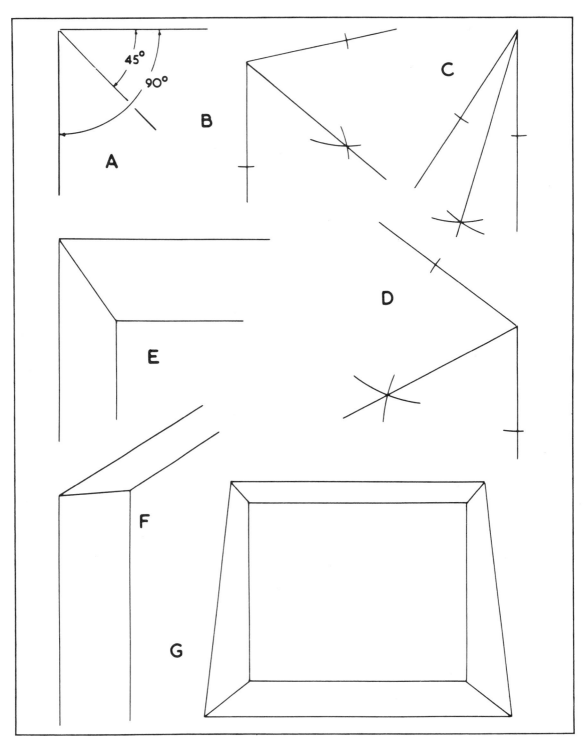

Fig. 11-2. A miter bisects the angle or divides the meeting surfaces of parts of different widths.

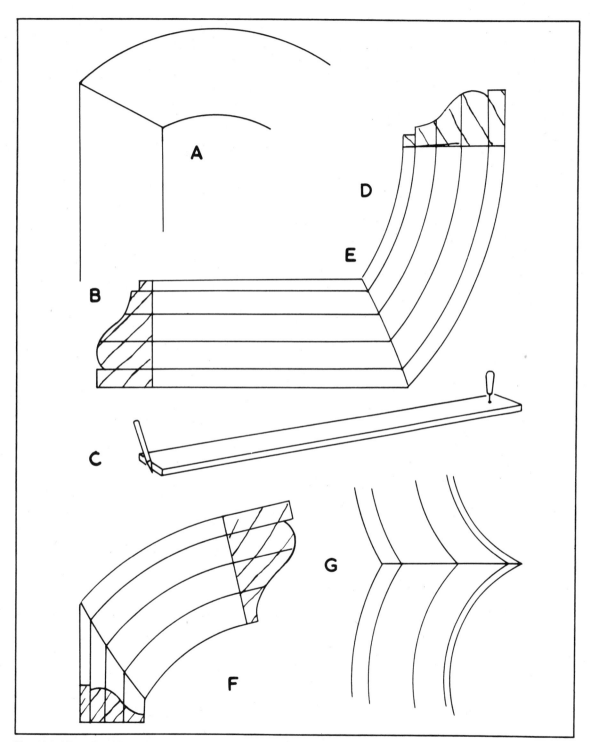

Fig. 11-3. Miters involving curves are not always straight.

Fig. 11-4. Trammel heads slide on a piece of wood, so they can be used for drawing curves of large radius.

form of shooting board with a central block to allow wood to be positioned either way (Fig. 11-6D). Another has the work the other way and is sometimes called a *donkey's ear* (Fig. 11-6E). A type of vise is called a *miter trap* (Fig. 11-6F).

A different and effective miter tool uses a swinging knife that makes a slicing cut either way. The sawed wood may be positioned either way for a smooth cut to be made with the grain (Fig. 11-6G).

PLAIN MITER

Two parts meeting in a miter may be glued (Fig. 11-7A), but the diagonal cut grain does not bond well with glue. In light picture frames where the load on each joint is not great, there may be a fine nail one way (Fig. 11-7B). Another may overlap the

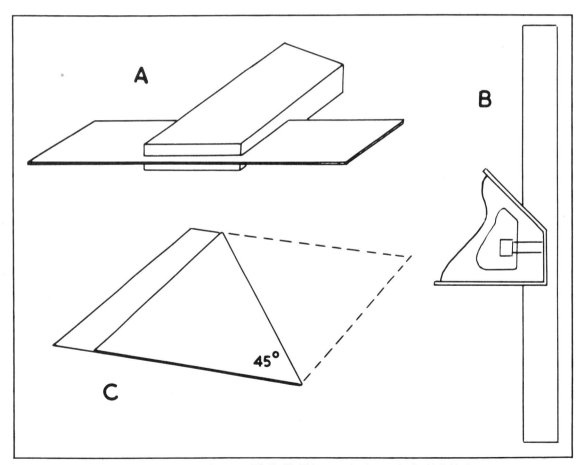

Fig. 11-5. A miter or combination square will mark 45° (A, B). This can also be marked with folded paper.

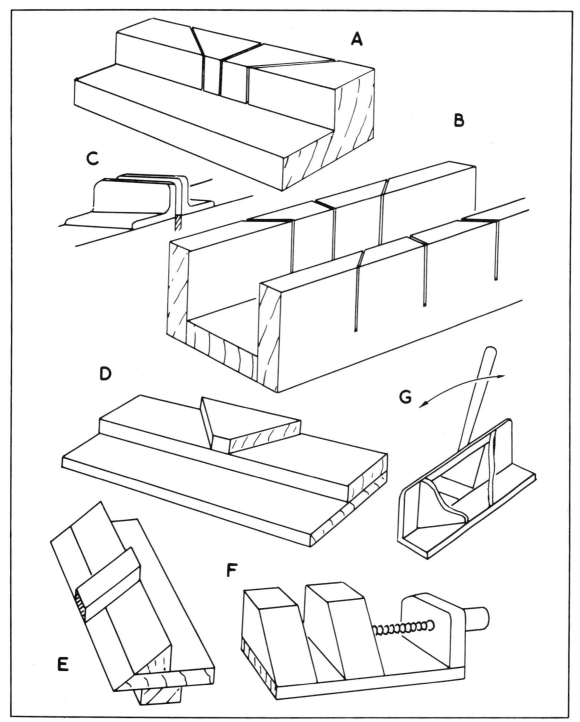

Fig. 11-6. A miter block (A) or miter box (B, C) will guide a saw for cutting miters. Devices are used to hold a miter for planing (D, E, F), or joints can be sliced (G).

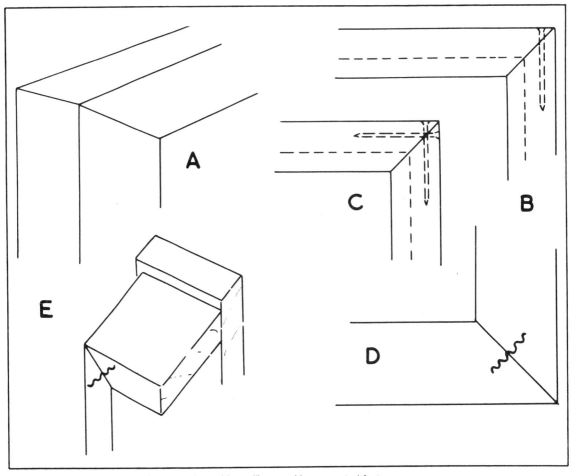

Fig. 11-7. A mitered joint may be strengthened by nailing or with corrugated fasteners.

other way (Fig. 11-7C). If the underside of a broad miter will not show, it could be reinforced with one or more corrugated fasteners (Fig. 11-7D). They could also be used under a miter between pieces on edge, where the top is secured to other parts, as in a furniture plinth (Fig. 11-7E).

There are corner clamps for pulling square miters together. One type has clamp screws for each piece. Another has a central screw to push the parts toward each other (Fig. 11-8). It may have jaws to fit into the rabbets of picture frame molding. Usually the part of the clamp where the frame corners meet is kept narrow so it is possible to drive nails. The corner can remain clamped while the glue sets.

DOWELED MITERS

Dowels between the meeting surfaces strengthen a miter joint considerably. Drilling must be carefully done (Fig. 11-9A). There is a problem in clamping, as the pressure must be square to the dowels. The best pressure comes from gluing on clamp blocks (Fig. 11-9B) that will have to be cut off later.

THROUGH DOWELED MITERS

If leaving the ends of dowels visible will not matter, the miter may be drilled across and dowels driven through (Fig. 11-10A). If the surface one way should be left plain, dowels can be driven into blind holes (Fig. 11-10B) diagonally, or you can drive them parallel with one side (Fig. 11-10C). The

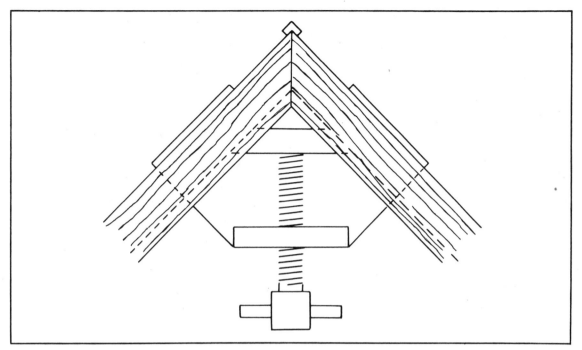

Fig. 11-8. A corner clamp pulls and holds mitered corners.

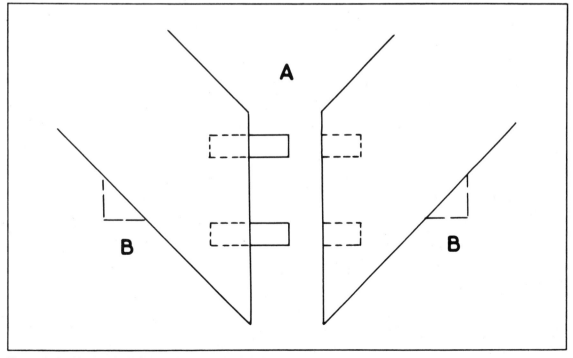

Fig. 11-9. A wide doweled joint may be strengthened with dowels.

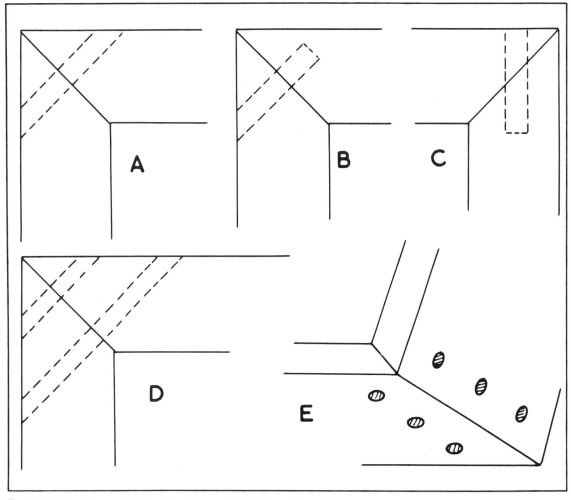

Fig. 11-10. Dowels may be taken through or partially into a miter.

inner dowel will be fairly long in a wide miter (Fig. 11-10D). Several dowels can be in an edgewise miter (Fig. 11-10E). Have the dowels too long and trim them level after the glue has set.

ANGLED DOWELED MITERS

Some plastic dowels are obtainable with two parts at 90 degrees (Fig. 11-11A). The advantage over straight dowels is that they allow a mitered corner to be pulled tight without the need for diagonal clamping. Holes have to be drilled opposite and square to each other. The dowels are glued into one piece (Fig. 11-11B). The other is brought to it (Fig.

11-11C). There can be hitting or clamping in the directions of the sides for tightening.

VENEERED MITER

A deep miter can be strengthened by diagonally grained pieces if strips of veneer are glued into saw cuts (Fig. 11-12A). The cuts may be square to the wood (Fig. 11-12B) or made diagonally (Fig. 11-12C). Saw cuts should be fairly deep and of a suitable width for the veneer. Pieces of veneer are glued in (Fig. 11-12D) and cut level afterward. The veneers will show in the finished joint, so the method is only suitable where that will not matter.

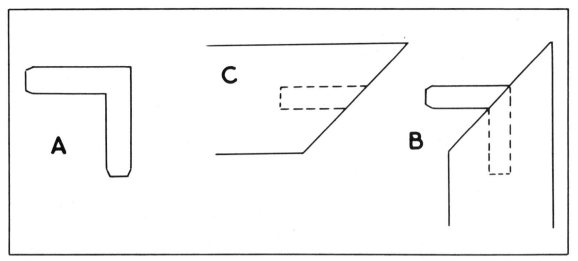

Fig. 11-11. Angled plastic dowels will strengthen a miter.

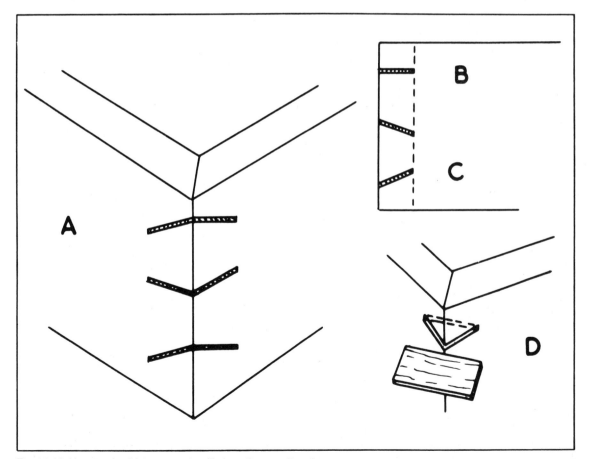

Fig. 11-12. Veneer glued into saw cuts will strengthen a mitered corner.

BLOCK REINFORCED MITER

Where only the outside surface will show, a narrow miter can be strengthened with a block glued inside (Fig. 11-13A). Screws could be used, too, and they may serve as clamps. The block is glued and screwed to one piece, then screws used to pull the other to it (Fig. 11-13B). If the inside will be seen occasionally, the block could be beveled to give a better appearance (Fig. 11-13C).

The block does not have to fit closely into the corner. It may tighten the joint better if its corner is cut off (Fig. 11-13D). Instead of a block, there could be a strut with a screw each way to draw the parts together (Fig. 11-13E).

STOPPED LAPPED MITER

A half lap at a corner (Fig. 4-6) may be cut to show a miter on one surface, but the halving details still show on the edges. If the strength of the half lap is required, but the edges and the front should show a miter, you can stop the lap behind the joint (Fig. 11-14A). The lap is made half the thickness and projects from the inner corner with stops in its width and length. Mark out the parts with miters on the front (Fig. 11-14B), but allow for the lap on the back (Fig. 11-14C).

Although the ideal joint would have every part meeting exactly as the joint is tightened, it is the miter that is important. Some clearance at the edges of the lap parts can be allowed, then they do not meet before the miter. If the back will not show, there can be screws and glue to hold the lap.

STOPPED TENONED MITER

If both sides of a miter will be visible and a strong

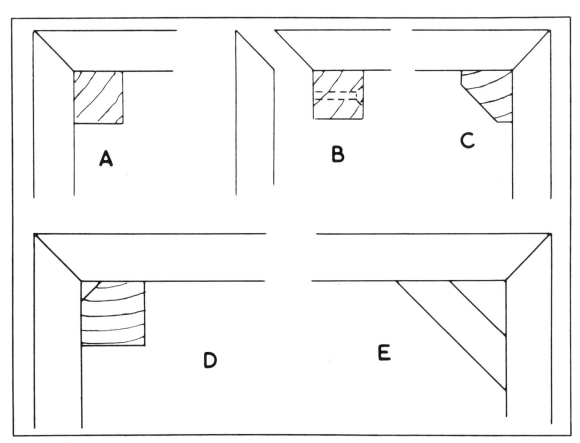

Fig. 11-13. There may be reinforcing blocks inside mitered corners.

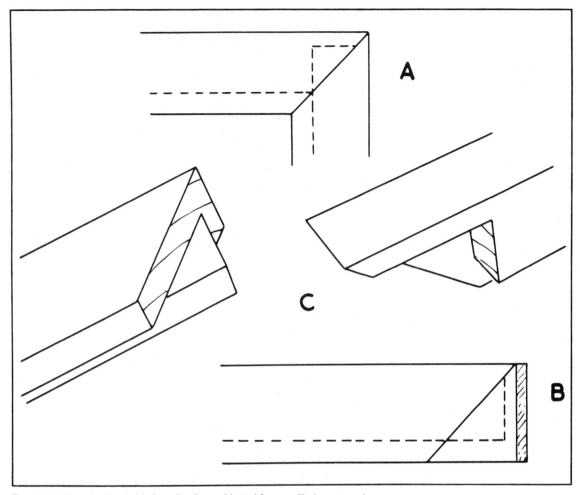

Fig. 11-14. A projection behind a miter in a rabbeted frame will give extra glue area.

joint is needed, a mortise and tenon joint can be incorporated. Both outer parts have plain miters, but at the center a tenon one part goes into a mortise in the other (Fig. 11-15A). It could be visualized as the stopped lapped miter joint with an extra mitered thickness behind it.

The mortise and tenon are one-third the thickness of the wood. Both pieces are marked with the miter cuts on both surfaces. One piece is marked with the tenon, too (Fig. 11-15B). After you have cut the outline, gauge the tenon thickness (Fig. 11-15C) and cut it. Cut the other piece on the miter line and gauge the mortise size (Fig. 11-15D). Drill and chisel out the waste. Note that this is square to

the strip surface. Be careful not to break out and damage the miter.

GEOMETRY OF COOPERED JOINTS

Coopered joints are miters between many similar parts that make up a cylinder or other curve. The edges usually meet as plain miters and are pulled and kept tight with metal bands. Although the parts may be finished as parts of a circle in section (Fig. 11-16A), their layout is with straight sections to make up a polygon of the desired number of sides (Fig. 11-16B). Curves may then be worked from the flat pieces.

A circle contains 360 degrees, so this has to be

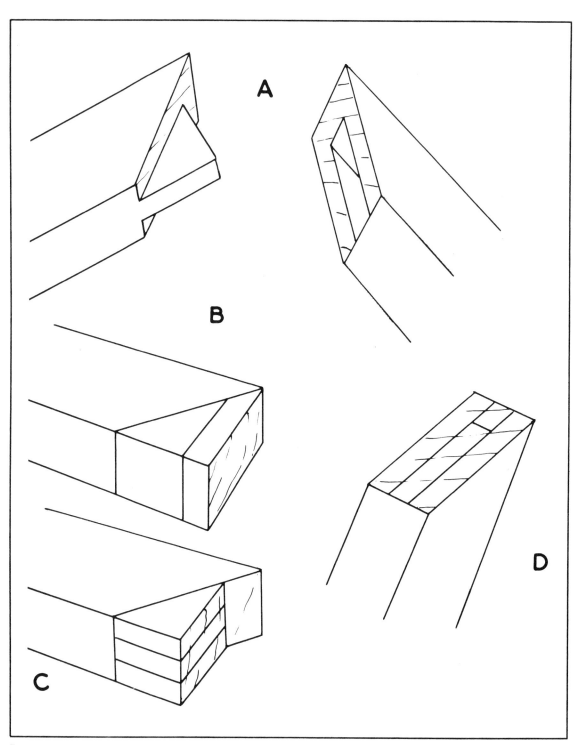

Fig. 11-15. Where the miter shows on both sides, it can be strengthened with a central tenon.

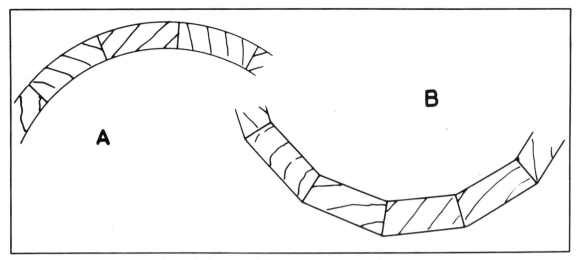

Fig. 11-16. A coopered joint is a form of miter cut radially.

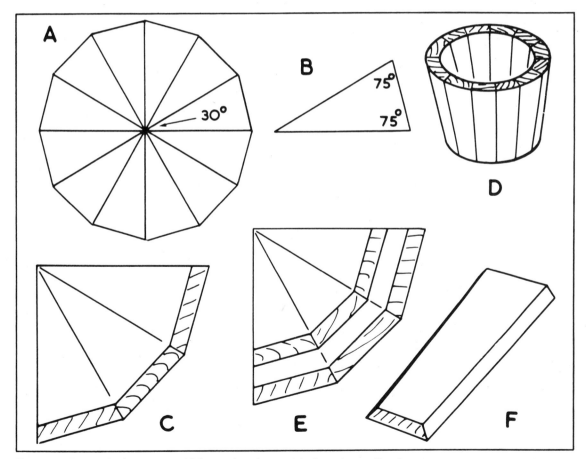

Fig. 11-17. The angles in a coopered joint are found geometrically and may allow for a taper.

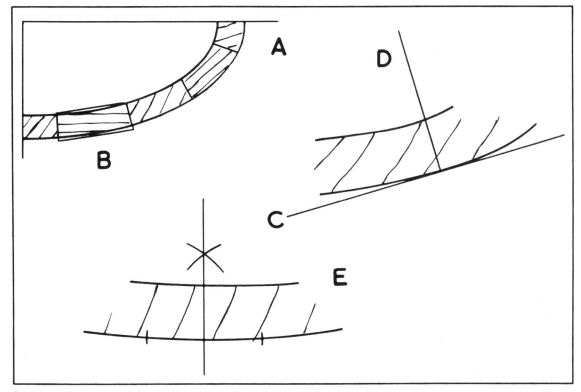

Fig. 11-18. Coopered joints come square to a tangent to the curve.

divided by the number of sides to project the shape of one or a group of sides. Suppose there will be 12 sides. The angle to project will then be 30 degrees (Fig. 11-17A). The sum of the three angles in any triangle must be 180 degrees. If you deduct 30 degrees from this, you get 150 degrees for the total of the other two. As they are equal, they must each be 75 degrees (Fig. 11-17B).

That gives you the angle of edge bevel for any barrel or other polygonal assembly made up of 12 sides, but it does not give you the widths of the pieces. You must set out the shape full-size or to scale. There is no need to set out the full circle unless you need to have an odd number of sides that cannot be divided. In this example a one-fourth circle will do (Fig. 11-17C).

If you are laying out a tapered shape, such as a bucket (Fig. 11-17D), the layout to obtain stave widths must be drawn for top and bottom (Fig. 11-17E). The end shapes may be joined for the

shape of each stave (Fig. 11-17F). In a barrel that is thicker at the center than the ends, the cooper works with center and end widths. The bevel of edge is obtained geometrically, but the curve in the length is estimated.

IRREGULAR CURVE MITERS

If a barrel or bucket is to be made elliptical or a curve other than round, each miter between staves will be at a different angle. This also applies to a flat frame made up of several pieces to give an elliptical or other curved outline. There is no way that the angles can be calculated, and the shape must be set out full-size or to scale. If it is symmetrical, you need only draw a part. One-fourth will be enough for an ellipse (Fig. 11-18A). Mark where joints are to come. Spacing will usually be determined by the thicknesses of wood from which the curved pieces will be cut (Fig. 11-18B).

Position draw tangents to the curve at each

joint (Fig. 11-18C). Draw lines square to the tangent at the point of contact with the curve (Fig. 11-18D). That indicates the miter line.

Another way of getting the same result is to step off marks equal distances each side of the miter position and strike crossing arcs from them (Fig. 11-18E). Do not step very far each side of the miter position; about the wood thickness will be enough. Otherwise, the angle will be affected by the different amount of curve. A line through the crossing arcs will be the miter.

If you have to make up part of a circle, but the radius is so great that you cannot reach the center, miters can be marked in the same way as for other curves with tangents or stepped compass marks.

There are tools for drawing lines square to curves, (Fig. 11-19), but they are more appropriate for marking wood already curved. Another use is for finding the center of a circular piece. The principle is the same as the geometric construction just described. There are two forms: two pegs with a blade bisecting a line between them (Fig. 11-20A) or a square cornered stock with a bisecting blade (Fig. 11-20B). A version is available as a sliding head on a combination square.

To find the center of a circle, the tool is pressed against the circumference. A line is drawn. This is repeated at another position and where the lines cross is the center. For marking miters or any other lines square to a curve, the tool is held against the curve, outside or inside, and a line drawn (Fig. 11-20C).

SPLINED MITER JOINT

Two parts meeting with a plain miter may both be plowed to take a spline (Fig. 11-21A). This could be a piece of plywood, although the greatest strength comes from a solid wood spline with its grain across (Fig. 11-21B). The ends of the spline will show in the finished joint, so this is only suitable where that will not matter. If it would be better not to cut the exposed edge, either inside or outside, the groove could be cut partway (Fig. 11-21C). If the method is used with both ends of the slots closed, the result is more like an inserted tenon across the joint (Fig. 11-21D).

Fig. 11-19. A center square is used for drawing lines square to a curved edge or for finding the center of a circular piece. There may be two pegs to bear against a curved edge, or an angled sliding head on a straightedge may be used in a similar way on curves of any size.

SPLINED COOPERED JOINT

When two parts meet with a miter along their lengthwise edges, a groove could be in each part similar to the previous example, except the proportions of the joint are different (Fig. 11-22A). It may be more convenient to use plywood or a spline with the grain lengthwise, but a cross-grained spline would be strongest.

A problem comes in clamping this joint. There may have to be glued clamp blocks provided outside to be trimmed off afterward. If the joint is part of an all-round assembly (Fig. 11-22B), there can be a circular clamp, or it may be possible to use rope around the parts and tighten with wood pushed through and twisted. Pad under the rope at the angles.

RABBETED HALVED MITER

If rabbeted wood has to be mitered and a joint is needed that is stronger than the usual picture frame type of miter with nails, screws, or dowels, the parts can be halved. Usually it is possible to arrange the cut to come inside the edge of the rabbet (Fig. 11-23A). Besides glue, you can drive one or more screws from the back.

The simple joint leaves end grain visible on

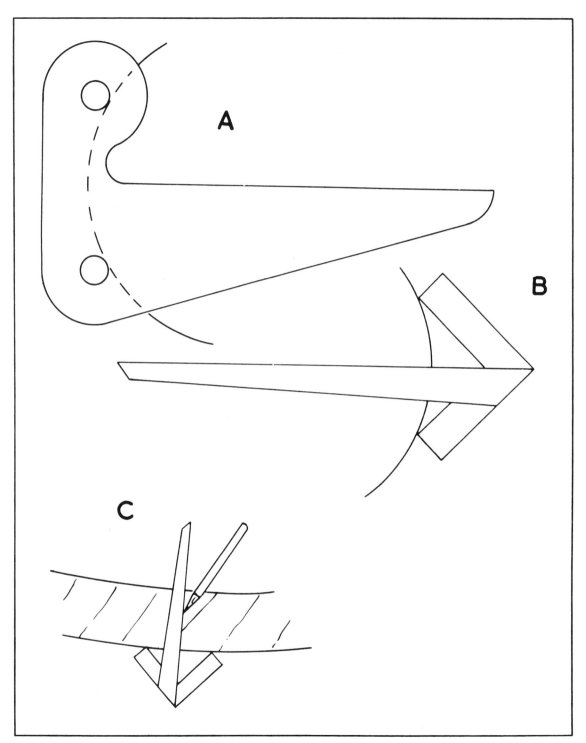

Fig. 11-20. Center squares rest against a curve so the marking edge comes square to it.

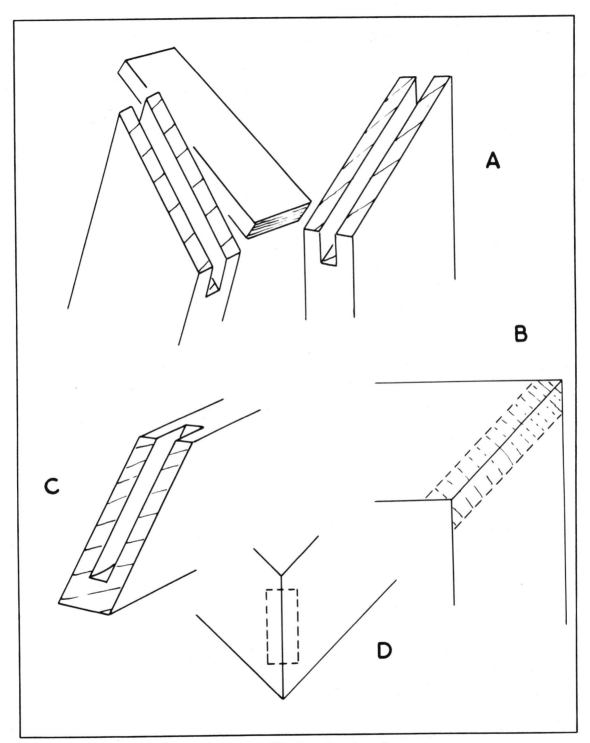

Fig. 11-21. Splines may be put across mitered joints, either through or stopped.

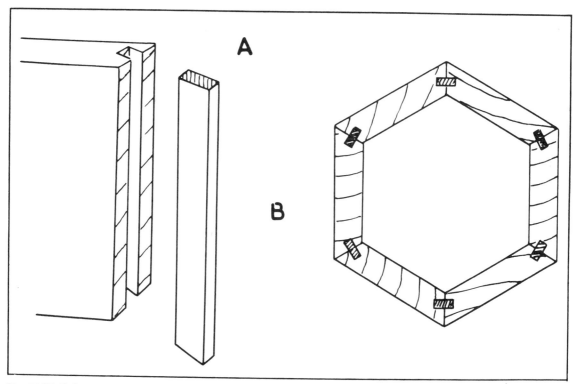

Fig. 11-22. Splines across coopered joints will strengthen them in the same way as a miter.

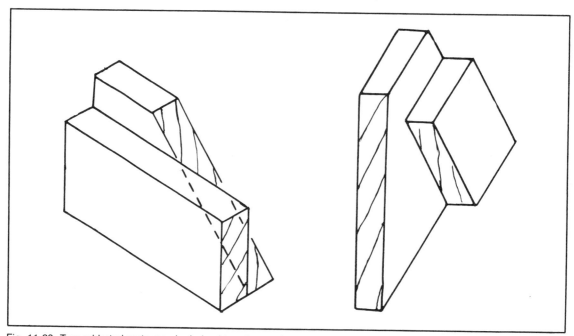

Fig. 11-23. Two rabbeted parts may be halved together and the wider parts cut with a miter.

one edge. If this is undesirable, the joint can be cut to hide it in the same way as described for the stopped lapped miter (Fig. 11-14).

RABBETED TENONED MITER

A tenon instead of a lapped piece can be in rabbeted parts if the rabbet is less than one-half the thickness and preferably near one-third thickness. If the rabbet is more than half the thickness, there has to be some awkward cutting to make a mortise and tenon joint of reasonable proportions.

There is some similarity between this joint and the rabbeted halved miter joint, but it is convenient to divide the thickness of the wood into three, although the proportions may be altered slightly to match the edge of the rabbet (Fig. 11-24). The tenon and its matching groove are shown outside the rabbet. If it is a form with the front molded to the rabbet, it is simpler to bring the tenon completely into the thickness of the rabbet, even if that means relative thicknesses differing from thirds.

If it would be better not to show end grain outside in one or both directions, the joint can be cut to hide the ends in a similar way to that described

for the plain stopped tenoned miter (Fig. 11-15). Screws or dowels may be driven into the joint from the back for extra strength.

MASON'S MITER

Where molding comes inside a frame of solid wood, as it may in a rabbeted frame, parts of the frame may continue through, usually with mortise and tenon joints. The molding will be mitered or at least it has the appearance of being mitered (Fig. 11-25A). This applies whether the molding is worked in the solid wood or is prepared in strip form and added.

Another way of dealing with the corner is to scribe one part of the molding over the other (Fig. 11-25B). See Chapter 6. One section of molding goes through, but the end of the other has to be shaped to fit over it. The appearance at the front is of a miter. Scribing is difficult to do with elaborate sections. A joint cannot be scribed if parts of the molding section are undercut. Scribing is only suitable for internal corners. The method cannot be used where moldings on the outside edge of a mitered corner are involved.

In stonework a mason may work a molding in a

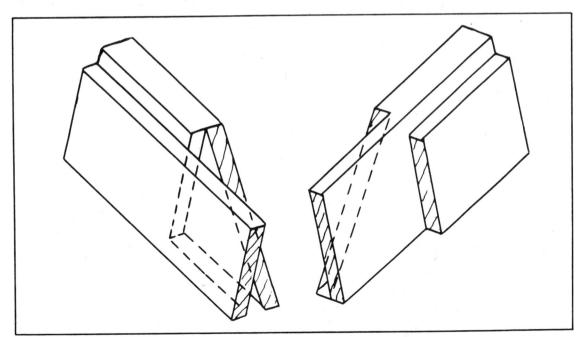

Fig. 11-24. If there is a narrow rabbet, a mitered bridle joint may be cut in the thicker part.

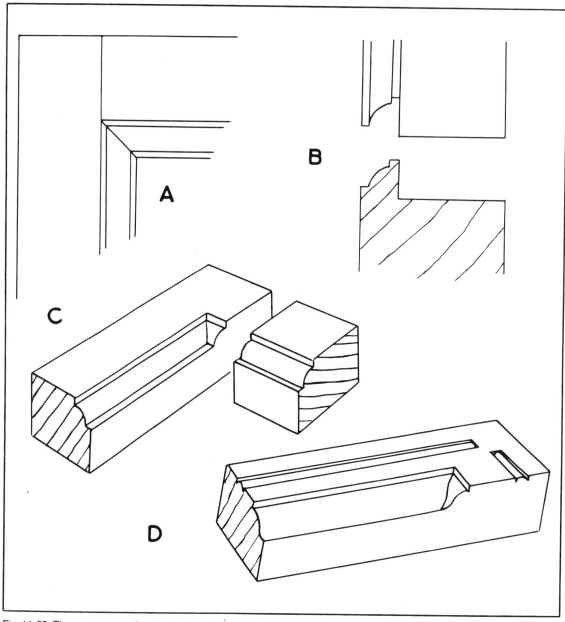

Fig. 11-25. The appearance of a mitered molding (A) may be given by scribing one piece over the other (B). A mason's miter is based on stonework, but it may be cut in wood when the return angle is cut in one piece (C, D).

different way (Fig. 11-25C) with the return cut in one piece so the other block butts against it to continue the pattern. A mason's miter was used by some old woodworking craftsmen and may have to be reproduced in restoration or reproduction of antiques, but otherwise it does not have practical applications today.

In stonework or antique woodwork based on it, surface patterns and edge moldings may be worked in one piece instead of a miter being cut. There is a

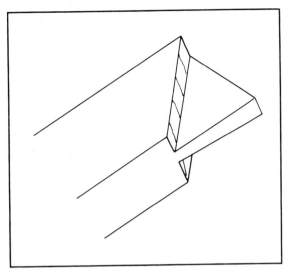

Fig. 11-26. A tenon through a bridle joint may be cut at a dovetail angle to provide extra strength in one direction.

If the tenon is to go through, it is marked and cut like a normal tenon, but one or both sides are tapered. It is simpler to taper one side (Fig. 11-26). If the tenon is cut and tapered first, the mortise may be made to suit. Only a slight taper usually is possible, unless the wood is very thick. This is enough to provide strength and a pull to close the joint as it is driven together.

SOLID KEYED MITER

Using pieces of veneer in saw cuts across a miter is a simple way of reinforcing the joint, but greater strength may be required. That can be provided by making keys of thicker wood. They can be let in like the veneers, but with larger slots (Fig. 11-27A), with one or more across the joint. The key strength is increased if the slots are deep, but cutting away too much for thick keys may weaken the main parts. Cut the keys too long and trim them after the glue has set.

Strength is increased by making the keys sloping in cross section to give a dovetail effect (Fig. 11-27B). The slope need not be much and can be on one or both sides of the key. A key fitted across a miter in this way is called a *feather*.

simple butt meeting (usually with a tenon in wood), so the design matches the other way (Fig. 11-25D) and is called a *bishop's miter*.

DOVETAIL TENONED MITER

A tenon on one part can be given a tapered section instead of having parallel sides. This can be arranged to resist pulling apart in one direction in the same way as a dovetail joint.

TAPERED MITER

A box or frame may be made with a taper square to

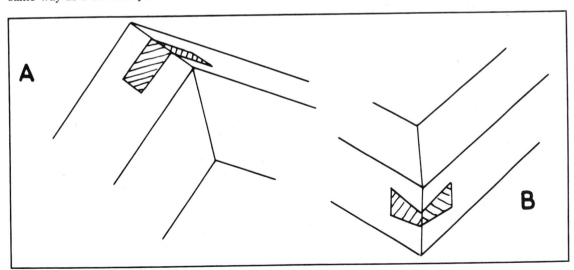

Fig. 11-27. A solid key may go across a miter (A) and is stronger if it is given a dovetail section (B).

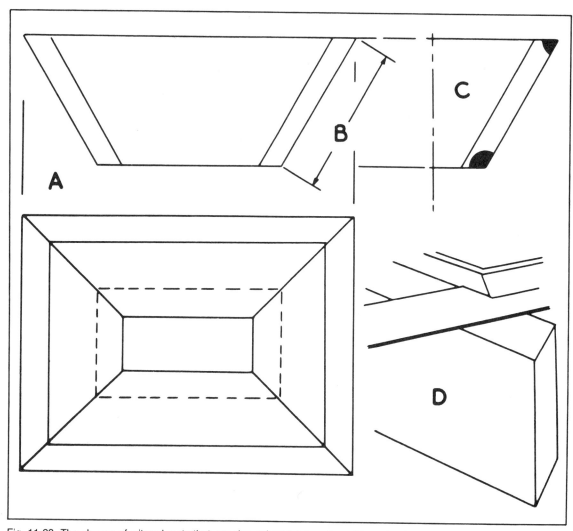

Fig. 11-28. The shapes of mitered parts that are also splayed outward must be set out geometrically.

the direction of the miter. There could be considerable depth, as in a box or hopper, or the whole thing may be fairly shallow, but flared, as in a frame that is wider at the front than the back.

Draw two elevations and a plan, either completely or half each view (Fig. 11-28A). You then can get the actual depth of each outside surface (Fig. 11-28B) and the angles of top and bottom edges (Fig. 11-28C). If the bottom is to be parallel with the top, allow extra width for planing that bevel. The drawings give you the lengths along the top and bottom outside edges. Mark these and the

corner angles with a miter or combination square held flat on the top and bottom surfaces (Fig. 11-28D). Draw lines between the inner ends of the miter marks on the inner surfaces. They will give you the inner surfaces of the cuts. If you need to test the miters after cutting, hold the miter square parallel with the top edge. The angle is different squarely across the surface. If you want to find this angle, the method is shown in Fig. 9-27.

REAR FEATHERED MITER

If the back of a plain miter does not show, the joint

238

can be strengthened with a spline or feather across the meeting surfaces. In the simplest form this is a small straight strip of wood with its grain across the joint. It is let into grooves as deep as may be cut without the risk of affecting the front surface (Fig. 11-29A). You can use more than one feather with wide boards. Giving the grooves and feather a slight taper will make the joint tighten when the feather is driven in.

The dovetail action of a butterfly feather will further strengthen the joint (Fig. 11-29B). This needs careful cutting, but if the feather is made first, it can be marked round on the miter. A slight taper in the depth will cause the parts to tighten as the feather is pressed in.

In some assemblies a butterfly feather at the front may be regarded as decoration. The effect could be heightened further by also using a dovetail spline across the corner (Fig. 11-27B) in a similar wood, possibly both contrasting with the base wood.

A rear feather could be used to strengthen some of the other versions of the miter joint. For instance, either type of feather could be used at the back of a lapped miter joint (Fig. 11-29C).

LIPPED MITER

When a corner brings the end grain of the parts together, one of the methods of strengthening just described can be used. If one of the parts has side grain, as when a rail comes to an upright part and a miter is needed, the strengthening can be arranged in the solid wood instead of being an inserted piece.

The rail may have a tenon into the other part (Fig. 11-30A) instead of a feather, which has to be kept fairly narrow to avoid weakening the end grain. If there is enough width for it, a dovetail is better (Fig. 11-30B) as it pulls the parts together and makes a close miter easier to achieve. If the rail is very wide, there could be more than one dovetail (Fig. 11-30C). The dovetails stiffen the end and help it to resist warping.

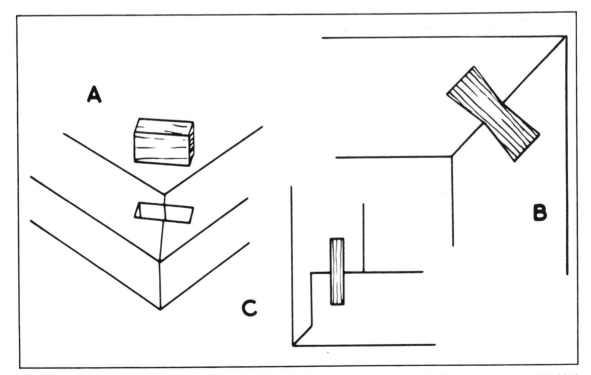

Fig. 11-29. A feather may go across the rear of a miter (A) and is stronger as a dovetail butterfly (B). It could also be used behind a lapped miter (C).

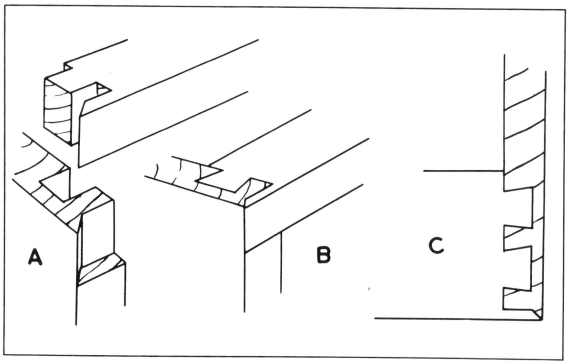

Fig. 11-30. A rail notched into end grain can have a lipped front.

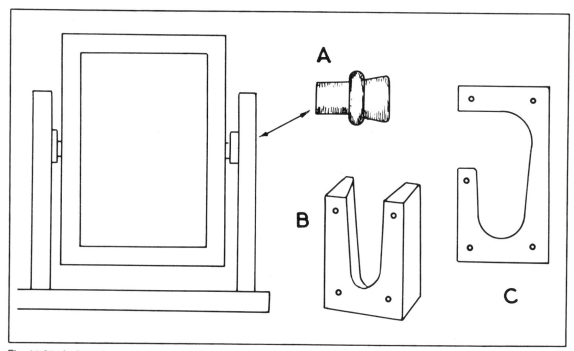

Fig. 11-31. A pivoted support gets increased friction by sloping the support and peg.

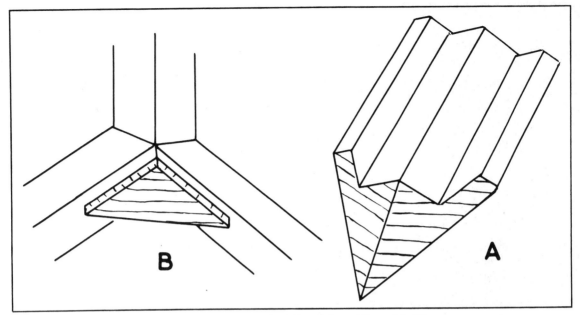

Fig. 11-32. Three pieces can be mitered (A), but they should be reinforced if possible (B).

DOVETAIL SOCKET

If a framed mirror is put in a stand so it can be tilted, the supporting arrangement should allow the mirror to be moved to any angle and preferably stay there controlled by friction. Supporting pivots will prevent the uprights opening or splaying in use, and an added advantage would be the facility for lifting the mirror out of its stand. Some metal pivots do not provide enough friction to hold the mirror angle without a strut, and they may allow the supports to spread so the mirror falls out.

This pivot is a turned hardwood peg with a dowel to fit into the side of the mirror frame, a shoulder to provide clearance, and an end turned to a dovetail taper (Fig. 11-31A). One form of socket is shaped like a U. Its inner edges are tapered to match the peg (Fig. 11-31B). Another version has an opening at the front (Fig. 11-31C). The tapered socket allows easy insertion, but at the bottom the peg should be a fairly tight fit.

THREE-WAY MITER

If three strips are to meet as in the corner of a glass-paneled showcase, where the angle each way is 90 degrees, the surfaces look best if they are mitered. The strongest corner includes a dovetail and a special mortise and tenon (Fig. 9-31), but for economy or speed it may be sufficient to use plain miters.

Mark the ends with 45-degree miters on their outer surfaces both ways. Cut these squarely inward until they meet (Fig. 11-32A). The section shown has rabbets for the glass, but the method is the same whatever the section. All three pieces are the same, but they obviously must be at the exact angles for a close fit.

This joint does not have the strength of the other one. It depends mainly on closely fitting glued surfaces, but there are ways of reinforcing it. The top and bottom of a showcase may not be visible normally, so thin triangular pieces can be added and kept back a little from the outside edges (Fig. 11-32B). At the bottom they will act as feet.

Glue two pieces and let the glue dry before adding the third. Otherwise, it is difficult to keep all the parts in line. Thin nails could be driven upward from each bottom piece into the upright. The triangular cover piece is put over the nailheads.

Chapter 12

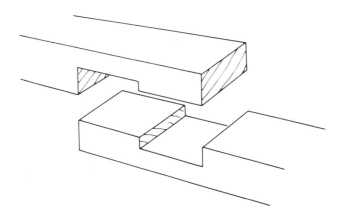

Scarfing

WHEN PIECES OF WOOD HAVE TO BE JOINED end to end, the collective name may be scarfing, but there are other names for particular joints. The method for joining the parts depends on circumstances. If an endwise joint is supported by being attached to other things, it does not have to be very strong. Nearly all of the joints have to allow the wood to continue through in the same section without projections, which makes it difficult to have enough strength in the joint, particularly if there is no other support. If it does not matter if there is thickening at the joint, a much stronger joint can be made.

You should have a piece of wood going right through in one piece where possible. No end-to-end joint can be as strong as solid wood, although some joints come close. In furniture and other wooden constructions of comparable sizes, there is usually no need for any form of scarfing as sizes are easily met with full-length pieces. It is in building and other large projects that pieces of wood have to be joined to make up lengths. In many cases the wood is of quite large section. When planning scarfing,

you should arrange the joints on or near supports so they are relieved of bending strains, which are the main contributors toward failure. A scarf a long way from supports may develop sagging, possibly some time after installation.

Many traditional scarfing methods were developed before strong waterproof glues. They are arranged to get the maximum strength mechanically and usually without glue. These joints still have uses, but where modern glues can be used, their strength is increased considerably.

SIMPLE SCARF

No glue can hold strongly on end grain only. The greatest glue strength comes between parts meeting on their side grain surfaces. If parts are to join so they finish in the same line, a joint has to be devised that gets the benefit of side grain while not weakening the parts with cuts. Sloping the meeting surfaces by at least 1 in 7 is sufficient to give good glue-holding surfaces (Fig. 12-1A). With suitable waterproof glues, this is accepted for making up lengths in boatbuilding. Glue does not bend exactly

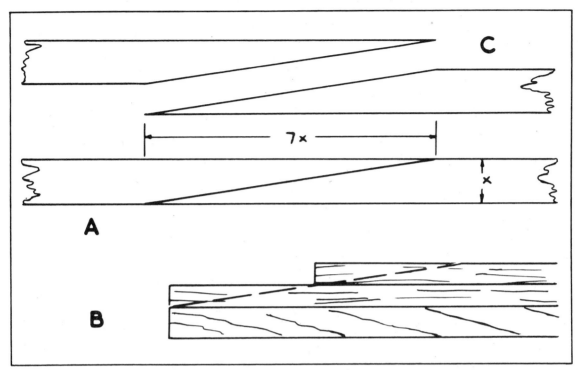

Fig. 12-1. Cutting ends at a long angle gives a good glue area in a scarf.

like the wood it joins, but this scarf can be used for wood that has to be sprung to moderate curves.

The two parts can be planed to match with minimal marking out by overlapping them by the length of the joint at the end of the bench or a stiff board (Fig. 12-1B). A straight slope taken to feather-edges will result in a good fit when the top piece is turned on the other (Fig. 12-1C).

This scarf is also used for joining pieces of plywood to make up lengths of panels, such as are needed when covering boat hulls. The bevels have to be carefully planed in the same way as suggested for long strips.

END LAP JOINT

The half lap joint can be used endwise. If the two parts will have other support, the joint need be no longer than the width of the wood (Fig. 12-2A). This gives enough area for glue and screws. If the joint has to provide stiffness without much other support, it is better to make the lap longer (Fig. 12-2B).

A weakness in this joint is the abrupt change of section, and that would be where breakage may occur. This can be relieved by tapering the ends (Fig. 12-2C), preferably fairly acutely for a glued joint. Strength should then be comparable with the previous joint, but it would be more difficult to cut accurately.

TAPERED END LAP JOINTS

The simple lap joint can be given some resistance to pulling apart by beveling the meeting pieces (Fig. 12-3A). This is a variation on the short simple lap, where other support is available. It reduces the thickness of the wood too much at the shoulders to be very strong in itself.

A taper the other way (Fig. 12-3B) has the advantage of not cutting away either part very much while providing glue surfaces similar to the simple scarf. This joint is used for joining planks in the skin of a boat. The joints are arranged the same way for a repair, with the outside thin edges pointing aft, so there is less risk of them becoming caught on any-

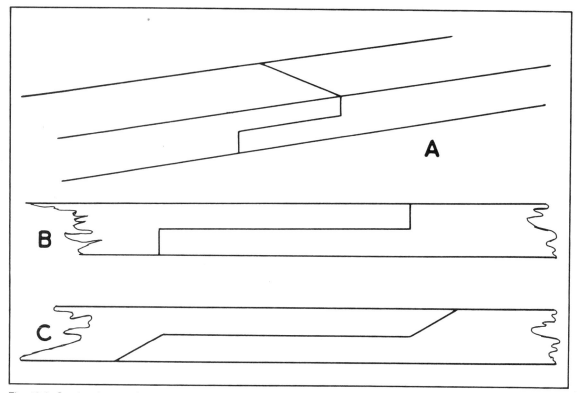

Fig. 12-2. Overlapping meeting ends gives increased glue area in a joint.

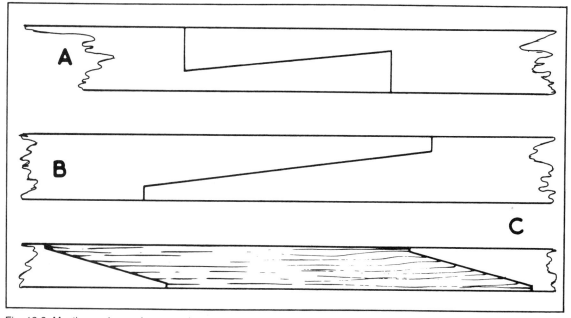

Fig. 12-3. Meeting ends may be tapered.

thing that might tear them back (Fig. 12-3C). Such a joint was developed for use with a sealant between the boards and strength provided by rivets or screws. It could be used with glue if the parts are made to fit close enough. The slope should be as long as can conveniently be arranged, but careful paring with chisels is needed. You should not have too slender a taper with softwood because of weakening at the thinner end.

ROOFING SCARF JOINT

A joint similar to the one used for boat planks is also used for extending purlins and other parts in the roof of a house. The wood section may be square or deeper than it is wide. As a guide to marking out, the center of the lap should be at half thickness (Fig.

12-4A). The taper chosen is moderate and may vary according to the thickness available. You could use wood screws, but bolts through are more common (Fig. 12-4B). In most situations the top surface has to follow through level, so bolt heads are either countersunk or let in. The underside need not be level, so it can be strengthened with more wood screwed on and drilled for the bolts (Fig. 12-4C). There may be a steel plate extending far enough to stiffen the joint (Fig. 12-4D). Putting a steel strap underneath makes it a plated scarf joint. A piece of wood underneath is a *fishplate*, and the result is a fished scarf joint.

BASIC FISHED JOINT

A joint can be made with strips of wood at each side

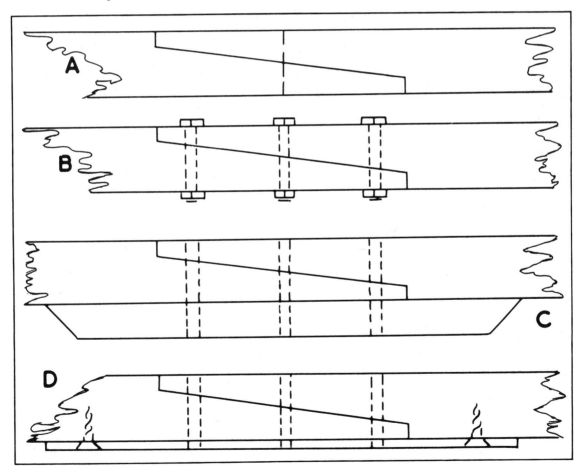

Fig. 12-4. In roofing joints parts may be bolted together and can be reinforced with wood or metal below.

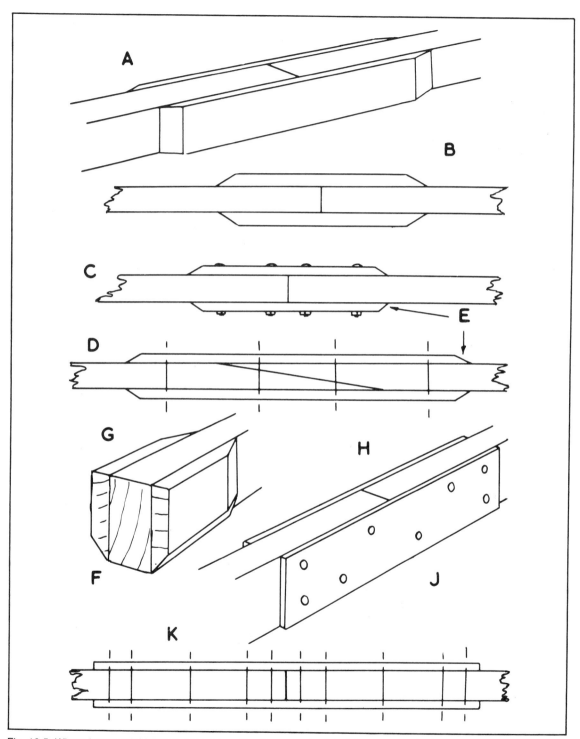

Fig. 12-5. Where increased thickness does not matter, there can be fishplates at one or both sides of meeting ends.

246

of the meeting ends. In most situations it is unnecessary for all four surfaces to follow through level. Suppose top and bottom have to be level, but the sides do not matter. Strips can be screwed or bolted on the sides (Fig. 12-5A). The longer the strips are, the less will be the risk of the joint sagging under load, and the stronger will be the joint. An overlap of about three times the depth on each piece may be considered reasonable (Fig. 12-5B).

The meeting ends may be cut square, then the joint secured with bolts (Fig. 12-5C). If glue is being used, the ends could be tapered to 1 in 7. The bolts are arranged to go through the laps and the full section wood beyond (Fig. 12-5D).

The ends of the fishplates could be cut square, but if they are visible, tapered ends would look better (Fig. 12-5E). Edges could also be tapered (Fig. 12-5F). If top or bottom surface will be bearing against other parts, though, the extra bearing surface of a flat edge may be preferable (Fig. 12-5G).

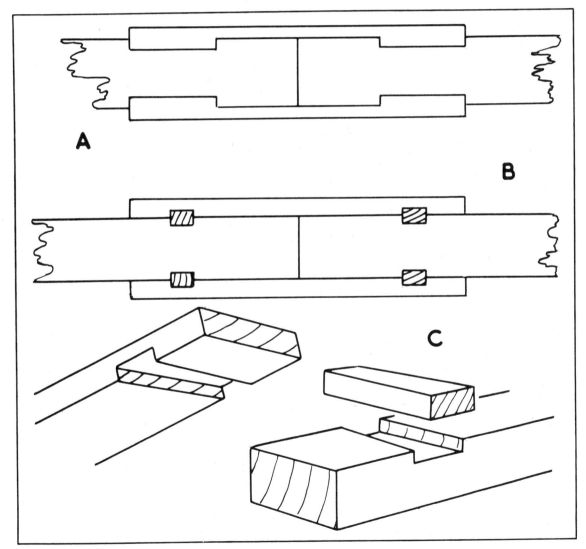

Fig. 12-6. Notched fished joints resist endwise loads.

The fishplates could be steel (Fig. 12-5H). If there is sufficient width, the bolt holes could be staggered to avoid getting them all in one line of grain (Fig. 12-5J). In any bolted joint of this type, whether using wood or metal, the bolts providing the greatest resistance to bending loads are those near the ends of both the meeting parts and the ends of the fishplates. In a large joint, they could usefully be arranged closer there than intermediately (Fig. 12-5K). For some stock sizes of wood used in building, there are special metal fishplates with edges turned over to either lap on the wood sur-

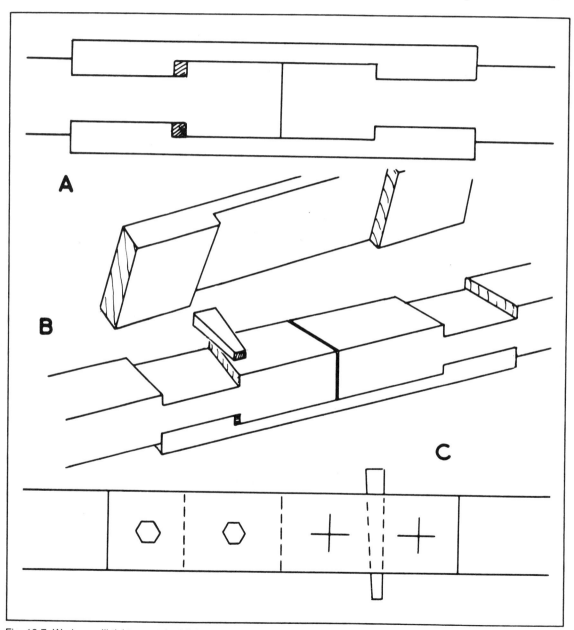

Fig. 12-7. Wedges will tighten notched fished joints.

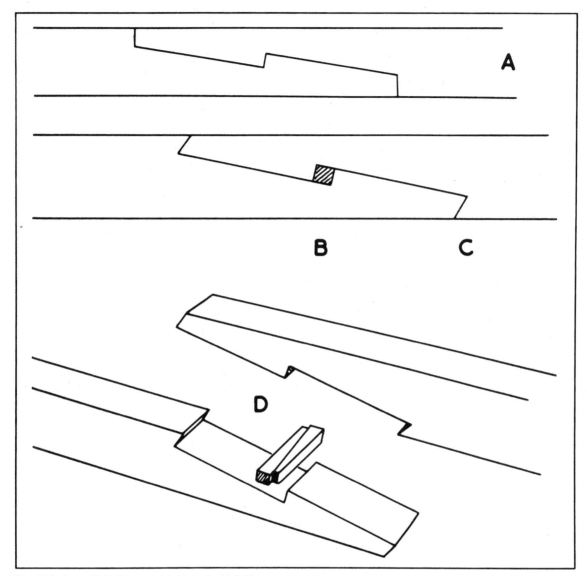

Fig. 12-8. A scarfed joint can be tightened with folding wedges.

faces or be let in if the surfaces have to be flush. The turned edges provide extra strength and resistance to bending.

NOTCHED FISHED JOINT

With the simple lap of the previous joint, only the bolts resist any tendency for the joint to move lengthwise. If there is much end load, the fishplates can be notched (Fig. 12-6A). There is no need to cut much out of the parts being joined, but the thickness of the fishplates must allow for the reduction in the center part. Bolts should go through both thicknesses. Notching may be in both fishplates, or it may be in one and the other left plain.

Another way of achieving a similar result is to let keys into the beams and the fishplates (Fig. 12-6B) at one or both sides. Even if the beams are softwood, make the keys out of hardwood. The keys could be parallel, but it helps in tightening if they are given a slight taper (Fig. 12-6C). Have a key too long, then plane it to a slight taper and use it to mark the shape of the pair of notches. Drive it in and cut off the surplus after the joint has been completed with tightened bolts. With any of these joints it helps to have the fishplates drilled, but then go through the beam by drilling through them from opposite sides. If you fit one bolt at a time, that will hold the parts for more drilling.

WEDGED FISHED JOINT

If it is important that the meeting ends are drawn tightly together, you can include one or more wedges to put on pressure before you drill for final bolting. In the notched fished joint, cut one of the notches to admit a wedge (Fig. 12-7A). Arrange one meeting edge square across and the other tapered (Fig. 12-7B). Make an overlong wedge to the same taper. Bolt the fishplates to the other part, then put in the second piece and drive in the wedge to draw the beam ends close (Fig. 12-7C) before drilling for the other bolts and cutting off the ends of the wedge. You may have a wedge on one side only, or you can get more pressure by wedging under both fishplates.

WEDGED SCARF JOINT

Ends that meet with a tapered scarf can include one or two wedges to pull the joint tight. In this case the tapered meeting surfaces are stepped. Without wedges this could be used to provide a lock (Fig. 12-8A), either glued or used with bolts.

The gap at the center is widened for wedge tightening (Fig. 12-8B). For a single wedge, the space must be tapered slightly so the wedge can force its way in and press the joint ends tight. Cut the ends so they meet in a V and not squarely, then there is less risk of one piece rising on the other (Fig. 12-8C).

A single wedge will work satisfactorily, but it puts on a one-sided load as it is driven. A better way of applying straight pressure is to use folding wedges. These wedges have matching slopes driven between parallel surfaces (Fig. 12-8D). If they are driven a little from each side, the resulting

thrust is parallel and considerable. For folding wedges, both parts are cut square across with a gap wide enough to start the wedges. The joint may be satisfactory with glue only. If bolts are used, one piece can be predrilled in readiness, but do not make the full holes until you have the joint driven tight.

TABLED JOINT

The end lap joint can be given a lock by notching the two parts into each other (Fig. 12-9A). If the two parts are cut each side of the center of the thickness, they will be equally loaded. Do not take out much, or the beams will be weakened at the shoulders (Fig. 12-9B).

Such a joint in house construction could be bolted through, or you could add fishplates on surfaces where the extra thickness would not matter. Strength is gained by making the joint reasonably long. The total lap could be five or six times the thickness of the wood. More strength can be provided with iron straps, which could be continuous rings, slid on and driven over the joint after the parts are mated, or pieces of strip iron, which are cut to bend over and be screwed on (Fig. 12-9C).

WEDGED V-SCARF

In heavy construction there is a variation of the wedged scarf joint that is related to the tabled joint. The two parts overlap with notches and are cut parallel, but with the meeting parts sloping (Fig. 12-10A). The amount of notching need not be very deep; it need be only about ¾ inch on a 2-inch depth.

Allow a gap where the notched edges come. Use this to take folding wedges (Fig. 12-10B) to force the tapered ends into the sloped shoulders.

This should make a very tight and firm joint, except there is a slight risk of sideways movement if there are heavy loads that way. The joint can be made to resist that by cutting the meeting parts with a V-shape (Fig. 12-10C). A fairly acute angle would give the greatest resistance to bending, but that would be difficult to cut accurately. With the wedge tightening, a more moderately angled V should be adequate.

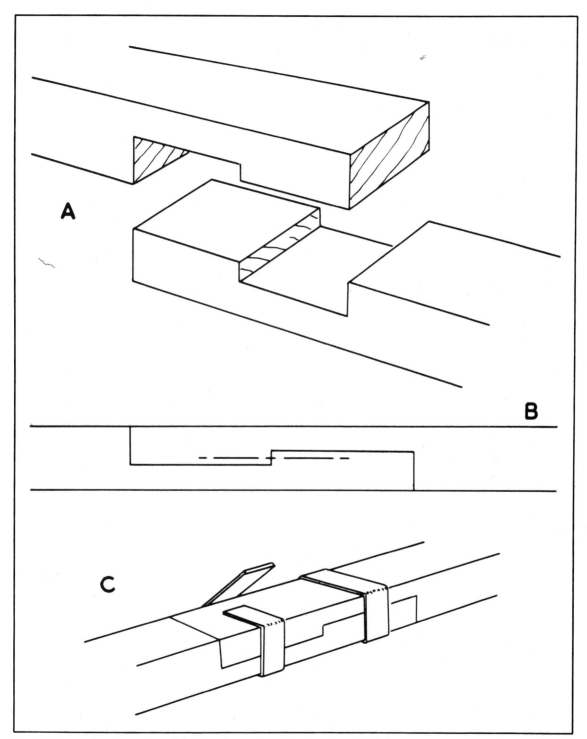

A

B

C

Fig. 12-9. Lapped ends may be notched together and can be strengthened with iron straps.

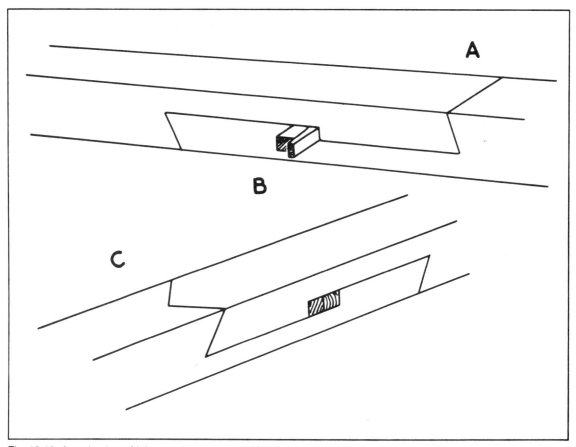

Fig. 12-10. A wedged scarf joint may have the ends V-shaped to maintain alignment.

TENONED SCARF JOINT

This is probably the best known end-to-end joint for wood of large section. It is similar to the previous joint, except for short tenons at the ends (Fig. 12-11A) instead of the meeting slopes.

The parts fit into each other by a similar small amount to that suggested for the wedged V-scarf, then the tenons and their mortises at the ends are half the wood thickness there (Fig. 12-11B). They need not go very deeply; slightly more than the tenon thickness should be enough. Wedging at the center will force the ends tightly into each other. Carefully cut the lengths so the tenons do not bottom before the shoulders have closed. Ideally, both close at the same time, but a little surplus in the mortise depth is better than a gap left at a shoulder, particularly if appearance is important.

DOUBLE TENONED SCARF JOINT

The ordinary tenoned scarf joint has considerable strength, but like the plain wedged scarf joint there is a slight risk of movement if sideways loads are great. Resistance to that could be provided by giving the parts V-ends (Fig. 12-12A), which requires some careful paring of the shoulders and mortises.

Another way of providing resistance to sideways loads has small tenons square to the main ones (Fig. 12-12B). They need not be very large and could be cut squarely or with tapered sides (Fig. 12-12C). The main tenons might also taper (Fig. 12-12D) to allow self-tightening as they squeeze in.

In any end-to-end situation where the parts are to follow through level on all four surfaces, these joints probably provide the strongest union, with a good resistance to deflection.

It is common to make the joints with the overlapping parts parallel with the top and bottom surfaces, but they could be given a slight taper. The taper should not be very much, but it avoids weakening by cutting away much at the shoulders, although it thins the tenons.

LAPPED MORTISE AND TENON END JOINT

One of the Japanese end-to-end joints has an arrangement of interlocking mortises and tenons, with a pair of wedges for tightening (Fig. 12-13A). It could go right through if the wood is thin, but if it is nearer square section the long tenon is about half thickness. The stub tenon outside it is full depth (Fig. 12-13B).

The tenon parts are marked parallel on both pieces. The mortises and tenons may be marked to match, but you have to allow for the wedge tightening. A little lengthwise clearance should be allowed for the parts to pull as far as possible into each other. The overall length of the joint is not critical; a long tenon about twice the width of the wood should be about right.

When you can see that the parts will fit, mark the recesses for the wedges. Their corners come on the joint line (Fig. 12-13C). Allow a slight taper in the depth and cut the wedges to match, so the parts are pulled together as the wedges get close to the bottom. If the parts are glued, coat all surfaces before driving in overlong wedges. They and the surfaces may be planed level to give a smooth attractive appearance to the joint.

CROSSBILL JOINT

This Japanese end-to-end joint gets its name from the crossbill finch, which has its beak ends overlapping. In side view the joint is very similar to a tenoned scarf joint (Fig. 12-14A), but in the other view the parts are angled in opposite directions on the two sides (Fig. 12-14B). The length of the joint should be at least twice the width of the wood.

Mark out the meeting parts all around (Fig. 12-14C). A limited amount of cutting can be done with a fine backsaw. You can saw as far as where the two beaks meet, but to go further you will have to pare with a chisel. The small tenons can be sawed, but the mortises are almost entirely chiseled.

The parts are locked together with a peg across the center. In the Japanese construction it has a square section (Fig. 12-14D), but it would be simpler to assemble the joint and drill through for a

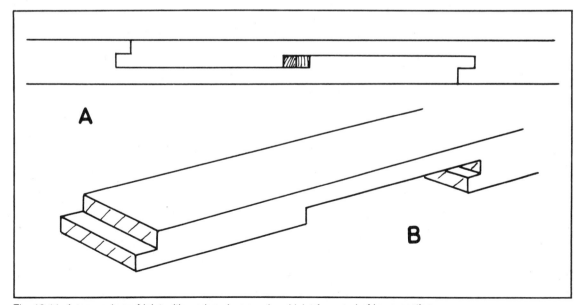

Fig. 12-11. A tenoned scarf joint with wedges is a good end joint for wood of large section.

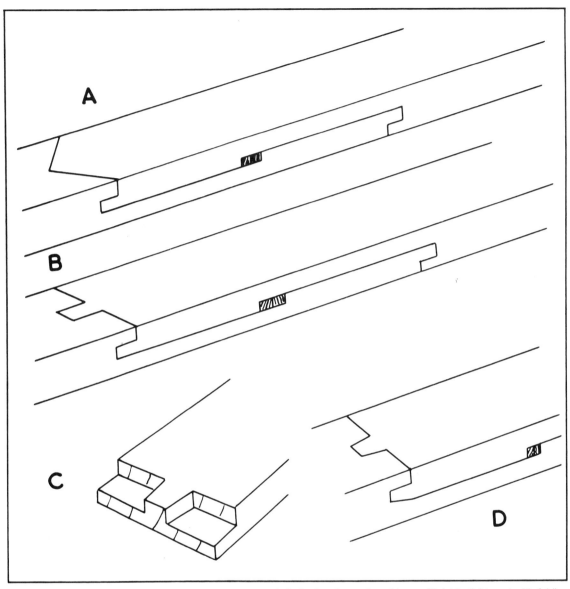

Fig. 12-12. Tenons both ways resist sideways movement in both directions when this scarf joint is tightened with folding wedges.

piece of dowel rod (Fig. 12-14E). You could also cut a tapered slot for a wedge or a parallel slot for folding wedges to tighten in the same way as described for several earlier joints.

In an exposed position this joint may be decorative if it is carefully fitted and the peg is in a contrasting color. It is not likely to be as strong as some of the traditional Western joints.

BUTT STRAPS

If pieces have to present a level surface on one side and the opposite side is unimportant, there may be no need for elaborate joints. It may even be impossible to make them if the meeting parts are wide panels rather than strips. In many cases you can let the edges meet and cover them inside with a piece called a butt strap (Fig. 12-15A). If the parts are straight strips, the butt strap may be quite long (Fig. 12-15B) and held with glue and screws. If the strips are to be sprung to a slight curve, the butt strap can be tapered in its length (Fig. 12-15C) so as not to affect the overall curve too much. An acute cut at the end makes a neater finish and avoids an abrupt change of section (Fig. 12-15D).

If plywood edges have to be joined, it helps to locate the joint over a solid part of the supporting framing if possible. Direct nailing may not be satisfactory (Fig. 12-15E), but it may be possible to include a wider cover piece (Fig. 12-15F). Most plywood is not thick enough to allow for screwing from the back, so nails or screws have to be driven from the surface to reinforce glue.

Plywood pieces often have to be joined to make up the lengths of panels on a boat's sides and bottom. If there is a curve involved, it is better to join the parts before bending than to make a joint in position. The latter is more likely to produce unevenness in the flow of the curve.

With the comparatively thin plywood used for a boat skin, there is not enough thickness to give a good hold to screws. It is better to use clench nailing and glue. If it is possible to apply overall clamping, it may be possible to use glue only. Usually with wide panels, though, you should have nails to give strength and to offer a clamping action as they are clenched.

Use similar plywood to the pieces being joined. Cut it wide enough for a double row of nails each side of the joint. Taper the outside well (Fig. 12-15G). Use thin nails with small heads—brass or

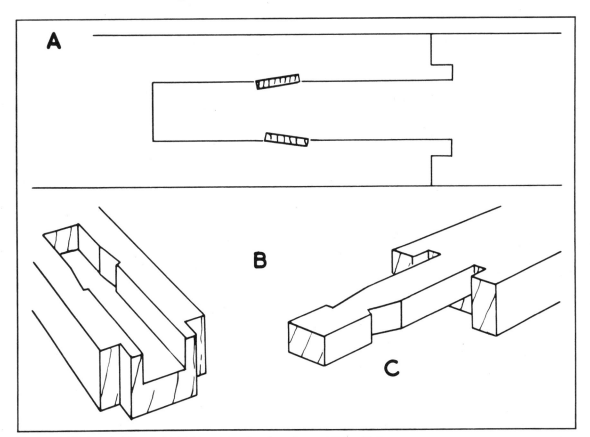

Fig. 12-13. Wedges pull the parts tight in a lapped end mortise and tenon joint.

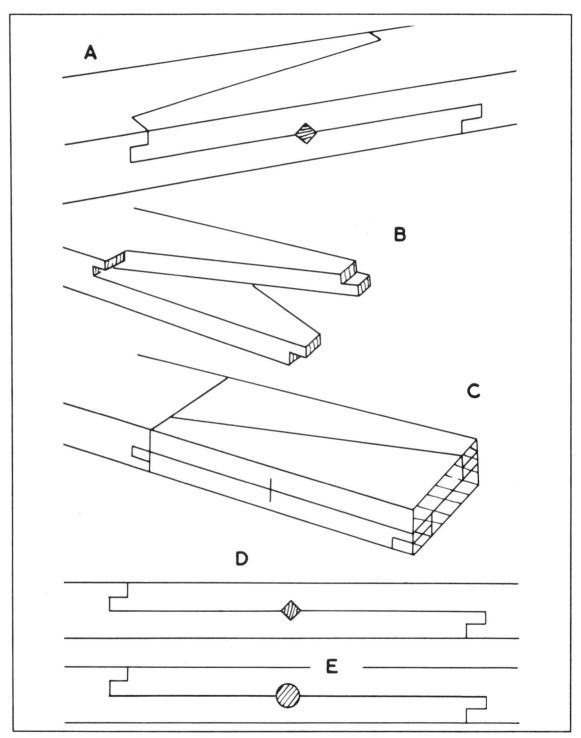

Fig. 12-14. A crossbill has fitted tenon ends and a peg or dowel across to lock the parts.

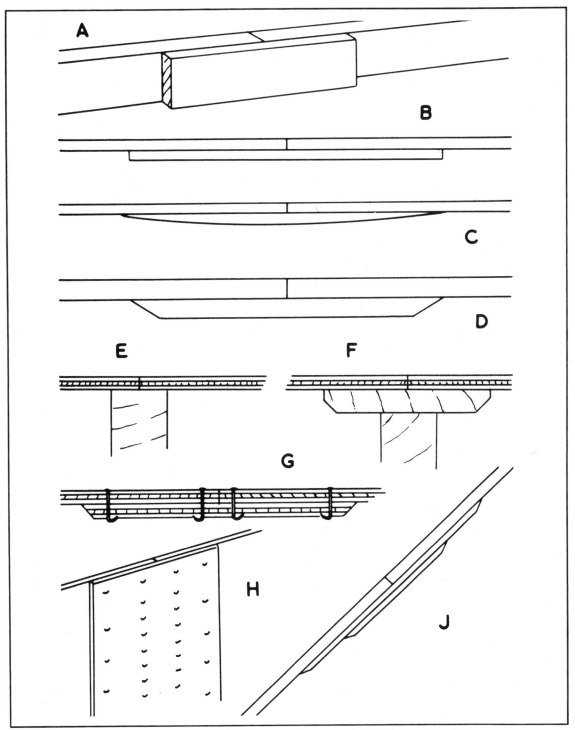

Fig. 12-15. Where only one face has to be level, there can be butt straps behind the meeting edges.

copper are suitable for boat skins—and space them closer on each side of the joint than further out (Fig. 12-15H). Nail from outside and clench inside. See Chapter 2.

A very wide plywood butt strap may offer some resistance to curving a boat skin, but other supports will usually pull the plywood to shape without variations in the curve being obvious outside. Too narrow a joint cover may cause more uneven curving. That will be particularly obvious when the skin is sighted along after finishing with gloss paint or varnish. Solid wood joint covers are more likely to distort the visible outside curves. If there is to be much curve in the plywood, the parts could be joined with solid wood prepared with its surface curved closely to the final shape. Another way of making the joint with the minimum risk of distorting the curving of the panel is to use two pieces of thinner plywood. Let one be much wider than the other and give the edges acute tapers (Fig. 12-15J).

BILLIARD CUE JOINT

A billiard cue is usually made of two pieces of wood. The long thinner end is of a comparatively light hardwood. A darker-colored heavier hardwood is at the thick end—sometimes with a weight inserted. The whole thing is round and tapered. The joint between the two pieces of wood is a sort of four-sided scarf (Fig. 12-16A). The finished joint looks rather complex, but the work is almost all straight saw cuts.

The long thinner part should be made first, and that may be rounded and tapered before cutting the joint. A typical size is 48 inches long with a taper from 1⅛-inch diameter at the joint to ⅜-inch diameter at the tip. Prepare the wood to a square taper. Reduce it to a regular tapered octagonal section, before taking off the corners and rounding it with abrasive paper pulled around and finally lengthwise. You can do final rounding and cleaning up after assembly, but it helps to get a good shape now.

The scarf may be about 7 inches long. At this distance from the thick end, measure the circumference with a strip of card. Prick through the overlap with an awl (Fig. 12-16B), then open the card and divide the distance between the holes into four (Fig. 12-16C). Put the card back and mark the four positions. Project along to the end. Midway between these marks square across (Fig. 12-16D). Draw lines from these positions to the original marks (Fig. 12-16E). These are the outlines of the cuts, which should go almost to featheredges (Fig. 12-16F). The thickness of a saw kerf, about 1/32 inch, should suit.

Have the cue rigidly held in a vise and saw close to the lines. Follow with a paring chisel or a rabbet plane. Check the straightness and squareness of the tapers.

The joint in the other piece has to be cut while it is a square section. After gluing it on, it is tapered round and matched to the other part. By doing that, it is possible to compensate for slight discrepancies and get the finished cue straight.

Mark the length of the scarf from the squared end of the piece (Fig. 12-16G). Draw tapers that match the other part on the four faces (Fig. 12-16H). Cut these with a fine saw by carefully working a little from each side so as not to wander from the lines. In that way you can probably get a good enough finish from the saw. You may have to do some trimming with a chisel. It may help in getting a close fit to take the sharpness off the inner corners. Mark the two parts if you make a trial assembly, so they go together the same each time. The square end should push closely on to the round part (Fig. 12-16J).

Glue the joint and make sure the pieces are pushed as tightly as possible. The four corners of the square part may try to lift. Pull them in with clamps or tie around tightly with cord or electrician's tape. When the glue has set, shape the square part to the other to see the full beauty of the joint in wood of contrasting colors.

HAMMERHEADED KEY

When fairly massive parts have to be joined end to end, particularly two curved pieces or a curved part to a straight part, you can use a hammerheaded key with wedges to exert considerable pressure on the meeting surfaces.

Inserted tongues can keep the parts in line

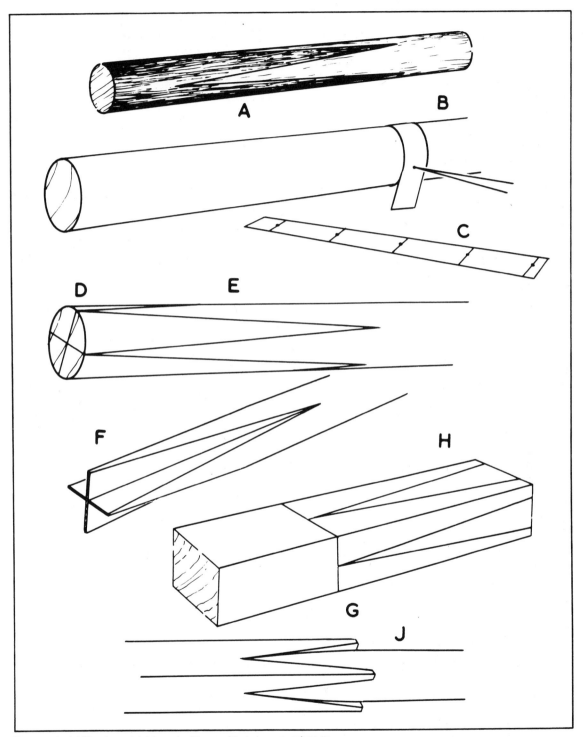

Fig. 12-16. A billiard cue joint is a double scarf between round parts.

(Fig. 12-17A). The key is close-grained hardwood and should be thick enough to at least go halfway through the parts being joined and long enough not to cause levering against very short grain in the parts being joined. The hammerhead ends could be parallel or tapered (Fig. 12-17B). Make the shoulders of the heads at slopes to suit the wedges that will be driven.

The amount of movement required is not much. Cut the recesses so there is some clearance beyond the hammerheads, and they will not reach the limit before the wedges have forced the meeting faces as tight as possible. Make the wedges of hardwood and keep them overlong to cut off later. Their size has to be judged to penetrate deeply under the hammerheads, as they must pass on the thrust for as near the depth of the hammerheads as possible. Holes may be drilled to let the wedge ends go further, so there is a full bearing surface. Mark on each wedge the maximum depth it may be expected to go as a guide when driving.

DOWELED AND KEYED SPLICE

When two pieces of fairly large sectioned wood have to be joined end to end and the joint may not be bearing against anything for support, as it would in a wall plate, the parts may be keyed to keep them in line. Dowels may be used to resist lengthwise loads (Fig. 12-18). The joint could be used for a wall plate, but then it might be too elaborate.

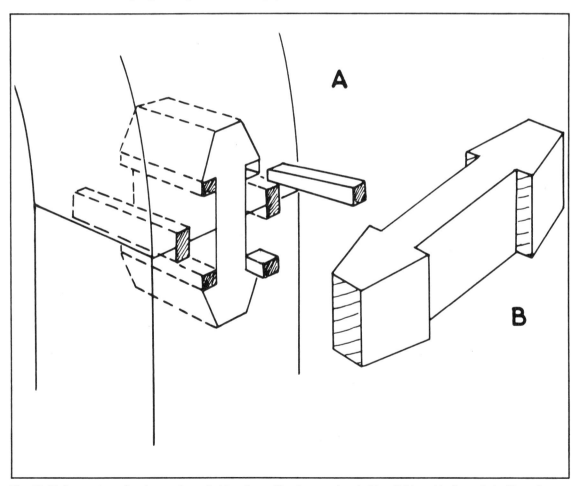

Fig. 12-17. Large shaped parts may be pulled together with a hammerheaded key tightened in its socket with wedges.

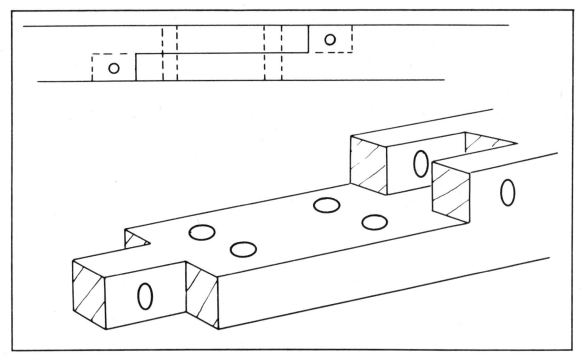

Fig. 12-18. Dowels may be used through two parts that interlock endwise.

Proportions depend on the size of the wood, but the keys should be long enough to allow for drilling through without the risk of grain breaking out. The spacing of the other dowels should put them reasonably far apart and not too near end grain. If the finished assembly will have to resist flexing, the greater the length, the stiffer it will be. More dowels could be in a very long joint.

Chapter 13

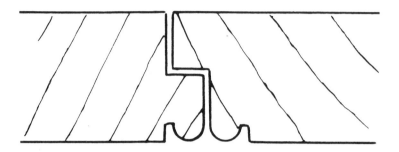

Shutting Joints

W HEN TWO PARTS MEET AND ONE HAS TO open and close on the other, there is a *shutting* or *closing joint*. The most common example is a door fitting into its frame or against the front of a cabinet, but there are others. These joints are often neglected, and unsatisfactory closing may spoil an otherwise good piece of woodwork.

If a door swings in an opening and there is nothing to limit its movement, the hinges and their screws will be strained and soon loosened. Something must stop the door at the right position. Some fasteners and catches may also act as stops, but it is more common to build in a stop, so whatever is provided to secure the door does just that and is not required to limit its movement, too.

RABBETED FRAME

A room door usually swings in a rabbeted frame (Fig. 13-1A). Its main function is to close the gap all around the door and prevent drafts, but it also acts as a stop. When the door is hinged, there should be enough clearance on that side for the door to close

without binding. At the other side the door can come close into the rabbet (Fig. 13-1B). The lock or other fastener should allow for the door to close tightly. Too much slackness will cause the door to be loose and rattle in a draft.

CABINET DOORSTOPS

If a door is arranged on the front of a cabinet, the cabinet side acts as a stop, and there is no need for anything else (Fig. 13-2A). In this case the top and bottom may overhang the door for a neat appearance (Fig. 13-2B).

If the door comes within the carcass parts, there could be a continuous stop for the door to close against (Fig. 13-2C), or the side might be rabbeted if it is thick enough (Fig. 13-2D). The alternative is one or more short stops. One piece could be near the middle or behind the catch (Fig. 13-2E). It may be better to put stops at top and bottom, either on the side or above and below (Fig. 13-2F). The latter is better if you want as clear an access to the interior as possible. Using short stops

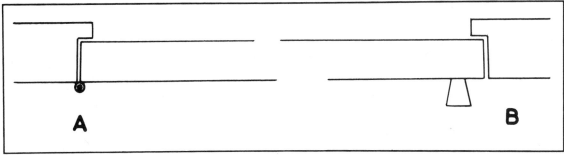

Fig. 13-1. Both sides of a door may close into a rabbeted frame.

leaves a gap through the edge of the door. It may not be much if the door is a good fit, but dust could pass through. A full-length stop is more dustproof.

The section of wood used for the stop need not be very thick. The front edge has to be square, but the rear edge may be beveled (Fig. 13-2G) or rounded (Fig. 13-2H).

If the door edge and the wood alongside are both flat, the gap between will be obvious, even when it is kept as narrow as possible. If the door is set back inside the stile (Fig. 13-3A), the gap is disguised. Another method of making it less obvious is to work a bead on the edge of the door (Fig. 13-3B), the stile (Fig. 13-3C), or both. If it is construction that may have that sort of decoration, molding could be on the edge (Fig. 13-3D). Similar treatment will have to be used on the hinge side, and it may be possible to allow the hinge knuckles to form part of a bead or other pattern worked on the edge of the wood.

DUSTPROOFING

An ordinary door closure may be sufficiently dustproof for most purposes. A cabinet containing valuable items or delicate things on display behind a glass door may need better treatment.

One way of dustproofing used for displaying jewelry and similar hinges has both sides of the door let into shallow rabbets. That may be sufficient at the hinge side, or a small fillet could be let into a plowed groove in the door edge so it closes into a matching groove in the side (Fig. 13-4A). The other side may have a plain rabbet, but closure is tighter if there is a bead worked in the rabbet and a matching hollow on the door edge (Fig. 13-4B).

In another treatment for the hinged side, the door is rabbeted and its projection goes into a groove in the cabinet side (Fig. 13-4C). The back of the groove must be beveled slightly to allow the door to swing. Making the groove wider for the same purpose would defeat the dustproofing purpose; the door and groove widths should match at the bottom of the groove. If the door swings on pivot hinges, its edge may be rounded, using the pivot center as the center of the curve. The stile edge is hollowed to match, preferably with a stop for the door to close against (Fig. 13-4D).

DOUBLE DOORS

If two doors meet at the center, their need for stops is the same as for single doors, but they cannot be arranged in the same way. There can be pieces at top and bottom (Fig. 13-5A), with straight front edges, but the other exposed parts should be beveled or rounded for the best appearance.

If there is a shelf, its edge may be far enough forward for it to act as a stop. Usually it is set back a short way, and there can be a stop put on it (Fig. 13-5B). This may be the only stop, or it can be repeated on another shelf or be used with top or bottom stops. More than two stops create an alignment problem, and you have to arrange them so they all come into action simultaneously.

A good way of fastening double doors is to have one or more bolts on one door to engage with a shelf (Fig. 13-5C) or top and bottom of the carcass. The other door then has a turning catch or other fastener to engage with the first (Fig. 13-5D).

The gap between a pair of doors is often more obvious than the gaps at the sides or on a single

263

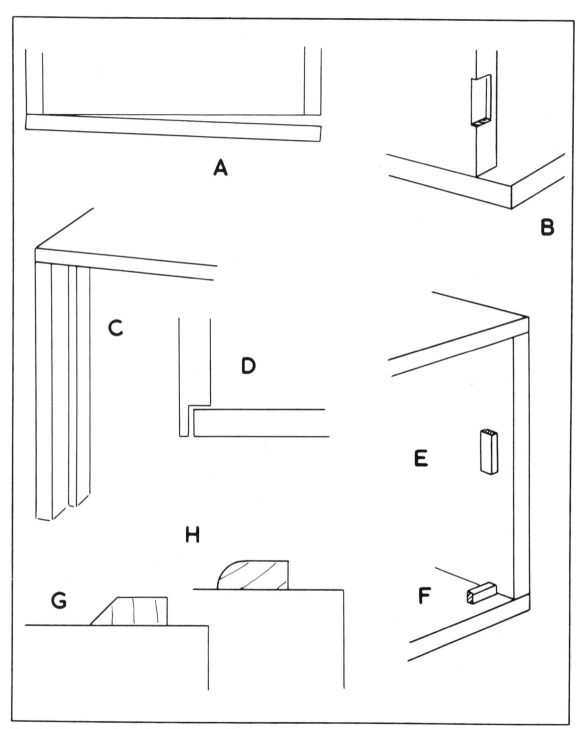

Fig. 13-2. A door may close in front of the sides (A) with its hinges let in (B). There may be a stop inside a case (C), or a rabbet may be the stop (D). Small stops can be fitted (E, F, G, H).

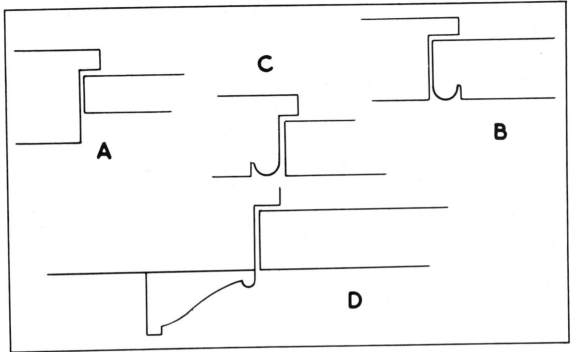

Fig. 13-3. A door joint can be disguised with a bead or molding.

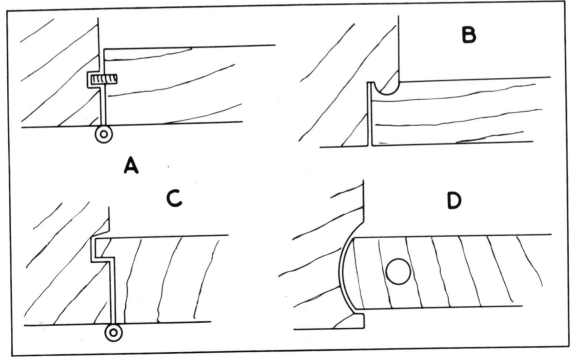

Fig. 13-4. A door can be dustproofed by arranging tight closures.

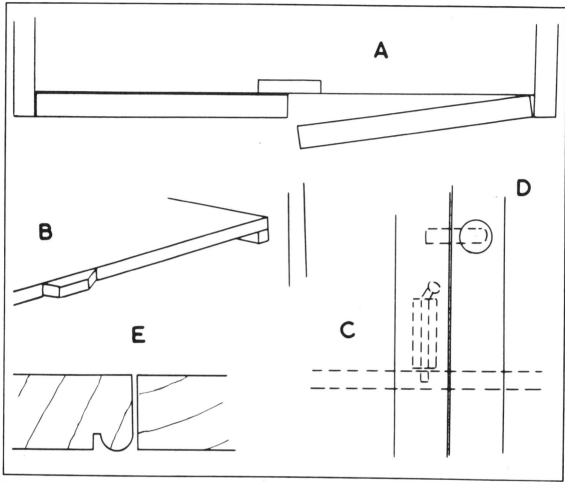

Fig. 13-5. Double doors may meet at a stop (A, B). One may be bolted (C) and the other held to it with a catch (D). A bead hides the meeting edges (E).

door. Usually it cannot be as close a fit because of shrinkage and movement problems. A bead on one edge helps to make the gap less obvious (Fig. 13-5E). For a balanced appearance, that would also have to be worked on the outer edges of the doors.

DUSTPROOFING DOUBLE DOORS

Meeting edges without any special treatment will allow drafts and dust through. A common treatment is to rabbet both doors so they fit into each other (Fig. 13-6A). If both pieces are the same width before rabbeting, one will appear wider than the other. If only the front is important, one piece may be made wider than the other by the amount of the

rabbet (Fig. 13-6B). If both sides of the doors will be equally visible, as they would in room doors, the parts will have to be the same width before rabbeting.

One way of disguising the difference in width is to work a bead, preferably the same width as the rabbet depth on the overhanging piece (Fig. 13-6C), on one or both sides.

Dustproofing is improved if the meeting rabbets are altered to interlock more closely. One form makes each part into a hook section (Fig. 13-6D). If the doors are hung to swing and meet closely, this helps to keep them in line and limit the amount of dust getting through. At one time there were pairs of molding planes available for cutting this joint, but now it is more appropriate to machining. A similar form is also used for glued edge-to-edge jointing (see Chapter 16).

Another way of improving the dustproofing a pair of rabbets is to put a tongue or slip into a groove in one part, with a rounded edge to mate with a groove in the other part (Fig. 13-6E).

Another method of getting a closer fit between the two doors, which is used by old-time cabinet-makers for larger work, involves gluing in tongues near the edges of each rabbet to go into hollow at the root of the opposite rabbet (Fig. 13-6F). This has the advantage of being cut with ordinary hand or power tools as all the cuts are rabbets.

ASTRAGAL JOINTS

Any of the previous joints can have their fronts cut with single or double beads (Fig. 13-7A) as decoration and to modify the appearance of the break between the edges. Another method, often used in older cabinetwork, has an applied piece of astragal molding covering the gap.

In the simplest form, the molding is glued half to one piece to cover the gap (Fig. 13-7B). That depends on a comparatively narrow line of glue, and it is better to use a rabbeted astragal strip that goes between and over the doors (Fig. 13-7C). If the door is too thick to take the molding full width, it may be rabbeted (Fig. 13-7D).

A modern variation on this has the applied strip rabbeted to admit the other door, but its front is a bead that projects forward of the main surfaces (Fig. 13-7E). A projecting bead does more to disguise the gap than one worked flush with the surface.

In some period furniture a brass astragal

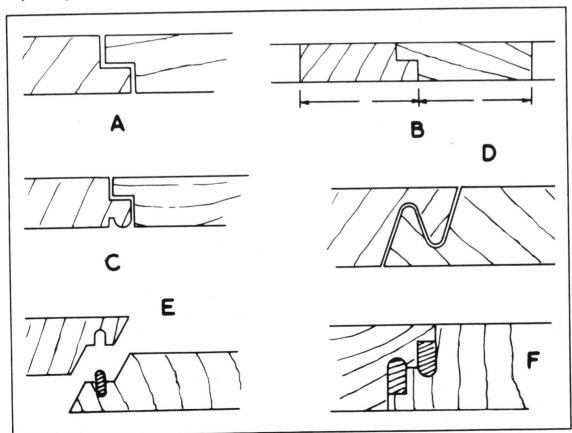

Fig. 13-6. Meeting doors may lap in several ways.

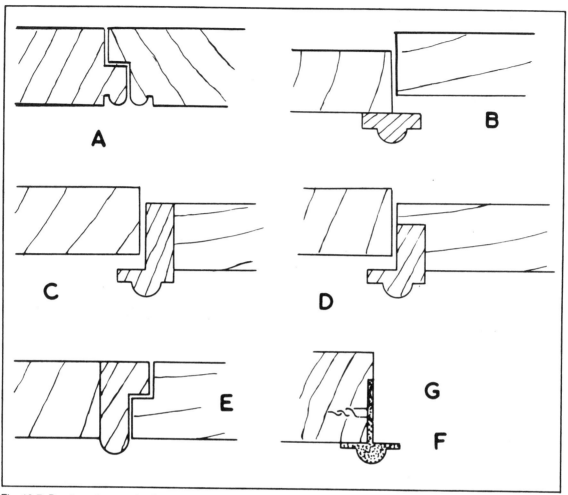

Fig. 13-7. Beads and astragal strips may come at meeting door edges.

molded strip with a projecting tongue will be found instead of the wooden strip. This lets into the side of one door (Fig. 13-7F) and is held with screws at intervals (Fig. 13-7G).

LIGHTPROOFING

If a door is expected to be lightproof, as one to a photographic darkroom, one of the self-adhesive plastic foam strips around the frame may be sufficient when the door compresses it on closing (Fig. 13-8A).

An alternative is cloth with a high pile, such as velvet or one of the synthetic alternatives to it. Beveling the edge of the door so it closes on to cloth

in the angle (Fig. 13-8B) is effective. At the hinge side the cloth may be folded and the edges glued into a groove (Fig. 13-8C), so the projecting roll compresses as the door closes on it. This could be done all around. Something similar could be arranged at the bottom of the door (Fig. 13-8D), although that is probably better lightproofed with something put against it after closing.

LIFT-OUT PANELS

Sometimes it is better to make a door removable to give maximum access to the interior or to fit it where there is insufficient space for it to swing. In that case gravity is used to locate the panel at the

268

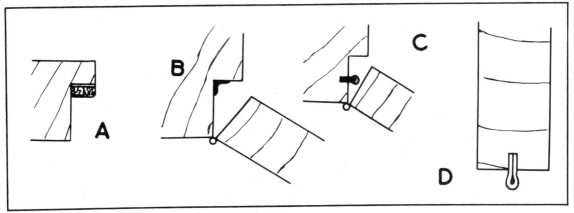

Fig. 13-8. If a door has to be lightproof, it can close on soft cloth or plastic strips.

bottom, and some sort of catch holds it in at the top. One method of fitting has a tongue worked across the panel bottom edge to engage with a groove in the frame (Fig. 13-9A). At the top the panel goes into a rabbet (Fig. 13-9B). Rabbets could be at the sides if dustproofing is important.

If there is a magnetic or ball catch at the top, or a turn button is used outside, the simplest handle is

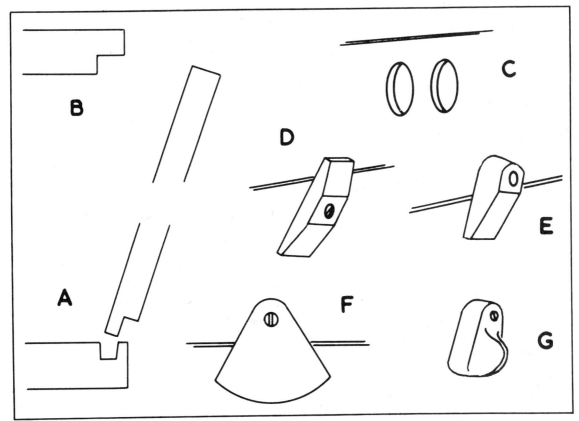

Fig. 13-9. A lift-out door (A, B) may have holes as a handle (C) and turn buttons to hold it closed (D, E, F, G).

one or a pair of holes large enough to put fingers through (Fig. 13-9C). Otherwise, there can be a knob or a strip handle.

A simple fastener, sometimes seen on locker doors that lift out from under boat bunks or benches, uses gravity to keep it closed. This is a variation of the turn button, which is normally balanced (Fig. 13-9D). A half button is neater and more likely to remain closed when hanging vertically (Fig. 13-9E), but the next step is to increase the weight of its lower end (Fig. 13-9F), so it falls to the closed position. It could be flat, or the weight could be increased even more by carving a handle (Fig. 13-9G).

DRAWER JOINTS

For the sake of appearance, a drawer should close level at the front. The guides, runners, and kickers (Fig. 13-10A) must be square to the front, so the drawer runs smoothly and squarely. Otherwise, it may be difficult to get the drawer closing with the front level.

If the drawer front overlaps the opening, that acts as a stop (Fig. 13-10B). Keep the rear of the drawer far enough forward so it does not hit the carcass back before the front closes tightly.

If it is a flush-fronted drawer, the stops must be arranged in another way. If the back of the carcass is stout enough, the drawer can come against it. In that case the drawer sides must be planed off until the front is level (Fig. 13-10C). If the drawer does not reach the back or the back is not stout enough to withstand the drawer being pushed against it stops may be on the runners (Fig. 13-10D).

In typical drawer construction the bottom is let into a groove, leaving a gap below it. This is sufficient for stops to be arranged on the rail below the drawer bottom. The stops can not be very thick, but for a drawer that is a reasonable fit in the opening they will function without the drawer riding over them. There could be one long stop, but it is more common to have two stops toward the sides of the drawer (Fig. 13-10E). During assembly the stops may be lightly nailed until the exact locations have been found, then they are glued and screwed.

Stops may come inside the top of the drawer front (Fig. 13-10F), either right across or a pair arranged toward the sides. Besides stopping the drawer at the right place when pushed in, stops can prevent a drawer from being pulled out unintentionally if the drawer back is kept high enough to come against the back of the stop (Fig. 13-10G). If the drawer has to be removed, lifting its front will allow the bottom to clear the rail and the back to be dropped below the stops. Rounding or beveling the rear bottom corners of the drawer sides will help removal.

Another advantage of the top stop is in dustproofing if it is carried right across. A square edge may be sufficient, but in good quality cabinetry the stop may be rabbeted and its round edge allowed to fit into a groove in the drawer front when that is closed (Fig. 13-10H).

A further precaution in dustproofing is to close the space below it and above anything else there. Otherwise, there may be nothing inside the runners and rails. This is simply done by including a plywood or hardboard panel in grooves (Fig. 13-10J).

DRAWER SECURITY

A drawer can be fitted with a lock, which would be necessary if valuables are put in it. Sometimes security is needed against a child pulling out the drawer or the drawer sliding open when a boat heels.

If the front of the drawer overlaps to hide the gap, the drawer sides can be notched to fit over the front framing (Fig. 13-11A). The top is given enough clearance to allow for the depth of the notch (Fig. 13-11B). When the drawer is closed, the notch prevents it from coming out until it is lifted clear (Fig. 13-11C). In prolonged use the notches in the drawer sides may wear, but that can be prevented by including a strip across under the bottom between the notch edges (Fig. 13-11D).

If the drawer comes above a compartment with a door, it may be possible to arrange a fastener inside to prevent a drawer from being pulled out without reaching inside to release it. Fit a piece

270

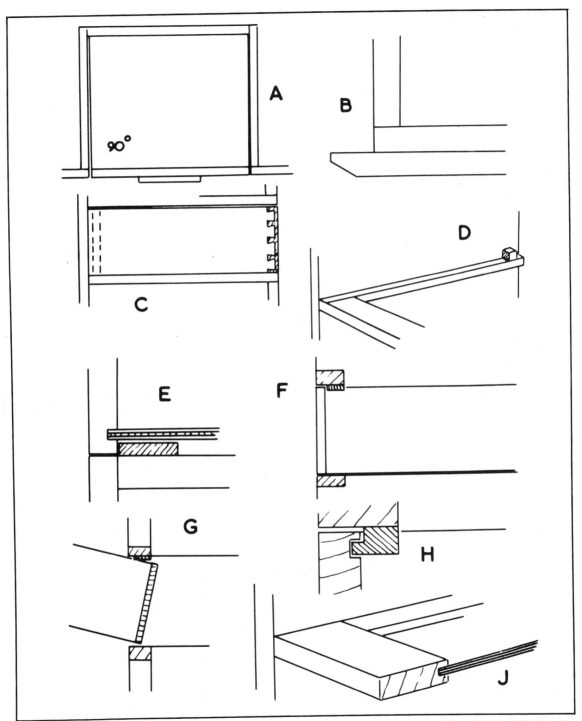

Fig. 13-10. A drawer may finish flush or overlap the front (A, B, C). A stop may be on a runner (D) or at the front (E). A similar stop at the top will prevent the drawer from pulling out (F, G, H). A panel provides dustproofing between drawers (J).

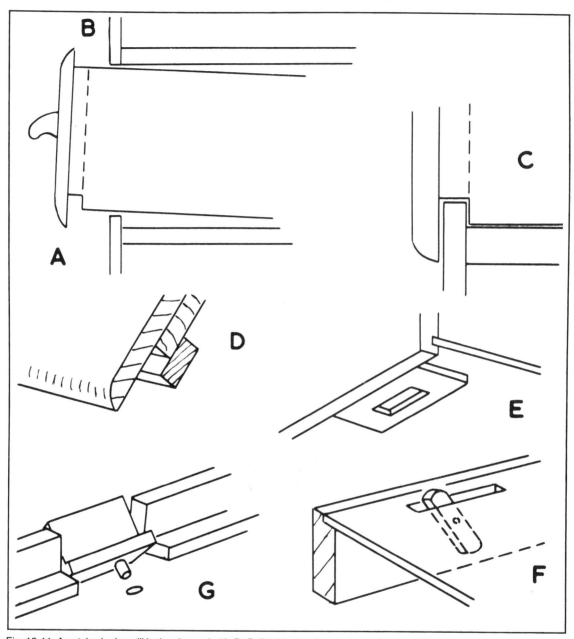

Fig. 13-11. A notched edge will lock a drawer in (A, B, C, D). A button from below will make a lock (E, F), or there can be a peg above (G).

under the bottom with a slot in it (Fig. 13-11E), then put a turn button inside the rail below to turn into the slot (Fig. 13-11F).

There are other possibilities, depending on the form of the piece of furniture. It may be possible to arrange a pull-out peg through the side into the drawer, possibly arranged inconspicuously as part of a pattern. For a top drawer, a section of the back above could be made to tilt and lift a stop (Fig. 13-11G).

Chapter 14

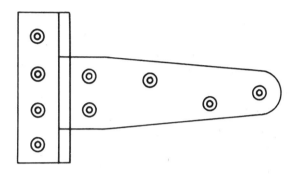

Hinged Joints

WHEN ONE PART HAS TO SWING OR MOVE in relation to another, it has to be provided with some sort of pivot or hinge. You have a choice of making a wooden pivot or of adding one or more metal hinges. Wood moving on wood will eventually wear, so wooden pivots may not be expected to last as long as metal ones, but they may have a sufficient life. Much depends on the type of wood, the bearing surfaces, and the frequency of operation. For instance, the pivot for a gateleg table could be of wood and be expected to last as long as needed. The hinge on a frequently used door would soon become slack if made of wood, and the hinges there are usually of metal.

Some metal hinges are designed for particular purposes, and others can merely be screwed to the surface. The most widely used hinge is the common butt (Fig. 14-1A). It is obtainable in many sizes from tiny examples for the lids of trinket boxes to others weighing several pounds. The metal may be iron, steel, brass, or aluminum. The hinges may be placed or treated in some way for protection and appearance.

There is a pivot pin in this hinge around which the sheet metal may be rolled (Fig. 14-1B). It is stronger if cast or machined (Fig. 14-1C) to form a knuckle. The two parts of the hinge knuckle are cut to fit into each other around the pin. Whatever the hinge metal, the pivot pin is often steel for the sake of strength, but for wet situations it should be nonferrous metal. In small hinges the pin only holds by friction. In larger hinges the ends may be riveted, or there may be some end caps shaped for decoration.

HINGE PRINCIPLES

A door or lid swings about the center of the pivot pin, so its location is important. If its center is exactly level with the two surfaces, the moving part should be able to swing through 180 degrees to come exactly flush with the other part (Fig. 14-2A). It is better to have the center slightly forward of the surfaces, then they will clear each other (Fig. 14-2B). The amount of clearance will be twice the amount that the pivot center is set forward of the surfaces.

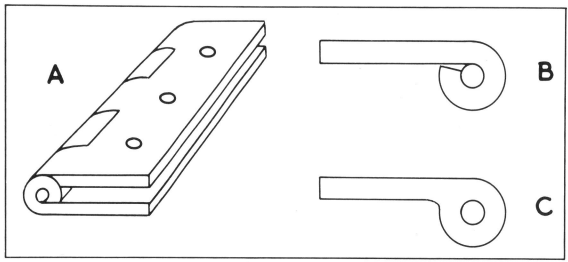

Fig. 14-1. A hinge has interlocking parts and may be folded metal or cast.

It is common to give more clearance than this by having the center of the pivot even further forward if there is no particular need for a close fit when open. If a hinge is put on the surface, its knuckle and pin will be entirely forward of the surfaces (Fig. 14-2C), so there will be a wide clearance when the moving part swings back (Fig. 14-2D). Hinges fitted between the parts can have their knuckles that far forward.

Keep the knuckles forward if the door has to clear projections on its frame. This can happen with a room door with molding around its frame. If the door is to swing right back, the hinge knuckle position has to be well out (Fig. 14-2E). Often there is no need for the door to go that far, so the pivot center may be further in (Fig. 14-2F). If the door opens against a corner wall, it does not have to go very far past 90 degrees, so the pivot center need not project much (Fig. 14-2G).

If two hinged parts bind, there are several possible causes. Hinges set too deeply into recesses will cause the wood parts to meet before they are fully closed (Fig. 14-2H). Packing one or both leaves of the hinge with stiff paper will cure this. The hinge could be screw-bound. If the screws are not sunk flush with the metal, they may meet before the door is closed (Fig. 14-2J). If the door closes into a rabbeted frame and the door is too far

in on its hinges, it surface may close against the rabbet before it is fully in.

All of the hinges along a joint must have their pins in line. Otherwise, the action will not be smooth. Movement may distort hinges or pull out screws. The hinges may creak with only slight misalignment. The problem is greatest with a long hinged edge having three or more hinges. A similar problem occurs if the door and its frame have an intentional curve. Hinges will have to be chosen that allow sufficient projection for all the pins to be arranged in line.

Besides the projection of the knuckle square to the surface, it is possible to adjust the clearance when swinging by moving the knuckle the other way. Usually the knuckle center comes midway between the two edges (Fig. 14-3A). If it is more toward the frame, the door may not open fully (Fig. 14-3B). If it is more toward the door (Fig. 14-3C), the swing will give a little more clearance than if the pivot point had been central. Not much adjustment is possible, as it is affected by the need to sink the hinge flaps into the wood. For the last case all of the letting in can be on the door, and the frame hinge leaf goes on the surface.

BUTT HINGED JOINTS

Common hinges close so their inner surfaces are

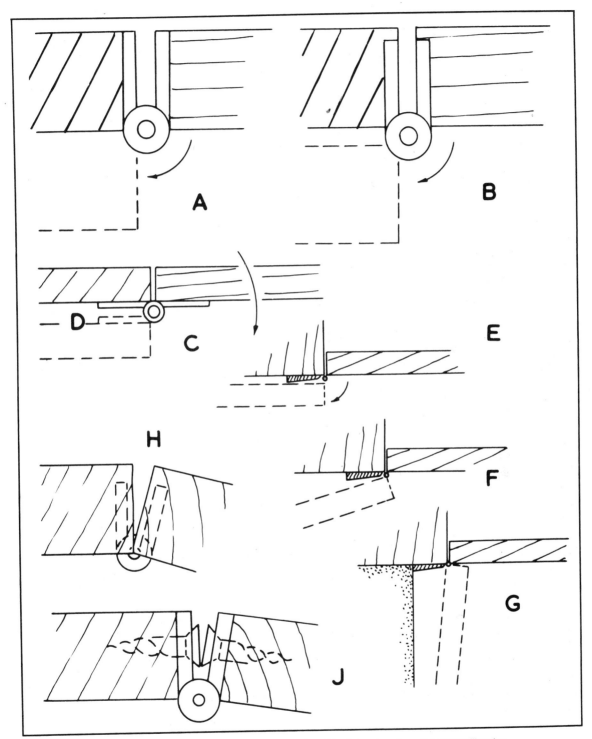

Fig. 14-2. Butt hinges fit between edges. The position of the knuckle determines how the door will swing.

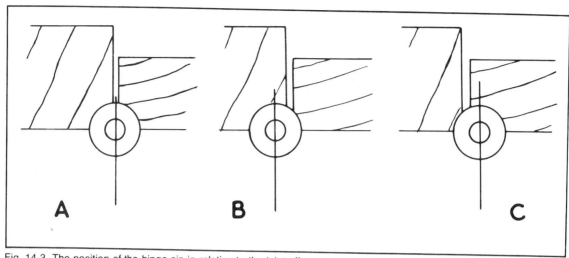

Fig. 14-3. The position of the hinge pin in relation to the joint effects the swing of the door.

parallel, but not quite touching (Fig. 14-4A) and open to not much more than 180 degrees, which is sufficient for most purposes. Hinges are available that swing further, and they are described later. The space between the closed flaps approximates to the clearance that will be needed between the two wood parts.

In the usual construction a hinge is let equally into each part (Fig. 14-4B). If the recesses are to be cut by hand, set a marking gauge to the width that will bring the knuckle into the right place (Fig. 14-4C). For the depth of each recess, set the gauge to the thickness of a flap. Cut the recesses with saw and chisel. Be careful not to go too deep or slope the cut. A router can be used, then the rounded corners squared with a chisel. Hinges can be obtained with rounded corners for fitting into routed recesses.

To increase clearance for screw heads that may not have finished exactly flush in their holes, and to provide a grip in the stile when most of the hinge may be let into the door with a deeper parallel recess, the other part slopes in from level with the surface (Fig. 14-4D). When the door is shut and the wood edges are parallel, the hinge is still slightly open.

When arranging hinges on a vertical joint, put the bottom hinge further from the bottom of the door than the top hinge is from the top of the door. If the spacing is the same, there is an optical illusion.

The bottom space looks less than the top one, which is less attractive.

For a box lid or other horizontal joint, the problem does not arise. Hinges can be arranged symmetrically along an edge. The size and number of hinges depend mainly on experience. Hinges are described by their length, but their width increases as lengths get bigger. It may be the width in relation to the wood that settles the choice of hinges. There should always be at least two butt hinges, however short the joint. A butt hinge made in a long piece is a piano hinge, which is named from its use on piano covers. It may be a preferable alternative to two or three butt hinges in some assemblies. You can buy piano hinges in long pieces undrilled.

BOX LID HINGES

You can hinge a lid or similar thing in any of the ways just described. Much depends on how far the lid is to open. If the knuckle lines up with the surfaces or only has a slight projection, the lid can swing back to be stopped by the box (Fig. 14-5A).

If the pivot center is kept in from the edge, the wood parts will meet before the lid has opened very far. This can be arranged for the box to provide its own stop when the lid is vertical, or at any other intended angle, by planing chamfers on the box and lid outside the hinge line (Fig. 14-5B). Stopped butt hinges are made that are arranged with projections on the knuckle to stop the hinge when it is opened to 90 degrees so it can serve the same purpose as chamfering the wood.

RISING BUTT HINGES

Hinges are made with the knuckle in two parts. The pin in one part can project into the other, but it can be removed. These hinges (Fig. 14-6A) allow a door to be lifted off. It helps in locating the door when it is being replaced if the pin on the lower hinge is longer and can be refitted first. This is particularly so with heavy gates. Putting the bottom parts together holds them while you locate the top pin and hole. Such large gate hinges are *gudgeons* (with holes) and *pintles* (with pins).

Those hinges serve if all that is required is the facility to lift off, but if the meeting knuckle surfaces are sloped (Fig. 14-6B), a door will rise as it is opened. This helps in increasing clearance over a carpet when a room door is opened. A secondary benefit comes in the self-closing action, as the weight of the door will make the parts of the hinge slide down the slope.

Make sure there is enough space for the lifting

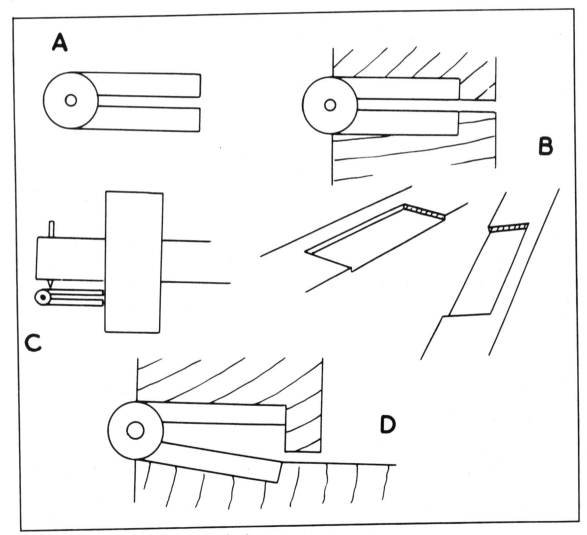

Fig. 14-4. A hinge may be let into one or both edges.

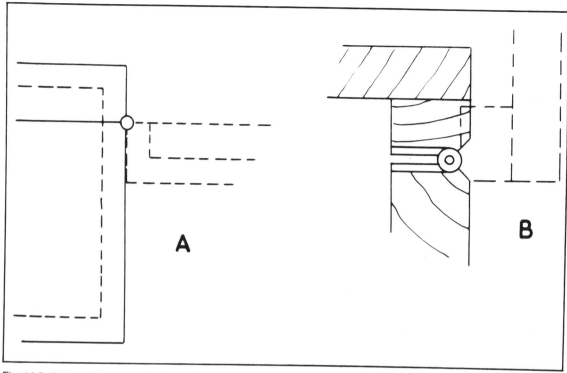

Fig. 14-5. A hinged lid may swing down (A) or be arranged with a stop (B).

and removal action. If the diameter of the knuckle is clear of the surfaces, there will be no trouble. If the knuckle is partly within the thickness of the wood, there will have to be some notching for the lifting hinge part to come clear.

SURFACE HINGES

Although the fitting of butt hinges let into the edges of the meeting parts is neat, sometimes it is better to put the hinges on the outside surfaces. Butt hinges in these positions are only appropriate in the crudest work where appearance is unimportant. Surface hinges with decorative outlines may match catches and handles to make a balanced attractive pattern on a door or box lid. These were used extensively in older furniture, and copies may be needed in reproduction of antiques. Screw holes are appropriately placed (Fig. 14-7A), and the outline is shaped. The finish is often bronzed, and screws with a similar finish are needed.

The single line of edge screws in a butt hinge

may not be enough to take the weight of a heavy or wide door. Wider hinges with extra holes (Fig. 14-7B) spread the load on more screws. Screws in edge-mounted butt hinges take the load in the direction of their length, and they may tend to pull loose or out completely (Fig. 14-7C). Screws through a hinge on the surface take the load across themselves and offer more resistance that way (Fig. 14-7D). If a door overlaps the side of a carcass, a butt hinge between also has the load on the screws in the door across their length and is stronger than the other way.

A strap hinge may be large and intended for heavy construction, with enough width for screw holes to be staggered to come in different lines of grain (Fig. 14-7E). Another version is narrow and parallel (Fig. 14-7F) so it can be used on wood edgewise (Fig. 14-7G), where it is let into the full width of the wood or a cut slot.

Another hinge for heavy weights, where one side of the assembly is not wide enough for a strap, is a T-hinge (Fig. 14-7H). The plain version is now used for heavy doors and outdoor construction, but there are many T-hinges with elaborately shaped outlines, piercing, and other decorations. These hinges and reproductions of them can be seen on chests, cupboards, and large heavy doors of medieval castles and houses.

SPECIAL HINGES

Many special hinges are designed to suit the needs of mass production furniture manufacturers. Some are described in Chapter 17.

An edge-mounted hinge is a pivot hinge (Fig. 14-8A) and goes under a door, with the lower part into the overhanging framing. A similar hinge may have a link between the two pivots (Fig. 14-8B), so it can be mounted on the edge on two parts, such as a draft screen (Fig. 14-8C), and allow them to swing on each.

For a similar situation where the hinges are to come on the edge, the hinge is made with two knuckles separated by a piece that allows the other parts joined to fold on each other (Fig. 14-8D). The double-folding screen hinge (Fig. 14-8E) mounts on the two edges, but its three lines of knuckles allow the screens or other parts joined to be folded closely one way, then opened and folded so their other surfaces meet. A double knuckle hinge is used for a room door that can swing both ways.

ACUTE ANGLE HINGING

Most hinged joints are square, but in a corner

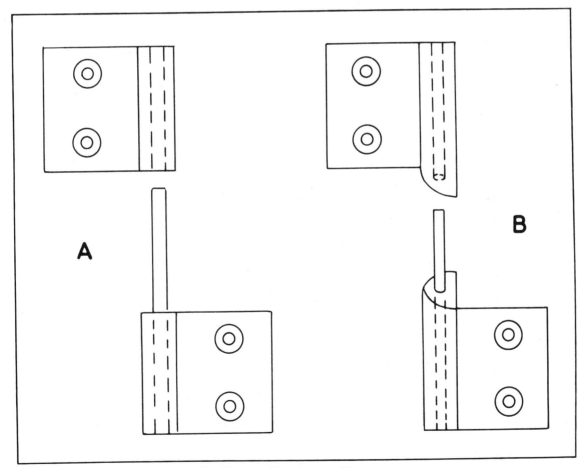

Fig. 14-6. A hinge may allow a door to lift off (A) or to lift as it opens (B).

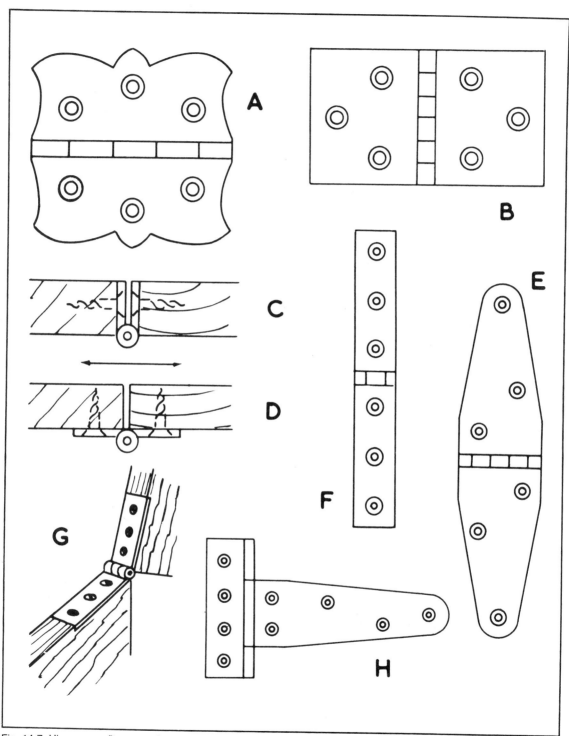

Fig. 14-7. Hinges may fit on a surface or be extended to allow for more screws.

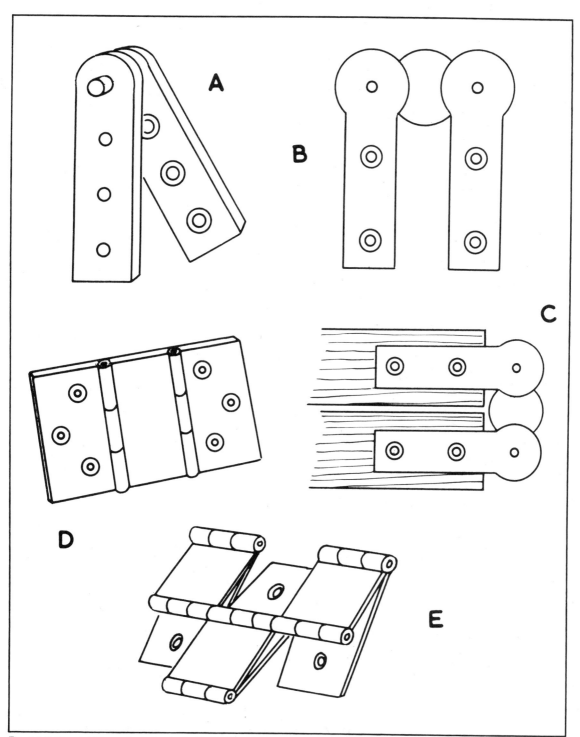

Fig. 14-8. Special hinges include pivots (A, B, C), a double knuckle (D), and a double folding screen hinge (E).

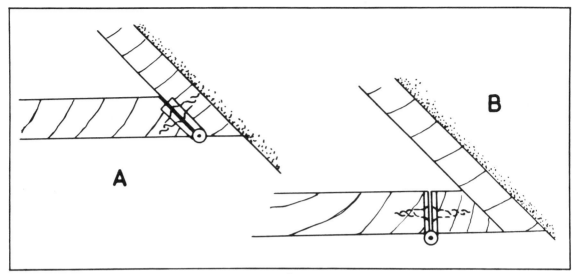

Fig. 14-9. At an acute angle you should have a narrow stile for stronger hinging.

cabinet or similar assembly the door meets the upright part at an angle less than 90 degrees. If a butt hinge is used directly between the parts, the screws into the door do not have sufficient wood to provide a grip. The thin wood edge may split (Fig. 14-9A).

It is better to provide a narrow stile (Fig. 14-9B), so the hinge will be screwed squarely. This does not restrict access to the interior. A similar piece at the other side allows the door to be cut squarely. It can carry a doorstop and allow a more convenient way of fitting a catch and handle.

RULE JOINTS

If a table is made with a drop leaf or flap hinged with the knuckle below the bottom surfaces, the parts swing open to expose a gap between their square edges (Fig. 14-10A). In better work the meeting surfaces are given a rule joint, which requires the use of a special backflap hinge. The name of the joints comes from the similarity of its section to the joint movement in some folding rules.

A backflap hinge is made like a butt hinge, but the gaps at the knuckle are cut back enough to allow it to open further than usual (Fig. 14-10B). The screw holes are spaced to allow for the overlap of the parts in this joint.

In the complete joint the hinge is let in with its knuckle upward. The permanent flat top has its edge curved, and the edge of the flap has a concave curve to move over it (Fig. 14-10C). The effect is to leave a molded appearance when the flap is lowered (Fig. 14-10D). If outer edges of the tabletop are given matching moldings, the general effect is uniform and more pleasing than the simple square-edged break on the hinge line.

To get the shapes of sections for the edges, you must draw the meeting parts full-size. The parts pivot about the center of the hinge knuckle, so draw the hinge first (Fig. 14-10E). The shoulder on the top comes vertically over the center of the knuckle, then a curve is drawn from this (Fig. 14-10F). The curve on the flap matches this, except for a small amount allowed for clearance (Fig. 14-10G).

Be careful to arrange the amount of curve so the screws into the flap enter solid wood far enough from the curve to avoid the risk of splitting, either during construction or in later use. Do not let the hinges in any deeper than necessary.

ROD PIVOTS

A door or flap may pivot on screws in a light construction preferably with washers under the head and between the parts (Fig. 14-11A). The screw

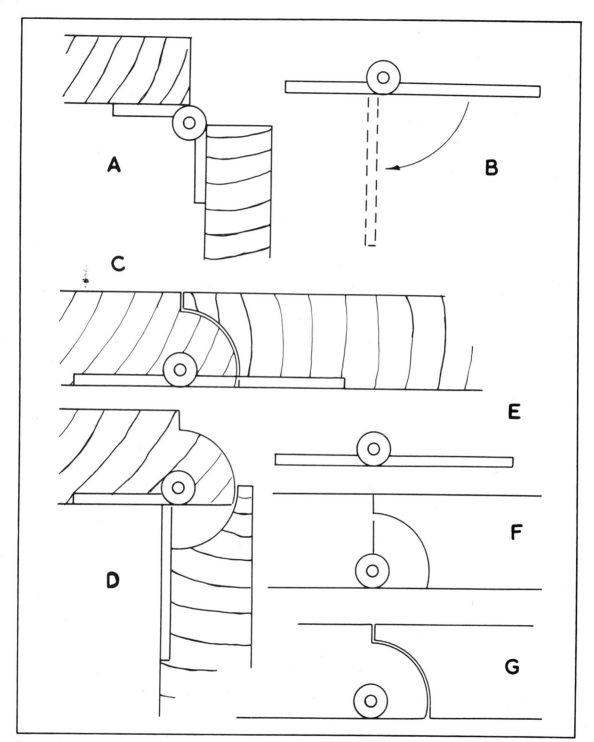

Fig. 14-10. A simple hinge on a table flap does not allow as neat an edge as a backflap hinge and a rule joint.

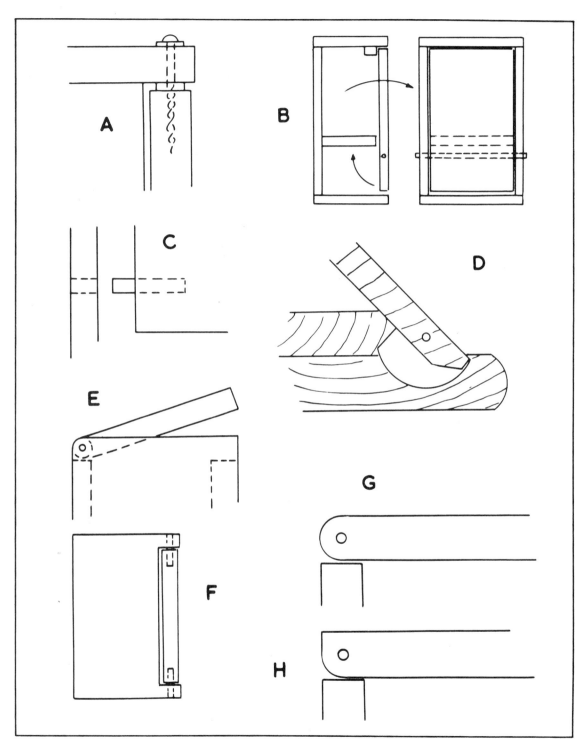

Fig. 14-11. Screws or pegs can be used as pivots instead of hinges.

threads grip the flap, so the screw turns in the other piece. The head might wear into bare wood after prolonged use. If the head needs to be countersunk, it could run in a tapered washer in the hole, or a cup washer can be used outside. The screw length should be chosen to give enough grip and have enough of its plain neck rotating in the outer piece. If thread comes there due to using a shorter screw, it will cut into the wood as it rotates.

Wood screws as pivots are unsuitable for heavier assemblies. It is better to use rods. A flap to swing down may have a hole drilled for a rod right through it (Fig. 14-11B). Much depends on the probable load. If support comes from an extension of the flap only and the outer end may sometimes have to resist much pressure, a through rod is better. A metal rod is better than a wood dowel one for a heavy load. In any case the wood rod needs to be thicker for sufficient strength, and the thickness of the flap may not be enough to take it. For end rods (Fig. 14-11C) in an assembly of moderate size, it may be possible to use thick nails shortened and driven into drilled holes.

The fall front of a writing desk may pivot in this way. There are metal fittings to screw to both parts and provided with the pivot between them. In better work the flap lowers to a level position, but it swings up so it is covered (Fig. 14-11D).

Similar rod pivots can be used for a box lid (Fig. 14-11E) or a cabinet door (Fig. 14-11F). Clearance has to be constructed, and there cannot be a very close joint. The lid or door edge must be rounded to a curve with its center at the rod center, so it will clear the other part as it swings (Fig. 14-11G). If the lid is to be stopped when upright, the curving may be partial (Fig. 14-11H).

Because there cannot be much wood outside the rod, keep the rod a small diameter and arrange the grain the same way as the rod, if possible, to avoid the risk of short edge grain breaking out.

FLY RAIL PIVOT

A variation on the rod pivot is seen in the fly rail sometimes used to hold up the flap of a folding table. The top rail is cut away, and a piece that fits is given a pivot so it can swing out under the raised flap (Fig. 14-12A). A screw or rod could be downward into the rail (Fig. 14-12B), this may be adequate as the usual loads on the fly piece do not strain the pivot much. It would be better if the rod extended upward into the tabletop (Fig. 14-12C), which means drilling a blind hole into the top and lowering it on to the rail, or a hole could be drilled upward from below (Fig. 14-12D).

If the ends of the fly piece are cut squarely and the pivot is central, it may be pushed open either way. Sometimes it is preferable for there to be more extension one way than the other. Then the pivot is arranged off-center. The ends are cut at an angle, so the piece can only be pushed open in the way intended (Fig. 14-12E). The extending end may be rounded or molded to improve appearance if it shows under the raised flap (Fig. 14-12F), and the slot in the rail may be shaped to match or left square.

GATELEG PIVOTS

In a gateleg table an assembly something like a gate swings out to support the raised leaf or flap (Fig. 14-13A). Sometimes metal hinges allow the gate to fold flat against the main assembly. It is more common for the gate to be made with its rails to fit between the main rails so it can swing on pivot rods—either wood or metal.

A rod may go partly into the lower main rail (Fig. 14-13B), and one may be taken fully through the top rail to permit assembly (Fig. 14-13C). That rod is hidden when the top is put on, and the gate cannot be removed. Alternatively, the top rod may only go a short way upward into its rail, and the full-depth rod may be taken through the bottom rail. That allows assembly after the top has been fitted. The bottom rod can be prevented from falling out with a screw through. It will still be possible to remove it and the leg, if ever necessary, without disturbing the rest of the table.

Where the gateleg swings against the main rails, there may be some notching to allow the folded assembly to clear the hanging flap. This is usually like a half lap joint, but it need be no deeper than necessary to get the leg far enough behind the flap.

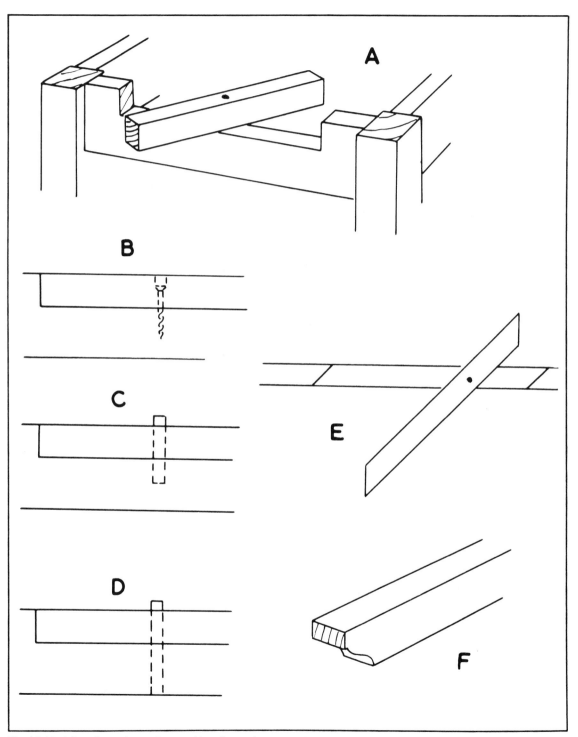

Fig. 14-12. A fly rail may be cut into a table rail to swing out and support a flap.

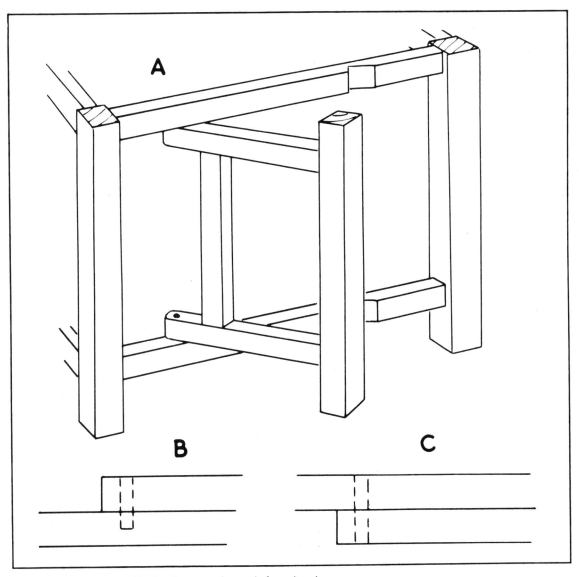

Fig. 14-13. In a gateleg table the pivots may be made from dowels.

FINGER AND KNUCKLE HINGES

A hinge made of wood is a knuckle joint hinge, but a simpler version is a finger joint hinge. The parts meet in a similar way to the finger joint used at the corner of a box.

In the simple finger hinge the ends are cut to fit into each other with the ends square (Fig. 14-14A) and enough clearance in the spaces for the parts to turn sufficiently (Fig. 14-14B). It is common to divide the depth of the hinge into an odd number of parts, so one piece comes outside the other on both edges, and to make the widths of the fingers about the same as the thickness of the wood, although that is not important. Deeper fingers may be better for softwoods, while a close-grained hardwood could have narrower ones.

A knuckle hinge joint is a more closely fitted assembly. In good work where the joint is visible,

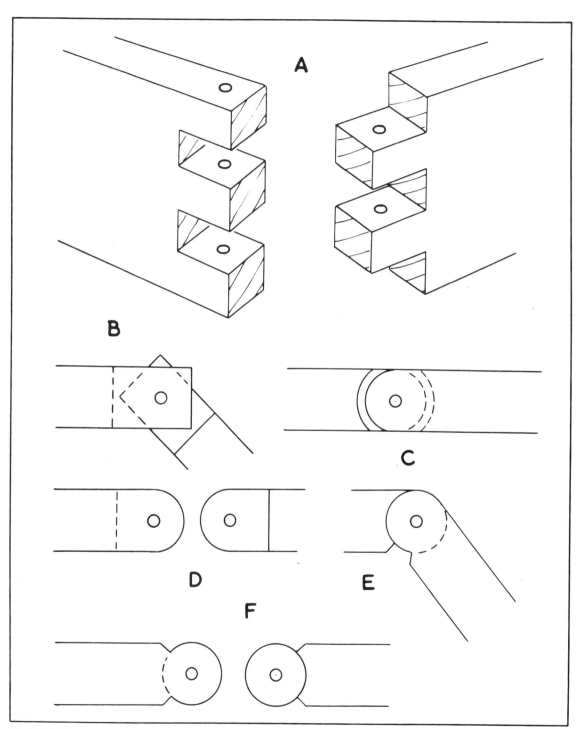

Fig. 14-14. A finger hinge has interlocking parts (A, B). A knuckle joint is more closely fitted and may be limited with stops in one or both directions (C, D, E, F).

the parts are matched (Fig. 14-14C), with the spaces hollowed to fit the projecting parts. The parts can be cut squarely where they will not show.

If the amount of movement required is not great, the parts can be made like the finger joint hinge, but with rounded ends (Fig. 14-14D). If the movement has to be greater one way than the other, the edges that side can be cut back (Fig. 14-14E). Greater movement both ways requires more cutting back, and a 45-degree slope both ways allows the joint to go from square one way through 180 degrees to square the other way (Fig. 14-14F).

The pivot rod should be metal and no thicker than necessary so too much does not have to be drilled out, and the short end grain is not put under too much strain. For most furniture construction, a rod ⅛ inch in diameter should do.

WEBBING HINGE

A simple and effective hinge can be made between parts that have to fold over each other in either direction by using fabric. Upholstery webbing or stout tape may be used. It is arranged to start on the back of one piece. It follows a figure eight path around the other piece and back to the surface it started on the first piece, spiraling just enough to clear its own edges (Fig. 14-15A). Tacks are driven through the ends and on the center around the other piece of wood. This allows the parts to fold on each other one way, then swing to fold similarly the other side (Fig. 14-15B).

Fabric can be used as a simple hinge. Some pioneer furniture and even gates were hinged with leather nailed on. Plastic-coated fabrics will flex almost indefinitely and have hinge possibilities. One possible use is over a lifting flap outdoors, where the material weatherproofs and acts as a hinge without a metal hinge underneath (Fig. 14-15C).

TAMBOUR FALL

Fabric is used with wood in a tambour fall. This was popular in desks. The tambour fall closed the desk, but it could be slid up to disappear when the desk

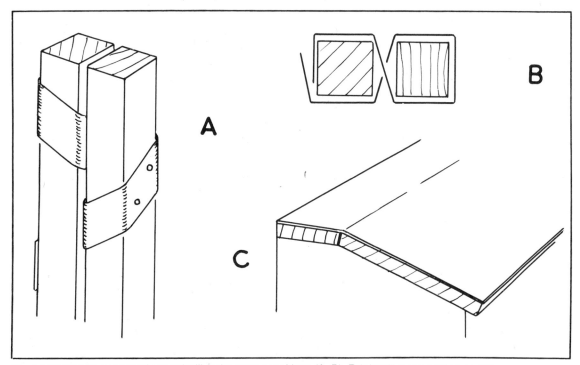

Fig. 14-15. Webbing wrapped around will make a two-way hinge (A, B). Fabric will make a lid hinge (C).

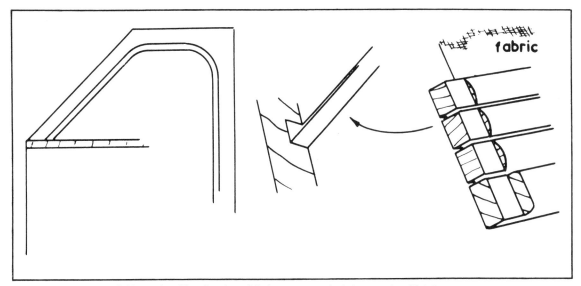

Fig. 14-16. A tambour fall is made with strips that slide in a groove gluded to a strip of fabric.

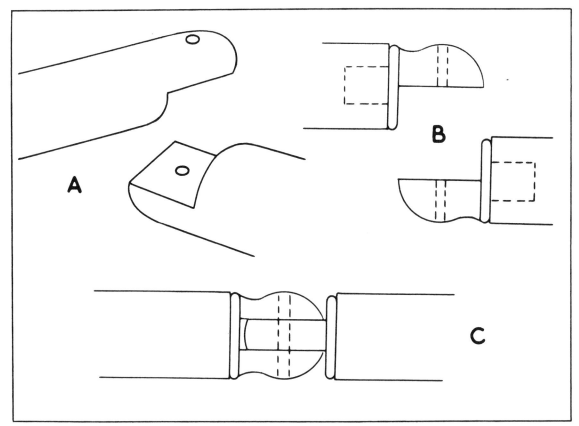

Fig. 14-17. A curtain pole joint (A) may be cut in the solid wood (A) or be made with turned pieces doweled in (B, C).

was to be used. Variations are found in some modern furniture.

In its assembly there is a narrow groove at each side into which go the ends of many narrow strips of wood and one thicker one to provide the edge and handle. All of these pieces are glued to flexible fabric that hinges between them as they follow the grooves. The strips have their ends reduced to slide in the grooves (Fig. 14-16).

CURTAIN POLE JOINT

If round rods have to meet and be arranged to pivot on each other, as in a curtain rail that will be adjusted around a recess, half can be cut from each end. A screw is put through centrally to form a pivot (Fig. 14-17A). When the angle has been adjusted, any projecting sharp edges can be trimmed off.

A better end has half balls making the pivot. They could be turned on the poles, but because of their lengths it may be better to turn them separately with dowels projecting to go into holes in the poles (Fig. 14-17B). Turn the ends as complete matching balls. Cut each in half to mate with the other, so whatever angle the poles move to the corner presents a neat appearance. If greater strength is needed in this assembly, the balls could be notched into each other like a bridle joint (Fig. 14-17C).

Chapter 15

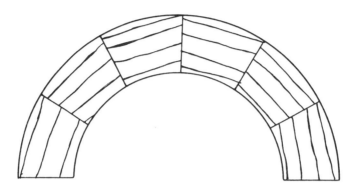

Curved and Laminated Joints

WOOD IS FLEXIBLE AS A NATURAL FIBROUS material, and some woods may be bent more than others. Some bending is possible without treatment. The bent part has to be held in shape, or it will spring back to straight or very nearly so. The amount of bend possible can be increased considerably if the wood is steamed, and it is more likely to keep its shape after drying. Steaming is used in many woodworking activities, such as making bentwood furniture and boatbuilding.

Wood to be steamed is enclosed in a container, where steam from a boiler is introduced and allowed to flow around the wood and be vented elsewhere (Fig. 15-1A). The wood is kept away from the sides of the container, so steam can get all around it. After a sufficient period, it is quickly removed and bent to shape. The bending may be a simple pull around a form (Fig. 15-1B), or a more complicated mold or form as described for later processes. It is then left to dry and set before being removed. It will spring back a little, so it is common to force it to rather more curve than will finally be needed. Windsor chair backs are curved in this way.

In some cases the steamed board will be held in place permanently by screws or nails. This happens with boat planking, where the steamed wood is quickly put in place and fasteners driven before it begins to dry.

Small parts may be made flexible by soaking in hot water instead of enclosing in a steam box. You can pour hot water over a part made of solid wood or plywood to give a little more flexibility and reach the intended shape. Steam and water reduce the risk of cracking, which may occur when dry wood is bent. If wood is bent while full of sap before seasoning, it can be left to season while held to shape.

SAW KERFING

When any piece of wood is bent, the outer fibers are stretched and the inside fibers compressed, while those at the central neutral axis do not get longer or shorter. Compressing is more difficult than stretching, so if only the outside of the curve will show and something can be done to ease the compression loads, the wood will bend easier and further without steaming or risking breakage.

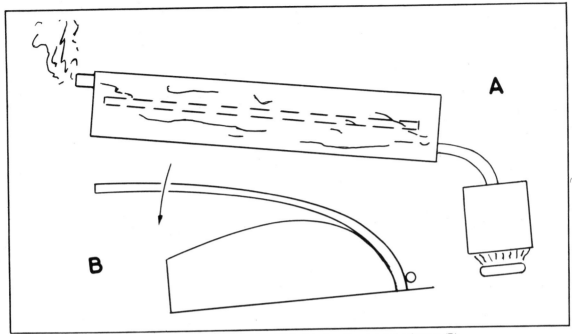

Fig. 15-1. Wood can be made more flexible by steaming (A) before bending around a former (B).

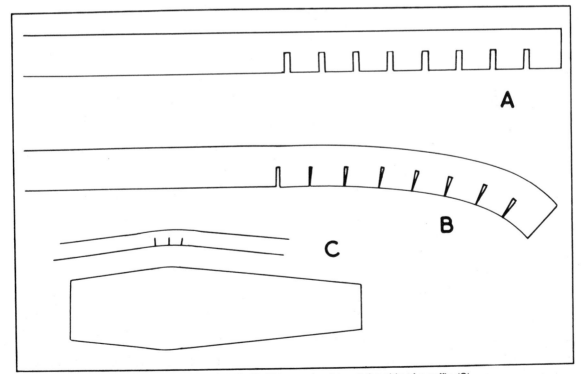

Fig. 15-2. Saw kerfs across wood help it bend (A, B). This may be done at the side of a coffin (C).

One way of reducing compression loads is to cut saw kerfs across what will be the inner surface (Fig. 15-2A). How close the kerfs are and how deep they are cut depend on the amount of curve to be given, but the cuts should not go halfway through. The kerfs close when the wood is pulled to a curve (Fig. 15-2B). The amount of possible curve is then affected by the widths of the kerfs, which depend on the set of the saw and how close the kerfs are, but they should not be too close or the wood between may crumble. For most curves, the kerfs can be about as far apart as the thickness of the wood.

Saw kerfing is still used in making of shaped caskets or coffins (Fig. 15-2C). The old-time craftsman had a very long backsaw for this purpose.

SLIT KERFING

Some strip wood parts are mainly straight, but they require curves at one or both ends. This happens with a canoe or boat keel that is straight or moderately curved, but at the end of the line sweeps up to form a stem or bow. In some constructions the stem is a separate piece joined on, but you can bend the one piece to form the straight and curved parts.

Sometimes it would be possible to steam and bend the end, but in another way the end is given several lengthwise saw cuts (Fig. 15-3A). If glue is put into the saw kerfs and they are pulled around a former (Fig. 15-3B), the wood will take the curve. The glue will hold it after it has set. Some excess length should be allowed for maintaining the curve right to the final end and for trimming later.

In that method of bending the wood loses some thickness due to the waste removed in the saw cuts. That may not matter, but if it is important that the thickness around the curve is kept the same as the straight part, pieces of veneer, with their grain across or diagonal, can be glued in and bent with the wood (Fig. 15-3C). Have them slightly too wide, so they can be planed level after bending.

LAMINATED CURVES

Some steamed solid wood requires considerable pressure to bend it. Forms and molds have to be strong, or you may find the mold bending in reaction to the wood you want to bend. This applies to a back for a Windsor chair, where the forms in production work are heavy metal assemblies.

An alternative to solid wood is an assembly of several layers of thinner wood bent together. This is laminating. The shape may be made up of many pieces of veneer, a lesser number of thin strips of

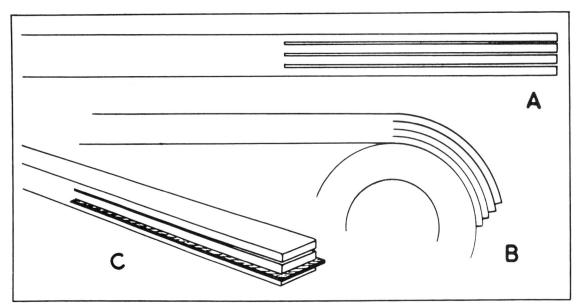

Fig. 15-3. Slits along the grain help bending (A, B). They may be filled with veneers.

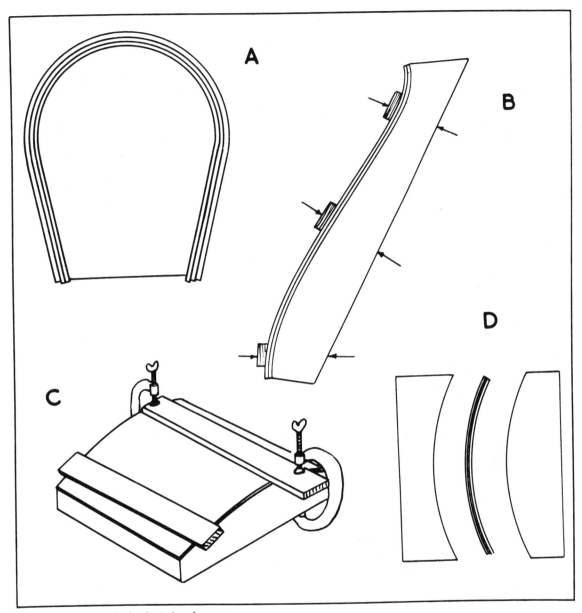

Fig. 15-4. Parts may be laminated on formers.

wood, or an even lesser number of pieces as thick as may be expected to bend dry. Whatever the number of pieces, they have to be bent around a form and held to it while the glue sets (Fig. 15-4A). The wood must not be steamed as most glues cannot grip damp wood.

In large construction, such as the curved beams for a roof, parts could be bent a few at a time. The inner layers could be allowed to set and be cleaned up before more layers are put on, but in most laminating of furniture-size parts, all the laminations are put on at one time. The glues used should normally be waterproof synthetic resins because of their great strength, although for some interior building laminations casein glue is used.

Take care to get enough glue where it is needed between the layers, but not to glue the assembly to the form or anything used to clamp it. Paper makes a good barrier. If the assembly rests against a baseboard as it is bent, that may be covered with newspaper.

For a straightforward moderate curve, the former may be solid wood. Pressure may be applied with clamps over scrap wood (Fig. 15-4B). If the strip is narrow, single clamps may be enough, but for much width there should be strips across between clamps (Fig. 15-4C).

This may be adequate for strips stiff enough to follow a curve between pressure points. If you are using veneers, it is better to have a mold in two parts, so pressure is uniform throughout the glue area (Fig. 15-4D).

If it is a lamination like a chair back, the mold may have a thick plywood base with the shape mounted on it. This could be cut away to admit clamps, or other ways of putting on pressure can be used. A wedge pressing against a piece of wood held down with a stout screw is simplest (Fig. 15-5A). Have a single screw at each place, then the wood block can pivot on it to match the wedge. It

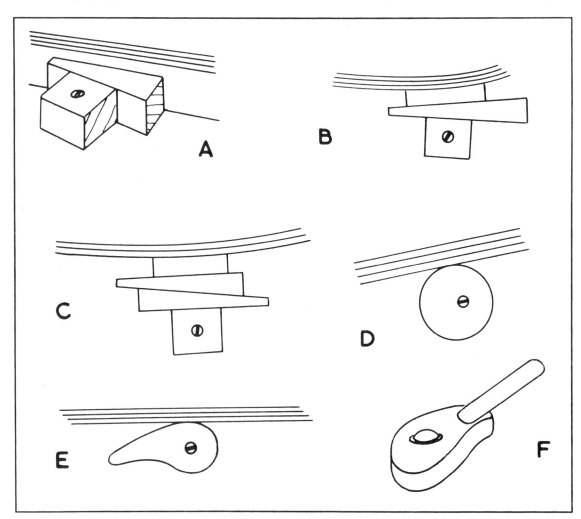

Fig. 15-5. Laminations may be held to formers with wedges (A, B, C) or cams (D, E, F).

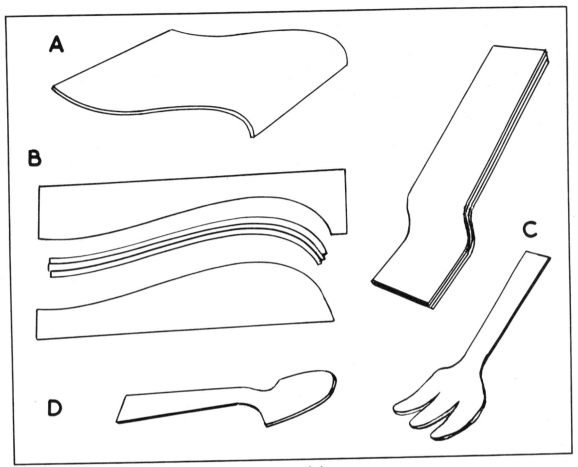

Fig. 15-6. Veneers can be laminated to make a chair seat or salad servers.

may help to include a shaped piece against the work and under the wedge (Fig. 15-5B). A pair of folding wedges will put on even more pressure (Fig. 15-5C).

Pressure may be applied quickly by using cams. If the work is fairly light, the cam may be just a circular block pivoting on a screw off-center (Fig. 15-5D). For more pressure it can be specially shaped (Fig. 15-5E), and for even more pressure the cam may be bolted through and provided with a lever (Fig. 15-5F).

MOLDED VENEERING

The word veneer when referring to cabinetwork means thin pieces of wood, probably 1/25 inch or less thick, but the term is applied elsewhere to wood cut up to ⅛ inch thick. Plywood is made of veneers laid with the grain of alternate layers across each other. This gives considerable strength in a comparatively thin piece. Molded veneering is really making plywood curved instead of flat. It is not always possible to lay veneers to a curved shape with their grains square to each other, but they can usually be arranged diagonally to each other and to the direction of curve to get the greatest strength.

With veneers in fairly wide pieces you can make parts curved in one direction, such as a simple chair seat (Fig. 15-6A). Three or more veneers could be pressed to shape in a two-part mold (Fig. 15-6B). In small assemblies the veneers could be pressed to a lengthwise spoon profile (Fig. 15-6C), then this is cut to make a salad serving set of spoon and fork (Fig. 15-6D).

If a compound curve is needed, the veneers have to take a curve in more than one direction. Each layer has to be made up of many narrow strips, which are fitted to each other and laid over a mold carved to the intended shape. An example is a molded racing kayak seat. For general use it may be fiberglass, but for top-class racing it is molded veneer. To get the body form shape, the strips of veneer are compressed as they are glued between shaped metal molds. Such seats are expensive.

An example of molded veneer construction is seen in boat hulls built this way. Such a hull has plenty of strength in the skin. There is no need for internal structure, except what is needed to fit out the boat. Large craft are built in this way, but a canoe or kayak hull can be built of three 1/16-inch layers of veneer and require no internal framing.

A mold has to be made in the intended internal shape, but it need not be close and can be built of spaced lengthwise strips on frames (Fig. 15-7A). Strips that will make the hog and the gunwales are laid in and attached to pieces that form the stem and stern. Over this goes a layer of polyethylene to prevent glue sticking to the mold.

The veneer is prepared in strips about 3 inches wide and long enough to go from the hog to a gunwale at an angle of about 45 degrees. Starting at the middle of the hull, a strip is cut at about 45 degrees. It is bent and glued to the hog and gunwale, then held there with temporary staples driven with a trigger tacker (Fig. 15-7B). The opposite side is treated in the same way. Further strips are laid alongside the first ones in both directions until all of the hull has been covered. A small hand plane is used to fit edges together as the work progresses. When the glue of that layer has set, all the staples through it are withdrawn.

Another layer is put on in the same manner, but in the opposite direction (Fig. 15-7C). This time glue is put between the layers. Staples are needed to hold the veneers in contact. When that glue has set, all the staples are removed. The surface is sanded smooth. Over that goes the third and last layer (Fig. 15-7D), usually diagonally in the same direction as the first, but the strips could be lengthwise. After the glue has set, the staples have

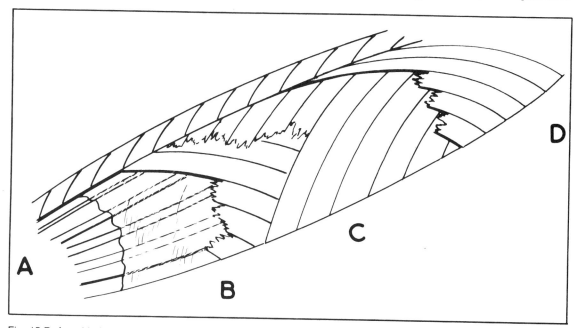

Fig. 15-7. A molded veneer boat hull is made by laying up strips of veneer in alternate directions over a mold made of lengthwise strips.

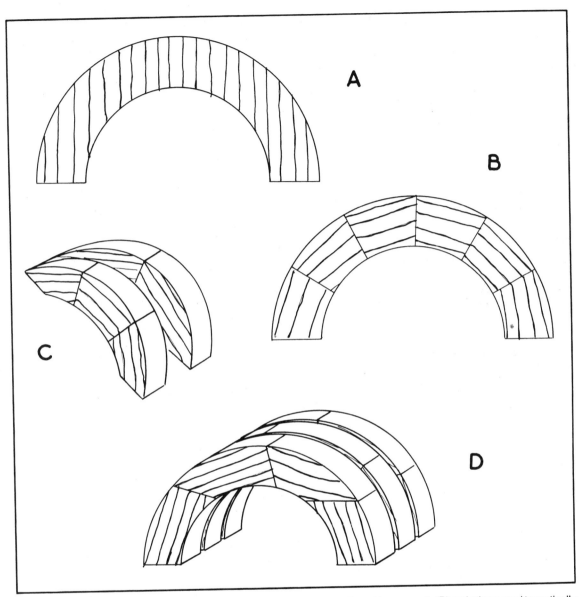

Fig. 15-8. To avoid short grain in a curve cut from solid wood (A), parts can be cut in segments (B) and others used to vertically laminate the shape (C, D).

been withdrawn, and the outside has been sanded, a wipe with a wet cloth will cause the staple holes to close. Final painting or varnishing can be done.

CURVED SECTIONS

Besides laminating by bending thin strips to shape with glue between, you can make some things in layers by a method sometimes called *vertical laminating*.

If an arched piece is cut from solid wood, part of the semicircle will have grain approximately in the shape of the outline. Square to that will be grain across the outline and parts in between with varying degrees of short grain, getting progressively weaker toward the extreme cross grain (Fig. 15-8A). For most assemblies, the weakness of part of the shape would make them unacceptable.

If segments are made so the grain follows the general direction of the outline (Fig. 15-8B), the problem of grain direction is solved, but you then have to join the parts. In a traditional wooden wheel the rim is made in this way and joined to the hub with spokes—two to each segment. A steel tire is shrunk around the whole thing, forcing the parts tightly together.

Another way is to make a similar layer, but arrange the joints so they are staggered in relation to the first ones (Fig. 15-8C). It is even better to have a third layer (Fig. 15-8D) to make up the required thickness. The parts butt against each other in each circle, but they need not be cut radially and can come as they will, unless a symmetrically patterned front is needed. The layers can be screwed together or dowels might be put through,

although with modern strong glues there should be no need for extra fasteners if the parts are a good fit and properly clamped.

JOINTED SEGMENTS

If a circle or part of it has to be made up with one thickness of solid wood, the segments have to be joined to each other. One way is to cut half lap joints (Fig. 15-9A), with enough overlap to provide a good glue area and space for screws driven from the back. If the wood is thicker, it would be better to use bridle joints (Fig. 15-9B) or to make finger joints, where there are equal amounts projecting from each part (Fig. 15-9C). Well-fitted finger joints, which may be machine cut, are probably the most satisfactory way of assembling this type of curved work.

BRICK SEGMENTING

If a curve is made up of many pieces of wood laid on

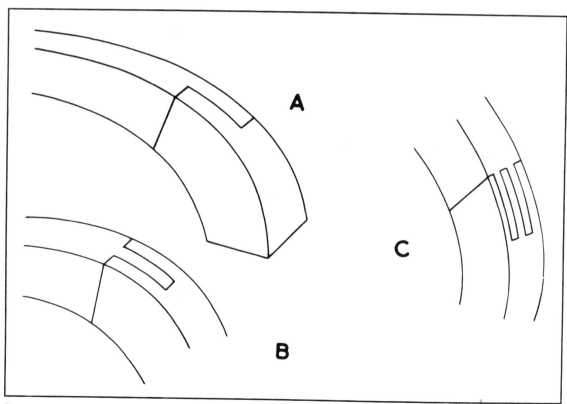

Fig. 15-9. For a curve to be built of joined solid segments, there are several ways of interlocking the parts.

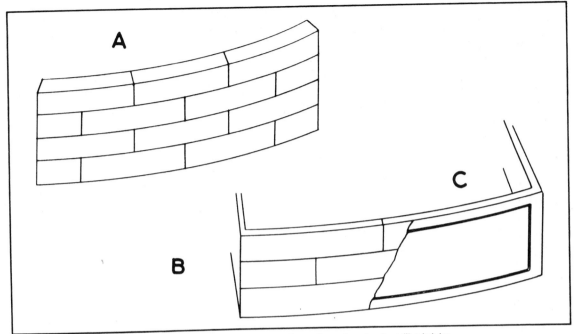

Fig. 15-10. For a shallow curve like a drawer front, pieces of wood can be glued up like bricks.

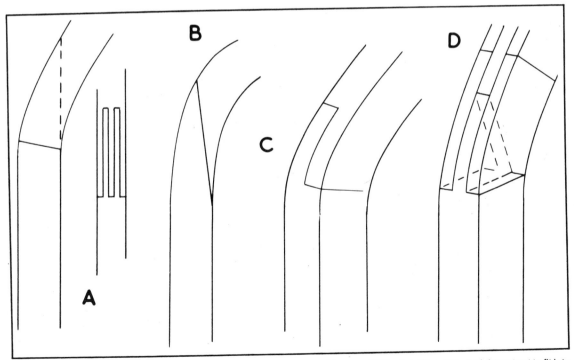

Fig. 15-11. Where straight parts join curves, there can be a finger joint (A), a scarf (B), a lap (C), or the straight part cut to fit into the curved laminations (D).

each other like bricks in a wall, this is brick laminating or segmenting. Pieces of wood are cut to similar sizes so the grain does not run off too much, then they are glued together with the joints staggered to make up the size required (Fig. 15-10A).

The method is used to make circular and elliptical rails under a table or dresser top. For a moderate curve the pieces may be quite long, but for tighter curves they are shorter, and in elliptical work their length will be different according to the part of the curve they form. Ends butt together. Curved drawer fronts may be made in this way, with a slight curve made up of fewer and wider pieces (Fig. 15-10B). Much depends on available wood and the capacity of the band saw.

In most cases the surface is not left exposed. It is covered with veneer (Fig. 15-10C).

CURVE TO STRAIGHT JOINTS

In many assemblies a curved part has to be joined to a straight one, as when an arch goes over two posts.

If possible, the curved part should be made with straight extensions. They can then be joined to the straight parts below where the curve starts, using bridle or mortise and tenon joints or even dowels. Because of the method of building up the curved parts, any straight extension may not have grain running down the way a joint has to be made, and it could be weak.

The upright part might continue up into the curved piece with fingers, which could be cut to slope upward toward the outside and give stiffness where needed (Fig. 15-11A). There might be a scarf sloping to meet the outside curve and shaped to match it (Fig. 15-11B). In some assemblies the upright part may be cut to make a form of half lap joint, continuing until it breaks through the curve, and the outside is shaped to match (Fig. 15-11C).

If the curved part is made up of vertical laminations, the straight part could be treated as a continuation of this and cut to match the layers of lamination. Make sure it goes far enough into the curved part to provide rigidity (Fig. 15-11D).

Chapter 16

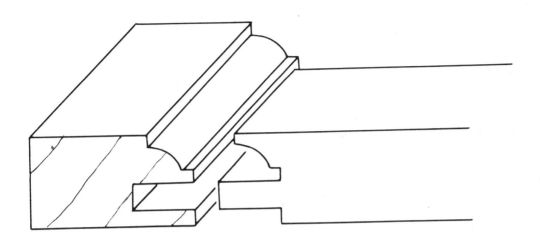

Joints for Machine Cutting

MOST WELL-ESTABLISHED JOINTS DATE FROM long before the arrival of even the most simple machinery, and they were cut entirely with hand tools. These joints have stood the test of time and are still favored, although some may now be partly or completely cut with power tools. Most of the joints described in this book are basically capable of being cut with hand tools, although some part of the process may be helped by power tools.

Some joints in heavy woodwork must have been very tiring to cut and fit, with only muscle power to work the tools. It must have also been difficult to achieve accuracy. A machine does not tire. It is capable of keeping up a standard performance almost indefinitely and sustaining accuracy to a standard for which it has been set. Many things can be cut or made with all their details identical, for at least as long as the cutting parts of the machine retain their edges.

Machines can mass produce many things besides furniture and other wood products. Most of us could not afford to pay for a similar piece of furniture made as a one-off, so we accept having the same thing as many other people. The individual craftsman, whether amateur or professional, can make a one-off piece, and he may prefer to use traditional joints. Some machine-made joints are really the mark of mass production. The maker of individual pieces of furniture will have to decide if his one-off work is to incorporate traditional joints or those which a knowledgeable observer may interpret as mass production.

MORTISING

A power drill is a better waste remover from a mortise than a chisel that has to be hit and levered. Some early attempts at using drills to cut mortises employed jigs to guide the drill. A series of holes was made that touched. The jig was adjusted to bring the new drilling positions midway between the first one, so further drilling removed the waste between the holes (Fig. 16-1A). This might have been good enough, or the mortise could be smoothed along its edges with a chisel. Ends had to

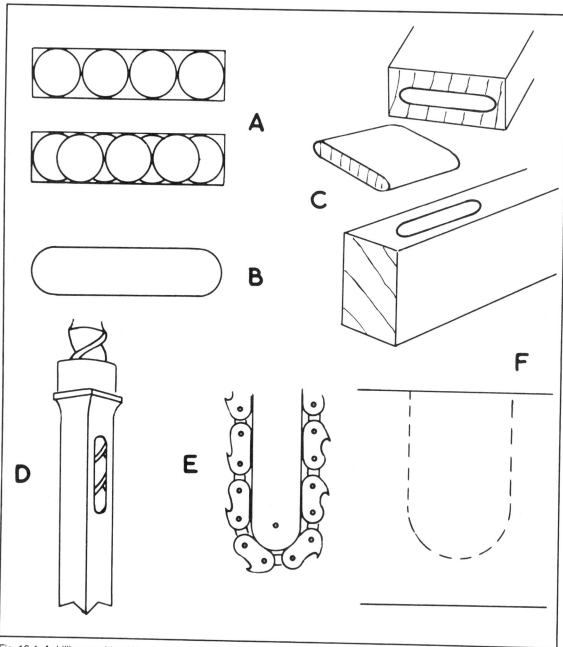

Fig. 16-1. A drilling machine (A) or a router (B) will remove most of the waste from a mortise. In machine work a tenon may be inserted (C). Special mortise tools (D, E, F) cut quickly and accurately.

be squared with a chisel, or the tenon was made rounded to suit the ends.

A drill does not cut on its side, but a router cutter can be made to cut on its end and its side. It may be moved along a mortise to trim the wood to a uniform depth and width. The finished shape is then similar to that produced with the drill jig, but much more cleanly cut and accurate (Fig. 16-1B). It still needs squaring if square-edged tenons are used.

An alternative is to cut mortises in both parts and use a loose tenon glued in (Fig. 16-1C). The tenon material can be machined in a long piece and cut off as required.

Square-ended mortises can be cut with a square hollow drill. This is actually a square tube made like four chisels with their bevels inward. Down this goes a twist drill (Fig. 16-1D). The tool is mounted in a machine like a drill press and brought down on the wood so the drill removes the bulk of the waste, and the square hollow chisel pares the round hole square. The tool has to be withdrawn and lowered again alongside the first hole. The process is repeated until enough squares have been cut to make up the required length of mortise.

For large mortises, one machine tool uses a cutter something like a chain saw. A chain runs around a sprocket that is lowered into the wood. The outside of the chain has cutters that remove the wood in the shape of a mortise (Fig. 16-1E). The bottom of the mortise is semicircular (Fig. 16-1F). A square-ended tenon can be inserted just as far as

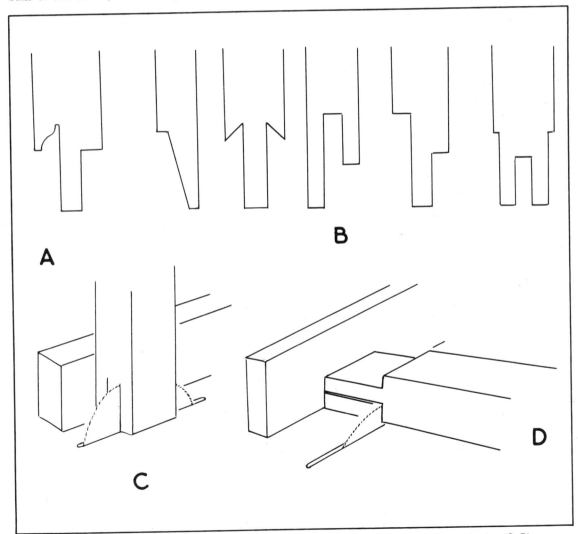

Fig. 16-2. A tenoning machine will cut other shapes besides tenons (A, B). A circular saw will cut tenons (C, D).

the curve if the wood is of sufficient depth or in thinner wood the end of the tenon can be shaped to go to the mortise bottom.

TENONING

In quantity production tenons are cut with a machine that does much of its work with circular saws. Two saws cut the sides of the tenon, then others cut the shoulders. When the machine has been set up to produce the first tenon to match its mortise, any number of tenons can be cut that will be identical to the first. If opposite ends have to be treated, the wood may be reversed for a second pass.

The machine can be fitted with cutters to produce other shapes on the end of wood. Scribing a shoulder over a molded edge on the mortised part is possible (Fig. 16-2A) no matter how complicated the molding, providing it does not include undercut sections. Simple chamfers can have matching shoulders. Long and short shoulders can be cut square or at angles. Other end shapes may be made (Fig. 16-2B).

A simple table saw may be used to cut tenons accurately if it has a fence and a rise and fall adjustment. The end of the wood must be cut squarely, either to actual final length or at a set amount of waste to be trimmed after assembly. Sides of the tenon are cut by setting the saw depth to the length to the shoulders and the fence to the distance of each cut from the surface (Fig. 16-2C). Shoulders are cut in a similar way by altering the projection of the saw and the distance from it of the fence (Fig. 16-2D). If all the stages in each piece are done at the same time, a large quantity of identical tenons can be cut.

BASIC EDGE JOINTS

Power saws and planers may be used to cut edges straight and square for simple edge-to-edge joints between boards. Most tongue and groove joint variations described in Chapter 10 can be cut by machine. These are usually cut by moving the wood against rotating cutters of the required profile. In some cases the cutter may be in a portable machine,

such as a router, and moved on the wood. As the shapes depend on the profile of the cutter, almost any shape is possible, depending on the pattern of the cutter. Undercuts cannot be worked. Parallel parts of much depth are liable to tear or become rough from the side of the penetrating cutter, so a tongue and groove may be given a taper (Fig. 16-3A). This need only be very slight, but it ensures a cleaner surface on the sides of the tongue and groove. Practically, it makes assembly easier and gives just as much glue area as a squarely cut edge.

The purpose of shaping edges is to provide a larger glue area than would be given by a straight cut across. Interlocking patterns also keep the surfaces in line when gluing, so the need to move the boards laterally in relation to each other is avoided. There may be a simple S-shaped section (Fig. 16-3B). The parts can have variations on the tongue and groove joint, as cuts do not have to be square (Fig. 16-3C). Thicker wood may have several tongues and grooves (Fig. 16-3D), so there is a firm interlocking.

Most of these joints are formed with the rotating cutter approaching at the edge. You can have it guided along the edge, but making its cut on the surface. That allows for what would be undercuts the other way, so shapes can be made with matching curves (Fig. 16-3E). This also serves as a shutting joint, both where two doors meet or at the closing side, where the edges can interlock as the door closes to make a draftproof joint (Fig. 16-3F).

INTEGRAL MOLDED EDGE JOINTS

Where much strength is needed between two parts meeting at an angle, they must be given mortise and tenon joints or dowels long enough to take the load. There are some places where a tongue not big enough to be called a tenon may be enough on the end of one piece. Matched rotary molding cutters can cut an end with a sufficient tongue to fit a groove and a scribed edge to cover a molding (Fig. 16-4). The groove may take a panel or be a short mortise just to take the tongue of the other piece. Cutters can make many types of molded edge, with tongue and groove behind them.

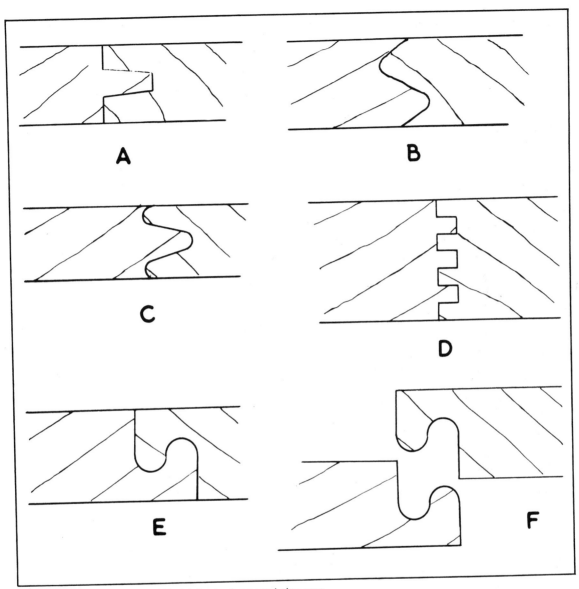

Fig. 16-3. Machine-cut interlocking joints give increased glue area.

CORNER JOINTS

In hand-cut corner joints take care to avoid putting loads on short grain. This is because of the weakness of grain that might break out during cutting or under later loads. Some short grain in a joint is acceptable, mainly because the method of machine cutting has little risk of breaking the short grain. The precision is such that it compensates in strength for the inherent weakness of short grain.

There may be a dado and rabbet joint (Fig. 16-5A), which is sometimes used along the grain in handwork, but may be cut by machine across end grain, where it is unlikely that there will be any load to force a levering action against the short-grained end. A further step is a dado, tongue, and rabbet joint (Fig. 16-5B), which lends itself to cutting with power tools, but would be difficult to cut accurately by hand. Although it includes short grain in the

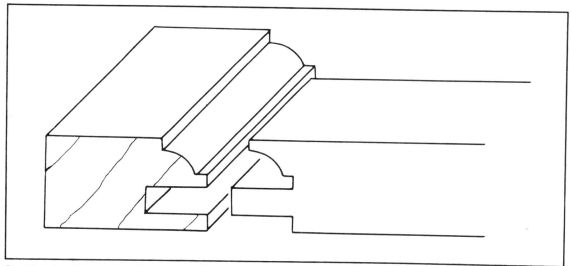

Fig. 16-4. A molding cutter will make matching molded and grooved joints.

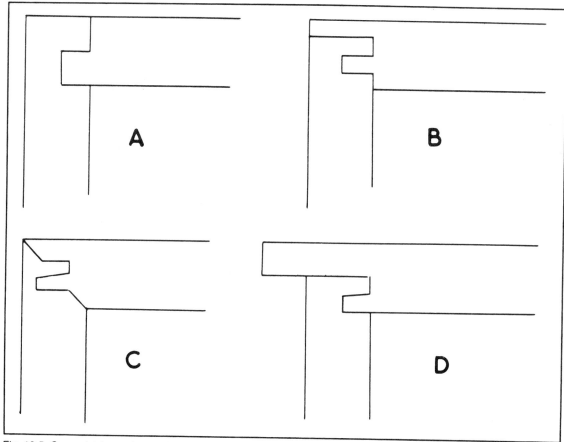

Fig. 16-5. Corner joints can be notched by machine in several ways.

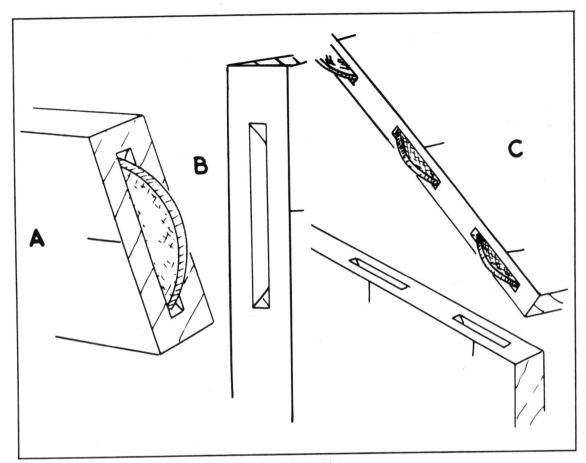

Fig. 16-6. A plate joint uses a compressed hardwood biscuit glued into recesses.

direction of the load, this joint is used for drawer fronts instead of dovetails, where the front is clear across and only a small amount of end grain shows at the drawer side.

A variation on this has a miter effect, so no end grain appears on the surfaces (Fig. 16-5C). The tapered interlocking tongues are stronger than if they had been cut with parallel surfaces, and they have a tightening effect as the joint is drawn together. The joint could be cut along or across the grain and would be suitable for the corner of a box or cabinet. At a drawer front it would give a clean appearance both ways.

Where the drawer front has to overlap the casing, the joint needs modification so it works in a rabbet that allows part of the front to extend (Fig. 16-5D).

Machine-made dovetails have been described in Chapter 9. Machines vary from portable jigs and cutters powered with an electric drill to more elaborate machines, but in most cases the result is a half-blind or stopped dovetail with the tails and pins the same width. Some machine tools will make through dovetails with tails and pins of different widths.

PLATE JOINTS

An alternative to dowels, short tenons, or tongue and groove joints is to use shaped pieces of compressed wood in curved slots. A tool with a cutter like a wide circular saw cuts identical recesses in both pieces. It is guided by register marks on the surface (Fig. 16-6A). A prepared shaped biscuit of compressed hardwood fits loosely into the recesses

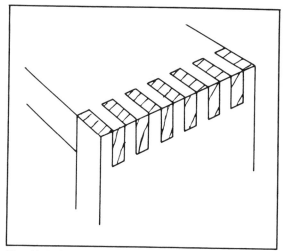

Fig. 16-7. Finger joints can be cut very accurately by machine.

(Fig. 16-6B). It has a crosshatch pattern to hold glue. Although the first fitting is loose, moisture in the glue causes the insert to swell and make a tight joint.

The joint may be used at a miter, either in a flat frame or as a long edgewise joint. It may come at a corner, or it could be used along an edge. Where the joint is long, there can be a series of hollows and inserts (Fig. 16-6C), each located between the mating pieces with register marks on the surface to line up with a central mark on the cutting tool. The machine makers provide prepared compressed hardwood biscuits to suit the recesses they cut.

Although this method is suitable for solid wood, it can also be used for manufactured boards. Other methods of joining might be unsuitable due to cut parts crumbling or breaking.

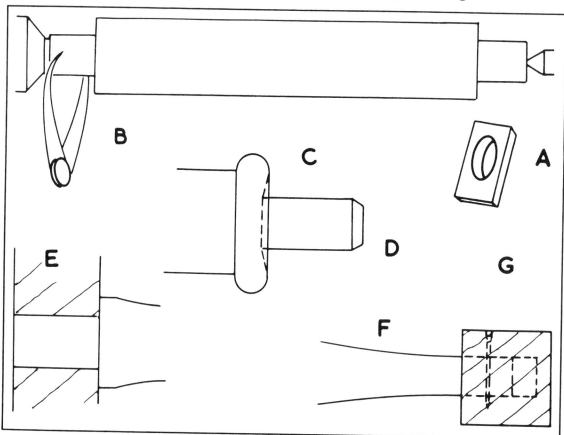

Fig. 16-8. Dowels may be made integrally on turned work (A, B). It helps to undercut (C) and bevel (D) for close assembly. There may be a shoulder (E) or a sliding end (F).

FINGER JOINTS

Interlocking fingers are used in some hand-cut construction, but the joint is particularly suitable where corners meet, as in a box, for cutting by machine. The tongues or fingers may then be made with precision difficult to achieve by hand, so a well-fitting joint may be regarded as a decorative feature. When the joint is cut by hand, there is a tendency to make the fingers wide to reduce the amount of work. The narrower fingers produced by machine look better and increase the glue area to strengthen the joint (Fig. 16-7).

TURNED JOINTS

One of the oldest machines is the lathe. It was used in a primitive form, with hand or foot power, to make round objects in wood and other materials. Dowels were turned on the part being shaped to fit into a round hole in another part. Variations on this are still used when turned parts are included in an assembly.

If a dowel is being turned at the tailstock end of the lathe, a piece of scrap wood with a hole in it can be used as a template (Fig. 16-8A) for getting the diameter correct. At the other end the size will have to be checked with calipers (Fig. 16-8B). Avoid a curve in the angle where diameters change, as this might prevent a close-fitting joint. It may be better to very slightly undercut or taper in the cut (Fig. 16-8C). At the other end a taper may be turned for easy entry into a hole (Fig. 16-8D). If the dowel goes into a blind hole, it should be turned short to leave a space beyond it. This is better than sawing to length after turning.

If the dowel is a reduced diameter so there is a shoulder (Fig. 16-8E), that sets the overall length exactly. This is what is wanted in most assemblies. The turned shoulder serves the same purpose as the cut shoulder of a tenoned part.

In some instances, such as with many chairs, allow some adjustment in the amount of penetration of the turned end into its hole. This happens with the lower chair rails where the top tenoned rails set the sizes there. The legs may slope, though, and the exact length of the lower turned rails is not easily determined. In that case the end of the rail comes to the joint with a slight taper and the last part parallel (Fig. 16-8F), so it can be moved in and out of the hole in the leg. In this type of assembly it helps to prevent movement when the size is determined and before the glue has set if a thin pin is driven inconspicuously across the joint (Fig. 16-8G).

Turned dowels may go into round parts, but dowels going into square parts is stronger due to the smaller cross section of the drilled part (Fig. 16-9A). The dowel should usually go more than halfway (Fig. 16-9B), unless it is into a large round section. If there are rails in two directions, they are better at different levels (Fig. 16-9C). Otherwise, the drilled part may be weakened too much. If they must come at the same level, the holes may be drilled into each other and the dowel ends mitered (Fig. 16-9D).

To give the greater strength of a square section, turned parts may have square parts left where the joints come. This is common and regarded as decorative (Fig. 16-9E). The dowel ends may then come at different levels or be brought together with miters, without weakening the leg to the dangerous point that might occur with a small round section (Fig. 16-9F).

A shouldered turned dowel end may hold a pillar, such as a lamp standard into a base (Fig. 16-10A), either into a blind hole or through and tightened with a wedge (Fig. 16-10B). It may be kept short and the wedge punched if the surface has to remain flat.

In some assemblies the turned part may have to appear to pass through a shelf or other flat part (Fig. 16-10C). One turned piece can be given a dowel long enough to go through the shelf and into a hole in the other turned part (Fig. 16-10D). Another way of dealing with this would be to drill both parts and use a separate dowel (Fig. 16-10E). That allows greater penetration into each piece, with greater strength, than might be possible to turn in the solid wood.

That method has only one turned part entering the shelf. Another way has one piece turned to fit into a large hole in the shelf, then it is drilled to take a dowel on the other part (Fig. 16-10F). The second

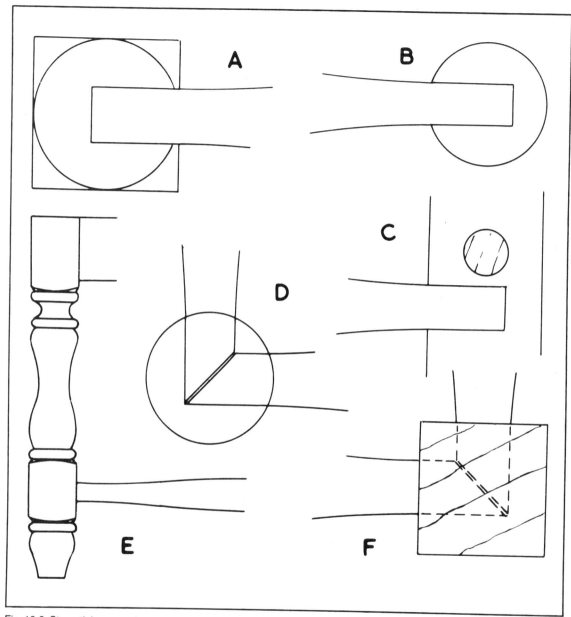

Fig. 16-9. Strength is greater in a square than a round (A, B). Dowels are better staggered (C) than meeting (D) in a round leg, but there is more strength if part of a turning is left square (E, F).

dowel need not be very much smaller diameter than the other end if the parts are close-grained.

SASH JOINERY

In the making of window frames and their surrounds, there are many places where the wood has to be worked to complicated sections. These could be made by hand, but it would be difficult and laborious. Today, such joinery is made in the shop, and the complete unit is taken to the site. All of the work is done by machinery. Joints involved include mortise and tenon and dado.

Examples are the rails and transom involved in an opening window. At the bottom the sill (Fig. 16-11A) is shaped to shed water that falls on it, with a lip turned out to prevent water going over the rear edge (Fig. 16-11B) and a groove to prevent it from running back underneath (Fig. 16-11C). There is a groove inside to collect condensation (Fig. 16-11D). Weep holes are drilled through at intervals to allow condensation to escape to the outside.

The window frame is notched into the rail. It may have a groove underneath to prevent water running back, or the water is better kept away with weatherboard (Fig. 16-11E) notched in to remove any risk of water creeping down the joint.

If there is one window above another, the transom (Fig. 16-11F) has rabbets for both windows, with hollows to discourage water from creeping back. The front edge extends far enough to throw water clear, and the way its edge is molded and grooved prevents water from creeping back (Fig. 16-11G).

TABLE SLIDES

Wood slides for an extending table need to fit into each other and preferably interlock so they do not pull apart sideways, as they could with plain tongues and grooves. A suitable joint would be difficult to make by hand, but with a spindle or router the

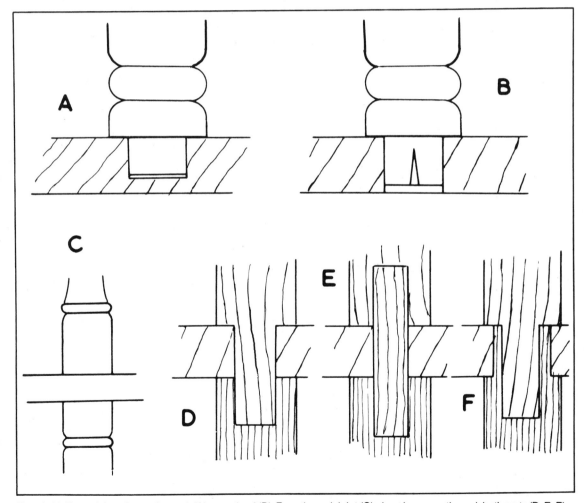

Fig. 16-10. Turned dowels may be sunk (A) or wedged (B). For a through joint (C), dowels may go through both parts (D, E, F).

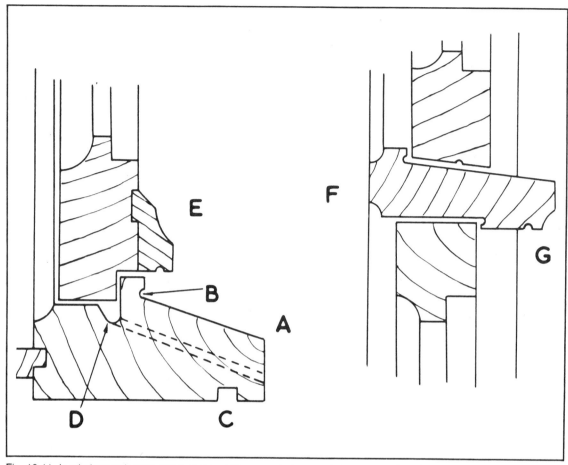

Fig. 16-11. In window sash parts many of the sections needed can only be cut satisfactorily by machine.

fitted parts can be shaped accurately (Fig. 16-12). As shown, there are three parts to the extension. The middle piece has to be shaped on both sides, but the others only need the groove on one and the projection on the other.

POCKET SCREWS

Pocket screwing has already been described for arranging screws upward from the insides of rails into tabletops (Fig. 16-13A), with the pockets cut by handwork with chisel and gouge. If many have to be made, they can be cut with a large bit (1¼ inch is suitable) and a simple jig in a drill press or an electric drill in a stand.

The jig is a stout piece of wood long enough to hold the rail without wobbling. It is cut with a groove to take the rail at an angle of about 15 degrees. Attached to it is a short strip to act as a big guide (Fig. 16-13B). The cutting width has to be arranged so the bit cuts a pocket as required. Use a Forstner bit or a sawtooth or multispur bit guided by its outside. The depth stop on the drill press will regulate the size of the pocket, which should take the full diameter of the head of a flat head screw.

TABLETOP FASTENERS

Wood buttons are commonly used for holding a tabletop to grooved rails so they will move if the top expands or contracts. Small metal joggled strips are an alternative. They are more compact, but work in the same way (Fig. 16-14A). The groove in the rail does not need to be much more than a saw cut.

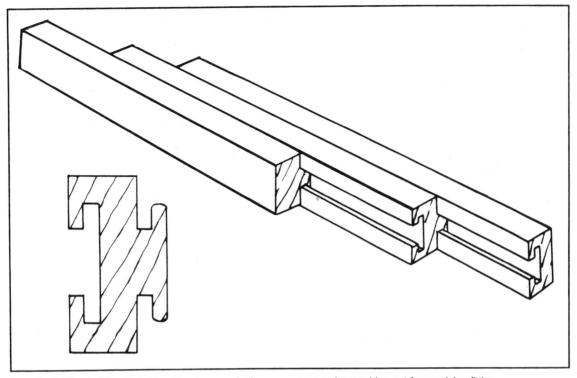

Fig. 16-12. Wood slides for table extensions or similar purposes may be machine cut for precision fitting.

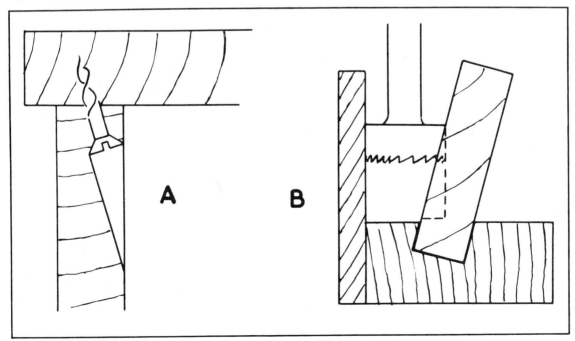

A

B

Fig. 16-13. Screw pockets may be cut on a drill press with a simple jig.

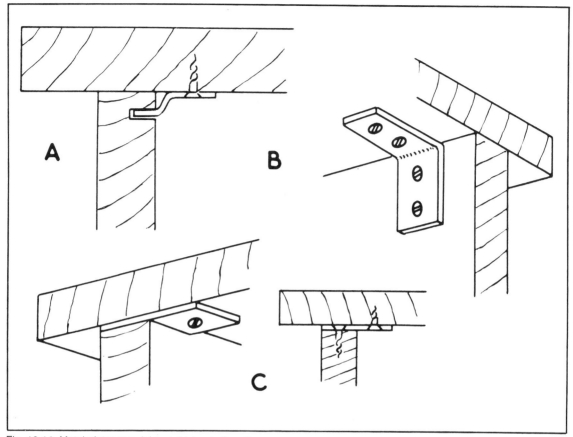

Fig. 16-14. Metal plates may join a tabletop to its rails.

Where the top is made of a manufactured board that does not expand or contract, the attachment can be more positive. Pocket screws or glued and screwed blocks inside may be used. Sheet metal brackets are an option (Fig. 16-14B). Flat metal screw plates can be let into the tops of the rails (Fig. 16-14C), either projecting inward only or on both sides if the top overlaps more.

Chapter 17

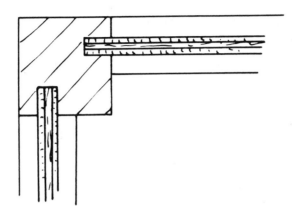

Joints in Manufactured Boards

THE INCREASING SCARCITY OF GOOD WOOD AND its rapidly escalating cost has been met by advances in wood technology, so many things that once would have been made of natural wood are now made of manufactured boards. These are all boards based on wood, but they make the maximum use of wide flat sheets. Plywood is best known, but there are hardboards and particle boards (chipboards), as well as other manufactured items to use with or in place of solid natural woods.

Plywood is made of many veneers glued together with their grains crossing. Some thicker versions have solid wood cores between veneered surfaces and are known as solid-core plywood or blockboard. Particle board is made of small chips of wood bonded together in a synthetic resin. For better work, the density of wood chips in relation to resin should be great. Hardboard is mostly ⅛ inch thick, with one smooth surface and the other showing a crossing pattern. It is made from wood, and its quality varies considerably. Inferior hardboard is little better than cardboard. One type is oil-tempered. It has a degree of water resistance and is one of the densest and best varieties.

The quality of manufactured boards governs what may be done with them. More involved joints are difficult or impossible in poorer quality boards. Particle board and plywood may be obtained with veneers of wood that may match adjoining solid wood parts, so the assembled effect may be of an entire solid wood construction. Hardboard is unsuitable for veneering. Because it has only one good side, it unsuitable where both sides need to present a good appearance. Plastic veneers and other plastic materials can be applied to provide kitchen and bar work tops.

BANDING OR LIPPING

The edges of the manufactured boards are unattractive, and they should be hidden where possible. Plywood and hardboard have taken the place of solid wood in such things as drawer bottoms, carcass backs, and door panels. They are stable, so no provision has to be made for expansion and contraction. In a solid wood door panel, space has to be left in the grooves for the wood to expand and contract in its width (Fig. 17-1A). A plywood or hardboard panel may still be fitted loosely for convenience in assembly, but it may go to the bottom of a groove (Fig. 17-1B). The only preparation would be a slight chamfer around the edge for easing in. As these materials are a uniform thickness, the fit in a plowed groove can be more precise.

Solid wood is stronger along the grain than across it, so where the load has to be taken across the grain there must be a sufficient thickness. The manufactured boards are uniform in their strength in all directions. When making something like a shelf, plywood could be thinner than solid wood in the same position. For the sake of stiffness and appearance, a rabbeted lip may be put along the front (Fig. 17-1C). A similar lip could be at the back or just a strip underneath (Fig. 17-1D).

As plywood has its layers of veneer with their grain lines square, any attempt to glue to the edge of a sheet will only get a good bond to the side grain and an indifferent one to the end grain. Even allowing for this, veneer may be glued satisfactorily to the edge of a thick piece of plywood (Fig. 17-2A). The more common way of hiding the edge is to use devices to give a better glue area.

One way is to plow a groove along the edge and fit a solid wood lip with a tongue into this (Fig.

17-2B). The tongue and groove increase the glue area, mostly side grain to side grain. In solid core plywood this gives a good bond (Fig. 17-2C), particularly where the end grain of the core is involved. A flat joint would be almost all end grain.

There are machine-made joints in which the banding is cut with a V-section. This may be used on plywood or particle board (Fig. 17-2D). It could also be given a tongue for greater strength (Fig. 17-2E).

Lips could be fitted with loose tongues. A tongue may be solid wood, preferably with its grain either straight across or diagonal to the width, but you can use thin plywood (Fig. 17-2F). Besides simple square and rounded lips, an edge could be molded (Fig. 17-2G) and could project some way (Fig. 17-2H). If there is much extension of solid wood, it ought to have support at the ends.

CORNERS TO SOLID WOOD

If a carcass is made up with four solid wood legs, panels between them can have their edge hidden easily. With the usual mortise and tenon jointed framework using horizontal rails, the plywood may be let into grooves both ways on the legs (Fig. 17-3A) to come central in the rails. If the surfaces are to be flush, thin plywood may be let into rabbets with the solid wood square (Fig. 17-3B) or rounded (Fig. 17-3C).

If the panels are thicker plywood or particle

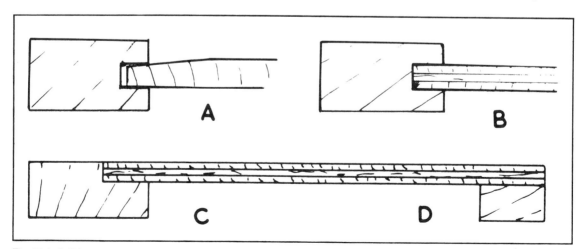

Fig. 17-1. Solid wood panels need space in grooves to expand and contract (A). Plywood does not move (B) and can be used with thicker wood for shelves (C, D).

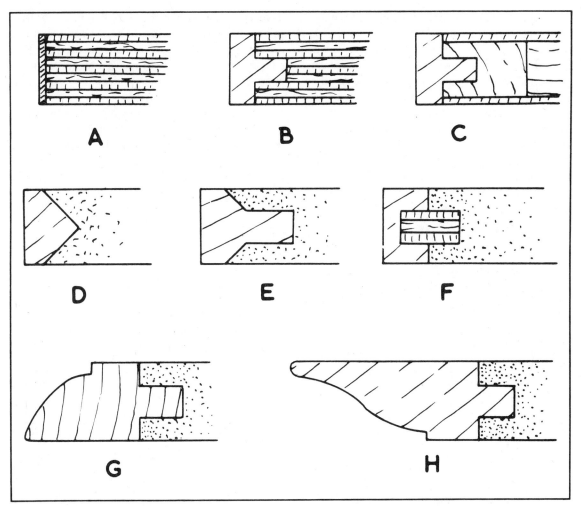

Fig. 17-2. Plywood may be edged with veneer (A) or lips (B, C). Special edges can be machined for particle board (D, E, F), which can be extended further (G, H).

board, the edges may be joined with loose tongues into both pieces both ways (Fig. 17-3D). This can be done when the panel meets a piece of solid wood and forms a corner with it (Fig. 17-3E).

If two pieces of particle board or solid core plywood are to meet so their outer surfaces extend to the corner, they will have to be mitered, but there is little strength in a plain miter. Dowels could be across the miter (Fig. 17-4A). It may be possible to plow grooves and insert a tongue (Fig. 17-4B). Take care to avoid the acute angle breaking away, whether the outer grain is parallel to it or across it. Particle board is inclined to crumble. In

most circumstances it would be better to have a solid wood corner piece.

If thin plywood panels are to meet with a miter, there has to be a reinforcing piece of solid wood inside (Fig. 17-4C). The joint is best made in two stages, with the solid wood first glued and maybe pinned to one piece. The other is brought to it (Fig. 17-4D). As with the thicker materials, the acute angled corner may break. It is better to have a solid wood corner if that can be arranged.

EDGING PARTICLE BOARD

Much particle board for furniture and other home

319

purposes is supplied already veneered on both broad surfaces and usually along the edges, either with genuine wood veneer, a plastic with a wood grain finish, or a plain white or other color plastic. These manufactured surfaces should be retained, but if the material is cut something has to be done about the exposed unattractive particle board. Manufacturers provide long tapelike strips of similar material to that already on the particle board, but slightly wider than the thickness of the board and with a heat-sensitive adhesive on the back.

This may be ironed on with a domestic clothes iron. Have the board supported with its edge upward. Cut a piece of banding slightly too long and have a piece of plain paper ready that is bigger than the banding. Have moderate heat on the iron and use it to press down on paper over the banding (Fig. 17-5). A little practice will soon show the amount of heat needed, but it is not critical. Pay particular attention to the ends and edges.

When the banding has cooled, trim the overhanging surplus. Special tools are available that work like small planes with a guide running on the surface to stop the cut when it is level, but any fine closemouthed plane can be used diagonally along the edge. You can use abrasive paper wrapped around a flat piece of wood and held slightly tilted to the main surface to avoid scratching it.

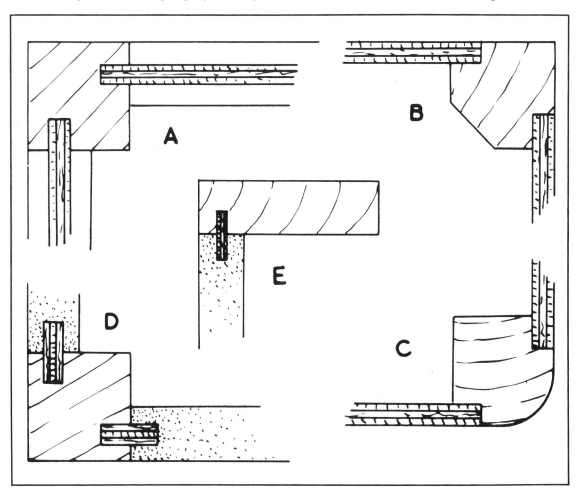

Fig. 17-3. Plywood panels may be let into rails and legs with grooves and rabbets. Plywood can also be grooved into particle board.

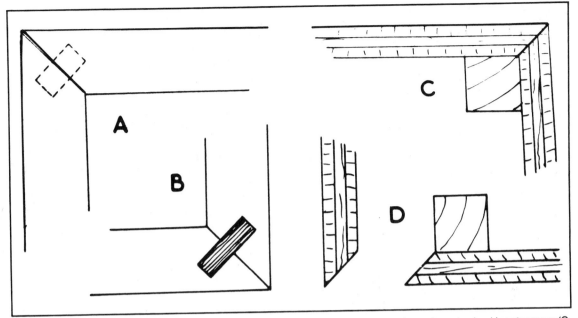

Fig. 17-4. Particle board or thicker plywood may be doweled or tongued (A, B). Thinner plywood needs a backing at corners (C, D).

PARTICLE BOARD CORNERS

The synthetic resin used in the manufacture of particle board does not bond well with all glues that are suitable for solid wood. Use urea formaldehyde glue—the waterproof type that is a favorite for boatbuilding. Polyvinyl acetate glues will also bond with it, but they are not as strong.

Glue needs a close contact if it is to make a strong joint. Most glues are not gap-filling to any significant extent, so a simple glued joint may seem theoretically adequate for some purposes. The practical difficulties of cutting an end to give a perfect fit against a surface (Fig. 17-6A) make that sort of joint normally inadvisable. Using a tongue

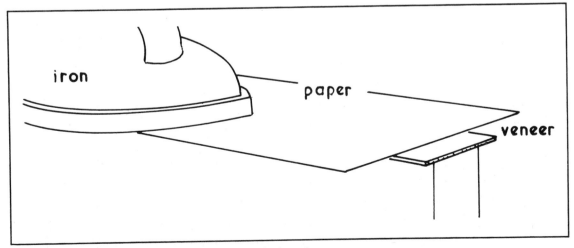

Fig. 17-5. Self-adhesive edging for particle board may be ironed on.

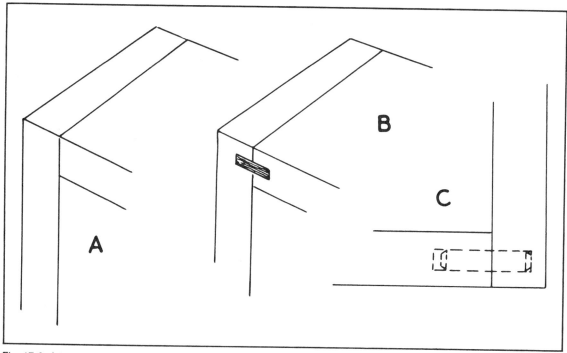

Fig. 17-6. A tongue keeps a corner joint in line, and dowels can also be used.

(Fig. 17-6B) improves the strength of the joint considerably, providing the grooves can be plowed cleanly. Notching one piece into the other also increases the glue area.

Particle board is unsuitable for such interlocking joints as dovetails and other types where one piece is cut to fit through the other. Some amount of grooving and rabbeting is possible, but fitting parts across leads to crumbling. There is no elasticity in particle board like there is in wood, so jointed parts cannot be sprung or forced together.

If one piece meets another at a corner or somewhere along the length, the most commonly used joint is with dowels. Plastic dowels are available, but wood dowels are satisfactory. The technique is the same as for wood doweling (see Chapter 7), preferably with the use of a jig. Drill as deeply as the material permits in the thickness. Allow a little extra length in the other part, so the dowel bottoms in the thin piece, and there is a little space to spare in the other (Fig. 17-6C). Tapering the dowel ends and cutting grooves are important. Wood is slightly porous and may absorb some air or

surplus glue around the dowel hole before splitting. Particle board is nonporous, and it could break out if pressure builds up ahead of the entering dowel.

Dowel diameter should be between one-third and one-half the thickness of the particle board. Have dowels close at the ends of a joint, but 3 inches or 4 inches apart across a joint should usually be enough.

PARTICLE BOARD SCREWING

You should not attempt to nail particle board. Usually this results in splits, even after a hole has been drilled for the nail. A nail must not be expected to cut its own way in. A hole must be drilled only slightly undersize and taken further than the nail will be expected to penetrate. Because of the need to drill almost as large as the nail diameter, there is little grip in a nailed joint, even if splitting does not occur. If dowels are not used, it is better to rely on screws.

Common wood screws will grip particle board, but you must drill to clear the unscrewed neck and a root diameter hole for the screwed part (Fig.

322

17-7A). In wood it is common to not drill right to the tip of the screw and leave it to cut its way into this last part, but in particle board the hole should be deeper than the screw will go (Fig. 17-7B).

Although the wood screw thread suits wood, it is not the ideal form for particle board. There are special screws for the material that look something like screws intended for sheet metal (Fig. 17-7C). The thread goes to near the head, so there is no plain part that needs a clearance hole. Gauge thicknesses are the same as for wood screws. You should choose lengths slightly more than would be used for joining wood parts of similar sections.

If a countersunk screw head is used, the hole must be countersunk fully for it. It cannot be expected to pull in much, as it would with most woods. An exposed screw head is unattractive. If it has to

be left visible, there are metal and plastic screw caps that act like washers under the head (Fig. 17-7D) and may have covers to go over the screw head, so they look neater than bare heads. Oval or round heads look better than flat ones.

It is better to counterbore the screw heads by drilling partly through the particle board so the head is sunk (Fig. 17-7E), then a plastic plug with a shallow head may be glued in (Fig. 17-7F). The plugs are obtainable in colors to match surface veneers.

Another way of using screws without going through the surfaces is to have strips of wood inside with screws both ways (Fig. 17-8A). For shelves and the undersides of parts that will not show, this is a good method of joining. The strips are best made of hardwood and need not be of large section,

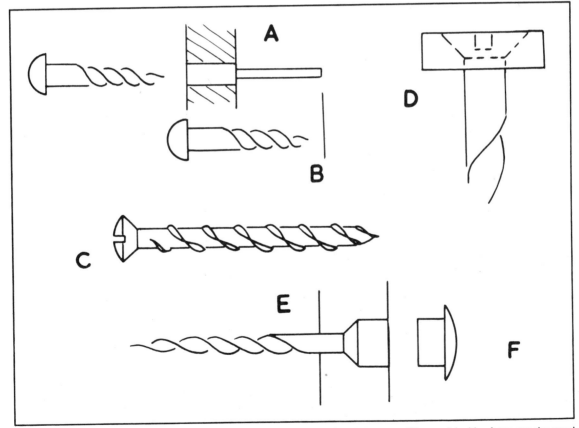

Fig. 17-7. Holes for screws must go full depth in particle board (A, B). Special screws (C) are advisable. A cap may be used under a screw head (D), or the screw can be counterbored and covered (F).

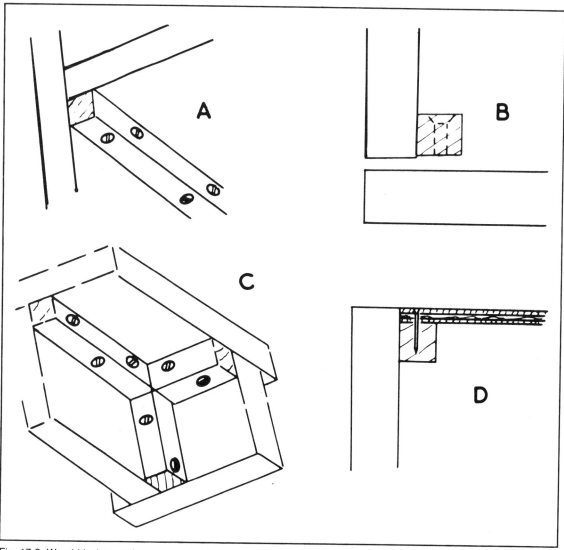

Fig. 17-8. Wood blocks may be screwed inside to secure joints in particle board.

providing they will take holes without splitting. Predrill them. Attach a strip to the piece that will butt against the other. It will help in drawing together a tight joint if the strip is kept back marginally from the end (Fig. 17-8B), then the screws the other way will get the maximum pull. Holes in the wood strip should allow the screws to slide through, but they should be drilled to suit the thread in the other part.

There can be strips behind a plinth along all the joints instead of dowels (Fig. 17-8C). Similar strips can be used at the back of a cabinet, where a piece of plywood or hardboard has to be supported (Fig. 17-8D). Although screws must be used into the particle board, there could be fine nails instead of screws through the back. In all of these joints there can be glue as well as screws, but the glue should suit the materials. If the panels have wood veneers, any of the usual wood glues are suitable, but otherwise follow the suggestions given earlier.

KNOCKDOWN FITTINGS

Much furniture is made so it can be taken apart. The parts may be solid-core plywood or particle board. The attachments have to be secure and positive. Many of them have value in making joints in permanent furniture that is unlikely to ever to be taken apart. The number of fasteners is always growing, but those described here are examples of the way furniture parts can be joined without the customary traditional joints.

One method of joining has some similarity to the screwed blocks just described. Two blocks made of nylon or other plastic has lugs for lining up and a central metal-thread screw. One piece screws to the piece overlapping part of a corner (Fig. 17-9A). The other screws to the piece to be brought to it (Fig. 17-9B), so the central screw can pull the parts together. To get a tight joint, the second piece needs to be located on its particle board so it finishes just clear of the other block when the screw pulls the parts tight. At least two pairs of blocks along each joint are needed. In a four-sided assembly they bring the parts tight and the overall shape true.

Another type of fastener takes the screwed joint a stage further by using an insert for the screw to enter. If a screw goes directly into particle board, it cannot be entered and removed several times without losing at least some of its grip. In one screwing alternative there is a nylon plug with a serrated outside that can be glued and driven into a slightly undersize hole (Fig. 17-9C). The other part is given a clearance hole for a screw with its point arranged to be self-tapping (Fig. 17-9D). As the screw is driven in, it cuts a thread in the plug to make a tight attachment that will still be effective after several withdrawals.

Another option is metal and is intended for take-apart solid wood or thick plywood parts. The insert is brass with a split in part of the length and a knurled entrance. The hole is already tapped to take its metal-thread screw. The insert is driven into a slightly undersize hole, and the knurled top grips the wood to prevent the part turning as the screw is driven (Fig. 17-9E). The screw is the normal type and does not need to be self-tapping.

Several methods of tightening rely on a cam action to pull prepared parts together. In the example (Fig. 17-9F) a special bolt with a spacer is screwed into a nylon insert in the overlapping piece. A hole in the other piece fits the spacer and leads the bolt into a large hole drilled partly through the wood or particle board. Into this hole goes a circular piece with a large opening to admit the head of the bolt and introduce it to an internal cam. When the circular piece is rotated with a screwdriver, the cam pulls on the screw head and draws the parts together.

Bolt tightening that pulls into any insert put into a hole in line with the pull depends for its strength on the friction and glue holding the insert. It would be better for the pull to come across the insert. That can be arranged if the screw goes into a metal dowel entered in a hole across the part (Fig. 17-10A). The bolt is a long one, and it may have a metal insert into a counterbored hole to spread the pressure from its head (Fig. 17-10B). As the metal dowel hole has to be drilled into an edge, this is not a fitting for wide boards, but it makes a very strong joint for holding rails to legs and similar applications.

For a secure attachment where the appearance on the far side is unimportant, but there is no space for the projecting end of a bolt and its nut, a T-nut (Fig. 17-10C) can be inserted in wood. An example is where the part with the nut comes against a wall. A hole to take it is drilled, and the nut is driven in so its prongs enter the wood. The threaded part penetrates well into the wood, so a bolt through the other part (Fig. 17-10D) can enter far enough to get a good grip without being exposed on the far side.

When several prefabricated units have to be joined together, you may be able to merely screw through one into the other, but it is better to use connecting screws where one part can be screwed into the other (Fig. 17-10E). The hollow part has ridges on the outside to grip the hole and resist turning. The other piece has a neck of the same diameter and a screwdriver slot for tightening.

FRAMING HARDBOARD

There is little stiffness in a piece of hardboard, and

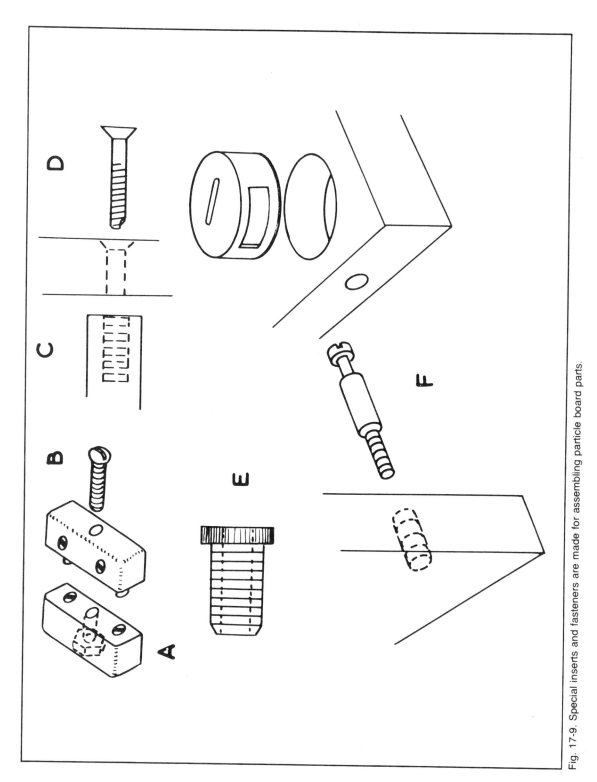

Fig. 17-9. Special inserts and fasteners are made for assembling particle board parts.

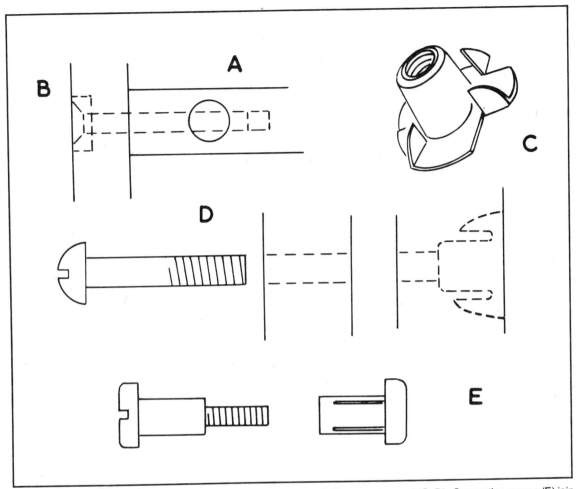

Fig. 17-10. A bolt may go into a metal insert in particle board (A, B). A T-nut can be used (C, D). Connecting screws (E) join parts.

any area much more than 1 square foot usually needs stiffening. Putting the panel into plowed grooves in a solid wood frame gives good support and may be used with rather larger areas, but if the panel is to form a flush surface there must be some strip wood framing behind it. The strips may be 1 inch square or larger, around the edges and intermediately, where necessary (Fig. 17-11A). In the crudest work the strips may merely butt against each other, but they are better halved or tenoned together. Glue will bond with the back of hardboard, but nails should also be used. Special fine nails with small heads intended for hardboard are available. They are colored so the heads are inconspicuous when punched level. Edges may be hidden with a frame (Fig. 17-11B), which can stand forward with a shaped edge and mitered corners if the assembly is a bulletin board or something similar (Fig. 17-11C). For the best edge protection, it may be rabbeted like a picture frame (Fig. 17-11D).

Hardboard is used for the two sides of flush doors. The solid wood framing should be stiff enough to keep the door in shape and with enough internal pieces to support the hardboard against knocks. Assembly can be with glue and special nails, but the edges at top and sides must be protected with banding (Fig. 17-11E) mitered at the corners. Room doors often do not have banding

327

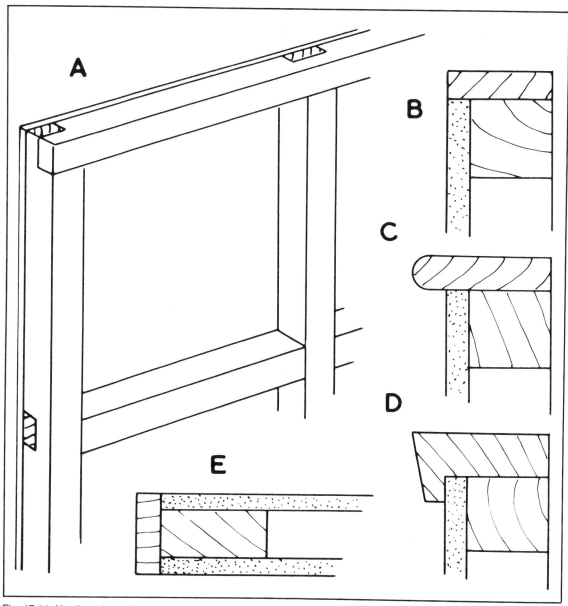

Fig. 17-11. Hardboard panels need wood stiffening, and it can be framed with wood.

across the bottom, but it could be added after the door has been checked for size and any surplus has been removed from the bottom edge.

PIERCED HARDBOARD

Hardboard panels may be bought with a pattern of holes drilled at regular intervals all over. The holes may provide ventilation if the panel comes over a space where air might otherwise become stagnant but a common use is in making racks for household and shop tools by using bent wire hooks.

The panel needs framing to keep it clear of the wall (Fig. 17-12A). Hooks may be bought to suit the many things that can hang from the panel, but they could be made from stout wire that is easily fitted through the holes. For most things there is a double bend in the wire, so it can be pushed in. Bringing it down into position prevents it coming out under load (Fig. 17-12B).

Hooks can be arranged to go into two holes where more support is needed. Wood or other parts can be made to hang special tools, and wire hooks are screwed behind them (Fig. 17-12C). Shelves may be hung in this way (Fig. 17-12D), but there is obviously a limit to what weight can be supported with wire through holes. For stronger shelving or racks for heavier tools, the holes can be used for screws from the back, preferably with washers to spread the load.

Most holes will be unused, although they provide a way to move racks about. If a panel of racks is needed for a particular arrangement, possibly with shelves and other things screwed on, holes might be drilled for wire racks just where they are needed in plain hardboard or plywood to avoid having many unused holes.

HOLLOW FASTENINGS

A problem with locating attachments comes in hollow assemblies, such as flush doors with hardboard or plywood surfaces or room walls made with panels mounted on studding. If the chosen position does not line up with studding or framing, you have to attach to a panel that is too thin to provide a grip in its thickness for a screw. You cannot get at the other side to use a nut and bolt or other fastener requiring action on both sides to tighten it.

For simply hanging a light load, you can use bent wire through a hole in the manner just described. There have to be stronger supports for most things.

Nearly all fasteners available for hollow as-

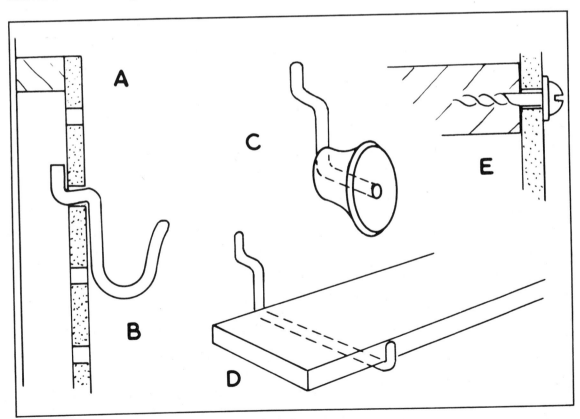

Fig. 17-12. Pierced hardboard will take wire hangers for tools.

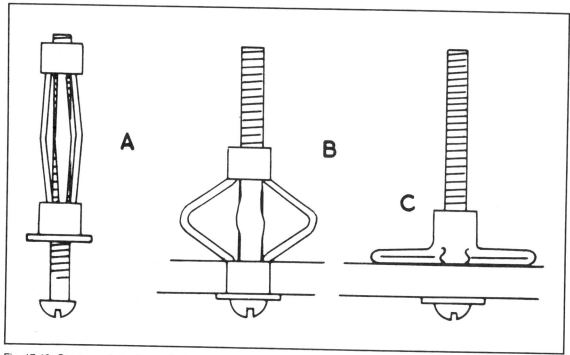

Fig. 17-13. One type of attachment for hollow walls has a part that expands when its bolt is tightened.

semblies have a piece to pass through the panel. A screw driven in expands that piece to pull back against the far side, with a similar effect to a nut. Some have a part that falls into place as it is pushed in. With some of these fasteners the inside piece falls off if the screw is removed, but other combinations leave that part attached to the wall for subsequent reassembly.

A common fastener is a hollow wall anchor, which may be metal or plastic. The main part is a tube with a lip at the front and a solid far end drilled for the screw. In between the tube is divided lengthwise (Fig. 17-13A). A hole has to be drilled so the part will just push in, and the lip prevents it from going right through. When the screw is entered, the tightening action spreads the cut tube as it is forced back (Fig. 17-13B) so it eventually comes flat against the far side of the panel (Fig. 17-13C). A metal fastener has a metal-thread screw, but some plastic plugs may be used with a wood screw.

There are some variations on the above pattern, but the method is similar. Some pieces that go through the panel have projections under the lip to prevent it from turning as the screw tightens. Another type has a pointed screw already in the outer piece, so the whole thing can be driven into soft material without drilling.

In a hollow door there may be insufficient space for the device to go in without reaching the far side. Smaller nylon plugs are made with springy arms for putting coat hooks and similar lightly loaded things on door panels. The plug is pushed into a hole. This closes the arms (Fig. 17-14A). The screw is entered with just a few turns to grip the plug (Fig. 17-14B), and it is pushed to get the plug right through when the arms spring out (Fig. 17-14C). Completion of tightening pulls them wide against the back of the panel (Fig. 17-14D).

Toggle bolts have a piece that goes through the hole and is arranged to move square to the panel at the far side. The toggle is made in the final shape and does not rely on expanding as it is pulled back. The hole needed is relatively large, so the thing being attached should be big enough to cover it. A washer over the hole may be needed.

330

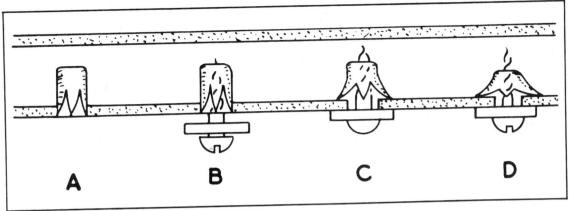

Fig. 17-14. A nylon plug will expand inside a hollow door.

One type of toggle bolt has two wings with a spring to open them. They go through the hole folded on the bolt (Fig. 17-15A), then open as they clear the far side and can be drawn back tight by screwing (Fig. 17-15B). In another type the toggle is in one piece, but it pivots on the bolt off-center or it is weighted one side, so gravity will cause it to fall into position behind the panel (Fig. 17-15C). The toggle may have teeth to dig into the back of the panel. The screw usually has a screwdriver head, but a heavy one may have a bolt head for a wrench. The threaded part may be a stud onto which a nut is tightened. With these fasteners and others, you need to draw back on the screw to bear the inner

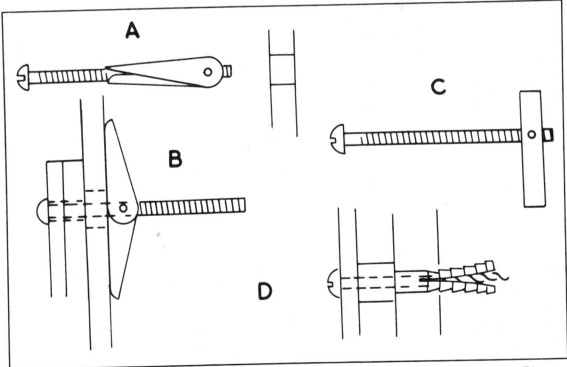

Fig. 17-15. Toggle bolts open inside a hollow wall (A, B, C). For a light load, there is a plastic expanding plug (D).

part against the panel during early tightening to prevent it from turning with the screw.

For fairly light loads, such as a perforated hardboard storage panel, plastic fasteners with serrated split ends expand enough to grip at the other side. One type is provided with a collar neck to hold off the panel a suitable amount (Fig. 17-15D).

PARTICLE BOARD EDGING

Besides lipping particle board with wood as already described, there are metal strips that give neat edges, particularly on work surfaces covered with melamine plastic. There are screw-on strips. Some have the screw heads exposed, but others have press-in plastic to cover the screws driven in a channel (Fig. 17-16A). The narrow lip does not project much. It covers and protects the top surface edge. The usual form is made of aluminum with a colored plastic insert.

Another type of molded edging has a serrated projection behind it (Fig. 17-16B). The serrated parts are shaped so they will push into a groove, but resist pulling out. The groove needed is no more than the cut of some circular saw blades. If one cut with a particular blade is not wide enough, there can be another pass at a slightly different setting.

A variation on this is a handle (Fig. 17-16C). It is attached in the same way to the full length of a drawer or door side and gives a good grip without projecting from the front surface. This handle is used in kitchen cabinets and other places where projecting handles might be a nuisance or obstruction.

PARTICLE BOARD HINGES

Although not impossible, letting normal woodworking hinges into the edges of particle board doors is difficult to do without breaking or crumbling. Very thin hinges are made so one leaf closes into the other. The total thickness is no more than the gap that would have to be left for clearance in any case (Fig. 17-17A). These hinges can be mounted directly on both surfaces. They are bent so the thicker knuckles stand outside and throw the door clear as it swings (Fig. 17-17B).

Many hinges are intended particularly for mass-produced furniture where the hinges are hidden or provide particular functions, but they are mostly simply screwed to surfaces. Some mount in metal or plastic inserts that are pressed and glued into the particle board, as described for knockdown fittings. One type uses a plastic plug in the particle board. The hinge has a screw into it, with one part with a projection mating with another, similarly attached to the other part (Fig. 17-17C). If a pair of hinges have the pins the same way, the door may be lifted off. Otherwise, the top hinge is arranged to point downward.

Some concealed hinges have parts that fit into large diameter holes in the surface. They have to be taken fairly deeply into the particle board. Diameters are 1 inch or more. There is a problem in making these holes without breaking out at edges or damaging the surface on the far side. Large woodworking drill bits are not very effective on particle board. Those with a long central point cannot be used as they would break through on the far

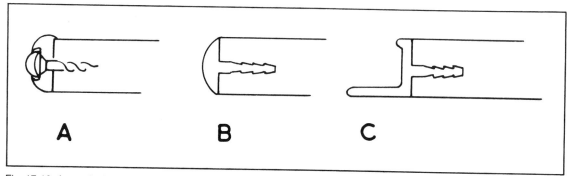

A   **B**   **C**

Fig. 17-16. A metal edging with a plastic filler may be screwed on a particle board edge (A). There are metal edges to fit into grooves (B, C).

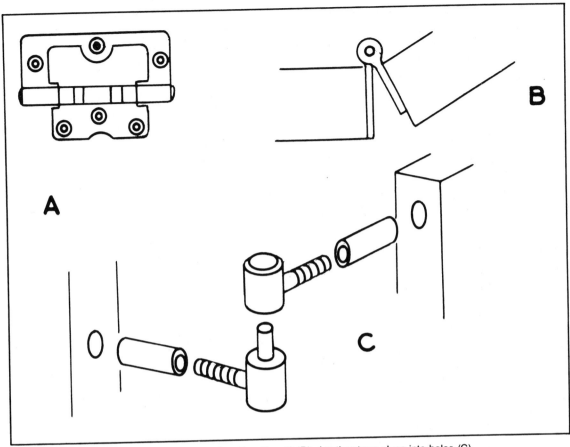

Fig. 17-17. A thin hinge has one part folding into the other (A, B). Another type plugs into holes (C).

surface. You may be able to use a Forstner bit, as that does not have a projecting center, but the resin soon blunts the edges. Special bits made for the purpose are more like metalworking end mills.

SHELF SUPPORTS

Particle board shelves may be screwed through the uprights of bookcases or similar assemblies. The heads are counterbored and covered with plastic plugs, but if the outside surface is to remain unmarked, there have to be inside methods of attachments. Cutting dado joints, as in similar wood construction, is impractical in this material.

If the shelves are to be at permanent positions, they may be doweled to the sides during assembly (Fig. 17-18A). This is the recommended method,

but if the shelves are to be adjustable in position or are to be added after other parts are permanently assembled, some other method of support has to be used.

Several supports are developments of the simple pieces of dowel rod pushed into holes below the shelf, as suggested for wood shelving. For particle board, it is better to line the holes with inserts. One type uses a pair of bushes or inserts glued and pushed into holes (Fig. 17-18B). A plastic stud with a sprung split end pushes in and has a small flat to come under the shelf (Fig. 17-18C).

It is better to use metal supports for heavier shelves. Metal sockets with lips line holes in the upright (Fig. 17-18D). The supports have an L-shape, so they can be used at the end of the shelf (Fig. 17-18E) and are almost hidden.

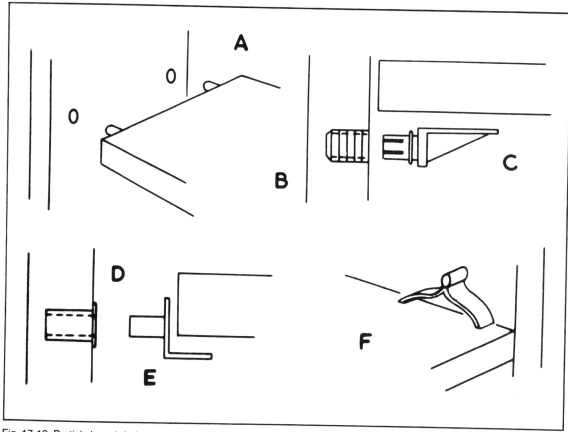

Fig. 17-18. Particle board shelves may be doweled (A), or they can be supported on special plugs (B, C, D, E) with a retainer above (F).

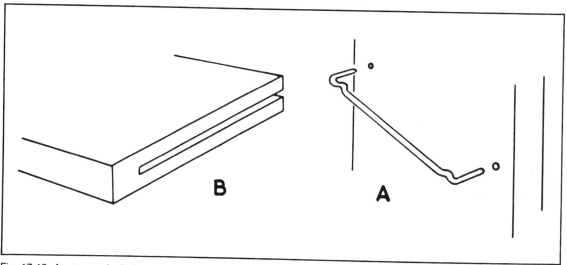

Fig. 17-19. A sprung wire in holes in the side and a groove in the shelf will make a hidden support.

If a shelf rests on supports, it might be lifted unintentionally during use, as the usual support does nothing to resist upward movement. Plastic sprung pieces are available that can be used above a shelf to keep it down. A plug goes into a hole or socket near enough to the shelf surface to cause the sprung ends to widen (Fig. 17-18F). It is still possible to move the shelf after pulling out the plug.

You can support a shelf with no projections so it appears doweled in by using a length of wire, which will fit in a series of holes in the side to allow height adjustment if required. The ends of the wire are bent to press into holes, and the shaping holds off the strip between the required amount (Fig. 17-19A). The shelf end has a groove cut deep and wide enough to suit the wire, but it does not have to be carried through to the front (Fig. 17-19B). There is no indication of the method of support when the shelf is in position, although it can be removed by pulling forward.

Glossary

architrave—Molding around a door or window.
arris—Meeting of two surfaces. A sharp edge.

backflap hinge—One that swings back further than a normal hinge.
baluster—Vertical pillar supporting a handrail.
bar—Intermediate member in a glazed frame.
barefaced—Not notched, as a barefaced tenon.
bargeboard—Inclined boards on the roof end at the gable of a house.
baseboard—Board around room at the bottom of walls.
batten—Narrow strip of wood.
beam—Horizontal load-carrying structural wood or steel member.
binder—Beam supporting floor joists.
bird's mouth—Angled notch in the end of one piece to fit the corner of the supporting strip.
blind—Not carried through, particularly holes and mortises.
bolt—Fastener screwed to take a nut.
box—Enclose.

bracket—Support for a horizontal surface from a vertical one.
butt hinge—Common hinge usually fitted to the edge of a door.
button—Small piece of wood turning on a screw to act as a catch.

cant—External splayed angle.
cant rail—Horizontal rail behind vertical boarding.
cantilever—Beam supported at one end.
capping—Cover strip, as at the top of a gate.
carcass—The main structure of a piece of furniture.
casement—Hinged or pivoted sash window.
cast—Twist.
ceiling—Lining in a boat. Top surface of a room.
chase—Grooving.
clamp—Device drawing parts together. Strip across a wide board to prevent warping.
clapboard—Overlapping boards outside house or forming a fence.

cleat—Small piece joining parts together.

coach screw—Large wood screw with head for wrench.

cock—Stand above surface.

cogging—One piece notched over another to prevent movement.

coping—See *scribing.*

cottered—Metal wedges used to tighten an iron band around a wood joint.

counterbore—To enlarge the top of a hole to let a screw head go below the surface.

countersink—Conical sinking at the top of a screw hole so the head finished with the surface.

cramp—See *clamp.*

dado—Groove.

diminishing—Reducing, particularly a door stile.

dog—Metal U-shaped double spike to draw boards together.

donkey—Quick-acting vise for thin material.

dormer—Window in an extension so it is vertical in a sloping roof.

draw—Pull together, as in drawbore or pin.

face marks—Marks applied to show a side and edge to work from.

fascia—Flat board edgewise, as at the edge of a roof.

fastenings (fasteners)—Nails and screws used for joining.

feather—Strip of wood used as tongue. Figure in wood grain.

featheredge—Wood thinned toward one edge.

fillet—Narrow strip of wood used as filling or to support a part.

fillister—Plane for cutting rabbets, with stops for width and depth.

fish—Join end to end with strips each side.

flitch—Log prepared for conversion. Beam made from two pieces bolted together.

flying shore—Temporary support between walls and not attached to the floor.

folding wedges—Two similar wedges used overlapping to apply pressure.

foxtail wedging—Wedges to spread the end of a tenon inside a blind mortise.

framed—Strips joined to form a carcass to be filled or covered with panels.

frank—Exposed. Reversed haunch in mortise and tenon joint.

gable—End of a building, follow the outline of the roof.

gauge—Marking tool or means of testing. Definition of size by numbers.

grating—Framework of crossing bars used as a floor.

groove—Any long narrow channel.

gunstock stile—Door stile tapered at the lock rail for wider panel above.

halved—Crossing pieces notched to fit into each other.

handed—Arranged in pairs.

hanging stile—The door stile to which the hinges are fitted.

haunch—A shortened part of a tenon.

heel straps—Metal straps around joints between rafters on tie beams.

hip—Roof with slope at the end as well as the sides.

horn—Extension beyond joint.

housing—Groove to take an end of a board in another. A dado joint.

inserted—Added, as when a tenon is set in the end as well as into a mortise.

jamb—Vertical side of a window or doorway.

jig—Guide for holding or shaping work.

joggle—Double bend. A horn.

jointing—Any joint, but particularly boards glued edge to edge.

joist—Horizontal members, particularly carrying floors or ceilings.

kerf—The slot made by a saw.

key—Wedge. Cotter. Veneer in slot across miter.

king post—Central upright in a roof truss.

knuckle—Pivot of a hinge.

laminate—Make up in layers, particularly in curved work.

lap—Overlap, particularly where part of a piece crosses another in a joint.

lath—Strip of wood of small section.

lipping—Facing an edge with a strip, as with solid wood on a plywood shelf.

locking stile—Door stile opposite to the end that is hinged.

lock rail—Rail across the door at the same height the lock will be.

louver—Opening with inclined boards across.

mansard roof—Roof with double pitch on both sides.

mason's miter—Mitered molding cut into the solid of one meeting part.

matched boarding—Boards tongued and grooved to each other.

meeting stiles—Door stiles that meet in double doors.

miter—Joint where the meeting angle is divided, as at the corner of a picture frame.

mortise lock—Lock that fits into a mortise in the edge of a door.

mullet—Groove block used for testing the edge of a panel that will have to fit another grooved part.

mullion—Vertical division of a window.

muntin—Vertical division between rails of framing.

nest—Fits into, as with a nest of tables.

newel—Post carrying the handrail to a flight of stairs.

nog—Wood built into wall for attaching to or supporting a shelf.

nosing—Semicircular molding, as at the edge of a step.

pallet—Wood frame for transporting goods. Slip of wood in brickwork for attaching to with nails or screws.

pedestal—Supporting post. Base for a column.

pegging—Dowels or pegs across a joint.

pilaster—Decorative half column fitted on a flat surface. Pier projecting from the wall.

pilot hole—Small hole drilled as guide for larger one.

pin—Fine nail. Rod through knuckle of hinge. Peg.

pintle—Vertical pin on which another part is pivoted.

planted—Attached molding or other part not worked in the solid.

plinth—Base of furniture. Bottom of column. Block at bottom of architrave.

plow—Tool for cutting grooves along grain.

plumb—Upright. Vertical.

purlin—Horizontal beams on rafters under roof covering.

quadrant—Quarter of a circle. Stay for flap or fanlight window.

queen post—Secondary upright in roof truss.

rabbet—Angular sectioned cut, as in the back of a picture frame.

rafter—Sloping member of a roof below its covering.

rail—Horizontal member in framing.

rake—Incline to horizontal.

return—Continuation around corner, particularly a molding.

rim lock—Door lock that attaches to the surface.

riser—Upright part of a stair tread.

rising butt hinge—Door hinge that lifts the door as it opens.

rod—Board with full-size details and used when marking out. Any slender pole. Obsolete measure of length (5½ yards).

router—Hand or power tool for leveling bottom of recess.

saddle—Seating for shaped part or end of one piece against another.

sash—Window frame carrying glass, which may be movable.

scribing—Cutting over a molding to give the appearance of a miter.

shingle—Wood tile.

shooting (shuting)—Making an edge straight.

shore—Wood prop. Temporary support.

shuttering—Woodwork in which concrete is formed.

shutting stile—See *lock stile*.

sill—Bottom horizontal member of framing.

skirting—See *baseboard*.

slat—Narrow thin strip. Horizontal rail in chair back.

soffit—Underside of eaves or stairs. Narrow ceiling.

sole—Bottom of plane and many other things.

spindle—Round slender part. Molding machine.

splat—Central upright part in a chair back.

splay—Spread out.

spline—Narrow strip of wood fitted into meeting grooves.

stile—Upright side of door or framing.

stopped—Not carried through, as in a stopped chamfer or rabbet.

stretcher—Lengthwise rail between lower parts of a table or chair.

string—Side support of stairs. Side of ladder.

stub—Shortened, as in a stub tenon.

stud—Vertical parts in hollow wall. Threaded rod. Nail with ornamental head.

tang—End of tool to fit in handle.

template—Shaped pattern to draw around when marking out.

tie beam—Horizontal piece across the feet of the rafters of a roof truss.

tread—Horizontal part of a stair that is stepped on.

treenail—Peg or dowel driven through a joint.

trellis—Crossing strips usually with a single nail at each crossing.

tusk—Projection, particularly a tenon extending through its mortise.

veneer—Thin wood usually glued over a thicker base as decoration.

waling—Horizontal piece tying together vertical boards.

wall plate—Wood along the top of the wall forming base for roof parts.

warping—Hollow and shrinking due to changes in moisture content.

weatherboard—See *clapboard*.

wicket—A small gate set in a larger one.

winder—Radiating step for change of direction in a stair.

winding—Twisting of a board in its length.

Index